Acquiring Clinical Judgment

A Workbook/Casebook

Acquiring Clinical Judgment

A Workbook/Casebook

to accompany

Theory and Design in Counseling and Psychotherapy

Susan X Day
Iowa State University
University of Houston

Patricia Andersen
Midwestern State University

LAHASKA PRESS
HOUGHTON MIFFLIN COMPANY
BOSTON   NEW YORK

Publisher, Lahaska Press: Barry Fetterolf
Senior Editor, Lahaska Press: Mary Falcon
Editorial Assistant: Lisa Littlewood
Project Editor: Robin Hogan
Senior Manufacturing Coordinator: Priscilla J. Bailey
Marketing Manager: Brenda L. Bravener-Greville

Lahaska Press, a unique collaboration between the Houghton Mifflin College Division and Lawrence Erlbaum Associates, is dedicated to publishing books and offering services for the academic and professional counseling communities. The partnership of Lahaska Press was formed in late 1999. The name *Lahaska* is a Native American Lenape word meaning "source of many writings." The small eastern Pennsylvania town of Lahaska, named by the Lenape, is the home of the Lahaska Press editorial offices.

Printed in the U.S.A.

ISBN: 0-618-19143-7

123456789- VHG -08 07 06 05 04

Contents

PREFACE

Acquiring Clinical Judgment is a supplement to *Theory and Design in Counseling and Psychotherapy* by Susan X Day. It augments the text by

- helping you study the chapter content in a condensed form;
- providing case examples with which to practice conceptualization and treatment planning;
- guiding your consideration of the interplay among personality, case, and theoretical orientation; and
- teaching you to read, with professional understanding, scholarly articles on counseling and psychotherapy.

Our focus is on helping you build the clinical judgment that will assist you in therapy and in academic pursuits. To this end, chapters in *Acquiring Clinical Judgment* include the following features:

Chapter Review

We summarize the main ideas of the chapter's theory and its practice.

Practice Test Questions

A self-test helps you assess your comprehension of the material. Answer keys appear in the back of the chapters.

Key Terms and Essential Concepts

Key ideas from the *Theory and Design* chapter are explained. These definitions help you review the theory and assist you in checking your work on Key Terms from the chapter. Terms and concepts are organized thematically to give your review coherence.

Graduated Practice with Cases

In the first three chapters, cases demonstrate the introductory concepts discussed. The case script for Chapter 1 shows the use of core conditions and an empirically supported treatment. Chapter 2 demonstrates the process of conceptualizing a case based on Kelly's personality constructs. Chapter 3 shows edited excerpts from a recorded discussion where experienced clinicians share ethical concerns arising in their counseling work.

In the cases provided for each of the theories described in Chapters 4–10, we begin by providing the case of a representative client and questions applying concepts to determine conceptualizations and choice of techniques. The second case, a core case, leaves more up to you regarding formulating thought and action appropriate to the situation. The third case emphasizes the interaction of therapist's style, client complaint, and theory and invites you to consider additions from theories outside the chapter. These three types of case example are further described below.

Representative Case

A case appropriate for the chapter's theoretical orientation is presented. These cases are drawn from aggregates of real counseling clients' situations.

Thinking About the Representative Case

Specific questions guide your thinking about the representative case. This will help you see the features that would be emphasized by a counselor of the chapter's orientation.

Check Your Thinking About the Representative Case

So that you can tell whether your responses to the questions were along the lines consistent with the theory under study, we provide some answers of our own.

Core Case

Core cases are repeated in several chapters demonstrating a number of ways to conceptualize client needs. The basic case description (see **D** below) is given in one chapter. When the case is shown the second or third time, different theoretical concepts are applied (see **A** below) and different plans (**P**) for future interventions are noted.

Data, Assessment, Plan

The three words above are a standard format used by psychologists in writing case notes. **D** designates Data, where the client's characteristics and symptoms are described. **A** stands for Assessment, where the clinician gives diagnostic impressions and conceptualizes client dynamics. **P**, or Plan, tells the plan for future counseling interventions and when applicable, client homework assignments.

Finding a Balance

Most counselors choose several theoretical approaches that suit their personality preferences. Integrating several approaches also allows a counselor to cover variations in client traits and clinical issues. A comparison is made among theoretical approaches showing how different preferences influence the work with the client.

Key Therapist Preferences

In this section, counselors' personal characteristics are identified and tied to concepts and practices used by the approach described in the chapter.

Case Example

A case is described that could clearly benefit from the theory and technique of the chapter, but could also lend itself to integration of other approaches.

Applying Therapist Preferences

This section demonstrates the counselor's preferences in action by describing what interventions might be used in therapy.

Comparison with Other Approaches

A comparison is made with other approaches showing how different counselor attributes and conceptual preferences might change conceptualizations.

Course of Therapy

Sometimes the full resolution of client issues is not complete using one of the three formats, so the case description is extended.

Exceptions

Chapters 5 and 12 have a core case as an example for the Finding a Balance section. Chapter 11, describing cultural systems does not discuss a comparison to other theoretical orientations. All counselors are expected to adapt theoretical conceptualizations and techniques to fit with clients' cultural backgrounds. Neither does Chapter 13 make comparisons to other approaches given the multiple possibilities of integrating numerous theories.

An Example of Published Research Using This Theory

Each chapter closes with a reprint of a published journal article that shows research based on the chapter's theory. These articles are annotated in text boxes, which explain conventions of scholarly writing, research design and methodology, and statistical analyses. Our intention is to guide students through relevant research materials while teaching them how to read research with understanding. Discussion ideas follow each article and include brainstorming questions about how other similar research might be performed.

Answer Key for Practice Test Questions

Answers to the practice test questions are located at the end of each chapter.

Acquiring Clinical Judgment

A Workbook/Casebook

CHAPTER 1

Effective Ingredients of Counseling and Psychotherapy

Chapter Review

The structure of counseling provides some basic interactional patterns and expectations. Most clients come to therapy with a conflict that may be interpersonal, intrapersonal, or derived from society. The goal of counseling is to create change for the client—a change in thinking, emotions and/or behavior. Since counseling involves a conversation between people, the personhood of the counselor is an important factor in the dialogue. The counselor's personality, his or her strengths and preferences, affect the choices in structuring the interaction. Extraverts may be more active in the counseling exchange; introverts may be more laid back. Values and philosophy of life as well as personal experiences affect counselors' reactions to clients and provide an underlying approach to counseling. Theories add a systematic methodology to therapy considerations; but from the personhood of the counselor comes the expression of the conceptual ideas. Counselors integrate their personal, stylistic preferences with their choices of theoretical orientations.

Empirical research supports the importance of the client-therapist relationship as critical to positive counseling outcome, contributing thirty percent to client change. The therapeutic alliance is one of the common factors affecting client change, along with healing setting, professional trust, therapeutic procedures, and a conceptual framework for the psychological work. Many common factors have been identified by experts, and both the counselor and the client play a part in the optimal combination of common factors.

Both the client and the counselor contribute to successful counseling. The client, who is distressed, who actively seeks treatment, and who brings positive expectations, is most likely to experience beneficial change. Counselors contribute to therapy by demonstrating nonpossessive warmth, genuineness, and accurate empathy to create a helpful relationship. The counselor also enhances hope, encourages emotional sharing, offers new learning, and facilitates improvement in the client's sense of self-confidence and self-efficacy. The counselor listens carefully to the client's verbal and nonverbal self-expressions, suspends judgment, notes common themes, and promotes behavioral change.

Empirically supported therapies, ESTs, or empirically validated therapies, EVTs, have been found to be effective in controlled studies where interventions are compared to no treatment or another treatment. Such literature demonstrates the value of pharmacological treatments for a number of disorders. However, only a small portion of a client's improvement is attributed to specific counseling interventions (8–15 percent). Still, reimbursement for managed care insurance plans require counselors to use ESTs associated with specific presenting concerns, and ESTs are considered the standard of care in liability suits. A reasonable compromise between the controversy emphasizing common factors vs. specific interventions would be to use ESTs within the context of a strong therapeutic alliance and other common factors. Theory provides the rationale that both the client and the counselor need to trust their counseling efforts. Theory also establishes a coherent framework for systematically applying ESTs.

Practice Test Questions

True or False: Consider each statement and try to explain in your own mind why it might not be fully true. Be sure to take into account any qualifying factors that might make the statement untrue. If you decide that the statement is fully true, circle **T**. Otherwise, circle **F**.

T   F   1.   An alliance between the client and counselor has been shown to make psychological work easier, but it is not necessary for client change.

T   F   2.   Myths, ritual, or procedures create faith in the therapeutic process for counselors and clients, but such hocus pocus is not necessary for client change.

T   F   3.   EVTs, or empirically validated treatments, is a more accurate term than ESTs, empirically supported treatments.

T   F   4.   ESTs researchers and common factors supporters generally don't argue about the efficacy of pharmacological interventions.

T   F   5.   Common factors advocates admit that a larger percentage of therapy outcome is due to ESTs rather than the therapeutic alliance.

T   F   6.   Tailoring counseling interventions to client characteristics eliminates the use of ESTs.

Multiple Choice: Circle the one letter next to the best answer to the following questions or to complete the sentence stems.

1.   The healing setting is characterized by the following:
   a.   an atmosphere of trust the client needs to tell the whole truth.
   b.   a competent professional counselor that the client can view as someone who knows what he is doing.
   c.   defined conditions and topics for counseling with a focus on the client, not the counselor.
   d.   all of the above.

2.   A coherent rationale, conceptual scheme, for counseling is defined as follows:
   a.   The counselor tells the client what is wrong and how to change.
   b.   The client disagrees with the counselor's diagnosis but is required to capitulate.
   c.   The counselor and client agree on what is wrong and what a good outcome would look like.
   d.   The right theory proven by ESTs utilized by the counselor regardless of client input.

3.   Client characteristics shown to contribute to positive outcomes in counseling include
   a.   positive expectations for therapy.
   b.   a feeling of complacency, not distress.
   c.   a high level of motivation related to consequences imposed by referral agent.
   d.   a considerable amount of time to devote to counseling assignments.

4. Studies showing the effect of training of counselors on therapeutic outcome show that
   a. clients seeing experienced counselors show no more improvement than clients seeing inexperienced graduate students or college professors.
   b. individual counselors do not improve their skills when they receive more training.
   c. training is one of the common factors shown to influence positive change for clients.
   d. clients seeing trained counselors improve, but those seeing untrained counselors stay the same.

5. The characteristics of the counselor and the contributions counselors make to facilitate client change include
   a. accurate empathy, nonpossessive warmth, genuineness.
   b. linking emotional arousal to DSM diagnosis.
   c. identifying the client's sense of self-loathing to interpersonal relationships.
   d. telling clients what they are doing wrong and predicting the negative consequences.

6. Choosing to follow ESTs vs. trusting the therapeutic impact of common factors is influenced by which of the following?
   a. Insurance companies insist counselors use ESTs for reimbursement purposes.
   b. Clients could sue if ESTs were called for and not used.
   c. ESTs are easier to learn than the convoluted theories.
   d. Common factors are enhanced by the systematic application of ESTs.
   e. a, b, and d
   f. a, b, and c

Core Case: Marianna Chavez

Core cases will be repeated in several chapters showing how different counseling approaches might work with the same client. Marianna, the client in this core case, will be conceptualized from the perspectives of Gestalt, behavioral and cognitive-behavioral approaches in chapters to come. In this chapter, a dialogue demonstrates core conditions and then an EST intervention. In the first part of the dialogue notice the establishment of the therapeutic relationship.

MARIANNA: Sometimes I'm so energized, like when I talk on a panel for diversity, and I explain to the audience how terrible it is in my country with the drug lords. How people die! Like my grandparents.

COUNSELOR: You're enthusiastic about political causes, but there is sadness too, in your expression.

MARIANNA: Yes, I feel sad.

COUNSELOR: You have memories, like with your grandparents?

MARIANNA: (Crying) Yes, I see them. I picture them in my head. They have been killed. There is blood.

COUNSELOR: It is very hard when you remember.

MARIANNA: (Continues crying) I remember a lot. For a long time I could forget, but now the pictures, I see them all the time. I'm so tired.

COUNSELOR: I see the struggle in your face. It hurts you a lot.

MARIANNA: (Quietly) Yes. I am afraid. Sometimes I don't leave my room. I just sit in the dark with the curtains covering the window.

COUNSELOR: The memories are so scary, you hide. You just feel fear and pain.

MARIANNA:	So many bad things happened. Like with men, boys.
MARIANNA:	(Loudly) I try to talk to my mother but she won't talk!!
COUNSELOR:	You want to talk about your memories. It's difficult when there's no one to talk to.
MARIANNA:	I have to get out of my hole! I want to be normal, date, like other girls.
COUNSELOR:	You're buried in your room, in the dark, in your painful memories. You want things to change.
MARIANNA:	(Sobbing) Yes, things have to get better.

Later, in the course of therapy: Marianna's fears have been conditioned by traumatic events in her life. The following shows the counselor using a behavioral therapy technique, systematic desensitization, to help her overcome an aversion to gold, a reminder of a trauma. This is an example of a well-grounded EST.

COUNSELOR:	Close your eyes. Place your feet flat on the floor. Adjust your position in the chair to get comfortable. When you are comfortable, nod your head.

Marianna nods.

COUNSELOR:	Now bend your ankles so your toes are pointing up to the ceiling. Press your heels down hard and tighten your feet and your calves. Press hard and tighten. Now, let go, let your feet rest comfortably on the floor. Feel the muscles relax. Your toes, your feet, your calves are relaxed.

Marianna rests her feet down on the floor.

COUNSELOR:	Now, press your thighs down into the chair and tighten the muscles, tight, press. Now, let go, let the muscles relax. Feel the looseness in the thigh muscles. And, relax, your feet relaxed, calves relaxed, thighs relaxed.

Marianna relaxes her legs and feet.

COUNSELOR:	Now press your buttocks together and press down. Tighten your buttocks, tight. Now let go, relax, feel the muscles relax. Now tighten your stomach. Pull your stomach in and tighten, tight and hard. Now, let go, relax the muscles. Relax. Relax your stomach, your buttocks, thighs, calves, and feet. Relax from your waist to your toes, relax. Breathe deeply, and let the air flow, in and out. In and out. Just relax.

Marianna relaxes.

COUNSELOR:	Now, raise your left hand up and bend your elbow. Press your elbow down into the arm of the chair and make a fist. Tighten your hand muscles in a fist. Tighten your forearm and upper arm muscles. Tight. Press down. And, tighten your fist. . . .
	Now, let go, let the arm muscles and your hands relax. Relax. Lay your arm back down beside you, and loosen your fist. Let your hand open and feel the fingers relax. Just relax.
	Now, raise your right hand up and bend your elbow. Press this elbow down into the chair and make a fist. Tighten you hand muscles in a fist. Tighten your forearm and upper arm muscles. Tight. Press down. And, tighten your fist. Now, let go, let the arm muscles and your hand relax. Relax. Lay your arm back down beside you and loosen your fist. Let your hand open and feel the fingers relax. Just relax.
	Feel the relaxation. Your fingers, hands, forearms, upper arms. Arms and hands relaxed. Thighs and calves, relaxed. Feet and toes relaxed. Toes, legs,

arms, all relaxed. Breathe deeply, and let the air flow, in and out. In and out. Just relax.

Marianna relaxes.

Counselor: Now tighten your back muscles. Press your back into the back of the chair. Feel your shoulders tighten. Then, tighten your chest and press back more. Tight. Tighten. . . . Now, relax. Let the muscles loosen and relax. Just let go. Feel the relaxation. Just relax. Chest, shoulders, back, stomach, all relaxed. Arms, hands, fingers, all relaxed. Thighs, calves, feet, and toes, all relaxed. Feel the relaxation. Breathe deeply, and let the air flow, in and out. In and out. Just relax.

Marianna relaxes.

COUNSELOR: Now pay attention to your eyes. Squint and tighten your eyes. Feel your face tighten up. Press your lips together and clench your teeth, jaw, tight. Feel the tightness throughout your face. Tighten your forehead. Tight, tight, all over your face. Now let go. Let the muscles loosen and feel the relaxation. Try to tighten your scalp. Tight. Feel the tightness. Let go, let your scalp, eyes, cheeks, lips, all relax. Feel the relaxation. Now, twist your neck to the right, lowering your head. Tighten the neck muscles. Tight. Let go. Let the muscles relax. Now, twist your neck to the right. Tighten the neck muscles. Tight. Now, relax the muscles. Just let go. Feel the muscles relax. Relax. Feel the relaxation in your neck, scalp, face. Relax. Feel your chest, arms, hands relax. Feel your stomach and buttocks relax. Your thighs, calves, feet, all relaxed. Relax. From your toes, legs, stomach, arms, back, chest, all relaxed. Your face, scalp, neck, relaxed. Feel the relaxation. Breathe deeply and let the air flow in, and out. In and out. Just relax. When you feel completely relaxed, raise your finger.

Marianna relaxes. She raises her finger.

Now I want you to imagine you are walking in the meadow. There's green grass at your feet. The sky is open and blue with a soft yellow sun. The air is clean and softly warm. You're walking on a path. Your body is relaxed and you're enjoying the lovely day.

If you feel anything other than relaxation, raise your finger.

Marianna relaxes, face composed.

You're walking in the sunlight, enjoying the day. You notice a small rock on the side of the path. The sun shines on the rock, and it appears to be a golden color. You kneel down to pick up the rock and hold it in your hand to look at it. If you feel anything other than relaxation, raise your finger.

Marianna relaxes, face composed.

The rock is shiny. Probably not gold. You toss the rock, raising your arm back, and throwing it ahead of you. The rock flies through the air and drops. If you feel anything other than relaxation, raise your finger.

Marianna relaxes, face composed.

Now you see another shiny object. A piece of jewelry. The sun shines on a medallion with a chain. It appears to be a golden color. You kneel down and pick up the necklace and hold it in your hand to look at it. If you feel anything other than relaxation, raise your finger.

Marianna looks composed, but she turns her head and holds up her finger.

O.K. Relax. Breathe in and breathe out. Jest let the necklace drop to the ground. Let it go. Let it slip from your fingers and fall to the ground, next to your feet. Step forward. Just let the necklace lay there on the ground and walk away. Notice the sun shining. The blue sky. The green meadow. Relax. Breathe in and breathe out. Relax. If you feel anything other than relaxation, raise your finger.

Marianna relaxes.

Now, in a moment you will open your eyes. But first, breathe in and breathe out. Feel the relaxation throughout your body and breath. Now when you are ready, open your eyes.

Marianna opens her eyes and reports she feels relaxed. She has experienced her first encounter with gold while relaxed. Gradual exposure during relaxation will desensitize her to the aversion to gold. Later, she will face more intense fears and deal with her other traumas.

Thinking About Marianna Chavez

1. How does the counselor show accurate empathy in the script?
2. While working with Marianna, how does the counselor combine the use of an EST and common factors?
3. How does Marianna want her life to change?
4. How do the use of core conditions and the EST of systematic desensitization help the client move toward her goal?

Check Your Thinking About Marianna

1. The counselor notes Marianna is enthusiastic about her political speeches but also shows a sad facial expression. The counselor reflects that Marianna has memories of loosing her grandparents and that recalling the memories brings pain and hurt. Marianna's responses indicate that the counselor's statements are accurately reflecting the emotional experience. Responding to the empathic understanding, the client continues to open up, describing her flashbacks and fear and revealing her withdrawal to her room. The counselor shows an understanding that hiding comes in reaction to Marianna's emotional trepidation. Finally, the counselor recognizes Marianna's need to talk about her difficulties and her desire to have a more normal life.

2. The counselor encourages Marianna to fully describe her emotional experience within the context of a helping relationship that is warm and understanding. Once an atmosphere of safety and trust is built, the counselor introduces and implements an EST (desensitization), demonstrating expertise by using a technique supported by research.

3. Marianna wants to move past her painful memories and to join her peers in a normal social life. She says she wants the flashbacks to end, and she wants to stop hiding in her room. She hints that relationships with men may be problematic, given her memories; but she wants to be like other young women her age and have dates.

4. The counselor's genuineness, empathy, and warmth create a helping relationship where Marianna feels comfortable sharing her feelings and her difficulties. The desensitization (an EST) is used to dissociate the negative association between gold and her pain. Releasing emotions and learning to respond differently to triggers for her memories will help Marianna put her past trauma behind her. She can move toward her goal of a normal social life as she lets go of her difficult past.

Example of a Published Research Article on Common Factors

Each chapter will contain a reprint of an article from a professional journal. The commentary in the boxes to the left of the article will help you understand the research and the format of the piece.

This article is a research summary on common factors.

> This is a research summary. The authors did not perform experiments themselves, but pulled together the results of many research studies and combinations of studies. This type of publication, also called a *review of research*, is extremely helpful in getting an overview of a topic and in building a list of studies to look up on the topic. The authors will cite the major works to date.

Research Summary on the Therapeutic Relationship and Psychotherapy Outcome

Michael J. Lambert and Dean E. Barley

Factors that influence client outcome can be divided into four areas: extratherapeutic factors, expectancy effects, specific therapy techniques, and common factors. Common factors have been shown to correlate more highly with client outcome such as empathy, warmth, and the therapeutic relationship than specialized treatment interventions. The common factors most frequently studied have been the person-centered facilitative conditions (empathy, warmth, congruence) and the therapeutic alliance. Decades of research indicate that the provision of therapy is an interpersonal process in which a main curative component is the nature of the therapeutic relationship. Clinicians must remember that this is the foundation of our efforts to help others. The improvement of psychotherapy may best be accomplished by learning to improve one's ability to relate to clients and tailoring that relationship to individual clients.

> *Outcome* refers to the end product of counseling and psychotherapy, so it could mean relief of symptoms, improvement in functioning, beneficial personality change, or a combination of these. There are many ways to define and measure outcome.

Psychotherapy outcome research has examined the relation between client progress and a variety of variables. These variables typically include extratherapeutic factors (e.g., spontaneous remission, fortuitous events, social support); expectancy (including the placebo effect); specific therapy techniques (e.g., biofeedback, hypnosis, systematic desensitization); and common factors, that is variables found in most therapies. The relative importance of these various factors in producing client change has been vigorously debated on theoretical and empirical grounds for over six decades.

This debate has been documented by extensive reviews of the outcome-research literature (e.g., Bergin, 1971; Bergin & Lambert, 1978; Gurman & Razin, 1977; Lambert, 1982; Lambert with meta-analytic summaries of this same literature (e.g., Andrews & Harvey, 1981; Lipsey & Wilson, 1993; Shapiro &

Reprinted by permission of *Psychotherapy*.

Bergin, 1994; Lambert, Shapiro, & Bergin, 1986; Luborsky, Singer, & Luborsky, 1975; Meltzoff & Kornreich, 1970) along Shapiro, 1982; Smith, Glass, & Miller, 1980; Wampold et al., 1997). Based on extensive reviews of the psychotherapy-outcome literature, we have drawn several conclusions about the comparative impact of the above factors on client outcome. These conclusions are summarized in Figure 1.

The estimates presented, while not derived directly from meta-analytic techniques, characterize the research findings of a wide range of treatments, disorders, and ways of measuring client and therapist characteristics. The estimates represent research findings that span extremes in research designs, and are especially representative of studies that allow the greatest divergence in the variables that determine outcome. The percentages were derived by taking a subset of more than 100 studies that provided statistical analyses of the predictors of outcome and averaging the size of the contribution each predictor made to final outcome. Figure 1 is offered as a painstakingly derived, albeit crude, estimate of the relative contribution of a variety of variables that impact outcome. This diagram highlights that, among those factors most closely associated with therapist activity, the common factors, or client-therapist relationship factors, are most significant in contributing to positive therapy outcome.

This figure illustrates the relative importance of the factors that influence client outcome. The reader will notice

> In making up Figure 1, the authors included the broadest range of types of studies possible. For example, they included research that defined and measured outcome in different manners. They also included a range of research designs. They were attempting to get the big picture.

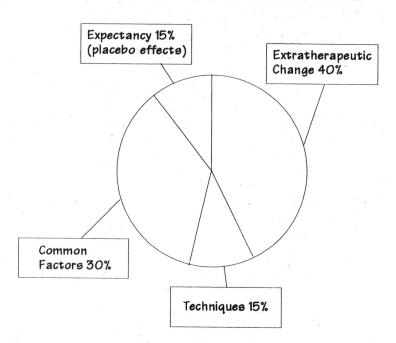

Figure 1.

Percentage of improvement
in psychotherapy patients
as a function of therapeutic factors

In research reports, you will often see the phrase "accounts for x% of the variance." This means that statistically, a certain variable was responsible for x percent of the change seen in the clients (in this article) or of the change in a group or other condition. Something that accounts for a small amount of the variance is not an influential variable. For example, therapist eye color probably accounts for zero percent of the variance in client outcome.

that a great deal of client outcome (40%) is attributable to factors outside of therapy. Expectancy effects and specific therapeutic techniques each account for only 15% of outcome variance. On the other hand, common factors, which include the client-therapist relationship, are more significant in contributing to client improvement and account for 30% of the variance in client outcome.

In discussing client-therapist relationship factors, it is difficult to conceptually differentiate between therapist variables (e.g., interpersonal style, therapist attributes), facilitative conditions (empathy, warmth, congruence), and the therapeutic alliance. These concepts are not mutually exclusive or distinct, but are interdependent and overlapping. The research in these areas is discussed fully in other articles in this special issue.

Therapist attributes have been carefully studied as a source of variation in client outcome. Research has documented clearly that some therapists are better than others at promoting positive client outcome in general and that some therapists produce better results with some types of clients than others (Lambert & Bergin, 1994; Lambert & Okiishi, 1997; Orlinsky & Howard, 1980). In spite of research designs intended to minimize therapist effects on outcome, differences attributable to the therapists are frequently found (Luborsky, McClellan, Woody, O'Brien, & Auerbach, 1985; Shapiro & Firth, 1987; Shapiro, Firth-Cozens, & Stiles, 1989).

Some research designs try to minimize the effects of individual therapists, so that they can see the effects of different treatments clearly. To minimize therapist effects, researchers might make sure all therapists follow the same script, or they might choose therapists all at the same level of experience, skill, or some other variable.

Clients often attribute their positive therapy outcome to the personal attributes of their therapist (Lazarus, 1971; Sloane, Staples, Cristol, Yorkston, & Whipple, 1975). For example, Strupp, Fox, and Lessler (1969) reported that patients who felt that their therapy was successful described their therapist as "warm, attentive, interested, understanding, and respectful" (p. 116). Similarly, in a comprehensive review of over 2,000 process-outcome studies since 1950, Orlinsky, Grave, and Parks (1994) identified several therapist variables and behaviors consistently shown to have a positive impact on treatment outcome. Factors such as therapist credibility, skill, empathic understanding, and affirmation of the patient, along with the ability to engage the patient, to focus on the patient's problems, and to direct the patient's attention to the affective experience were highly related to successful treatment.

The three facilitative conditions are associated with Carl Rogers and are also called "the core conditions" and just "the conditions."

These are similar to the three facilitative conditions proposed by the person-centered school. The three conditions are empathic understanding, the degree to which the therapist is successful in communicating personal comprehension of the client's experience; positive regard, the extent to which the therapist communicates nonevaluative caring and respect; and congruence, the extent to which the therapist is nondefensive, real, and not "phony."

Several reviews of the research on the facilitative conditions and client outcome have been completed. Lambert,

In the study of counseling, features can be scored or rated from different points of view. For example, the therapeutic relationship could be judged and scored by the client, by the therapist, or by an outside rater watching the session or a videotape. The client's rating of the relationship is more closely related to outcome than the outside raters'.

DeJulio, and Stein (1978) reviewed 17 well-designed and executed studies and concluded that these studies presented "only modest evidence" that such factors relate to outcome. Greenberg, Elliott, and Lietaer (1994) conducted a meta-analysis of four studies that examined the correlations between therapist ability to facilitate (provision of the facilitative conditions) and client outcome. The overall correlation between the three conditions and client outcome in this analysis was .43. Other reviewers (Gurman, 1977; Levant & Shlien, 1984; Mitchell, Bozarth, & Krauft, 1977; Patterson, 1984) have suggested that the relationship between therapist interpersonal skills and outcome is more ambiguous than originally postulated. Much of this ambiguity results from the way the proposed relationship factors have been measured. Research findings indicate that client-perceived relationship factors, rather than objective raters' perceptions of the relationship, obtain consistently more positive results (e.g., Cooley & LaJoy, 1980; Gurman, 1977; Miller, Taylor, & West, 1980). What appears to be vital is that the client feels understood, accepted, and prized in a way that is meaningful to that particular client (Bachelor, 1988). The therapeutic alliance has a broader definition than the facilitative conditions and includes the client's contributions to the relationship. The therapeutic alliance is often conceptualized as having three components: tasks, bonds, and goals. Tasks are the behaviors and processes within the therapy session that constitute the actual work of therapy. The goals of therapy are the objectives of therapy that both client and therapist endorse. Bonds include the positive interpersonal attachment between therapist and client of mutual trust, confidence, and acceptance (Bordin, 1976, 1989; Hatcher & Barends, 1996; Safran & Wallner, 1991).

Reviews of the research have consistently reported a positive relationship between the therapeutic alliance and outcome across studies, even though there are some instances where it fails to predict outcome, or where associations were nonsignificant (Gaston, 1990; Horvath & Greenberg, 1994; Horvath & Luborsky, 1993; Horvath & Symonds, 1991; Krupnick et al., 1996; Martin, Garske, & Davis, 2000). Horvath and Symonds's (1991) meta-analysis of 24 studies reported that 26% of the difference in the rate of therapeutic success was accounted for by the quality of the therapeutic alliance.

Practice Implications

In managed-care environments, accountability is emphasized, and empirically supported psychotherapies (Task Force, 1995) and manual-based interventions (Wilson, 1998) are often advocated. Therapists must indeed make every effort to stay current with new technical developments in the field, including specialized treatment techniques. However, it is imperative that clinicians remember that decades of research consistently demonstrate that relationship factors correlate more highly with client outcome than do specialized treatment techniques (Castonguay, Goldfried, Wiser, Raue, & Hayes, 1996). This is not to say that therapists should not focus on improving therapeutic techniques. The major points to be made here are that therapists need to remember that the development and maintenance of the therapeutic relationship is a primary curative component of therapy and that the relationship provides the context in which specific techniques exert their influence.

Given the importance of the facilitative conditions and the therapeutic alliance for successful treatment outcome, training in relationship skills is crucial for the beginning therapist. Successful training in the communication of empathy mandates that clinicians adapt their response style in accordance with how each particular client defines or experiences helpfulness. Clinicians may also improve client outcome by adapting their own interpersonal presentation to match other salient client variables that impact the therapeutic relationship (e.g., stage of change, client motivation, attachment style), as also presented in this special issue.

A constant emphasis on the therapeutic relationship is also recommended in continuing education for licensed professionals. Frequent evaluation of relationship factors is vital for experienced clinicians, and such factors should be specifically stressed during ongoing training, peer consultation, and supervision. Clinicians are advised to watch for a reduction in their ability to empathize and relate to clients that can indicate professional stress or burn out. For therapists to be effective, it is essential that they take care of themselves so that they are better able to care for clients.

It is clear that some therapists are better than others, at least with some clients. This is probably related to the therapist's contribution to the therapeutic alliance, especially in working with severe cases. Emphasizing relationship and other common factors in practice and research is likely to enhance client outcome far more than the current focus on specific techniques.

> After reviewing supportive research, the authors make their argument for a focus on relationship factors. They are making clear their stance on the common factors versus empirically supported techniques question. They believe that training of counselors needs to put the therapeutic relationship in the foreground, not mastery of specific techniques.

References

Andrews, G., & Harvey, R. (1981). Does psychotherapy benefit neurotic patients? A reanalysis of the Smith, Glass, and Miller data. *Archives of General Psychiatry, 38,* 1203–1208.

Bachelor, A. (1988). How clients perceive therapist empathy: A content analysis of "received" empathy. *Psychotherapy: Therapy, Research and Practice, 25,* 227–240.

This reference list includes some of the classic works on what makes psychotherapy effective.

Bergin, A. E. (1971). The evaluation of therapeutic outcomes. In A. E. Bergin & S. L. Garfield (Eds.), *Handbook of psychotherapy and behavior change* (pp. 217–270). New York: Wiley.

Bergin, A. E., & Lambert, M. J. (1978). The evaluation of outcomes in psychotherapy. In S. L. Garfield & A. E. Bergin (Eds.), *Handbook of psychotherapy and behavior change: An empirical analysis* (pp. 139–189). New York: Wiley.

Bordin, E. S. (1976). The generalizability of the psychoanalytic concept of the working alliance. *Psychotherapy: Theory, Research and Practice, 16,* 252–260.

Bordin, E. S. (1989, April). *Building therapeutic alliances: The base for integration.* Paper presented at the annual meeting of the Society for Exploration of Psychotherapy Integration, Berkeley, CA.

Castonquay, L. G., Goldfried, M. R., Wiser, S., Raue, P. J., & hayes, A. M. (1996). Predicting the effect of cognitive therapy for depression: A study of unique and common factors. *Journal of Consulting and Clinical Psychology, 65,* 497–504.

Cooley, E. F., & Lajoy, R. (1980). Therapeutic relationship and improvement as perceived by clients and therapists. *Journal of Clinical Psychology, 36,* 562–570.

Gaston, L. (1990). The concept of the alliance and its role in psychotherapy: Theoretical and empirical considerations. *Psychotherapy, 27,* 143–153.

Greenberg, L. S., Elliott, R., & Lietaer, G. (1994). Research on experiential psychotherapies. In A. E. Bergin & S. L. Garfield (Eds.), *Handbook of psychotherapy and behavior change* (4th ed., pp. 509–539). New York: Wiley.

Gurman, A. S. (1977). The patient's perception of the therapeutic relationship. In A. S. Gurman & A. M. Razin (Eds.), *Effective psychotherapy: A handbook of research* (pp. 503–543). New York: Pergamon.

Gurman, A. S., & Razin, A. M. (Eds.). (1977). *Effective psychotherapy: A handbook of research.* New York: Pergamon.

Hatcher, R. L., & Barends, A. W. (1996). Patients' view of the alliance in psychotherapy: Exploratory factor analysis of three alliance measures, *Journal of Consulting and Clinical Psychology, 64,* 1326–1336.

Horvath, A. O., & Greenbero, L. S. (Eds.). (1994). *The working alliance: Theory, research, practice.* New York: Wiley.

Horvath, A. O., & Luborsky, L. (1993). The role of the therapeutic alliance in psychotherapy. *Journal of Consulting and Clinical Psychology, 61,* 561–573.

Horvath, A. O., & Symonds, B. D. (1991). Relation between working alliance and outcome in psychotherapy: A meta-analysis. *Journal of Counseling Psychology, 38,* 139–149.

Krupnick, J. L., Stotsky, S, M., Simmons, S., Soyer, J., Watkins, J., Elkin, I., & Filkonis, P. A. (1996). The role of the therapeutic alliance in psychotherapy and pharmacotherapy outcome: Findings in the National Institute of Mental Health Treatment of Depression Collaborative Research Program, *Journal of Consulting and Clinical Psychology, 64,* 532–539.

Lambert, M. J. (1982). *The effects of psychotherapy* (Vol. 2). New York: Human Sciences Press.

Lambert, M. J., & Bergin, A. E. (1994). The effectiveness of psychotherapy. In A. E. Bergin & S. L. Garfield (Eds.), *Handbook of psychotherapy and behavior change* (4th ed., pp. 143–189). New York: Wiley.

Lambert, M. J., Dejulio, S. S., & Stein, D. M. (1978). Therapist interpersonal skills: Process, outcome, methodological considerations and recommendations for future research. *Psychological Bulletin, 85,* 467–489.

Lambert, M. J., & Okiishi, J. C. (1997). The effects of the individual psychotherapist and implications for future research. *Clinical Psychology: Science and Practice, 4,* 66–75.

Lambert, M. J., Shapiro, D. A., & Bergin, A. E. (1986). The effectiveness of psychotherapy. In S. L. Garfield & A. E. Bergin (Eds.), *Handbook of psychotherapy and behavior change* (3rd ed., pp. 157–212). New York: Wiley.

Lazarus, A. A. (1971). *Behavior therapy and beyond.* New York: McGraw-Hill.

Levant, R. F., & Shlien, J. M. (Eds.). (1984), *Client-centered therapy and the person-centered approach: New directions in theory, research and practice.* New York: Praeger.

Lipsey, M. W., & Wilson, D. B. (1993). The efficacy of psychological, educational, and behavioral treatment: Confirmation from meta-analysis. *American Psychologist, 48,* 1181–1209.

Luborsky, L., McClellan, A. T., Woody, G. E., O'Brien, C. P., & Auerbach, A. (1985). Therapist success and its determinants. *Archives of General Psychiatry, 42,* 602–611.

Luborsky, L., Singer, B., & Luborsky, L. (1975). Comparative studies in psychotherapy. *Archives of General Psychiatry, 32,* 995–1008.

Martin, D. J., Garske, J. P., & Davis, M. K. (2000). Relation of therapeutic alliance with outcome and other variables: A meta-analytic review. *Journal of Consulting and Clinical Psychology, 68,* 438–450.

Meltzoff, J., & Kornreich, M. (1970), *Research in psychotherapy.* New York: Atherton Press.

Miller, W. R., Taylor, C. A., & West, J. C. (1980). Focused versus broad-spectrum behavior therapy for problem drinkers.

Journal of Consulting and Clinical Psychology, 48, 590–601.

Mitchell, K. M., Bozarth, J. D., & Krauft, C. C. (1977). A reappraisal of the therapeutic effectiveness of accurate empathy, nonpossessive warmth, and genuineness. In A. S. Gurman & A. M. Razin (Eds.), *Effective psychotherapy: A handbook of research* (pp. 482–502). New York: Pergamon.

Orlinsky, D. E., Grave, K., & Parks, B. K. (1994). Process and outcome in psychotherapy—noch einmal. In A. E. Bergin & S. L. Garfield(Eds.), *Handbook of psychotherapy and behavior change* (pp. 257–310). New York: Wiley.

Orlinsky, D. E., & Howard, K. I. (1980). Gender and psychotherapeutic outcome. In A. M. Brodsky & R. T. Hare-Mustin (Eds.), *Women in psychotherapy* (pp. 3–34). New York: Guilford.

Patterson, C. H, (1984). Empathy, warmth, and genuineness: A review of reviews. *Psychotherapy, 21,* 431–438.

Safran, J. D., & Wallner, L. K. (1991). The relative predictive validity of two therapeutic alliance measures in cognitive therapy. *Psychological Assessment: A Journal of Consulting and Clinical Psychology, 3,* 188–195.

Shapiro, D. A., & Firth, J. (1987). Prescriptive vs. exploratory psychotherapy: Outcomes of the Sheffield psychotherapy project. *British Journal of Psychiatry, 151,* 790–799.

Shapiro, D. A., Firth-Cozens, J., & Stiles, W. B. (1989). The question of therapists' differential effectiveness: A Sheffield psychotherapy project addendum. *British Journal of Psychiatry, 154,* 383–385.

Shapiro, D. A., & Shapiro, D. (1982). Meta-analysis of comparative therapy outcome studies: A republication and refinement. *Psychological Bulletin, 92,* 581–604.

Sloane, R. B., Staples, F. R., Cristol, A. H., Yorkston, N. J. I., & Whipple, K. (1975). *Short-term analytically oriented psychotherapy vs. behavior therapy.* Cambridge, MA; Harvard University Press.

Smith, M. L., Glass, G. V., & Miller, T. I. (1980). *The benefits of psychotherapy.* Baltimore: Johns Hopkins University Press.

Strupp, H. H., Fox, R. E., & Lessler, K. (1969). *Patients view their psychotherapy.* Baltimore: Johns Hopkins University Press.

Task Force on Promotion and Dissemination of Psychological Procedures. (1995). Training in and dissemination of empirically validated therapies. *The Clinical Psychologist, 49,* 3–23.

Wampold, B. E., Mondin, G. W., Moody, M., STICH, F., Benson, K., & Ahn, H. (1997). A meta-analysis of outcome studies comparing bona fide psychotherapies; Empirically, "all must have prizes." *Psychological Bulletin, 122,* 203–215.

Wilson, G. T. (1998). Manual-based treatment and clinical practice. *Clinical Psychology: Science and Practice, 5,* 363–375.

Discussion Ideas

1. The authors include "the placebo effect" in expectancy factors. What are placebo effects in counseling situations? Why is it harder to find a placebo effect in counseling than in medical treatments?

2. Give examples of some extratherapeutic factors that might influence client progress.

3. What would you trust most as data on the level of therapeutic alliance--ratings from the therapist, from the client, or from outside judges? What are the advantages of each type of rating?

4. List the adjectives that describe the effective therapist in the article. In your experience, which four or five are the most important? Why?

Answer Key for Practice Test Questions

True/False		Multiple Choice	
1.	F	1.	d
2.	F	2.	c
3.	F	3.	a
4.	T	4.	a
5.	F	5.	a
6.	F	6.	e

CHAPTER 2
Theory and Case Analysis

Chapter Review

A theory is a set of related principles that describes phenomena or facts and can be used to make predictions about how the phenomena will occur in the future. Checking the accuracy of predictions can test the theory, and if the forecasts are born out, the theory can help us comprehend how events happen, guiding our actions for similar situations. Counseling theory organizes, articulates, and integrates the factual knowledge and experience of a number of people in the field. Theories are never fully proven empirically, though they can be disproven, and testing across situations is necessary.

Experience allows clinicians to contextualize and situate the client so irrelevant information is excluded and important information is parsimoniously used to look at deeper, essential client themes. Theory is made up of such insights, offering a coherent structure that can be trusted as plausible. Theory illuminates the underlying links and potential causes of client dynamics. Conceptual systems explain the vagaries of twists and turns in therapy, providing clues when the process has derailed and showing how to get back on track. Knowing theory helps therapists choose alternative techniques within a framework that can be explained and trusted by the client.

Case conceptualization is basically a mini-theory about a specific client describing the client's presentation, both healthy and unhealthy behavior, relevant descriptive information, the presenting concern, appropriate historical experiences, interpersonal style, environmental factors, and personality characteristics. With a full client description, theory offers explanations for client dynamics and what change is needed to deal with difficulties.

Some conceptualizations are taken from personality theory such as Kelly's constructs that summarize how people psychologically construe their views of the world. The client's social setting and relationship network includes a person's background perspective of intimate relationships, cooperative activities, social themes and patterns, acceptable climates for complaints, and roles played that support others. External social influences include how others see the person, group identifications, political and social issues, and areas where the person is included or excluded. Patterns of speech and versatility of thought and activities are other social identifiers. The person's economic resources affect psychological constructs including those dependencies that define the individual's basic lifestyle requirements. Finally, turning points in a person's life force the individual to change constructs during transitional periods.

In determining conceptualizations, a number of aids help clarify and expand counselor thinking. Predictions about clients are kept in therapists' personal notes, rather than in permanent records. Diagrams of the client's cognitive structure can be helpful. Brainstorming possible hypotheses and thinking in metaphors facilitate creative explanations. Psychological tests

16

organize the multiplicity of variables to consider. It can also be useful to collect client materials such as journals, drawings, and the like. Counselors bring to mind loose associations about the client during free moments and sometimes gain new conceptualizing insights. However, it is important to remember that the counselor's inferences, drawn from her life experience, may not be applicable to the client's life. Keeping in mind differences and similarities between the counselor and the client prevents misinterpretations. Protecting notes with appropriate security measures is also critical.

DSM diagnoses are helpful, not to categorize the client, but to help the clinician consider relevant factors for disorders. Diagnostic questioning defines the severity of problems and offers clues for some treatment planning, if not full conceptualizations. DSM categories include Axis I for presenting problems; Axis II for personality disorders; Axis III for medical conditions; Axis IV for environmental or psychosocial difficulties; and Axis V for GAF, 0–100 scale for a global assessment of functioning.

Therapists observe client characteristics and behavior and make inferences regarding the client's personality and psychological issues. A clear, undistracted focus on the client's appearance, nonverbal behavior, facial expressions, and common themes builds a picture of the client as a person. However, when making inferences, it is easy for the counselor to make errors in interpretations, such as inferring that client problems have a single cause to the exclusion of other factors, diagnosing based on the counselor's new learning or personal experiences, selecting evidence to confirm bias, attributing behavior to character flaws without factoring in external influences, and making unsubstantiated correlations. However, the possibility of inferential errors does not mean clinicians can afford to avoid all inferences, since case conceptualizations require searching for underlying patterns. The study of theory informs clinicians so inferences have some basis from knowledge in the field.

PRACTICE TEST QUESTIONS

True or False: Consider each statement and try to explain in your own mind why it might not be fully true. Be sure to take into account any qualifying factors that might make the statement untrue. If you decide that the statement is fully true, circle **T**. Otherwise, circle **F**.

T F 1. Clinicians should not remember previous clients when conceptualizing and choosing techniques for new clients.

T F 2. Case conceptualizations integrate information about the client into a coherent form that explains current and past behavior.

T F 3. To maintain efficiency, case conceptualizations remain the same once formed.

T F 4. DSM-IV-TR is based on ideas from a number of theories.

T F 5. Usually we attribute our own behavior to our personality and the behavior of others to situational factors.

Multiple Choice: Circle the one letter next to the best answer to the following questions or to complete the sentence stems.

1. Which of the following are inferential errors to be avoided in conceiving case conceptualizations?
   a. We become too tied to a single-cause etiology without considering other explanations.
   b. A compelling point of view is dismissed in favor of multilayered theoretical interpretations
   c. We observe two situations as related and assume other explanations might be more plausible.
   d. a and c
   e. a, b, and c

2. In making accurate observations of a client, our inferences are best supported when
   a. we have experienced our own neuroses so we know how it feels and operates.
   b. the information is based on many observations across situations..
   c. we are observing socially desirable traits that everyone wants to imitate.
   d. clients have complex pathology so we can easily detect their impairment

3. Which of the following are valid criticisms of the DSM?
   a. It encourages clinicians to treat clients according to the diagnostic label.
   b. Clinicians can observe a set of symptoms and determine follow-up questions to ask.
   c. Health-care paperwork follows the client and diagnoses may not be accurate.
   d. DSM diagnoses are more precise than client reports.
   e. a and b
   f. a and c

4. Which of the following are recommended aids for case conceptualization?
   a. Predictions regarding client behavior between sessions should be noted in the formal case record.
   b. Draw a map of the client's problems, thoughts, behaviors, and situation with arrows showing the relationships among the factors.
   c. Determine the diagnosis and stick to it for maximum treatment efficiency.
   d. Generate a metaphor for your sense of the relationship with the client.
   e. a and b
   f. b and d

5. Kelly's theory of personality constructs does not include which of the following?
   a. social setting and network of relationships, including support systems and significant relationships
   b. characterizing the client by external sources, such as others' opinions, group membership, and conflicts caused by societal influences
   c. physical resources, such as income and lifestyle dependencies
   d. use of language, range and variety of activities, thoughts, sex habits
   e. all of the above
   f. none of the above

6. A *theory* is a set of principles that
   a. explains some phenomena or facts.
   b. predicts how phenomena will occur in the future.
   c. is tested by checking accuracy of predictions.
   d. proves what decisions and actions will work under any conditions.
   e. a, b, and c
   f. all of the above

Representative Case: William Phillip

Counselors conceptualize cases by arranging client information into a meaningful framework to give both the therapist and the client the rationale, or structure, for the client's psychological work. In each chapter describing specific approaches, a representative case will demonstrate how one client's dynamics and situation represent a particular theory's concepts. After the case description, questions will stimulate your thinking about the client.

The following representative case illustrates specific personality constructs as described by Kelly. Consider your own impressions, building a case conceptualization and compare your thinking to the author's.

A young man age 21, William, has recently decided to quit the golf circuit where he has spent three years trying to qualify for PGA status. His appearance suits a country club environment: name brand casual dress with subdued colors; neat, trim physique; blond, well styled haircut. He speaks softly and, with ease, using descriptive phrases, such as, "sailing through life." He describes his family as "well off" economically, but certainly "not rich."

William presents himself for counseling two years after his father's death.

His father, a corporate executive, was an alcoholic. After a number of years, the father became increasingly dysfunctional, lost his job, and was admitted to a treatment center. He left treatment without medical recommendation and came home. William, the youngest sibling of three, felt a strong bond with his father since the two shared a passion for golf and spent many hours together on the course. When his father came home, only William believed the Dad's rationale that "he could lick this disease on his own." William watched over his father, trying to make sure his Dad didn't drink. One day, William was absent from home briefly to run an errand, and when he returned, his father was gone. William found him, drowned in a nearby lake.

William's older brother took over the family's finances and managed to put things in order so William and his mother were able to maintain their lifestyle. The recent downturn in the stock market has made the financial situation more precarious. The brother tried to take on a mentor role and advised William to attend college as a business major. William insisted on following the dream he shared with his father, to enter the golfing circuit. Given his limited success at golf, William feels he has dishonored his father's memory. In addition, William is "pre-engaged" to a young woman whose family belongs to the same country club where William and his father golfed. His fiancée will graduate from college in a year and expects to marry. William is extremely jealous of his girlfriend's social activities, knowing that other young men from their social set may be better able to provide the appropriate lifestyle for her. Whenever William and his fiancée are not together, he questions her every action.

William attributes his depressive symptoms to his discouragement with his golf game. For six months William has become increasingly sad, crying at times with no precipitating event. His concentration has progressively worsened; guilty feelings have become, at times, overwhelming, and he feels insecure much of the time.

Thinking About William

1. How would you describe William's social environment? In what ways does his family background affect his view of life? What are the social habits of his world? What kinds of complaints are acceptable? What roles does the client understand as important in his life?

2. How would other people in William's life describe him? What external events in society have affected his life?

3. How does the client express himself? How versatile are his thinking and participant activities?

4. What economic resources does the client have? What economic dependencies has he developed?

5. What are the major biographical turning points in William's life? What predictions would you have for William's future?

Check Your Thinking About William

1. William's family income represents an upper-middle or lower-upper-class category. His father's income provided a home in an exclusive neighborhood, complete with a lake and country club. Complaining about psychological pressures was not acceptable. Although his father has died, William's role as a good son, making his father proud, was and continues to be a primary one. Fitting in with others in the suburb and looking forward to a similar lifestyle with his childhood sweetheart is his picture of how his life should turn out in the future.

2. William's brother would describe him as too sensitive and unwilling to move forward in life. People within the family's social group would describe him as a nice young man from a nice family, but maybe somewhat naïve and ineffectual. The stock market downturn is a societal event affecting his life.

3. William's use of language sounds as though he is better educated than a typical high school graduate. His thinking and activities have not expanded beyond his background, though he is coming to a point where he needs to take on more adult responsibilities.

4. William has few economic resources. His mother's income through her husband's estate has supported the two of them for several years, but it sounds as though such an arrangement may soon become impossible. Yet William's growing up experience has created dependencies for a higher level of income than he can earn for himself.

5. William's father's death has been the major turning point in his young life on a number of different levels. Psychologically, he has been clinging to an unrealistic determination to fulfill his father's dream. He has not come to terms with the loss of his father's support, his idealized image of his father, and the implications of the death for his future. However, his recent admission that he has to give up the goal of becoming a professional golfer, and his recognition that he may not be able to fulfill his fiancée's expectations for an early marriage, suggest some reality testing is happening. He has sought counseling help in spite of a social prohibition against acknowledging the need for help, suggesting he may be willing to change his view of life. With some effort to gain an education, he could develop a realistic career identity and take responsibility for his future.

Example of a Published Research Article on Case Conceptualization

The following research article is about case conceptualization. The commentary in the boxes to the left of the article will help you understand the research and the format of the piece.

Relation Between Years of Psychotherapeutic Experience and Conceptualizations, Interventions, and Treatment Plan Costs

Stephen Mark Kopta, Frederick L. Newman, Mark P. McGovern, and Richard S. Angle

Abstract

> How will your case conceptualizations change as you become a more experienced counselor? This research attempts to find patterns among less and more experienced therapists.

In this study we investigated the relation between years of experience and psychotherapists' conceptualizations, interventions, and treatment plan costs. Thirty-eight therapists evaluated two case vignettes containing a psychosocial history and therapy session material. The therapists answered open-ended queries concerning their conceptualizations about the patient, intervention strategies, and treatment recommendations. Independent clinical raters rated the responses, using the Psychotherapy Judgment Rating Scale. Conceptualization and intervention categories associated with the psychodynamic orientation were positively related to years of experience. Categories not associated with the psychodynamic orientation demonstrated negative relations. In contrast to less experienced therapists, the more experienced therapists were more facilitative, rated the patients as more disordered, and recommended more costly treatment plans.

> The authors explain three reasons why their topic is important. Most research articles begin in this way, arguing that the study's results are valuable in solving some problem or resolving a controversy.

As the psychotherapist's experience increases, how are his or her tendencies to assess and treat patients modified? Auerbach and Johnson (1977) noted that answers to this question may help to improve training methods, determine the validity of using less experienced therapists in psychotherapy research, and provide information concerning the socialization process of therapists. Fiedler (1950) found that therapists, regardless of theoretical orientation, become more similar as experience increases. Reviews of studies indicate that increasing experience facilitates some therapy processes such as therapists' empathy (Auerbach & Johnson, 1977) and patients' satisfaction (Beutler, Crago, & Arizmendi, 1986). In this study we present data showing the relation between years of psychotherapeutic experience and therapists' conceptualizations, interventions, and costs of recommended treatment.

The participating counselors represented a range of theoretical orientations and years of experience. All had graduate degrees and worked in APA-approved programs.

To understand more about how the rating scale was constructed, how it is used, and how reliable it is, you would look up the Kopta et al., 1986, article from the Reference list at the end of this article.

This is an example of *correlational research*. Variables are not manipulated by the experimenter. Levels of association between two or more already existing variables are analyzed. Positive correlations meant that with years of experience, levels of these variables went up. Negative correlations meant that with years of experience, levels of these variables went down. That is, the negative correlations point to variables more common among counselors with less experience.

Method

The subjects were 38 psychologists (20 male and 18 female) from three clinical internship programs approved by the American Psychological Association (APA). They averaged 8.8 years of experience in practicing psychotherapy; the range was from 2 to 40 years. About half of the sample (47.4%) held doctorates; the rest were master's-level therapists. There were 10 psychodynamic therapists (*M*= 9.4 years' experience), 6 cognitive-behavioral therapists (*M*= 6.7), 6 family systems therapists (*M*= 12.7), 3 gestalt therapists (*M*=10.3), and 13 eclectic therapists (*M*= 7.3). The therapists indicated their orientations by noting which theoreticians most influenced their current practice and with which school of psychotherapy they identified.

The therapists completed two case vignettes that we mailed to them. Each 10-page vignette contained a psychosocial history and a process-like description of a therapy session for a different fictitious female patient suffering from anxiety and depression. At designated points in the vignette, the therapists responded to open-ended queries on their conceptualizations about the patient, the therapy process, and their recommended verbal interventions.

The responses were rated by 3 trained clinical raters: 2 Ph.D. clinical psychologists and 1 masters-level clinician. The raters used the Psychotherapy Judgment Rating Scale (PJRS: Kopta, Newman, Govern, & Sandrock, 1986). Conceptualization and intervention categories of the PJRS are listed in Table 1. Each category was defined and rated on a scale from 0 (*no focus or evidence*) to 6 (*complete focus or evidence*). Kopta et al. (1986) presented the specific rating procedures used by the raters, reliability data for the PJRS, and category definitions.

In addition, the therapists rated the severity of patients' problem(s) (1 = *no difficulty* to 7 = *extreme difficulty*) and level of (1 = *low* to 10 = *high*). They also recommended treatments from a checklist of modalities/ settings, as well as number of outpatient sessions and partial or inpatient days. We computed treatment plan costs by cross-multiplying the number of units of a recommended modality/setting by the unit of service cost for that modality/setting. For instance, the cost of a treatment plan suggesting 20 days of inpatient care at $230.00 per day followed by 30 individual therapy sessions at $45.00 per session would be $5,950.00.

Results

To determine the relation between years of experience practicing psychotherapy, independent of theoretical orientation, and the PJRS categories, we computed partial correlations. We used a Bonferroni correction to maintain the experimentwise alpha at $p < .05$ for 28 correlations;

Table 1.
Partial Correlations of Years' Experience
with PJRS Categories

Category	

Conceptualization

In most tables, the correlations (*r*) are shown with asterisks to indicate the probability levels of each correlation. The more asterisks, the more likely the result was not due to chance but to some other factor—in this case, years of experience. The *ns* means that the correlation was not significant—the result could have happened by chance.

Unconscious (processes)	.52***
Conscious cognitive (processes)	–.47***
Overt behavior	ns
Biochemical (factors)	ns
Environmental influence upon patient	ns
Patient influence upon environment	us
General anxiety	ns
Depression	ns
Distant past-childhood (events)	.36***
Past-adult (events)	ns
Present (events)	–.27*
Therapist-centered (experiences)	.51***
Patient-centered (experiences)	–.46***
Responsibility for cause—external	.27*
Responsibility for cause—internal	–.34*
Responsibility for change—external	ns
Responsibility for change—internal	ns

Intervention

The *p* value of a statistic tells you how likely it would be to find this result only by chance. A *p* less than .05 means that this result would happen fewer than 5 times out of 100. A *p* less than .0018 means that it would happen fewer than 18 times out of 10,000. The Bonferroni correction asks for a smaller *p* value for a result to be considered significant, and is used when multiple comparisons are made at once.

Approval	.49***
Disapproval	ns
Directive (responses)	–.30*
Nondirective (responses)	us
Interpretation	ns
Information giving	ns
Questioning	ns
Empathy	.42**
Support	.46***
Criticism	ns
Reflection	ns

Note. PJRS = Psychotherapy Judgment Rating Scale. The nonsignificance level is *p* > .05. For the 28 PJRS correlations, the Bonferroni corrected alpha level for *p* > = .05 is .0018. Correlations noted as *p* < .001 met this criterion.
*p <.05.   **p <.01.   ***p < .001.

therefore, the individual correlations shown in Table 1 can be interpreted as significant if $p < .0018$.

In regard to the PJRS variables, significant positive correlations were found between years of experience and unconscious processes, therapist-centered experiences, approval, and support; furthermore, positive correlations with distant past—childhood events, external responsibility for cause, and empathy approached significance. Years of experience correlated negatively with conscious cognitive processes and patient-centered experiences; present events, directive responses, and internal responsibility for cause tended to show a negative relation.

With variation in theoretical orientation held constant by a partial correlation procedure, years of experience was positively associated with degree of problem severity ($r = .48$, $p < .001$), as well as with treatment plan costs ($r = 31$, $p < .05$; $n = 36$). We found a negative relation between years of experience and level of functioning ($r = -.37$, $p < .01$).

Discussion

The more experienced therapists in this study demonstrated conceptualization and intervention patterns consistent with the psychodynamic theoretical literature and with the psychodynamic therapists in Kopta et al.'s (1986) study: In contrast to less experienced therapists, they focused more on the unconscious, on early childhood events,[*] and on material related to the therapist or the therapeutic setting; they gave less attention to conscious thinking, present events in the patient's life, and material related to the patient's life situation outside the therapy setting; and they recommended intervening in a less directive manner.

These results support findings of Wogan and Norcross (1985) who reported a positive relation between years of experience and psychodynamic techniques, as measured with a therapists' self-report questionnaire.

We found other relations to years of experience that were not associated with a psychodynamic orientation. For instance, as the level of experience increased, the therapists displayed more approval, empathy, and support. These results may help to clarify earlier contradictory findings. For example, Auerbach and Johnson (1977) cited studies in which more experienced therapists displayed higher levels of these qualities than did less experienced therapists. However, Wogan and Norcross (1985) obtained no relation between their "Rogerian" component and years of experience.

The partial correlation procedure removed the effect of the leanings each therapist would be expected to have, due to the orientation they reported. In this way, everyone started on common ground, statistically.

The Discussion section usually compares the results with other similar studies.

The more experienced therapists were *both* more psychodynamic and more Rogerian than the less experienced. The common factors of approval, empathy, and support are associated with Rogerian orientations. The emphasis on the unconscious, early childhood, and the relationship with the therapist are associated with psychodynamic orientations.

---

[*] Some of our results, although not significant according to the Bonferroni criterion, replicate previous findings. In such cases, we have interpreted the correlations according to the unadjusted alpha levels.

A distinct finding was that in contrast to less experienced therapists, the more experienced therapists viewed the patients as more disordered; that is, they rated problem severity higher and level of functioning lower. In addition, they also recommended more costly treatment plans. Do psychodynamic tendencies influence therapists to view patients in a more pathological light and, consequently, as being in need of more intensive treatment? The results of earlier studies are mixed. Researchers using videotaped "patients" showed that psychodynamic therapists rated the patient as more disturbed than did behavioral therapists (Langer & Abelson, 1974) and gave a more pessimistic prognosis than did behavioral or cognitive therapists (Houts, 1984). Yet Kopta et al. (1986), who studied most of the therapist sample in this study (i.e., 33 of the 38 therapists), found no differences between psychotherapeutic orientations in problem severity and level of functioning ratings. They did find that the psychodynamic therapists recommended costlier treatment plans than did other therapists.

One interpretation of our finding is that the differences in therapists' conceptualization and intervention tendencies were due to the experience process itself. For example, over the years therapists may find unconscious influences, transference behavior, and early childhood factors as more interesting and challenging features of the treatment process. As experience increases, therapists may learn to be more perceptive of the nuances of interpersonal communication that make them more facilitative in their approach. Other plausible explanations can be found in the literature. Wogan and Norcross (1985) indicated that older therapists, including nonpsychodynamic ones, are more likely than their younger colleagues to have received training in psychodynamic therapy. Also, Beutler et al. (1986) suggested that more experienced therapists may represent a self-selected, more facilitative group than do therapists of the same generation who left the profession earlier because of poor skill development and frustration.

This study contained some limitations that were noted by Beutler et al. (1986). First, level of experience was not considered independent of formal training. In fact, 17 of the 38 therapists were clinical psychology interns; however, all of these interns reported having 2 or more years of clinical experience before beginning their internships. Also, as mentioned earlier, amount was not distinguished according to type (e.g., theoretical orientation) of experience so that the influence of earlier, perhaps theoretically different experience could not be identified.

Our findings strengthen the argument that experience relates positively to psychodynamic and facilitative treatment processes. Future researchers should make methodological adjustments so that experience can be delineated in regard

> Beutler et al. discussed some of the problems of studying therapist variables in a chapter he wrote before this research study was done. Some of these problems, the authors admit, are limitations of their current study.

to the developmental process of training and changes in
theoretical orientation.

References

Auerbach, A. H. & Johnson, M. (1977). Research on the
therapist's level of experience.(In A. S. Gurman & A. M.
Razin, Eds., *Effective psychotherapy: A handbook of
research* (pp. 84–119). New York: Pergamon.)

Beutler, L. E., Crago, M. & Arizmendi, T. G. (1986). Research on
therapist variables in psychotherapy (In S. L. Garfield &
A. E. Bergin, Eds., *Handbook of psychotherapy and
behavior change* (pp. 257–310). New York: Wiley.)

Fiedler, F. (1950). The concept of an ideal therapeutic
relationship. *Journal of Consulting Psychology, 14,* 239–
245.

Houts, A. C. (1984). Effects of clinician theoretical
orientation and patient explanatory bias on initial clinical
judgments. *Professional Psychology: Research and
Practice, 15,* 284–293.

Kopta, S. M., Newman, F. L., McGovern, M. P. & Sandrock, D.
(1986). Psychotherapeutic orientations: A comparison of
conceptualizations, interventions, and treatment plan
costs. *Journal of Consulting and Clinical Psychology, 54,*
369–374.

Langer, E. J. & Abelson, R. P. (1974). A patient by any other
name . . . : Clinician group differences in labeling bias.
Journal of Consulting and Clinical Psychology, 42, 4–9.

Wogan, M. & Norcross, J. C. (1985). Dimensions of therapeutic
skills and techniques: Empirical identification, therapist
correlates, and predictive utility. *Psychotherapy: Theory,
Research and Practice, 22,* 63–74.

Discussion Ideas

1. List the data that was collected from the participating counselors in this research study.
   Why do you think each type of data was considered relevant?

2. The materials in this study were written vignettes, or stories, and written responses from the
   therapists. Do you think that using the written form could have affected the results? Why
   or why not? What other methods could be used in doing this kind of research? What are
   their advantages and disadvantages?

3. What are three possible explanations for the association of psychodynamic approach with
   years of experience? These are given in the Discussion section. Do you find one of these explanations more believable than the others? Explain your preference.

4. The more experienced therapists viewed the clients as more disordered. How can you explain
   this finding?

Answer Key for Practice Test Questions

True/False

1. F
2. T
3. F
4. F
5. F

Multiple Choice

1. a
2. b
3. f
4. f
5. e
6. e

CHAPTER **3**

Ethics in Psychotherapy, Counseling, and Research

Chapter Review

ACA (American Counseling Association) and APA (American Psychological Association) set ethical standards for member counselors and psychologists. Both codes apply principles used to make professional decisions for the practice of counseling, teaching, consultation, and research. ACA emphasizes human development, client welfare and rights, confidentiality, family involvement, career and employment needs, respect for diversity and differences, dual relationships (including the prohibition of sexual intimacy), group work, fees and bartering, termination, and use of computer programs. APA sets principles regarding competency, integrity, professional and scientific responsibility, respect for people's rights and dignity, concern for other's welfare, and social responsibility.

Counselors set the client's needs as primary, assuring that services do no harm and that clients are respected. Counselors carefully assess the therapy process to make sure the client's needs are being met and that the counselor's issues do not drive the choice of questions, topics and interpretations. Counseling is terminated when client needs are met or when the therapist recognizes that therapy is not working for the client.

Clients are informed as to what they can expect in counseling, and the limits of confidentiality are explained. Confidentiality cannot be upheld if the client threatens harm to another, when child abuse is reported, when suicidality is imminent, or when clients sign a release for records or consultation. Sometimes, counselors are employed to evaluate a client's mental condition for an agency or the courts, so clients are told that the counselor represents the agency, not the client. Children and some adults are not legally competent to give informed consent, and permissions are gained from parents or guardians. When it is not reasonable to gain informed consent, the counselor acts in the best interest of the client.

Counselors avoid dual relationships, those situations where the counselor would serve more than one role in a client's life. Friends or family members cannot be clients because the counselor could not be objective in a counseling relationship. Clients and their counselors are discouraged from becoming friends during or after counseling because the power differential between therapist and clients would carry over to the friendship. Also, the client retains an image of the counselor that would be tainted if informal contacts occurred after counseling sessions ended. Sexual intimacy with clients is, of course, the ultimate violation of the dual role prohibition. However, the arousal of sensual feelings is not uncommon in therapy, and counselors must then seek consultation to analyze the source of such feelings and decide what to do.

Using standardized tests in education and counseling is sometimes criticized as categorizing people with scores rather than seeing them as human beings. However, tests can be a useful tool in counseling. The information indicated by an instrument can help clients gain insights. However, tests are only useful if they are assigned for a legitimate reason, and the instrument chosen serves the intended purpose. Also, to learn the appropriate administration and interpretation of specific tests and/or coursework supervision is needed. The best practice in interpreting tests involves clients in an interactive process where the client points to scores, discusses the meaning, and describes examples from her life. Tests must be determined to be reliable and valid, and, if widely used, will provide a manual. To use instruments, publishers require proof of educational background, and counselors are obligated by ethical standards to provide security for the test's content. Test results are kept secure so nonexperts cannot gain access to them. Psychologists write reports summarizing results when others need the information, recognizing that raw results are open to misinterpretation.

Belmont Principles To Guide Research protect human subjects in empirical studies. These ethical guidelines describe how participants should be treated. Subjects are given the respect accorded to autonomous individuals who have the right to choose to participate or not and to be told about the experiment's activities. To the extent that participants act without full awareness of the study's methods, it is the duty of the researcher to protect them. Investigators must decide whether some risks are justifiable given the need to gain knowledge that would be of benefit to humankind. Harm to participants is limited, minimizing the impact and the time a negative impact could be expected to last. With limited impact, some negative consequences might be tolerated for the greater good of learning how to help others in the future.

Two safeguards are expected when professionals make ethical choices. The first is to document the decision-making process in clinical notes, keeping an ongoing account as the situation develops. It is important to record the ethical principles involved and the thinking behind the course of action taken. The second is to discuss the situation with other professionals to check your own thinking and then document the consultation.

Cultural sensitivity requires counselors to make adaptations to their practices when clients demonstrate differing values and orientations. Socioeconomic and religious rules may dictate that adult clients accede to the authority of parents, for example. Discrimination due to sexual orientation and minority group status may affect a client's psychological symptoms, and counselors need to factor in such external pressures when diagnosing and choosing interventions. Training in cultural differences may offer some insight regarding many client characteristics, but practitioners must guard against stereotyping all individuals within a group when cross-cultural attributes are assumed. Expressing an interest in a client's ethnic background is most often perceived positively and can encourage the client to explain what factors are relevant to him. The following topics are ones that may be relevant in the client/counselor dialogue: primary spoken language; family roles; sex roles and differences; independence; spirituality; definitions of success; methods for dealing with conflict; cultural history; money issues and economic class; and acculturation.

Practice Test Questions

True or False: Consider each statement and try to explain in your own mind why it might not be fully true. Be sure to take into account any qualifying factors that might make the statement untrue. If you decide that the statement is fully true, circle **T**. Otherwise, circle **F**.

T F 1. It is ethically appropriate to accept professional services from a client.

T F 2. It's O.K. to tell someone a client is seeing you for counseling as long as you don't reveal what the client talks about.

T   F   3. If a former client invites you to her wedding, it's necessary to attend.

T   F   4. It's not ethically appropriate to invite a friend to become a participant in a research study.

T   F   5. Having sexual thoughts about a client is terribly wrong.

T   F   6. A couple in marital counseling reports the wife slaps and bruises the husband regularly, but since the clients agree the action is of no importance, it's appropriate for the counselor to say nothing about it.

T   F   7. A parent asks to see the items his child missed on an I.Q. test to determine which questions require further learning. Since the parent's motive is in the child's interest, it's ethical to show the parent the test.

T   F   8. It is not appropriate to help clients with low socioeconomic status by giving a diagnosis that a third party will pay for, regardless of the accuracy of the diagnosis.

Multiple Choice: Circle the one letter next to the best answer to the following questions or to complete the sentence stems.

1. Ethical practice regarding client welfare in the ACA code of ethics includes which of the following?
   a. Counselors create dependent relationships with clients.
   b. Counselors determine appropriate counseling plans and tell clients what's best.
   c. Counselors review counseling plans to make sure the client is compliant.
   d. Counselors enlist family understanding and involvement in counseling.

2. To respect diversity when serving clients, counselors
   a. follow the general attitudes of the community in determining what actions are considered discriminatory.
   b. do not consider sexual orientation as a characteristic requiring sensitive attention in counseling.
   c. consider how their own cultural/ethnic/racial identity impacts their values and beliefs about the counseling process.
   d. actively try to understand the diverse backgrounds of clients until graduate training is complete.

3. Client rights include
   a. disclosing to clients what to expect in counseling and what risks may occur.
   b. a promise to uphold confidentiality under all circumstances.
   c. an understanding that counseling is always mandatory.
   d. the right of minors to participate in counseling without parental consent.

4. Which of the following are considerations for dual relationships with clients?
   a. Dual relationships are easy to manage by professionals with good judgment.
   b. Counselors do not have counseling relationships with people who they evaluate or supervise.
   c. Sexual relationships with former clients is permissible six months after termination.
   d. Regularly attending family events with a client would not entail dual role implications.

5. Which of the following are relevant factors in assuring there is no exploitation of a former client when engaging in sexual intimacies with a client two years after counseling has been terminated?
    a. the depth and length of the counseling relationship
    b. the client's psychological history
    c. the client's current mental status
    d. all of the above

6. In charging client fees, counselors are ethically bound to do which of the following?
    a. Make sure the client understands the fee when the session is over.
    b. Accept an exchange of services or goods for counseling fees.
    c. Contribute a portion of their services for little or no fee.
    d. Use a collection agency or the court system when the client doesn't pay.

7. When counselors terminate or refer a client, they are required to do which of the following?
    a. During interruptions such as vacations, the counselors arrange for therapy through another source when it is in the best interest of the client.
    b. If a counselor is not trained for a particular counseling issue, she makes sure the client is not aware of the limitation, so the client will trust her.
    c. Counselors terminate counseling only when the client agrees, not before.
    d. When the client is not benefiting from counseling, the counselor should not raise the issue of termination until the client says something.

8. Which of the following are appropriate guidelines when using computers in counseling services?
    a. The computer program is determined to meet the needs of the client.
    b. The client understands the purpose and limits in using the computer program.
    c. Follow-up services are provided to clarify misconceptions and to determine further client needs.
    d. all of the above

9. APA Principles and Code of Conduct includes which of the following?
    a. striving to maintain high standards of competence for psychological work
    b. seeking to promote integrity in research, teaching, and counseling
    c. maintaining personal conduct that enhances the public's trust in psychologists
    d. all of the above

10. Psychologists respect for clients and concern for client welfare includes
    a. trying to eliminate the effect of biases on their work.
    b. performing their roles secretly when conflicts occur.
    c. recognizing power differentials between themselves and others.
    d. a and c
    e. a and b

11. Social responsibilities for psychologists include
    a. trying to advance science and to avoid the misuse of their work when undertaking research.
    b. complying with only those laws they think serve the best interests of clients and the public.
    c. awareness of responsibilities to the community where they work and live.
    d. a and b
    e. a and c

Ethical Discussions

The following are edited excerpts taken from a recorded discussion among experienced counselors discussing ethical issues arising in therapy work.

Wedding Invitation

SAM:	This dual relationship thing, what about getting an invitation for a client's wedding? Now, the only reason I would bring that up – I don't think I would go, but I know one where – Donna, I think your client died some years ago. Didn't you go to the funeral?
DONNA:	Well, I was late. But yes, I went to the church.
SAM:	But you did it out of respect.
DONNA:	I went there, but I didn't go to the funeral, no. I went to the church. Bob attended the funeral.
LIZ:	Ann and I attended a funeral for a client's daughter from group.
DONNA:	I have one on my desk now. It's an invitation to a high school graduation from one of my teens. He is really dying for us to come. He doesn't have parents, and he begged Ted and me to show up.
LIZ:	I've had wedding invitations, too.
DONNA:	I went to a client's graduation from MATC. Others I have turned down.
LIZ:	I got supervision about the wedding invitation, and the feeling at the time seemed to be that there was really nothing wrong with attending the ceremony but don't go to the reception.
SAM:	What was the rationale?
LIZ:	Well, at the reception, the first question will be how do you know the bride or groom? And, what, do you lie?
TODD:	From what I understood our teacher to say, we need to determine if it is going to be therapeutic or would it be beneficial for the therapist to go? Or will it hurt the client?
PAT:	So, it's not ethically wrong to go. It would be a clinical decision.
TODD:	Yeah it would be up to the clinician to decide if it was going to cause harm or be a distress for him.

Cross-Cultural Domestic Slapping

PAT:	What about the couples counseling: The husband admits he frequently slaps the wife, both agree that in their culture this behavior is considered appropriate for keeping the wife in her place. What do you do?
SAM:	Well, I feel that if you continue on, you're condoning what they're doing.
PAT:	So you don't continue on being the therapist?
SAM:	You aren't their therapist anymore.
SUZANNE:	At all? Or do you see them individually?
SAM:	I don't know, but it's got to be addressed. Even though it might be okay in their culture. I would go with my judgment, and say I can't do this. I can't condone

you, even it it's all right in your culture. It's not all right with me, and I think I would lose a lot of objectivity.

PAT: Right. So what would people do with the culture piece? When they're saying it's acceptable in their culture.

SAM: I guess what I'd try to do to get them to realize that I understand what their culture is, but now they're going to get into trouble for it here. Start it off as a legal thing: You will get into trouble if you do it here, and we don't condone it here. I mean, diversity is involved, and you still have to respect their culture, but I sure don't understand it, and that's why I need to realize –. That's why I go to the legal aspect, I guess, but at least they know, and it's hard to argue with that forum even if they disagree with it.

JEN: I might just start by trying to understand how it fits into the culture, by having them educate me to some degree on their culture and then hopefully share in the educational component of it too and then still make clinical recommendations.

TERRY: And also look for variability within the culture. There have got to be some people that aren't slapping.

SAM: That's a great idea; looking at it in that way.

LIZ: Yeah, it might be more tolerated in that culture, but that doesn't mean that it's really acceptable.

JEN: I think that's where the therapy comes in, in helping them see something different. I mean, that's what we do.

LIZ: Because I would think that it would be important in that session that that's sort of your teachable moment. Because you could lose them. I mean, if you say you're not going to do couples work, the husband may be completely gone, and unless she calls the police or something, how is he going to get treatment, just because you recommend it?

RON: And maybe one of the lessons that you sometimes get out of ethics is that, as much as we'd like it to be, it isn't always black and white, that sometimes there is a certain mess to it, but that's why we are professionals and look at these issues and try to ameliorate the mess as much as possible.

Exploring Ethics

Find another helping professional (or a professional-in-training) to discuss ethical dilemmas with, focusing on a problem either of you experience in practice or in your reading. If you need a topic provided, discuss one of the situations introduced at the beginning of Chapter 3 in your textbook. Take notes on your discussion (or transcribe a recording of it). Trade notes or transcriptions with at least one other student so you can see another pair's exploration.

Example of a Published Research Article on an Ethical Exploration

The following article is on ethical exploration. The commentary in the boxes to the left of the article will help you understand the research and the format of the piece.

Engaging Non-Attending Family Members in Marital and Family Counseling: Ethical Issues

S. Allen Wilcoxon

This article features an examination of the ethical issues affecting decisions far serving client when systemic intervention is indicated but critical family members resist engagement. Discussion focuses on conceptual and empirical information concerning engagement for systemic intervention as well as possible solutions to ethical dilemmas that affect treatment decisions.

> In this type of article, a common ethical problem is discussed from several points of view. The discussion is valuable to the many counselors who confront similar problems repeatedly in their practice.

Dilemma. A troubled wife requests counseling for marital difficulties, noting that her husband is unwilling to participate in sessions.

More than ever, counselors are focusing their attention on the marital and familial contexts that influence the individuals for whom they are providing services. This trend has led to changes in the format and content of counseling services as well as the introduction of new concepts and terminologies such as the *family system* and *systemic intervention* (Searight & Openlander, 1984). The systemic perspective offers a framework for describing the complex yet predictable patterns of interaction within a family unit. As with any system, no single member may successfully alter relationship characteristics in a marital or familial unit without some reaction from the other(s) within that system.

> According to ethics codes, counselors must provide the most effective treatment they can, and this requirement presents a problem when the most effective treatment proven is couples or family counseling, yet only one individual is willing to come in for treatment. This article considers the therapist's ethical dilemma in such a situation.

The literature supports systemic intervention as opposed to traditional, single-client intervention (Gurman & Kniskern, 1981). Many couples or families, however, are not amenable to services using this format. The counselor wishing to employ treatment-of-choice services may face an ethical dilemma. One's commitment to systemic intervention must be examined in relation to commitment to providing services for motivated, troubled individual clients constituting that system. In such instances, one faces a dilemma concerning convictions about the autonomy of individuals (both attenders and non-attenders) versus the impact and durability of changes in a systemic format of services.

Reprinted from S. Allen Wilcoxon, "Engaging Non-Attending Family Members in Marital and Family Counseling: Ethical Issues," from *Journal of Counseling and Development*, 64 (1986), 323–324.

Related Professional Literature

Conceptual Literature

> From a client-centered perspective, the client should determine who is included in treatment, and the therapist should not impose his or her preferences, even when the couple or family would ideally be seen together. Haley does not agree with this perspective.

Many practitioners schooled in the client-centered perspective of serving clients may believe that the engagement issue represents imposed counselor values or preferences. Haley (1976), however, stated that the practitioner's effectiveness may be severely impeded by not assuming from the outset a strong, directive stance in providing systemic services.

Napier and Whitaker (1978) observed that two important "battles" transpire in serving couples and families. The *battle for structure* involves issues of structure and administrative control (e.g., participants in sessions, scheduling, fees), whereas the *battle for initiative* involves motivation for change and accountability for resistance to changes. These authors stated that the first battle must be "won" by the professional, whereas the second must be won by the client system. Napier and Whitaker (1978) maintained that an important issue in the battle for structure is that of engaging both spouses (for marital intervention) or the entire family system (for familial intervention) before services are provided. Thus, they advocated withholding services until the battle is won. (There is a difference between withholding services and denying services: The first is an intervention strategy and the second is unethical but may be remedied by referral.)

> One tactic is to withhold services until all the parties in a system (couple or family) agree to come in. Withholding is a therapeutic tactic in itself because it forces the system into confrontation. However, in effect it denies therapy to clients who desire it, and it colludes with the parties who do not want it. In other words, non-attenders get their way because therapy does not proceed.

Acknowledging the conceptual and treatment significance of withholding services, Teismann (1980) stated that this tactic features an important ethical liability because services are withheld from motivated spouses or family members. He also maintained that the tactic suggests or promotes the illusion of an alliance between the professional and the non-attenders.

Empirical Literature

Because of space limitations, the more salient features of empirical investigations concerning systemic intervention are summarized. These conclusions are primarily found in Gurman and Kniskern (1981) and Wohlman and Stricker (1983).

> Research supporting family and conjoint (couples) therapy is summarized here. The fact that research supports a certain treatment means that the counselor is ethically constrained to deliver that treatment if possible.

1. Familial intervention is at least as effective as individual intervention for most client complaints and leads to significantly greater durability of therapeutic changes.

2. In some instances, specific forms of familial intervention are significantly more effective than individual intervention (e.g., structural family therapy with substance-abuse complaints).

3. The presence of both parents (especially noncompliant fathers) in familial intervention significantly improves chances for success.

4. In cases of marital complaints, conjoint intervention has been shown to be nearly twice as effective as individual intervention with one spouse.

5. Marital or familial services not employed in a conjoint or systemic format may promote negative therapeutic effects (i.e., problem exacerbation rather than problem resolution).

The conceptual as well as the empirical literature seem to converge to support the efficacy of systemic intervention. In light of these findings, engaging non-attending spouses and family members becomes a primary task plus an ethical responsibility for the counselor attempting to provide treatment-of-choice services.

Service Considerations and Ethical Issues

The counselor wishing to employ systemic services faces a variety of service considerations, which are the basis of the ethical dilemma mentioned above. These considerations include the following:

1. Win the battle for structure or provide services for any component of the system.

2. Avoid any chance of negative therapeutic effects or compromise and attempt to engage non-attenders through success with attenders.

3. Work only on individual issues with attenders or do not "chop up the system."

4. Withhold services or refer for nonsystemic services.

5. Operate on the theory that "some changes are better than none" or that systemic intervention is associated with greater durability of therapeutic change.

6. Systemic intervention is not a panacea, but empirical evidence supports systemic intervention as the treatment-of-choice.

7. Insistence on a systemic format implies the promise of success; however, there are no assurances, only generalizations from investigations.

Proposed Solutions

The ethical dilemma presented raises questions of the necessity of engagement as well as the tactics to accomplish that end successfully. As yet, there is no definitive solution for either issue. Napier and Whitaker (1978) observed that responses to resistance frequently lead to "losing" the battle for structure and accepting responsibilities for the battle for initiative. Withholding services until participants are engaged has been a rather controversial tactic, although O'Shea and Jessee (1982) wrote that "to do so is highly responsible, competent professional practice" (p. 6).

Teismann's suggestions allow the counselor to see the willing client while still focusing on the preferability of seeing both or all involved parties.

Teismann's (1980) suggestions seem to offer a compromise that many counselors may find more ethically attractive than withholding services. He suggested tactics such as (a) an agreement between counselor and non-attender(s) for a single, private session in exchange for a single, conjoint or systemic session; (b) brief sessions with the attending members or spouse that focus only on plans for engaging the non-attender(s); (c) audiotaped or videotaped samples of sessions for review by non-attenders; and (d) an agreement for short-term services (one to three sessions) for the motivated members or spouse. Teismann (1980) also advocated using leverage from referral sources and cancellation when all participants fail to convene.

For marital services, Wilcoxon and Fenell (1983) proposed giving the attending spouse (during the second counseling session) a letter containing a summary of research findings on one-spouse marital intervention and an invitation to the non-attending spouse to become involved in services. This letter also contains a request for both spouses' signatures to verify their understanding of the risks of one-spouse intervention. This technique has helped to ensure informed consent, but, more important, it has proven effective in engaging non-attending spouses. An adapted version of the letter format has been suggested as a means of engaging non-attending parents for systemic intervention with children in school settings (Wilcoxon, 1984).

Counseling ethics are often based on the principle of respect for the clients, which implies giving them full information about the pros and cons of the treatment they consent to receive.

Some may find the letter method to be the most ethically attractive technique because the burden of responsibility for engagement and choices about potential negative therapeutic effects falls on the system members. Although the professional is not completely absolved of ethical liability, a signed statement of informed consent regarding potential hazards of less-than-optimal services may be acceptable for those willing to provide services to motivated family members. For many, this "solution" may seem to be no solution. If, however, one interprets the literature as definitive support for the systemic modality, to provide services in a less-than-optimal format may be a violation of personal ethics and professionalism. Providing meaningful intervention services (or the failure to do so) in that setting may lead to subsequent engagement of non-attending family members or spouses

The justification for viewing engagement as such a critical issue is that, within the systemic perspective, engagement is not simply a prelude to intervention; it is intervention. Weltner (1982) noted that even as few as one to three sessions may have a meaningful impact on a familial system because of the energies involved in attending as well as the resultant insights that may effect changes. From this perspective, to engage is to serve.

Frequently, a counselor's strategy in an ethical dilemma involves devising a series of steps, with each one depending on how the previous step works out. In this case, the goal remains the same: to provide optimal treatment for the couple. A counselor who feels that it's unethical to continue with the wife alone, even with a signed letter, should refer the wife to another professional who is willing to see her alone.

Dilemma Resolution

To resolve the dilemma presented at the beginning of this article, the counselor may consider the following steps:

Step 1: Agree to see the wife, urging her to invite her husband (if only to offer his comments). This session should be brief with principal focus on the necessity of conjoint services.

Step 2: If Step 1 does not engage the husband, the counselor may obtain the wife's permission to contact her husband and emphasize the importance of conjoint services. If she agrees, the counselor may invite the husband to one individual session to discuss his perspective as a prelude to subsequent conjoint services (this would occur before the wife's second session).

Step 3: If the wife refuses Step 2 or if her husband does not respond favorably, the counselor may provide a letter for husband and wife to sign, indicating their understanding of risks in one-spouse marital counseling (this tactic is designed to engage both spouses). The counselor will not continue professional services until the signed letter is returned. The counselor provides referral information so the couple can engage other services if desired.

Step 4: If Step 3 fails to engage both spouses but the wife returns with the signed letter, the counselor may continue in one-spouse intervention with the wife (hoping to engage her husband at a later time) or postpone or refer until both spouses are successfully engaged for conjoint services.

References

Gurman, A., & Kniskern. D. (1981) Family therapy outcome research: Knowns and unknowns In A. Gurman & D. Kniskern (Eds.), *Handbook of family therapy* (pp. 742–775). New York: Brunner/Mazel.

Haley, J. (1976). *Problem Solving Therapy*. New York: Brunner/Mazel.

Napier, A., & Whitaker. C. (1978). *The family crucible*. New York: Harper & Row.

O'Shea, M., & Jessee, E. (1982). Ethical, value, and professional conflicts in systems therapy. In J. Hansen & L. L'Abate (Eds.), Values, ethics, legalities, and the family therapist (pp. 1–22) Rockville, MD: Aspen Systems.

Searight, H., & Openlander, P. (1984). Systemic therapy: A new brief intervention model. Personnel and Guidance Journal, 62, 387–390.

Teismann, M. (1980). Convening strategies in family therapy. *Family Process, 19,* 393–400.

Weltner, J. (1982). One- to three-session therapy with children and families. *Family Process, 21,* 281–290.

When you examine the reference list of an article, you can discover books and journals that expand on topics related to the discussion in the article. For example, you may have never before heard of the useful journal *Family Process*. This would be a journal you wish to include in your own literature searches.

Wilcoxon, A., & Fenell, D. (1983). Engaging the non-attending spouse in marital therapy through the use of therapist-initiated written communication. *Journal of Marital and Family Therapy, 9,* 199–203.

Wilcoxon. A. (1984, November). *Engaging family members in counseling: Uses of a letter.* Paper presented at annual convention of the Southern Association for Counselor Education and Supervision, Nashville.

Wohlman, B., & Stricker, G. (1983). *Handbook of family and marital therapy.* New York: Plenum Press.

Discussion Ideas

1. Summarize the basic ethical dilemma explored in this article.

2. What is the difference between withholding counseling services and denying counseling services? What are the ethical problems with each of these strategies?

3. Why might the letter format suggested by Wilcoxon and Fennel (1983) engage non-attending spouses and parents in treatment? What is the effect of having to sign such a letter?

4. What is *engagement,* and why is it so important?

5. What other situations have you encountered, or can you imagine, in which you might want to involve a spouse or family members in order to provide the best treatment for an individual seeking counseling?

Answer Key for Practice Test Questions

True/False		*Multiple Choice*	
1.	F	1.	d
2.	F	2.	c
3.	F	3.	a
4.	T	4.	b
5.	F	5.	a
6.	F	6.	c
7.	F	7.	c
8.	T	8.	a
		9.	d
		10.	d
		11.	e

CHAPTER 4

Psychoanalytical and Psychodynamic Approaches

Chapter Review

Early in the twentieth century, Sigmund Freud introduced seminal concepts including the primacy of developmental stages in childhood that determine adult character and the existence of unconscious dynamics that influence all human behavior. The unconscious distributed a limited amount of energy between three subparts, the *id, ego,* and *superego.* Conflicts between the id's pleasure seeking and the superego's moralistic perfectionism created anxiety that was managed by the ego. Developmental stages in Freudian theory followed patterns reflective of the workings of the unconscious. A major influential pattern was the *Oedipal/Electra* complex where sexual desires for opposite sex parents was redirected to embrace appropriate sex role identities. *Psychoanalysis,* as a therapy, was designed to uncover such unconscious patterns so that the patient could consciously acknowledge hidden desires. Making the unconscious conscious was expected to release anxiety from internal conflicts, and to free up energy for the ego to deal with external realities. Interpretations were based on the *transference* and *countertransference* relationship, as well as patient's *free associations* and dreams. In therapy, psychoanalysts presented a blank slate so patients could project past relationships onto the therapist.

   Psychodynamic approaches built on Freudian concepts, de-emphasizing some aspects of the original theory and adding new concepts. In *ego psychology,* Anna Freud added social influences and theorized that the ego had its own purposes such as creativity and mastery. Therapy based on ego psychology examined the ego's defenses revealing patients' underlying fears and loosening the unconscious patterns. Therapists were more engaged with patients than psychoanalysts.

   In *Object Relations* theory, development is based on interaction patterns between the child and parents, and less on the internal dynamics of unconscious energy. The child forms unconscious ways of viewing others as objects. In healthy development, the child starts with a dependent relationship on the mother object who provides for all needs. Children grow to a point of independence where the self-concept is constant and interactions have stability, even when others do not always meet their needs. Therapy helps those who have experienced ineffective parenting and who have developed unreliable object representations. Pathological object relations are conceptualized as the basis for narcissistic, borderline, or schizoid personality disorders. To transform the client's internal structure, the therapist provides a positive parental object. Therapists forgo full interpretations of the transference relationship allowing the client to vent anger without reacting. After anger is released, patient and therapist examine the experience, and the client learns alternative ways of feeling and relating.

40

Self psychology is a branch of object relations theory emphasizing the self concept as an internal object. For a positive self-image, parents reflect back to the child their accurate reading of the child's activities and efforts, providing a mirror image of the child to the child. Such mirroring, along with praise and empathic comments, promotes a *grandiose self* object where the children see themselves as perfect and the center of attention. In healthy development, young children also idealize parents and internalize an *ego ideal* that serves as both a conscience and an image of the perfect outcome for strivings. When effective internal objects are not developed in childhood, they cannot be refined for adult maturity; and with such deficits, adults continually seek relationships to provide *mirroring* and/or idealized individuals who will convey worth or power. Therapy seeks to change internalized objects through an *empathic* relationship. Clients gain the corrective emotional experience of being parented anew. Clients gain better self-images learning to deal with reality and to pursue healthy goals.

Jungian analytic psychology adds another function for the unconscious. In addition to a personal unconscious, Jung described the *collective unconscious* that contains knowledge of historically universal experiences shared by people across all cultures. Within the collective unconscious are *archetypes*, characters playing roles in dramas common to the human condition and relayed to people through religious writings, spiritual rituals, and different forms of art. Although Jung emphasized a humanistic psychology of growth and self-actualization, he also described human struggles. Jung wrote that people project a positive *persona* to display the best aspects of themselves and hide their *shadows*, or the socially unacceptable parts. In therapy clients confess the secrets hidden from public view and accept interpretations of transference and countertransference. Dreams are also interpreted to reveal the client's unconscious dilemmas, archetypal enactments, and solutions to current issues. The progress of therapy can be determined by the changing themes of dreams. The healing counseling relationship relieves unconscious turmoil and helps the client to become self-actualized.

In the initial stage of analytic and dynamic therapy, the transference relationship is established and interpreted as the therapist makes inferences from client statements, behavior, and feelings. Much of the content of early clinical sessions involves examining childhood experiences. Which interpretations are shared with the client depends on the therapist's clinical judgment as to what the client can accept and what would be therapeutically useful. When an analytical conclusion appears close to the conscious surface, an interpretation is termed a *confrontation.* Clients may defend against the analysis by denying interpretations or employing ways to avoid the material, and such *resistance* will also be interpreted. As the relationship develops and resistances weaken, therapy enters the middle stage when clinical material is reprocessed and *worked through.* Progress is indicated by the client's willingness to understand interpretations and implications, gaining insight, and adjusting attitudes and perspectives. When the psychological work approaches completion, the *termination* stage takes place. Termination takes a number of sessions to allow plenty of time for client and therapist to review client changes, the progress of their relationship, and to provide closure.

The primary critique of psychoanalysis and psychodynamic therapies is the lack of evidence from controlled studies that would prove that they are effective. However, many concepts from psychoanalytic thought have been supported by experiments. Other criticisms include sexist attitudes, consistent blame of mothers, and insensitivity to marginalized cultural groups and sexual orientations.

Practice Test Questions

True or False: Consider each statement and try to explain in your own mind why it might not be fully true. Be sure to take into account any qualifying factors that might make the statement untrue. If you decide that the statement is fully true, circle **T.** Otherwise, circle **F.**

T F   1. Concepts from Freudian psychoanalytic theory are used by many therapists today.

T F   2. Both psychoanalytic and psychodynamic theories of development are deterministic.

T F   3. The hydraulic model of psychic energy means feelings that cannot be openly expressed will come out in other ways.

T F   4. Neurotic anxiety is a fear that the person is violating moral values.

T F   5. Defense mechanisms are pathological ways to protect a weak ego.

T F   6. Ego psychology and the psychodynamic approach broke away from Freud's psychoanalytic theory.

T F   7. According to object relations theory, a three year old develops a mature dependence on the mother or caretaker.

T F   8. Parents should be careful to make sure a toddler does not develop a grandiose self concept.

T F   9. The anima represents the feminine side of a man, and the animus is the male of a woman in Jungian psychoanalytic theory.

T F   10. A client showing up late for therapy sessions is always making a conscious choice to resist the interpretations of the therapist.

Multiple Choice: Circle the one letter next to the best answer to the following questions or to complete the sentence stem.

1. Analyzing dreams entails the therapist and client determining
    a. the manifest content.
    b. the latent content.
    c. the meaning of symbols.
    d. the condensation of symbols.
    e. all of the above.

2. To provide a corrective emotional experience for clients with inadequate parenting, the therapist
    a. calmly accepts the client's outbursts without responding punitively.
    b. mirrors the client's affect while offering praise for progress.
    c. monitors the client's achievements while pointing out mistakes.
    d. a, b, d
    e. a, c, and d

3. Narcissistic personality disorders develop because parents do which of the following?
    a. lose interest or abandon the child
    b. provide good role models of appropriate behavior
    c. respond to child's temper tantrums by creating Time Outs
    d. Provide mirroring for the child's activities
    e. a and d

4. According to psychoanalytic theory, the function of the ego is to
    a. mediate and find solutions for the conflicts between the id and the superego.
    b. manage impulses so healthy social interactions can occur.
    c. deal with external demands through effective use of language, competency and judgment.
    d. a and b
    e. a, b, and c

5. Which of the following is a term for repetitive interpretations that help clients overcome unconscious patterns?
   a. *transference*
   b. *countertransference*
   c. *working through*
   d. *termination*

6. What is the difference between repression and suppression?
   a. Repression is an effort to remind yourself to do the right thing; suppression is the effort to stop yourself from the actual act.
   b. Suppression is forgetting something you don't want to do and repression is remembering when you don't want to remember.
   c. Repression is forgetting something you don't want to remember and suppression is remembering when you don't want to remember.
   d. Repression is forgetting unconsciously and suppression is deliberately forgetting what you don't want to remember.

7. Which of the following is an example of regression?
   a. An 8-year-old starts to suck his thumb when a new baby brother is born.
   b. The boss throws a temper tantrum when an important deadline is missed.
   c. A freshman on Christmas break refuses to keep his parents' curfew.
   d. a, b
   e. a, b, and c

8. Which of the following is a description of the "good enough" mother?
   a. When a baby cries, the mother always responds immediately.
   b. The mother usually does not meet the baby's needs for food and cuddling.
   c. For a toddler, she sometimes does tasks for the child and sometimes watches the child try to do the task himself.
   d. The mother is a good role model and gets very upset when she makes mistakes.
   e. b and c

9. *Object constancy* refers to unconscious representations that are
   a. consistent, knows when others are good and when they are bad.
   b. able to remember the good in people even when others are frustrating.
   c. honest representations of parenting as effective or deficient.
   d. objective in analyzing good and bad and honest in telling others.
   e. constant in knowing when personal behavior is bad.

10. Insight, according to psychoanalytical therapy, can be described as
    a. bringing feelings that were not accessible to the client into the open.
    b. creating structural changes in the unconscious.
    c. bringing the unconscious into conscious awareness.
    d. necessary and sufficient for people to change.
    e. all of the above

11. Which of the following is not a technique of psychoanalytic or psychodynamic therapy?
    a. free association
    b. dream analysis
    c. interpretations
    d. behavioral diary

12. To maintain an analytic stance, which of the following would the psychoanalyst do?
    a. Analyze the client's behavior according to religious tenets.
    b. Share experiences from his own life with the client.
    c. Enter the client's emotional world to establish empathy.
    d. Reframe an interpretation so the client could accept it.
    e. a, b, and c

13. Which of the following is a goal of therapy for object relations therapists and self psychologists?
    a. to create healing interactions between the therapist and the client
    b. to build ego strength
    c. to help client's accept reality and tolerate frustration
    d. to increase the client's ability to pursue healthy goals
    e. all of the above

14. Which of the following is a Jungian concept?
    a. regression
    b. persona
    c. splitting
    d. grandiose self

15. Which of the following is a criticism of psychoanalytic and psychodynamic therapies?
    a. The therapy methods have not been show to be effective by controlled studies.
    b. The therapy concepts are sexist and not open to cross-cultural distinctions.
    c. The concepts are not found to be applicable by counselors using other theories.
    d. a and c
    e. a and b

Key Terms and Essential Concepts

Psychoanalytic: Sigmund Freud attempted to explain psychological symptoms through a pioneering theory. Psychoanalytic concepts describe the inner world of human beings and how unconscious strivings influence personality and behavior. Freud perceived that biological drives required complex controls if people were to maintain civilized and moral behavior. An elaborate system of *unconscious* subparts (*id, ego, superego*) played out the struggle between instinctual drives and societal restraints while also trying to cope with life demands. The closed energy system distributed psychic energy between the personality subparts. Freud also perceived that sexual drives originated in childhood and were hidden from awareness as societal propriety required. He proposed a sequence of psychosexual developmental stages where the unconscious kept the desires out of awareness and redirected energy into appropriate adult roles. Deviations from normal development caused internal struggles and mental symptoms. Finally, he proposed a treatment method called *psychoanalysis* to bring the unconscious conflicts into awareness and to free the patient from internal pain and psychological neurosis.

Drives: Innate energy to satisfy biological determinants, such as sex and aggression.

Unconscious: A part of the psychoanalytic and psychodynamic psychological structure that remains out of awareness but still influences all a person is and does. It contains memories of experiences, wishes, and impulses.

Id: The home for biological drives contained within the structure of the unconscious and operating by the pleasure principle of satisfying all urges.

Superego: The seat for societal messages limiting the expression of innate urges and acting according to moral restraints and perfectionistic standards.

Ego: The third space within the psychoanalytic personality structure that observes and takes into account realistic considerations, while negotiating the clashes between the id and the superego.

Reality principle: Problem-solving utilized by the ego to manage internal conflicts and external demands.

Pleasure principle: A biological standard of reacting impulsively to satisfy appetites without consideration of others or future oriented consequences.

Anxiety: Generalized fear that, if severe, can impair one's ability to function. Freud proposed that neurotic anxiety was caused by a fear that id forces would overpower the ego's ability to contain impulsivity.

Oedipal stage: A psychosexual period of development (age 3–6) where a boy desires a proprietary relationship with his mother without interference from his father. In fear of retaliation from the father, the boy resolves his urges by identifying with the father and establishing the appropriate male sex role for future heterosexual relationships.

Electra complex: A psychosexual syndrome for girls paralleling the Oedipal experience of boys during the same age period of 3–6 years. A girl wants to take her mother's place with her father but fears mother would punish her for such thoughts. To manage the anxiety created by her desires, the girl identifies with her mother and takes on the feminine sex role.

Penis envy: A Freudian term describing the disappointment of girls when they discover they do not have a male appendage and resulting in the limitations of women's superego development. Horney countered the sexist concept by suggesting womb envy for men.

Ego theory: Sigmond Freud believed that the ego managed the conflict between the id and the superego. Anna Freud and Erik Erikson added to psychoanalytic thought by expanding the functions of the ego. This became a school of thought known as ego psychology. Kohut extended ego theory even further in self psychology.

Ego psychology: Anna Freud expanded her father's concept of the unconscious by introducing the influence of social factors on psychological development, and by emphasizing the ego and its defense mechanisms. Therapeutic interpretations focused on the patient's defenses to encourage greater choices for perceptions and flexibility for behavior. Eric Erikson extended ego psychology further by describing *psychosocial* developmental stages throughout life and adding healthy ego functions such as mastery and competency

Ego strength: The ability of the ego to manage internal conflicts so the person can cope with life demands and pursue healthy goals.

Interpretation: Psychoanalytic and psychodynamic therapists interpret for clients the meaning of internal dynamics revealed in counseling session. Interpretations come from theoretical concepts endorsed by the therapists.

Defense mechanisms: Unconscious methods used by the ego to adapt to realistic considerations while also reducing internal anxiety. Many defense mechanisms provide healthy functions when not rigidly applied. Defensive patterns can also redefine reality in unhealthy ways or pathological ways.

Sublimation: A defense mechanism that transforms socially unacceptable desires into socially useful behaviors.

Repression: A defense mechanism that unconsciously stifles a painful experience so the memory is kept out of awareness.

Denial: Disregarding negative realities to such a degree that the conditions avoided do not exist in the person's awareness at all.

Regression: When a person who typically behaves at one maturity level performs actions characteristic of an earlier stage of development. Such behavior defends against the requirement of coping at the appropriate level of responsibility.

Fantasy: Creating a vision of pleasant circumstances to escape mundane realities.

Rationalization: Creating logical explanations that make the cause of an event sound acceptable. One way of rationalizing is to point to external causes and, therefore, protect one's self from blame.

Reaction formation: To avoid recognizing unacceptable impulses, the person subscribes to the exact opposite inclination.

Projection: A person attributes his own characteristic onto other people, defending himself by believing others are the same way, or by negating the characteristic for himself thereby displacing the trait.

Suppression: Consciously forgetting as a defensive maneuver to manage the feelings related to a difficult situation or incident.

Emotional insulation: A person unconsciously protects herself against unwanted feelings by creating an attitudinal shield of not caring.

Displacement: A person has feelings aimed at one person but directs those feelings to someone or something else. In this way, direct confrontation is avoided.

Identification: A person admires characteristics of another person, and so she aligns with the admirable figure to overcome her own limitations and to take on new traits.

Psychodynamic: Psychodynamic theories retained basic Freudian ideas such as the unconscious and childhood development as critically influential. However, the description of how the unconscious works changed. Instead of maintaining the hydraulic principle of energy transferred between subparts of the unconscious, dynamic theories describe social introjects and emphasize an internal process revolving around the ego or the self.

Object relations theory: This post-Freudian theory proposes relational constructs or objects in the unconscious as the structure that affects human development. The child retains an imprint of the relationship with the primary caretaker and projects the representation onto all future relationships. When parenting is deficient, the object relations embedded in the unconscious is problematic and the person exhibits psychological difficulties. Relational objects can be inconstant, or not dependable, when based on neglectful parenting. An adult with a problematic childhood history will forever project inappropriate prototypes onto others. When parenting is sufficient, the child develops through a sequence of stages where the child gradually grows from dependence on parents to personal independence.

Object relations psychology: Therapists using object relations theory provide reparenting experiences for clients so that positive objects can be internalized by clients.

Objects: A term used in object relations theory to denote internal images of other people. When we are infants, other people are merely objects that provide food and other necessities. Childhood reactions to others are distilled into mental constructs and these mental images become a permanent part of a person's internal world

Self-theory/psychology: Extending the concepts of object relations, self psychology focuses on the unconscious self object which is emphasized more than relationships with others. The healthy self develops from early parenting that results in feelings of self-worth, an ego ideal of what the self can become, and a conscience that limits self-expression to societal standards.

Self: A continuing inner sense of our personhood that organizes our perceptions of our experience. Includes feelings of worth, individuality, our relationship to others and the world, and our basic comfort or anxiety level.

Mirroring: Self psychology describes the mirroring process typical of good parenting where the child's behavior is reflected back to the child with praise and empathy. Such reflective interactions help the child build a positive self-image.

Grandiose self: Through mirroring the child by age 3 develops an object called the *grandiose self*, denoting the self as perfect and the center of attention. The grandiose self object becomes the source of ambition, energy, and self-esteem.

Ego ideal: The internal object from self-psychology that represent the perfect self if it were achievable. The ego ideal is developed through the process of idealizing parents.

Idealization: A second basic need for the developing child in self psychology is a view of parents as powerful and flawless. The idealization provides an internalized object representing that part of the self striving for perfection and acting in good conscience. Idealizing the parent results in an ego ideal that subconsciously serves as a motivator for worthy goals, and competency and it acts as a conscience.

Splitting: One reason for reenacting inappropriate relational patterns as an adult is that immature object development prevents realistic assessments of how others react. Immature object relations may cause a person to interpret interactions and other people as all good or all bad. The object relations are said to be splitting, categorizing others as either positive or negative without an ability to hold constant the memory of the good in a relationship when disagreements or bad things happen. *Splitting* may also occur with the self-image that is judged with black or white evaluations. The person himself is seen as all good or all bad. Such a lack of integration causes disruptions in relationships and an unstable identity.

Object constancy: The psychological ability to remember the good in a person or the self even when disappointed or frustrated. Objects are integrated with both good and bad qualities and can then be held as a constant. If parenting is inadequate, according to self psychology, the underlying dynamic of seeking a protector or an admirer who could meet the need for a *grandiose self* or an *ego ideal* is reenacted in adulthood.

Therapy stages: The process of therapy follows a pattern where the client gradually gains more trust in the therapist and the counseling activity. Psychoanalytic and dynamic therapies describe the beginning stage as the period where the transference relationship is established and initial interpretations occur. Interpretations would entail therapist's inferences about the client's unconscious patterns as shown in the counseling interactions and in the material shared by the client. Psychoanalysts might also use the technique of free association where the client tells whatever enters his mind, revealing a pattern of associated thoughts. Psychoanalysts might also interpret dreams, said by Freud to be the "royal road to the unconscious." In the middle stage of therapy, the client becomes accepting of the interpretations, willingly brings in confirming material, and is said to *work through* psychological difficulties. Dynamic therapists would act as positive parental objects providing the client with a corrective life experience, meaning the new interaction would correct misperceptions about the self and others. Object relations therapy could include controlled regression where a child would return to an earlier stage of development in order to experience positive parenting. The ending stage is titled *termination*, the time when the client reviews the progress made and says farewell to the therapist.

Transference and countertransference: Both analytic and psychodynamic therapies presume the client will project unconscious relational material onto the counselor. In analyzing the projections, clients work through the accompanying feelings and begin to develop new ways of seeing themselves and others. The counselor also relates to the client with unconscious reactions. Since the focus of therapy is on the client, the counselor is careful to prevent his own material from interfering with the client's counseling experience. Hence, analytic therapists try to maintain a nonresponsive stance to limit countertransference and promote transference. Dynamic therapists, however, come from an empathic posture and use their own reactions to understand the client's impact on others for interpretations of transference and countertransference.

Insight: When a client becomes aware of unconscious material, thus bringing the unconscious into the consciousness, then the client has gained insight. This is the primary goal of psychoanalysis since understanding previously buried patterns changes the interplay between the id, superego and ego. The ego can then manage internal presses and have more energy for dealing with external realities.

Resistance: Insights gained in therapy challenge clients to face frightful issues and to make difficult changes. Clients may use a variety of avoidance behaviors to protect themselves from dealing with tough interpretations and the implications of needed change.

Working-through process: When the client accepts the therapy process and no longer resists, the counseling interaction flows smoothly, the client shares willingly, insights are gained, and the psychological effort to change proceeds. Clients resolve some issues, gain new perspectives, and practice new behaviors.

Neutrality: A term used to describe the therapist's ability to maintain an objective viewpoint in analyzing the client's issues according to psychoanalytic principles.

Abstinence: Psychoanalysts refrain from psychologically participating in clients' expressions of feelings, wishes, and fantasies.

Anonymity: Psychoanalysts present an anonymous front for the client, revealing nothing personal about themselves. With the therapist maintaining a blank slate, the client is free to project feelings from past relationships.

Free association: A psychoanalytic technique whereby the client speaks whatever comes to mind. The sequencing of topics implies underlying meanings and reveals unconscious material.

Empathy: Self psychologists reject the neutral and anonymous stance of psychoanalytic therapists by deliberately entering the client's inner world and gaining an understanding of life experiences from the client's perspective.

Corrective emotional experiences: A life event that allows a person to gain a new perspective on a past experience. The term is used by self psychology therapists to describe the process of reparenting clients. The term is also used to describe experiences outside of therapy that change perceptions so that the person feels differently about similar situations.

Analytical psychology: Jung's theory of psychodynamics that adds to the unconscious another layer of a collective knowledge shared by all human beings and representing historically universal experiences for people across all cultures.

Archetypes and collective unconscious: Jungian psychoanalytic theory conceives the unconscious as containing both a personal level and a level of communal knowledge passed on from previous generations. Artistic creations and spiritual traditions transmit values and dramatic roles that are embedded in unconscious memories. Archetypes represent universal roles that play out in common interactions that appear in different cultures.

Persona: A Jungian term for the public mask individuals show to the world which censors personal attributes and desires that may be socially unacceptable.

Shadow: The term from Jung that represents the dark side of the self with unacceptable desires that a person tries to hide from others.

Anima and animus: According to Jung, each woman's unconscious contains a male archetype, the animus. The female archetype for men is the anima.

Self-actualization: The process of a person becoming all she can be, living up to her true potential and contributing to society. A basic tenet of Jung's theory and other humanistic philosophies.

Introspection: A person examining her own internal world

Confession, Elucidation, Education, Transformation: The stages of Jungian psychoanalytic therapy. Stage one involves the client sharing life experiences and telling secrets not typically told to others. The second stage includes the therapist analyzing the transference and countertransference relationship with the client gaining insight into unconscious material. In the third stage, the therapist helps the client translate insights into his current life and in the fourth stage, the client seeks self-actualization interacting with the therapist on an equal level where both are affected.

Dream analysis: A major technique in Jungian therapy where interpretations reveal the client's unconscious dilemmas, archetypal enactments, and solutions to current issues. The progress of therapy is evaluated by the changing themes of dreams.

Termination: The process of ending and completing therapy. Typically, termination includes a review of the gains accomplished by the client, some reminiscing of the progression of the relationship, and a sense of loss experienced by both the client and the counselor.

Developmental stages: Different theories describe a sequence of childhood learning that requires progressively more complex skills and cognitive functions. Each level of learning is typically seen as a stage of development that must be completed before the next stage can be approached. For psychoanalytic thought, stages follow biological functions; for ego psychology, stages follow psychosocial influences; for object relations, stages follow the increasingly sophisticated interactions between the child and caretaker.

Humanism: A philosophy maintaining that human nature is basically growth-oriented and that all people possess the growth potential to express their worth in positive, constructive ways. When human beings do bad things, it is because their basic nature has been thwarted in some way.

Deterministic: A belief system proposing that human life is programmed by antecedent occurrences such as pre-birth destiny or early childhood. Lives unfold according to preset patterns and are not open to influence once the pattern is set.

Narcissistic personality disorder: An adult self-absorbed personality pattern where narcissists overestimate their own needs and lack empathy for others. Results from impoverished mirroring and lack of parental idealization so the self is the primary object of the person's inner world.

Borderline personality disorder: A personality disorder characterized by instability in both self-concept and interpersonal relationships, featuring dramatic moods swings and impulsivity. This is said to be caused by neglectful parenting and continual childhood frustration whereby the child becomes angry and projects anger onto parents. The child internalizes a world view of danger, and as an adult continually acts out in defense against the imagined hostility of others.

Schizoid personality disorder: A group of disorders where people experience a limited range of emotions, lack interest in relating to others, and show hardly any emotional expression. Theoretically caused by blocked ego development when a child received little love and was prevented from giving love.

Representative Case: Psychoanalytic Approach: Clyde Clanders

This representative case fits well with the psychoanalytic approach. Questions and answers follow to encourage the development of clinical thinking within the paradigm.

A 52-year-old male came to therapy shortly after entering an extramarital affair. Clyde spent much time explaining to the counselor that his lover had initiated the liaison and he would never have suggested sexual relations on his own. Although he felt guilty for betraying his wife and children, he also said his wife deserved his infidelity since he was certain she had been unfaithful several times. He described a chaotic upbringing as an only child where his mother pampered him and his father punished him severely for minor offenses. Clyde attended college and earned a degree in finance and later a CPA license (certified public accountant). Although he had once held dreams of becoming a stockbroker on Wall Street, his adult life had been spent meeting family and community responsibilities in a small city in the Midwest. Clyde seemed bewildered seeing himself in an affair, saying he knew he was risking everything he has invested in: his reputation, his family, his own morally-based self-respect. Yet he felt driven to continue the forbidden relationship and was very animated in describing his excitement. He easily admitted a part of the excitement was the clandestine nature of the meetings, even smiling at the thought that his wife and his lover's husband were being duped.

Thinking About Clyde

Imagining yourself as a Freudian psychoanalyst, can you frame an interpretation explaining why a conservative middle-aged man would have an affair? **Hint:** Consider what stage of development Freud emphasized. How would an affair enact an unconscious desire?

Course of Therapy

The transference relationship involved the client competing with the female therapist by trying to find better interpretations than she suggested and by solicitous overtures that cast the therapist into a feminine stereotype. Over time, therapy revealed that his Oedipal struggle was never resolved. The client was eventually able to admit to incestuous feelings for his mother and his rivalry with his father. His father was now in his eighties and still the client needed to compete and demonstrate how he was a better man. His mother had died two years prior to starting therapy, and the client missed her terribly. He repeated many times that his mother was a true lady. The client began to see his affair as a delayed attempt to enact the unconscious incest drama, and he lost interest in the liaison. His need to compete with his father also diminished.

Eventually, the client recognized that his disappointment in his wife stemmed from his fantasy that she would replace his mother. With coaching from the therapist, the client began to open intimate conversations with his wife, sharing some of his new insights and listening to his wife describe her experiences. She confessed to one brief affair but also disclosed that she had several close relationships with male friends in her loneliness. She resented the client's constant jealousy and was relieved to learn he was coming to terms with his own libido urges rather than projecting his own frustrations onto her. Neither partner considered divorce an option since both shared religious convictions prohibiting ending the marriage. The couple sought marriage counseling following the husband's individual therapy.

Check Your Thinking About Clyde

Unresolved Oedipal issues involved the client wishing for a career and a wife he could never have.

Representative Case—Psychodynamic Approach: Barry Radisson, Schizoid Genius

This representative case fits well with the psychodynamic approach. Questions and answers follow to encourage the development of clinical thinking within the paradigm.

A frantic, tall and thin, 36-year-old male comes to counseling at the urging of his sister who accompanies him. He has quit his job as an architect working for a small firm building apartment complexes. He created the master plan and received an award for the innovative design that demonstrated technical advances combined with low cost features. Now that the building is proceeding, Barry refuses to make certain required adaptations. He has spent the last three weeks isolated in his home reading crime novels, watching horror movies, and playing computer war games. He corresponds on the Internet with a woman regularly and describes her as his fiancée. His sister is concerned because the Internet contact has suggested visiting soon and the sister is certain a visit would be disastrous. Barry has never married though he has had several engagements that were all broken prior to the weddings.

Barry is detached and describes his business partners with contempt saying they lack vision. He is unconcerned with his job loss and adamant in his refusal to compromise on his vision for the building. He also refuses to sue for a portion of the profits in the project since the original design was his, as his sister insists he should. Barry's sister describes the family background as chaotic. Their mother was alcoholic and treated Barry "as her little pet." The mother would leave the children alone when she went out drinking, and then would bring various men home to her bedroom. Once the loud revelry ended, and her latest sexual partner left, the mother would come to her son's room. Dressed in lingerie, the mother would bring her son to bed with her. In the morning she would angrily banish him from her room. The father was a successful salesman who spent a lot of time out of town. When he was home he was extremely impatient and very critical of the children who did not keep the home as clean and well organized as he expected. The parental marriage was stormy, but the father was very indulgent of the mother whom he adored. The sister described Barry as placid and nonreactive to the disruptive family dynamics, though he was extremely sensitive to his mother's erratic moods.

Thinking About Barry

1. How does Barry's childhood interactions with his mother affect his object relations?
2. What treatment would an object relations approach call for?

Course of Therapy

During early therapy sessions Barry seemed tongue-tied, stumbling over his words, and sat in silence for long periods. He seemed to be appreciative of the therapist's sincere respect for his descriptions of his internal world but fearful that the understanding would be withdrawn. The skilled clinician did not prod and did not distance himself from bizarre descriptions of architectural designs for urban farmers but instead seriously considered meanings Mr. B was expressing. Instead of pathologizing, the counselor normalized the client's talent. A warm therapeutic space was created, and Mr. B began sharing openly. His inner world was filled with fears of hostility from others. He showed little empathy for others, though he was acutely aware of how others reacted to him. Gradually, Barry was open to carefully presented interpretations of the transference relationship and could understand his fears as related to his mother's inappropriate behavior and his father's criticism. He could relay his confusion about his mother's double messages and his sense of helplessness. Mr. B began to hear limited interpretations of the countertransference effects of his distancing and distrust.

However, the therapist began to realize that the relating skills Mr. B was demonstrating in counseling were not being transferred to his life outside therapy. Dealing with the Internet relationship demonstrated that the exchange did not qualify as a true connection. Eventually, the client was able to start his own consulting business and a real dating relationship without bolting. Although he remained placid, he was able to manage his fears of being consumed by the exchange with his dating partner. He genuinely cared for his partner and shared an active, orgasmic sex life, though he remained apathetic during intercourse. His partner and he never married nor lived together, but they maintained an arrangement that seemed to suit them both.

Check Your Thinking About Barry

1. Barry withdrew from the family chaos and his mother's inappropriate attentions as a child and continued his distancing defense in adulthood.

2. The therapist's respect, taking Barry seriously, normalized Barry's interactive object templates. The warm holding atmosphere and interpretations of the transference/countertransference relationship reparented Barry so he could relate better to others.

Core Case: Mrs. A

The following case study was published by the Alfred Adler Institute (1969)[*]. Here the case will be described from a psychoanalytic and psychodynamic approach as a comparison to the Adlerian Psychology approach in the next chapter. Later, Mrs. A and her family will be a case study for systems therapy.

The format follows a standard layout used by psychologists in writing case notes. **D** designates **Data**, where the client's presenting concerns and symptoms are described. **A** stands for **Assessment**, where the clinician describes diagnostic impressions and case conceptualization concepts. **P**, or **Plan**, tells the plan for future counseling interventions and when applicable, client homework assignments.

D: A 31-year-old woman who has been married eight years and has two male children, ages 4 and 8. Her husband works in the stock room for a department store and is unhappy with his job. During a war he lost an arm and his disability has thwarted career ambitions. For the last year and a half, Mrs. A has suffered from obsessive fears of death, negating previous symptoms of compulsively cleaning to overcome fears of dirt and germs. She has dreams of angels surrounding a coffin. She also fears knives and has suicidal ideation as well as thoughts to harm others. She thinks about hitting her husband or any other adult, including strangers, who annoy her. She imagines physically hurting her 4-year-old son. She does hit her children without provocation and says she is sorry afterwards.

---

[*] Adler, A. (1969). *The Case of Mrs. A (The Diagnosis of a Life-Style)*. Chicago, Illinois: Alfred Adler Institute.

Mrs. A was the second child in a family of eight children, with one older sister in an array of four older girls and four younger boys. When relaying her family history, Mrs. A bitterly reported that her parents were neurotic. The father physically abused the children in the name of discipline. The oldest daughter was beaten most often and was withdrawn in her behavior. When the father was drunk, he would also beat his wife and threaten to slice the children's throats. Frequent conflicts occurred between Mrs. A and the oldest brother. Mrs. A earned good grades and was liked by her classmates.

After leaving school, she worked as a live-in domestic maid, but she had to leave her job because she became ill. After she returned home, her father attacked her with a shovel because he was angry that her return added to his household expenses. Mrs. A escaped being hit over the head with the shovel by running away and hiding in a graveyard. She returned to domestic service until she took a job in a munitions factory.

She met her husband in the hospital where he was recovering from his amputation. Their engagement period included Mrs. A's jealousy of Mr. A's popularity and Mr. A's inconsiderate behavior. However, she became pregnant and they married within weeks. Mrs. A's first experience of suicidal ideation occurred when she was pregnant out of wedlock. She was disappointed at the birth of each of her sons because she wanted a daughter. At several points in the marriage, Mrs. A has lived separately from her husband, taking her children to live with her. She returned home to care for her husband when he suffered a nervous breakdown. Sexual relations between husband and wife have been intermittent for most of their marriage, since Mrs. A has little desire. With her obsessive fear of death and the looming threat of harm to the children now dominating the family, no sexual intimacy occurs. The husband spends most of his time watching Mrs. A so the children are not harmed and she does not attempt suicide.

Psychodynamic Approaches

A: Mrs. A suffers from severe anxiety stemming from physical and emotional abuse in childhood. From an object relations perspective Mrs. A's parenting was defective and she was likely frustrated as an infant when her needs were not met. She projected her anger onto her caretaker mother and introjected objects that cannot be trusted and are hostile. Her stormy and manipulative relationship with her husband and her opposition to her children and even strangers demonstrates her immersion in a world of interpersonal hostility. Emphasizing basic trust issues and therapeutic constancy is paramount.

Self psychology would also approach Mrs. A as limited in ego development without effective parental mirroring and with a negative idealization process. If her parents did provide some attention, it apparently stopped short of developing a grandiose self-object when the first son was born. Mrs. A shows object splitting in her image of angels as all good compared to her image of herself as deserving punishment at times but also worthy of redemption at other times. Other defenses are primitive.

Consider borderline personality disorder with obsessive compulsive features and subsequent treatment.

P: Treatment would require predictable structure maintained with calmness regardless of Mrs. A's reactions. She requires the development of a positive transference, but interpretations must be limited and carefully framed particularly in the initial stages of therapy. Acceptance of her fears and understanding her inner struggles could reduce her open hostility, but manipulations can be expected to continue for some time. Countertransference reactions must be not only controlled but also not interpreted for some time. Consider controlled regression treatment.

Psychoanalytic and Ego Psychology

D: Mrs. A's symptoms reflect considerable anxiety stemming from unconscious conflicts. Her superego is quite demanding as shown by her judgments of her parents, husband, and children. Very likely she judges herself with equal harshness. Her instinctual fears from the id are not fully in control; she fantasizes about harming others and herself. She has not resolved her psychosexual drives. Clearly she competed with her brother for her father's attention and wished she could be male. She never gained appropriate feminine maturity since her development was arrested and she declined to identify with her ineffective mother. Her father's abuse intensifies Electra impulses, and her fixation with knives represents a phallic symbol for what she cannot have. Her compulsive behaviors provide symptoms designed to control her severe anxiety. Her death wish reflects her underlying guilt—her perception that she deserves punishment for her hostility. She seeks redemption through death as shown by her dream with angels surrounding a coffin.

A: Ego psychologists would note ineffective defense mechanisms. She uses regression by creating a situation where she requires the care of others rather than fulfilling the age-appropriate role of mothering her children and caring for her husband. She projects her anger regarding a neglected childhood onto others and uses displacement by becoming angry with strangers. Mrs. A's treatment would not focus on Oedipal processes. Her own death wish is a reaction formation stemming from her desire to hurt others. She uses fantasy to dream of angels rescuing her in death.

P: Plans for both psychoanalytic and ego psychology would entail developing the transference relationship and offering interpretations timed to coincide with the client's ability to accept unconscious truths.

For Further Consideration: Object relations developments in recent times have shown that interpreting the transference/countertransference relationship would be contraindicated for Mrs. A. A major task for the therapist would be to manage his reactions or countertransference issues. What kind of interactions would Mrs. A likely bring into therapy? Mrs. A's psychosocial development is considered to have been limited at an early stage where basic parenting was deficient. Therefore, psychologically she is unprepared for observing and understanding her interactions on the level of transference and countertransference. She would hear interpretations as criticisms, and such interaction with the therapist would reinforce her view of the world as hostile. Without any prompting, she will project anger onto the therapist who will need to calmly allow the stormy scene to occur without reacting. Reflecting on her fear would be the appropriate clinical response after the storm subsides. Only after Mrs. A begins to trust the therapist as a person who reacts differently than what she expects of others will she be able to trust input that suggests she could have a different impact on others.

Finding a Balance

Most counselors choose several counseling approaches that suit their personalities and theoretical preferences. In this section, the counselor's personality characteristics are identified and tied to concepts and practices. Then a case is described. Then, another section shows how the counselor's preferences would play out in working with the case. Finally, a comparison is made showing how other approaches with different preferences might deal with the case. Integrating several approaches might cover varying counselor preferences and differing client issues better than any singular approach.

Key Counselor Preferences

1. Psychoanalytic and psychodynamic therapists enjoy determining abstract symbolism and analyzing clients' unconscious patterns in keeping with theoretical concepts. They have confidence in the truth of interpretations based on abstractions.

2. Psychodynamic counselors have a talent for and an appreciation of timing interventions in therapy. The therapist develops a transference relationship, considers which interpretations can be accepted by the client, when to trigger transference reactions, and when to offer interpretations to the client. The traditional psychoanalytic therapist prefers the stance of structuring the therapeutic interaction.

3. The therapist is capable of great self-restraint and can maintain a holding space for the client, regardless of the client's projections onto the therapist. For example, a client may experience rage against a tyrannical father from her childhood and project her anger onto the therapist, who would not retaliate but would instead act as an understanding, caring parent.

4. The therapist chooses to interpret some client defenses and to draw parallels between current concerns and historical issues. The therapist's preference is to focus less on solving current concerns and more on interpretations derived from historical events. Present issues can be resolved if they occur in the transference relationship, but those problems not experienced in the therapy relationship may not be fully examined.

5. Therapy requires working through the transferences and is not complete until the analyst is confident the process is complete. The therapist prefers that the client gain a full understanding of the origins of his issues and how they are played out in his life. Emphasizing a change in behavior is not a therapist's inclination.

6. Psychoanalytic and psychodynamic therapists view human development as set in childhood and accept that many patterns will not be amenable to change.

Case Example: Bob Berrigan

Bob, age 34, comes to therapy following his fourth divorce. He explains with great animosity that his wealthy father was paying for his analysis. He goes on the explain that this is the only time in his life that he has ever asked his father for help. He has only resorted to counseling as a last resort since he seems unable to get his life together.

It is obvious that Bob was resistant to therapy, but his initial defensive presentation fades as he describes his childhood. He was born as a fraternal twin; his sister was "simple" and he was her protector. His father owned several elegant restaurants and had become, over the years, quite successful. As a child, Bob watched his parents working hard in their first restaurant while he took care of his sister. He described his sister as beautiful, kind, and always grateful to him for his attention as well as admiring him without reservation. His parents fought vehemently, usually in the restaurant kitchen, after the business closed for the evening. One vivid memory included his mother, face contorted in anger, throwing a knife at his father, and saying, "I work like a dog for you and those bastard kids of yours." The knife landed in his father's chest and blood spewed everywhere. His father was taken to the hospital in an ambulance. In the confusion the children were hiding in a pantry while Bob held his sobbing sister. No one noticed the children until the next morning when the cook came into the pantry for ingredients. Years later at his mother's funeral, Bob learned from an aunt that he and his sister were actually born to his father's mistress. Bob was 17 when he was told the family secret. This was when he left home for college. Bob still cares for his sister, who lives in a group home and who still admires and loves him unconditionally.

Bob has been unable to hold a job consistently throughout his adult life. Usually he has worked in fast-food restaurants as an assistant manager, and he's been fired because he defends employees who have made mistakes or who have been disliked by other employees. He cynically notes that those employees he has tried to help usually don't thank him or appreciate his efforts. He even wonders if they need or want his help, but his conscience won't allow him to ignore the need to defend them. He survives on a small inheritance provided for his sister and himself from his stepmother's estate. He has refused much contact with his father who has offered to give him a restaurant to manage. Bob describes his marriages as uneventful until they dissolve without any reason from his perspective. Bob appears emotionally insulated except for hints of anger at both his parents. His dreams reflect fantasies where he and his sister are royalty, the king and queen, served by others.

As the therapeutic relationship developed it became apparent that object constancy for Bob was an issue. His descriptions of his wives revealed an inability to integrate their faults with their caring for him. He rarely criticized his wives, though his anger seeped out and they would confront him. His conflict avoidance was so strong, however, he always disclaimed any anger. Also he would displace his frustrations with employees' performance deficits onto the primary manager, allowing himself to remain calm and nonplused when mistakes disrupted business. His ego strength was too low to allow himself to express feelings directly or to develop realistic career plans.

Eventually, when the analyst opened the subject of canceling therapy sessions for two weeks for his vacation, Bob appeared angry. The therapist noted B's feeling and refused to accept B's denial, pressing the issue until Bob broke down and raged against the analyst, who accepted the tirade. No interpretation of the transference was made at this time as the analyst soothed Bob, saying his feelings were understandable and the therapist was sorry that Bob was hurt. The next confrontation occurred when the therapist pressed Bob on his lack of attention to his career goals, and again the counselor accepted the rage saying it was understandable that Bob felt criticized. Finally, the analyst allowed Bob to misinterpret a statement as siding with Bob's father and gave an explanation that sounded like the father. Bob broke down and in his rage accused the therapist of ruining his life through neglect and uncaring. The therapist interpreted the accusation as actually for Bob's father and Bob, for the first time, admitted his projection.

Therapy continued with interpretations of Bob's childhood experiences and the parallels in Bob's life and in transferences in therapy. Bob began to accept the interpretations and was able to note similar current experiences. The analysis was complete when Bob could express annoyance with his sister and the pressure he felt to maintain her idealization of him. He began to curb his fears and anxiety when he felt others were hurting him, and he learned to express himself in a range of interactions with others. Although his rage against his father diminished, he chose not to establish a relationship with him; and though he was able to maintain employment, his career identity was never fully established. He saw therapy as helpful in explaining his background, and he felt better about himself.

Applying Counselor Preferences

Using the previously listed psychodynamic preferences, how did the therapist manage therapy with Bob Berrigan?

1. The therapist enjoyed determining the symbolism of Bob's inner dynamics as stemming from the lack of constancy in his relationships with his parents. Bob's pattern of object relations was repeated in his adult relationships, giving the therapist material for determining the course of therapy. Bob benefited from a review of his childhood, gaining insight into his early life experiences.

2. The therapist demonstrated excellent skill in developing the therapeutic relationship, timing interpretations, and in managing the transference. The transference relationship allowed Bob to reenact the template of defending himself against his pain and anger against his father, as he has in his marriages.

3. The therapist showed an ability to maintain self-restraint and a warm holding pattern for Bob to experience his childhood pain. The transference relationship also allowed Bob to project his basic anger against his father onto the therapist, who did not retaliate but instead acted as a parent who understood Bob's hurt.

4. The defenses of projecting emotions onto others and emotional insulation were worked through in therapy, and Bob's interactions with others improved. Although Bob's working life undoubtedly benefited from improved relationships, the therapist chose not to examine current career identity concerns.

5. The therapist chose the length of therapy and was confident that his interpretations and the transference relationship provided therapeutic healing. Bob benefited from the therapist's choices but might have gained further change if his behavioral and cognitive habits were also considered.

6. The therapist's belief that Bob's life path was fully established in childhood may have limited Bob's growth and may have been a factor in allowing career issues to remain stagnant.

Comparison with Other Approaches

Individual psychology: Adler's approach shares an emphasis on childhood influence with the psychodynamic approach. However, the interpretations drawn from early experiences do not depend on the existence of an unconscious. Accordingly, the necessity of creating a transference relationship is not assumed. Individual psychology also assumes personality is not predetermined, and clients can change current issues. The length of therapy does presume enough time for a life review and current implications but not for reenacting childhood templates. Career issues and other current concerns would receive attention.

Person-centered and Gestalt: These approaches presume clients can raise childhood influences, if clients determine historical factors are relevant. Bob and his view of his own internal process would determine the content of therapy sessions. Interpretations would not be a part of therapy. Bob's anger would be explored, his attitudes toward others and his work would likely be examined, but the therapist's opinions would be withheld in favor of the client determining his own approach to his own life. The present would be emphasized rather than the past.

Existential and Transpersonal: Meanings as Bob determined would be emphasized rather than interpretations. Childhood would be only as important as Bob and his beliefs dictated. Bob's responsibility for his own life would be stressed, as would his spirituality.

Behavioral and Cognitive-Behavioral: These approaches would thoroughly examine Bob's current behavior and his thinking patterns, determine what habits created difficulties, and create interventions for change. Childhood stories would not be examined and the therapeutic relationship would be based on a mutual alliance, rather than presuming a transference process.

Example of a Published Research Article on Psychoanalytical Theory

This published research article is on psychoanalytic theory. The commentary in the boxes to the left of the article will help you understand the research and the format of the piece.

Effects of Subliminal Activation of Oedipal Fantasies on Competitive Performance: A Replication and Extension

Robert Palumbo and Irene Gillman

> The first two paragraphs are the abstract, a summary of the article.

A subliminal psychodynamic activation experiment was conducted in which the effects of five subliminal stimuli were sought on the dart-throwing performance of male subjects. The stimuli consisted of the following messages, each accompanied by a congruent picture: BEATING DAD IS OK, BEATING DAD IS WRONG, BEATING HIM IS OK, BEATING HIM IS WRONG, and PEOPLE ARE WALKING. The first two stimuli were intended to activate competitive motives within the context of the Oedipus complex; the next two, competitive motives outside that context; and the last was intended as a control stimulus.

BEATING DAD IS OK led to greater dart-throwing accuracy than each of the other four conditions, which in turn did not differ from each other. This finding replicated a result reported by Silverman, L. H., Ross, D., Adler, J., and Lustig, D. (J. Abnorm. Psychol., 87: 341–357, 1978) and is in keeping with the formulation that the activation of Oedipal motives can affect competitive performance. Neither a subject variable (fear of success) nor the differential effects of two experimenters was found to interact with stimulus conditions in affecting dart scores.

> Because this article appeared in a medical journal, a different citation style is used. Each source is numbered and can be found in the Reference list by number. In APA style, the sources are listed by first author's last name, alphabetically.
>
> In both styles, content notes are marked with superscript (raised) numbers.

Since the early 1950s, there has been considerable interest in experimentally studying the influence on behavior of factors outside of awareness through subliminal stimulation methods. (See Dixon [1] for an encompassing review.) One extensive program of research in this area is that initiated by Silverman (4, 5) in what has been termed "the subliminal psycho-dynamic activation method"—an experimental method for testing psychoanalytically posited relationships between unconscious conflict and behavior. As Silverman (5) has elaborated, psychoanalytic theory requires such experimental tests because clinical data have not allowed for the resolution

Robert Palumbo and Irene Gillman, "Effects of Subliminal Activation of Oedipal Fantasies on Competitive Performance: A Replication and Extension," from *Journal of Nervous and Mental Disease*, 172 (1984), pp. 737–741. Reprinted with permission of Lippincott, Williams & Wilkins.

A tachistoscope is a machine that projects images at rapid speeds. The exposure of 4 milliseconds is considered to be too short for the image to enter conscious awareness, but long enough to be perceived unconsciously (subliminally).

The experiment tests psychoanalytic theory, which says that all boys go through an Oedipal period, in which they first compete with their fathers and then identify with them. The competition makes them feel guilty and anxious. This study tests whether those unconscious feelings about competition with fathers can be stimulated to affect dart-throwing performance.

The authors list four purposes for adding to the current number of experiments based on the dart-throwing study. They add new features to their experiment to check other explanations for the previous variable dart-throwing results: this experiment will see whether fear of success, or the experimenter's manner, affect dart-throwing performance outside of the effect of subliminal messages.

of differences *among* psychoanalytic clinicians, let alone *between* psychoanalytic clinicians and clinicians of other theoretical persuasions. Silverman has cited over 50 articles and doctoral dissertations reporting that the 4-msec tachistoscopic exposure of verbal and pictorial stimuli presumed either to intensify or diminish unconscious conflict, when compared to 4-msec exposure of neutral stimuli, have influenced behavior in ways that are consistent with psychoanalytic theory.

Whereas most of these experiments have involved clinical populations, one series involved unselected male college students engaged in competitive dart throwing. Silverman's interest here was in introducing an easy-to-carry-out experimental paradigm that could demonstrate a psychodynamic relationship consistent with psychoanalytic theory. Silverman et al. (7) reported three experiments in which the 4-msec exposure of the message BEATING DAD IS OK, accompanied by a picture of an older and younger man smiling at each other, led to significantly higher dart scores than the message BEATING DAD IS WRONG, accompanied by a picture of the same two men frowning. These investigators conceived of the former stimulus as sanctioning a derivative Oedipal wish and the latter as condemning the same wish. Assuming that competitive performance can be influenced by remnants of unresolved oedipal conflicts that are present in most men, they interpreted their results as consistent with the idea that competitive performance can be affected by the degree to which Oedipal conflicts are intensified or diminished.

In the summary paper cited above, Silverman (5) reported that, whereas the great majority of subliminal psychodynamic activation experiments conducted by independent investigators have reported positive results, this has not been the case for the dart competition studies. Of nine investigations conducted outside of his laboratory, about one half have replicated the original findings (e.g., Hayden and Silverstein [2]), while the others have failed to replicate (e.g., Heilbrun [3]).

The following study was undertaken with the following aims in mind: a) to seek an independent replication of the results reported by Silverman et al. (7); b) to add experimental stimuli that would have bearing on the specificity of the Oedipal interpretation that Silverman et al. (7) gave to their experimental results; Silverman et al. acknowledged that their findings were "only consistent with the psychoanalytically based formulation . . . rather than as corroborating it . . . in order to claim the latter, further experiments would have to be carried out, and variations in stimulus content would have to be introduced in order to determine if it is the specifically Oedipal elements that produced the effects" (p. 343); c) to determine whether a subject variable, fear of success, would distinguish subjects who demonstrated the experimental effects from subjects who did not; it is quite possible that there are notable differences among subjects in their vulnerability to Oedipal conflict and that those high on the fear of success variable are particularly prone to such conflict; d) to investigate whether there are experimenter differences in eliciting stimulus effects, as it is conceivable that different experimenters, by virtue of their manner and behavior, are more or less apt to arouse Oedipally related fantasies and feelings. Thus, the answers to the last two questions could have bearing on the inconsistent results cited above for the dart-throwing experiments.

Methods

Subjects

Subjects were 40 males from Berkeley Claremont Business College, all of whom came from English-speaking homes. They ranged in age from 22 to 46 years, with their mean age 28.6 and mode age 28.

Procedure

Subjects volunteered for the study following an announcement of a "dart tournament" in which prize money would be given for the three highest scorers. Subjects were seen individually in a single session in which they first read and signed an information sheet that stated the following:

There are many things that affect a person's competitive performance. One important group of factors, we believe, is the way in which people react to faint or indistinct experiences. By experimentally studying this group of factors in people involved in competitive situations we hope to better understand how performance may be hindered or improved.

If you decide to participate in this study, you will be asked to throw darts at a dartboard, respond to some questions, and look at flickers of light that will be made by words and pictures very rapidly exposed. From past experience with these and similar procedures we do not expect them to have any negative effect on you. But we do expect to learn a great deal about competitive behavior.

If you agree to participate in this study, you can change your mind at any time and withdraw. Such a decision will be in no way held against you. All the information you provide will remain strictly confidential.

The subject was then administered the Fear of Success Scale (FOS) developed by Sadd, Lennauer, Shaver, and Dunivant. The procedure for the remainder of the session closely followed that reported by Silverman et al. (7). This began with a "priming procedure" in which the subject filled out a questionnaire tapping his feelings toward and

> This is an *informed consent* document. It gives the participant an idea of what they will experience, assures them of the right to withdraw without penalty, and promises confidentiality. Notice that the exact nature of the research question is veiled, so that the participants are not influenced in advance.

These tests typically call forth stories and images related to child-parent relationships.

Counterbalanced means that the critical stimuli were presented in all possible orders to balance out the possible effects of fatigue and practice. Each participant received the stimuli in one of the 120 possible orders.

relationship with his father and mother, the administration of Rorschach card IV, Thematic Apperception Test (TAT) cards 6BM and 7BM, and a story recall task, all of which were designed to activate oedipal themes.

After eight practice dart throws, the subject looked into the eyepiece of a tachistoscope and was given the first "round" of exposures to the subliminal stimuli. A picture was first presented for 4 msec from the stimulus field followed by a 3-sec interval when a blank slide was viewed, followed by the 4-msec exposure of a verbal message. This sequence was repeated three times. The subject then threw eight darts.

This same procedure was followed for 10 "rounds" which included five "neutral baseline" conditions alternated with five "critical" conditions. The baseline stimuli consisted of the following verbal messages, each accompanied by a congruent picture: PEOPLE ARE STANDING, PEOPLE ARE HEARING, PEOPLE ARE TALKING, PEOPLE ARE LOOKING, and PEOPLE ARE THINKING, always presented in that order. The order of the five critical conditions, on the other hand, was counterbalanced.

The verbal messages for the critical conditions were: BEATING DAD IS OK, BEATING DAD IS WRONG, BEATING HIM IS OK, BEATING HIM IS WRONG, and PEOPLE ARE WALKING. The pictorial accompaniments for the first two conditions were the ones cited earlier. The pictures accompanying the two BEATING HIM messages were of two young men looking at each other, smiling and frowning, respectively. The pictorial accompaniment of PEOPLE ARE WALKING was of two men side by side.

The PEOPLE ARE WALKING condition was used by Silverman *et al.* (7) as a control, and in one of their three experiments this condition produced dart scores that were significantly lower than those following the BEATING DAD IS OK condition and significantly higher than those following BEATING DAD IS WRONG. In the other two experiments, the control condition, while producing mean dart scores between BEATING DAD IS OK and BEATING DAD IS WRONG, was significantly different from only one of these and in the studies that have replicated the Silverman *et al.* (7) results, there too the only consistent significant result was that BEATING DAD IS OK produced higher scores than BEATING DAD IS WRONG.

The BEATING HIM stimuli were designed to test the specificity of the Oedipal explanation, if the result for BEATING DAD IS OK vs. BEATING DAD IS WRONG was replicated. That is, if such a result was forthcoming, with there being no difference between BEATING HIM IS OK and BEATING HIM IS WRONG, this would support the formulation that Oedipal motives were involved. On the other hand, if the two BEATING HIM stimuli produced results paralleling the BEATING DAD stimuli, nonpsychoanalytic explanations (see Palumbo) might more parsimoniously account for the results.

Exact specifications for the experimental materials are given so that this research setting can be compared with others. Also, other researchers will be able to replicate the study precisely.

The experimenters were *blind* to what cards they were presenting the participants to avoid the effect of experimenter bias. Experimenters could not change their manner of presentation according to type of stimulus.

The task described was given to make sure that the stimuli had not entered the participants' conscious awareness. Therefore, any influence the stimuli had was considered unconscious.

Stimuli were presented through an electronically controlled Scientific Prototype two-field tachistoscope. Subjects looked through the eyepiece at a fixation point on a blank field and the stimuli were exposed from the second field. The viewing distance was 34 inches. The illumination level for the stimulus field was 5 foot lamberts; for the blank field, 10 foot lamberts; and the ambient illumination also was 10 foot lamberts. The verbal messages were printed on white cards over two lines that occupied a space approximately 2⅙ X 1 inch. The pictorial stimuli were 3 X 2-1/2 inch line drawings.

An American-style dart board was used, this consisting of seven concentric circles with the bull's-eye marked 100 and the others radiating progressively from the center marked 80, 60, 40, 30, 20, and 10. The board was hung from a wall 98 inches from the throwing line with the bottom of the board 58 inches from the floor.

There were two experimenters, both male graduate students in their 30s, and each was randomly assigned one half of the subjects. They were blind to stimulus conditions, selecting stimulus cards by code letters printed on the backs by someone not otherwise involved in the study.

To test for the subjects' being blind to stimulus conditions, a discrimination task was administered to all 40 subjects at the end of the experiment. A subject was given 10 trials in which, under the same conditions as in the experiment proper, he was asked to distinguish the flashes made by one of the picture-message pairs from those made by another with the particular pairs randomly selected. Following Silverman *et al.* (7), the following instructions were given:

There's one more thing we're going to do. I have two sets of slides here and I want to see whether you can tell them apart when I flash them on at the same speed I did during the experiment. Try as hard as you can because the person who does the best on this will win a $5 cash prize. I am going to show you four pairs of exposures of one set of slides, which will be followed by four pairs of exposures of either the same set or a different set. After the second set of four exposures and after each set after that I want you to tell me whether you think the set you just saw was the same or different than the set right before it. Okay, now if you would put your eyes up against the viewer, we can get started. During this task, please don't look up; keep your eyes focused into the machine. Here's four exposures of the first set of exposures. Now I'm going to show you four more exposures of either the same or different set. Just say "same" or "different" to indicate what you think.

All subjects performed within chance limits on this task—that is, the number of correct discriminations ranged between three and seven for the 10 trials *(p > .10; two-tailed)*. (This was congruent with the subjects' spontaneous comments during the experiment proper in which they maintained that all they could see were flickers of light.) Thus there was no evidence that conscious partial cues were available to the subjects.

Results

An analysis of covariance was carried out with the baseline scores as the covariate. In this analysis there were three independent variables: subliminal condition (five critical stimuli); fear of success, with the subjects divided into high, moderate, and low groups (13, 14, and 13 subjects, respectively, in each group); and experimenter effects (two experimenters). The results of this analysis appear in Table 1, which also contains the mean baseline and critical dart scores for each of the five conditions.

The only significant effect was for stimulus conditions. Newman-Keuls tests were then carried out (using adjusted cell means) to determine which differences among the five conditions accounted for the significant condition effect. BEATING DAD IS OK was found to have produced significantly higher dart scores than the other four conditions ($p < .05$ in each instance). No other significant difference emerged.

> This analysis of covariance takes out the effect of each dart thrower's original skill (baseline score) so that the effect of the stimuli is what remains. The analysis then examines the average scores to check for meaningful differences among dart scores from each stimulus. When meaningful differences are found, the follow-up tests (Newman-Keuls) show exactly what groups differ from each other. In this case, scores from one stimulus stood out from all the others. The other stimuli did not produce meaningfully different scores compared with each other.

Table 1

Analysis of Covariance (BMDP2V), with Two Grouping Variables FOS (Three Levels), and Experimenter (Two Levels), Including Repeated Measures

Source	Subjects	df	Mean Square	F	p
FOS(A)	10.78125	2	5.59063	.10	.907
Critical messages (B)	258.67285	4	64.66821	2.80	.029
Experimenter (C)	188.98828	1	188.98828	3.43	.073
A x B	209.23901	8	26.15488	1.13	.347
B x C	73.96588	4	19.49139	.80	.528
A x C	92.07813	2	46.03096	.84	.443
A x B x C	337.91796	8	42.23975	1.83	.077
Error	3123.12500	135	23.13425		

Stimulus	Mean Baseline	S.D.	Mean Critical	S.D.
BEATING DAD IS OK	49.02	9.67	53.52	8.99
BEATING HIM IS OK	52.27	9.60	51.82	8.23
PEOPLE ARE WALKING	52.15	9.64	51.22	7.91
BEATING HIM IS WRONG	50.27	11.09	50.67	9.79
BEATING DAD IS WRONG	51.10	9.47	51.50	9.74

Discussion

> The authors summarize their conclusion succinctly.

The main finding from the Silverman *et al.* (7) experiments is replicated in the current study. The subliminal presentation of the word-picture stimulus BEATING DAD IS OK resulted in significantly higher dart scores than the stimulus BEATING DAD IS WRONG. Thus, this study, together with four other reports of successful replications (Carroll [6]; Glennon [7]; Hayden and Silverstein [2]; Lonski and Palumbo [8]), support the contention that the subliminal activation in college men of ideas sanctioning success in competition with father lead to better dart-throwing performance than the activation of ideas condemning success. As subliminal psychodynamic activation phenomena are highly counterintuitive *(cf.* Silverman *et al.,* chapter 6), it is important to note that four of the five replications (all but Glennon [7]) were conducted by investigators independent of Silverman. This argues against the positive results these studies have reported being attributable to experimenter bias, as does, of course, the double-blind controls used in these studies.

> The authors next discuss the results of their added features: grouping participants by *fear of success*, using two different experimenters, and including the competitive but non-Oedipal stimuli, BEATING HIM IS OK and BEATING HIM IS WRONG.

Do the findings from the current experiment shed light on the nonreplications *(e.g.,* Heilbrun [3]) of the findings by Silverman *et al.* (7)? By examining the differential stimulus effects for subjects showing high, medium, and low fear of success, and by examining the effects elicited by two experimenters, there was an opportunity to investigate whether subject and experimenter variables influenced stimulus effects. Inasmuch as the analysis of covariance failed to show any significant interactions between these variables and stimulus effects, this study can claim no solid support for the relevance of these variables. However, an interesting lead for future research was suggest by a *post hoc* finding. As is detailed in Palumbo, 4 subjects scoring low on FOS (the bottom third of the distribution) showed a clear-cut effect in the hypothesized direction for BEATING DAD IS OK vs. BEATING DAD IS WRONG ($p < .01$), whereas those scoring high on this variable (the top one third of the sample) showed no effect (with the nonsignificant trend in the opposite direction). As it was the BEATING DAD IS OK stimulus that carried this effect (it was this condition rather than BEATING DAD IS WRONG that differed from the control condition), this finding could imply the following. In order for the OK condition to serve its function and sanction derivative Oedipal wishes, subjects have to be free of fears of success because such fears can prevent the sanction from "taking." However, as this result was not predicted and as the overall *F* for the fear of success by stimulus condition interaction was not significant, a replication of this finding would be necessary before it could be viewed with confidence.

The new conditions introduced in this experiment, the stimuli BEATING HIM IS OK and BEATING HIM IS WRONG, produced results that were no different from those of the

> According to psychoanalytic theory, "winning Mom" sexually is the focus of the Oedipal conflict with the father. Another study examined the effects of subliminal messages about "winning Mom," the *libidinal* element of the Oedipal struggle.

> Unlike most articles published in psychology journals, this one (from a medical journal) does not include a section on limitations of the study.

control condition. The positive result for BEATING DAD IS OK in conjunction with the absence of results for BEATING HIM IS OK, argues for the former message being effective because of its specifically oedipal connotations. Similar conclusions were drawn from the findings of two other studies. Lonski and Palumbo (8) found effects for BEATING DAD IS OK vs. BEATING DAD IS WRONG, but not for BEATING MOM IS OK vs. BEATING MOM IS WRONG. Hayden and Silverstein (2) obtained effects for the stimuli WINNING MOM IS OK vs. WINNING MOM IS WRONG, intended to stir up motives related to the *libidinal* side of the oedipus complex, but obtained no effects for WINNING DAD IS OK vs. WINNING DAD IS WRONG. The current findings, particularly when considered together with the results from the two studies just cited, allow us to go beyond the conclusion of Silverman *et al.* (7). The earlier data, based solely on the BEATING DAD stimuli, were said to be only *consistent with* the formulation that oedipal motives can affect competitive performance. The data from the more recent studies can be said to offer more direct support for this same conclusion.

Summary

The experiment reported has provided further evidence that the psychodynamic relationships that have been inferred by psychoanalytic clinicians can be examined in the laboratory by the use of the subliminal psychodynamic activation method. In contrast to most of the studies that have used this method (summarized in Silverman [4, 5]), the current investigation used a nonclinical population and a psychodynamic relationship clearly emerged. The activation of an unconscious idea that sanctions oedipal competition allowed college men to perform more skillfully in dart throwing.

References

1. Dixon, N. *Preconscious Processing.* John Wiley & Sons, New York, 1981.
2. Hayden, B., and Silverstein, R. The effects of subliminal Oedipal stimulation on competitive dart throwing. Psychol. Res. Bull., 23:1–12, 1983.
3. Heilbran, K. Silverman's subliminal psychodynamic activation: A failure to replicate. J. Abnorm. Psychol., 89:560–566,1980.
4. Silverman, L. H. Psychoanalytic theory: The reports of my death are greatly exaggerated. Am. Psychol., *31:* 621–637, 1976.
5. Silverman, L. H. The subliminal psychodynamic activation method: Overview and comprehensive listing of studies. In Masling, J., Ed., *Empirical Studies of Psychoanalytical Theories*, Vol. 1. Lawrence Erlbaum Associates, Hillsdale, N. J., 1983.

6.   Silverman, L. H., Lachmann, F. M., and Milich, R. H. *Search for Oneness.* International Universities Press, New York, 1982.

7.   Silverman, L. H., Rosa, D., Adler, J., and Lustig, D. Simple research paradigm for demonstrating subliminal psychodynamic activation: Effects of Oedipal stimuli on dart-throwing accuracy in college males. J. Abnorm. Psychol., *87:*341–357, 1978.

Notes

1. Hofstra University, Hempstead, Long Island, New York. Send reprint requests to Dr. Palumbo, 915 Hillside Avenue, New Hyde Park, New York 11040.

> Independence from an earlier researcher is important in replications and extensions of his or her study, like this one. The replication should be conducted outside the influence of the earlier researcher. This separate pursuit is especially important when the earlier researcher is famous in the field.

This investigation was conducted for the first author's doctoral dissertation at Hofstra University under the second author's sponsorship.

The authors wish to thank Lloyd Silverman for his assistance in preparing the manuscript. It should be noted, however, that the study herein reported and the dissertation on which this manuscript was based were completed independently—that is, without any contact with Silverman and his associates.

2. See Silverman, L. H., Lachmann, F. M., and Milich, R. H. (1982) for an extensive account of how this method evolved, the rationale advanced for how it can meaningfully address psychoanalytic psychodynamic propositions, and the application of the method to an issue that Silverman and his colleague have become increasingly interested in through the years: the role of unconscious symbiotic or "oneness" fantasies in enhancing adaptation.

3. Sadd, S., Lenauer, M., Shaver, P., and Dunivant, N. Objective measurement of fear of success and fear of failure. Unpublished manuscript, New York University, 1976.

4. Palumbo, R. The fear of success in adult males: The effects of subliminal messages derived from two theoretical models. Unpublished doctoral dissertation, Hofstra University, 1979.

5. The assumption of homogeneity of regression was tested and found to be valid so that an analysis of covariance could be carried out.

6. Carroll, R. Neurophysiological and psychological mediators of response to subliminal perception. Unpublished doctoral dissertation, St. John's University, 1979.

7. Glennon, S. The effect of functional brain asymmetry and hemisphericity on the subliminal activation of residual Oedipal conflicts. Unpublished doctoral dissertation, New York University 1983.

8. Lonski, M., and Palumbo, R. The effects of subliminal stimulation on competitive dart throwing performance. Unpublished manuscript, Hofstra University, 1978.

9. The absence of an effect for BEATING HIM IS OK also supports the contention that subliminal psychodynamic

activation effects are not a function of the structural configuration of the stimuli because there are minimal differences between this stimulus and BEATING DAD IS OK. The negative results on the discrimination task argue against the current findings being explainable in terms of conscious partial cues, but one might still argue that the *subliminal* registration of differential structural configurations may be responsible for subliminal psychodynamic activation effects. The difference in this study between the impact of BEATING DAD IS OK and BEATING HIM IS OK makes this possibility increasingly remote.

Discussion Ideas

1. In what way is this study a *replication* of earlier research? In what way is it an *extension*? What are some reasons why a researcher would want to replicate exactly another researcher's study?

2. Reread our explanation of the Oedipal struggle. Do you agree that this experiment tested whether Oedipal subliminal messages influence behavior? Why or why not? Can you think of any other explanation for the results of this experiment?

3. Why were all the participants males? Would it be worthwhile to do the same experiment with women participants? Why or why not?

4. Why did the authors include five "neutral baseline" conditions?

5. Why do you think the experimenters presented both a picture and a verbal message for each condition, instead of only pictures or only words?

Answer Key for Practice Test Questions

True/False

1. T
2. T
3. T
4. F
5. F
6. F
7. T
8. F
9. T
10. F

Multiple Choice

1.	e	11.	d
2.	d	12.	d
3.	a	13.	e
4.	d	14.	b
5.	c	15.	e
6.	d		
7.	d		
8.	c		
9.	b		
10.	e		

CHAPTER 5

Adlerian Psychology

Chapter Review

Adler's theory emphasizes the social influences affecting each individual, starting with the impact of family dynamics during early childhood. Interacting with siblings and parents each child operates from a particular social position, creating an identity within the context of these early relationships. The child also interprets early experiences and determines general conclusions about life and his position with others. Without effective parenting, children often establish a cognitive template based on limited perceptions and supported by fictitious generalities and private logic. Sometimes discouraged by hurtful incidences, the child creates strategies designed to protect him from feeling a sense of inferiority. With effective parenting, children still vie for positions within the family social unit, with each person sandwiched between other family members and each viewing life from a specific vantage point. Yet healthy strivings develop into cognitive structures supporting cooperative interactions, achieving mastery, and making useful contributions. Such early learning, either discouraged patterns or healthy ones, become the basis for unique, personal worldviews that dictate particular behavioral patterns and establish subsequent individual lifestyles.

Later in life, new experiences and interactions can be distorted to fit the person's cognitive sets and early social motivations, or can be opportunities to test the effectiveness of established behavioral patterns. Change in lifestyle patterns occurs only with great difficulty when the person recognizes mistaken views and is self-motivated to create a personal transformation. Therapists, as facilitators of individual change, determine the underlying patterns of the client's behavior and cognitive structure. Counselors analyze the client's lifestyle and interpret the client's unique motivations, encouraging the client to see that earlier conclusions are faulty. As clients review their interpretations of experiences, they may be unable to generate alternative views. With support, however, clients realize the interpretations they have given to life events could have alternative explanations and that interpretations have been colored by personal needs. Various techniques are used to change faulty thinking (reframing, the question, push-button, role playing, brainstorming, humor) and to establish new behavior (acting "as if," task setting, catching yourself, paradoxical intention).

The goal of therapy, and for the mental health of individuals, is to create useful lifestyles that contribute to society. Useless attitudes and behavior can be overcome through encouragement—helping individuals gain the courage to change. Healthy attitudes and behaviors recognize the need for all people to cooperate with each other to achieve goals that promote the common good.

Practice Test Questions

True or False: Consider each statement and try to explain in your own mind why it might not be fully true. Be sure to take into account any qualifying factors that might make the statement untrue. If you decide that the statement is fully true, circle **T**. Otherwise, circle **F**.

T F 1. Adler agreed with Freud that human behavior is driven by unconscious dynamics.

T F 2. Adlerian counselors assume that childhood experiences determine an adult's style of life.

T F 3. The goal of therapy is always to restructure personality.

T F 4. Memories of past experiences are consistent with a person's current self-concept.

T F 5. Dreams reflect struggles with current issues without realistic restraints.

T F 6. Adler wrote that reexperiencing childhood events releases a client's emotional blocks.

T F 7. Reframing cognitive patterns will automatically change behavior.

T F 8. Changing established behavior and thinking is easy once a client gains new insights.

T F 9. Social interest means achieving status in the community and on the job.

T F 10. Relationships with siblings have little impact in forming a child's identity.

Multiple Choice: Circle the one letter next to the best answer to the following questions or to complete the sentence stems.

1. Style of life analysis includes examination of
    a. early recollections.
    b. sibling array.
    c. childhood sexual fantasies.
    d. mistaken perceptions.
    e. a, b, and d

2. The purpose of *the question* in Adlerian therapy is to
    a. collect information regarding the family of origin.
    b. determine the goals of therapy.
    c. focus the client's attention toward positive outcomes.
    d. a and c
    e. b and c

3. An Adlerian therapist would describe the cause of personal problems as
    a. the product of an innate death wish.
    b. a pathological process of mental illness.
    c. the result of receiving encouragement.
    d. the natural consequence of mistaken ideas..
    e. c and d

4. What is the sequence of human experiencing from an Adlerian perspective?
    a. First we feel, then we think, then we act.
    b. First we think, then we feel, then we act.
    c. First we act, then we feel, then we think.
    d. none of the above

5. According to Adler, which of the following is an accurate statement regarding a sense of inferiority?
    a. A few children feel inferior because parents are too critical.
    b. Overcoming a sense of inferiority is easy.
    c. Protecting one's self from feeling inferior can cause psychological symptoms.
    d. A sense of inferiority is overcome by doing better than everyone else.
    e. b and c

6. A sense of superiority is described as
    a. a positive mindset creating success for the individual.
    b. a positive attribute motivating a person to do well.
    c. an unfortunate attribute of the human condition.
    d. a striving that could be useful or useless.
    e. a, b, c

7. Acting *"as if"* is a strategy designed to
    a. provide release from tension.
    b. rehearse new behaviors.
    c. help a client forget trauma.
    d. establish confidence even if change is impossible.
    e. b and d

8. *Private logic* refers to
    a. the rationalizations people use to protect their self-esteem.
    b. logical conclusions that make sense to most people but are not shared openly.
    c. using logical reasons to make a point and gain individual status.
    d. privately determining what logic will be well-received by others.

9. The counselor/client relationship in Adlerian therapy is characterized as
    a. one in which the counselor determines the correct diagnosis and prescribes the appropriate treatment.
    b. a collaborative working interaction between the client and the counselor.
    c. one in which the counselor makes no comments and serves only as a sounding board for the client.
    d. one in which clients gain awareness and make their own interpretations of the purpose of their symptoms.

10. What is meant by the Alderian term *basic mistakes?*
    a. self-defeating cognitions and attitudes that underlie the style of life.
    b. major difficulties that include life-threatening behaviors and traumatic experiences
    c. faulty perceptions that create difficulties for the person over and over again
    d. a and c
    e. b and c

11. Within an Adlerian tradition, a constructivist approach in counseling is characterized by
    a. an assumption that individuals can determine their own life course.
    b. a conceptualization of client difficulties constructed by the counselor.
    c. the counselor's collection of information and interpretation of unconscious dynamics.
    d. b and c

12. A person's *style of life* includes
     a. the general direction, or movement, of a person's effort to meet life tasks.
     b. the basic cognitive sets and feeling patterns established in childhood.
     c. positive intentions and healthy interactions characteristic of the person.
     d. self-limiting concepts related to self-image and life expectations.
     e. all of the above
     f. none of the above

13. A phenomenological theory suggests that
     a. what life is actually like is less important than how the person perceives life to be.
     b. to determine the truth, it is vital that all the evidence be collected before coming to a conclusion.
     c. what separates human beings from other species is their consistent use of objective reasoning.
     d. life is replete with unique phenomena that cannot be understood as consistent patterns.

14. As a holistic theorist, Adler made the assumption that
     a. complex human beings are best understood by assessing each symptom separately to make sense of multiple factors.
     b. personality development occurs in age-segmented blocks with each time frame so distinct that a person may seem like different individuals at different ages.
     c. everything about an individual (thinking, behavior, feeling, attitudes) is directed toward a life goal.
     d. none of the above

15. The *push-button* technique is described as
     a. a guided imagery exercise designed to teach the client to relax.
     b. clients imagining pushing a button before recalling a pleasant memory.
     c. clients imagining pushing a button before recalling an unpleasant memory.
     d. clients realizing their current feelings are under their control.
     e. b, c, and d

Key Terms and Essential Concepts

Phenomenological: Adler wrote that reality was based on subjective interpretations of life experiences. Each individual maintains a personal worldview by approaching new experiences through a biased lens, ignoring contradictions and emphasizing what reinforces original concepts. Reality is seen through the eyes of the beholder. Since individuals process information with unique perceptions, objective analyses are difficult

Existential: Each person is responsible for creating the meaning of his existence. For Adler, people determine life's purpose through their interpretations of their experience. At any point in life, interpretations of previous experience can be changed and new concepts can be chosen to direct life in the future.

Holistic: Adler viewed personality as a holistic unit. Feelings, thinking, and behavior coalesce into a unified whole, an integrated personality with a distinctive perspective. Human beings function as a unified whole where all the elements of the personality are interrelated. Behavior is goal driven, designed to meet personal and social ends and to maintain the integrity of individual identity.

Style of life: Adler sought to understand the unifying motivations for individual personalities by discerning what underlying goals the person may be seeking. Analyzing the sibling array, family interactions, and early recollections from an individual's childhood exposes the most simplistic motives at the core of personality. From such early experiences a basic life script is set and is then reenacted throughout adulthood. Psychological symptoms stem from general mistaken ideas about life or from faulty cognitive sets within the characteristic structure. The style of life may be ineffective attempts to overcome difficulties. To transform a person's life, the basic script requires change. The script is further developed in adulthood through efforts to meet major life tasks: creating a loving, intimate relationship; making contributions through work; participating in the larger community; and for some Adlerian authors, establishing a relationship with self; and developing meaning through spirituality.

Social interest: When clients experience painful symptoms, it is because their attitudes and behavior are not appropriative for a cooperative social order. Skewed thinking often includes separating self from others, as when someone blames another, or tries to look better than others, or tries to protect the self from rejection. Positive mental health requires belonging through social connections and making useful contributions to the common good. As social beings, a selfish orientation negates the basic human need to be a part of the community. Self-absorption is useless because it blocks both individual growth and societal progress. Psychologically, self-interest is served when everyone cooperates for the betterment of all.

Family constellation: The group formed by the parents and other influential adults as well as the children. The sibling array is organized in a hierarchy with the oldest first, middle children next in descending age order, and finally the youngest.

Sense of inferiority: As children grow in awareness of the family constellation it is obvious to them that adults and older siblings function better and know more. Feeling inferior at the beginning of life is therefore a common experience and coping with a sense of inferiority is one of life's major psychological tasks.

Strivings for superiority: Adler defined mechanisms to overcome feelings of inferiority as *striving*, or an individual's movement, that could be positive or negative. Ideally, with effective parental training, overcoming inferiority motivates the child to strive for socially appropriate behavior and task mastery. However, many circumstances conspire for children to develop mistaken ideas and coping mechanisms to protect themselves from feeling inferior or from others recognizing their inadequacy.

Fictional self: Each person constructs a self-concept stemming from personal observations and interpretations of others' reactions. Individuals may cast themselves in consistent roles, such as victims, leaders or heroes, to play out the goals of their lifestyle. Of course, consistent casting for one's self requires casting others in counter roles, such as villains, followers, or damsels in distress.

Life script: Adler also described the self in the center of a fantasy drama where the person strives to overcome obstacles and deal with life events.

Fictional finalism: Since the cognitive constructs developed in childhood reflect a person's inner experience, not actual reality, people construe life events to fit the fictional script that inevitably proceeds toward a predetermined final conclusion.

Constructivist: A modern term reflecting the Adlerian concept that each person "constructs" her own life. A person's life story includes the interpretations of experiences that are used to develop a personal style of life.

Private logic: Adler discerned that unique individuals employ distinctive explanations for their experiences, and they come to idiosyncratic conclusions when interpreting life events. Private logic rationalizes individualistic worldviews and lifestyles. When considered from the individual's perspective, the train of thought makes sense in its own way, though others may not agree that the personal logic is reasonable. Adler believed that the common sense of the community is useful, and private logic is useless when it serves only the individual's purposes.

Discouragement: When individuals proceed from mistaken ideas, new experiences will bring natural consequences as negative feedback. If the person cannot adjust his thinking and behavior, consistent negative consequences will be disheartening, though the person may not understand his own responsibility for the chain of events.

Encouragement: To break a continuing pattern of negative consequences from reoccurring, the individual must gain the courage to change his thinking and behavior. Support from others offers hope and instills a belief that new cognitive sets and actions will result in positive experiences. Adler believed negative self concepts and psychological symptoms develop when a person is discouraged, feeling stuck in a life without hope for any change. Counseling reverses discouragement through interventions that instill hope, create better life visions and provide corrective experiences. En*courage*ment contains the word *courage,* and reflects Adler's characterization of the effort and support needed to make basic psychological changes.

Growth model: Theories based on assumptions that human beings develop over time, and that individuals can direct the change in their own lives. In contrast, deterministic models, such as a psychoanalytic approach, presume patterns are set at certain ages and change is not under conscious control. Also in contrast, a medical model presumes that psychological difficulties follow a pathological pattern similar to physical disease. Growth models do not presuppose illness, but rather learning deficits, mistaken ideas, or others factors that can be controlled by the individual. Therapies for growth models also approach difficulties holistically rather than treating symptoms as medical practices often do.

Basic mistakes: Few people gain adult identity without convictions based on mistaken impressions developed from the limited perceptions of childhood. Such mistaken ideas are bound to create negative consequences and psychological strains. From a vantage point of broader awareness and greater discernment, an adult can change basic mistakes in thinking.

Early recollections: Scenes remembered from childhood are constructed to reinforce themes inherent in the style of life. When such memories are analyzed they reveal how the person approaches life, with resolute leanings on polarities such as directing life vs. passivity, optimism vs. pessimism, or expressiveness vs. silence.

"As if": To facilitate change, a person can pretend she already thinks and acts differently. Rather than focus on the strain and effort of breaking old habits, playing a new role establishes new behaviors and helps the person realize new possibilities are possible.

The question: Adler described a technique designed to quickly focus the client's attention on a better future beyond presenting concerns. The therapist asks the client, " If I could magically eliminate your symptom immediately and completely, what would be different in your life?" The client describes a vision that doesn't contain the difficulties blocking the client's growth. A version of the question is used in solution focused brief counseling.

Representative Case: The Perfectionist Child (PC)

PC is a Hispanic child, the third among an array of five siblings. At 13, she is the oldest girl with two older brothers, the oldest being 15 and the next 14. Both older boys have been sent to reformatory for purse snatching with a local gang. The fourth child, another girl three years younger than PC, is retarded; and the youngest, at 9 years, is a hyperactive boy, who is also placed in a special class. Both parents work two jobs at minimum wage and English is the second language for all family members. Each day PC delivers her sister and youngest brother to their classrooms. Cleanly dressed and groomed, they all carry their lunches. She takes off her siblings' coats and boots, checks their notebooks, pencils, and so on, and leads each to their assigned seats. When PC is in her own classes, her assignments are exceptionally neat and thorough. She never volunteers but always answers questions if asked, usually with an exact quotation from the textbook. Occasionally her eyes close and she appears to drift into sleep momentarily. PC does join other girls from her neighborhood for lunch and on the playground and though she rarely speaks, she smiles and nods. Recently, PC received scores for aptitude and achievement tests in preparation for choosing next year's high school courses. PC's tests validate her ability to pursue a college preparatory track. Her plan is to graduate high school by 16, taking as many science classes as she can, and to attend junior college to become a nurse. She hopes she can be a nurse by the time her sister finishes school, since she plans to take her sister with her when she goes to an impoverished area in South America as a Catholic missionary.

With the onset of her menstrual cycle, PC asked to see the school psychologist. She is frightened because she feels unable to perform all her daily tasks of childcare and schoolwork according to the high standards she expects of herself. She is fearful her younger siblings will end up like her older brothers without her exacting care. She worries that her parents will suffer terribly if any more of their children have difficulties. She does not want to disappoint the nuns from her church. She prays constantly hoping she is good enough for an intercession from God.

Thinking About PC

1. How would an Adlerian counselor conceptualize PC's personality, interaction style, and family/cultural influences?

2. Assume that the counselor has decided to use group counseling with experiential exercises. What kind of activities could you design that would teach PC helpful life lessons?

3. What is the source of PC's perfectionism? What techniques could be useful in changing her need to do everything perfectly?

4. Why do PC's constructs begin to fail her when she starts her menstrual cycle?

Check Your Thinking About PC

1. PC is the middle child of an Hispanic family that prizes family cohesiveness and has strong role descriptors for boys and girls. An atmosphere of discouragement occurred when the older boys were sent away. PC became the child caretaker in keeping with the parents' need to work long hours and her female role. PC is excessively quiet because she doesn't want to say something wrong and publicly shame her family. She has sought refuge in her religion and has gained support from the nuns and religious concepts. However, she has interpreted church messages to be extensions of the requirement to do everything perfectly.

2. Interactions in a group could help PC feel safe to openly express herself to her peers. In listening to others, she could learn that other clients and their families also experience

difficulties. In supporting others PC could feel useful. Activities such as planning a meal, creating a group sculpture, constructing a collage or role-playing a scene where PC speaks up spontaneously could help her learn different ways to participate in interactions. She could learn that less than perfect expressions would not be disastrous.

3. PC felt the need to save the family by taking perfect care of her siblings and through perfect school performance. Her culture reveres a perfect model of self-sacrifice and taking care of others. While respecting the cultural influences, PC could be shown through behavioral experiments demonstrating that self-care could contribute to her being available for others. Her youngest brother's overactive behavior might improve without her meeting his every demand and allowing him to experience his own frustration. Expressing her own needs to friends and to her parents could help her learn that others do not expect her to take on responsibility for everyone. In opening a dialogue in family meetings PC may also hear appreciation for all she has contributed building her self esteem and putting her standards into perspective.

4. The onset of PC's menstrual cycle may have stirred feelings and thoughts previously absent or easily ignored. For example, the idea that she is a woman and capable of romance and motherhood may be quite threatening, since she has so far seen herself as living to serve her existing family. Sexual feelings may also be threatening in that they might disturb her pre-set plan for the future and her self-control.

Core Case: Mrs. A

The following case study was published by Alfred Adler Institute (1969)[*]. Here the case will be described from an individual psychology approach as a comparison to psychoanalytic and psychodynamic approaches in the last chapter. Later, Mrs. A and her family will be a case study as an example of systems therapy in Chapter 10.

The format follows a standard **DAP** layout used by psychologists in writing case notes. **D** designates **Data,** where the client's presenting concerns and symptoms are described. **A** stands for **Assessment,** where the clinician describes diagnostic impressions and case conceptualization concepts. **P,** or **Plan,** tells the plan for future counseling interventions and when applicable, client homework assignments.

D: See Core Case: Mrs. A in Chapter 4

A: Mrs. A suffers from a severe anxiety disorder stemming from physical and emotional abuse in childhood. As a child she overcame her older sister's defense of submission and competed with the oldest son. Her personality reflects movement to overcome danger and her lifestyle is an attempt to dominate others. In all likelihood, she experienced great fear in the family violence perpetuated by her father and determined she would never be dominated and would control others instead. Although she demonstrated the basics of cooperation as a well-liked achieving student, a domestic servant, and factory worker, her symptoms became prominent when faced with the life tasks of becoming a partner and then a mother. Mrs. A shows no empathy for her husband, who is also discouraged. Husband and wife compete for victim's status, who is suffering more and needs to be taken care of. Mrs. A has no experience with or models for effective child-rearing practices and she acts out her frustration by hitting others.

---

[*] Adler, A. (1969). *The Case of Mrs. A (The Diagnosis of a Life-Style).* Chicago, Illinois: Alfred Adler Institute.

P: Early recollections and lifestyle analysis would undoubtedly bring out Mrs. A's early fears and her childhood lack of basic safety. She may express anger, given that her resentment of her parents is readily present and therapeutic understanding could build an alliance. Praise for her cooperative efforts and her strength in refusing to submit, as her sister did, could be encouraging. She might also, in time and with emotional support, accept the interpretation that she has successfully achieved her goal of controlling her husband and family. Using the push-button technique could help Mrs. A build an awareness that she can control her emotions despite frustration. Using *the question* could build a vision of effective parenting and social interactions that would be satisfying. The therapist and Mrs. A could brainstorm strategies for training her children to learn cooperation, and parenting education could include role playing to rehearse effective behavior. Eventually, Mrs. A could be encouraged to compensate for her own negative parenting by becoming an effective parent herself. Marital counseling is needed to help Mr. and Mrs. A encourage each other and to become parenting partners.

Finding a Balance

Key Counselor Preferences

1. Adlerians are more pragmatic and less patient with abstractions that are not shown in the client's story than are psychoanalytic and psychodynamic therapists. Individual psychologists do not hold much stock with the concept of an unconscious or its control of the person's internal psychology or external behavior. Lack of awareness is possible, but the expectation is that the client will recognize interpretations from the life narrative.

2. Although Adlerians are very humanistic in their demeanor and interactions, they have a strong belief that the client is responsible for constructing his inner life and his outward behavior. Client's attitudes, feelings, and cognitions serve a purpose and are goal-driven, and personal goals must align with the common good to be healthy. The individual psychology therapist is kindly but firm in expectations that the client will suffer negative consequences when attitudes and behaviors are not in the social interest.

3. Individual psychologists are impatient with the idea that catharsis is necessary or that emotional processing would need extended periods of time. Although the therapist expresses empathy for the original childhood situation and the client's interpretation of his place and events, emotional release is only useful to understand the person and his goals, and is not an end in and of itself.

4. Adlerians are typically big picture thinkers. The goal of therapy is to understand the overall structure of an individual's personality and social interactions. Although full lifestyle analysis is not required in every case, some abbreviated form of inquiry is used to gain a view of the whole personality and its personal and social purposes.

5. Adlerians are result oriented. Cognitive restructuring and behavioral change are expected. The client shows symptoms because of mistaken ideas and beliefs leading to emotional strains and socially useless behavior.

6. The counselor clearly expects the client to overcome attitudes and actions that are not in the social interest. Although Adlerians are consistent in encouraging clients without judgmentalism, they believe mental health is defined by cooperative attitudes and behavior for the common good. An Adlerian patiently maintains a stance of encouragement for the individual with acceptance of negative consequences for inappropriate ideas and behavior. An emphasis on the social interest also often means Adlerians are involved in social causes and political activity designed to improve society.

Core Case: George Gordon

The case of George Gordon is a core case. We will revisit it again in Chapter 12 when we consider it with transpersonal therapy. The case is described here from an individual psychology approach.

A very well dressed middle-aged man, age 45, presented himself for therapy, saying, "It's time for me to feel better." His previously successful .com business crashed in the recent recession. He had experienced business failures in the past and was now impatient to move on and start a new venture. Unable to focus his attention and energy, he was uncharacteristically spending much time reflecting on his life and caught in a swirl of confusing feelings. He brokered mergers of companies to enhance profits for stockholders, creating stockpiles of money for further investments. Though he was exonerated when the SEC investigated his firm for insider trading, he expressed bitter anger at the suggestion of legal limits to "free" enterprise.

The client is divorced and has no current significant relationship or any children. His descriptions of life experiences were crisp, to the point, and ended with conclusions sounding like an annual report to a board of executives. His first marriage ended because his wife, "an asset" early in his career, had become a "liability." His mistress of ten years understood he would not marry because, "marriage was not a profitable enterprise." Then, she broke the "contract" by demanding they wed, and he refused.

His father was killed in World War II, and he was the only child raised by his mother who worked as a dental assistant. His earliest recollection was a scene at his grandparents' home where he and his mother lived. Dressed in drum major's uniform with a tall pointed shiny hat, he marched with high steps around the backyard, raising his staff up and down. Several uncles followed him, laughing, beers in hand following the moving rhythm of the client's staff and saying, he was certainly a magnificent leader. His mother came out of the house, surveyed the situation and inserted herself in line directly behind her son. She patted his shoulder from behind to indicate he should march down the driveway to the front of the house. As mother and son marched out of the backyard, she looked back and said to her brothers, "My son will become a millionaire and leave all you bums behind."

Recent recurring dreams involved the client sitting on a wooden bench on a railroad platform; sitting and watching train after train go by without his moving or doing anything, just watching. The client's symptoms entailed features of an agitated depression: ennui rather than characteristic energized activity; irritation with others rather than typical charming interaction; lacking goals; and slowed mental activity. He expected therapy would renew his energy and his ability to focus his attention on new tasks.

Applying Counselor Preferences

Using the previously listed Adlerian preferences, how would a counselor proceed with George Gordon?

1. An individual psychology counselor would prefer identifying easily understood themes such as George's mother treating him as a leader bound for success in the drum major scene. Interpretations based on his life narrative rather than unconscious drives would probably be appealing to George.

2. While being sympathetic the counselor would insist that George accept personal responsibility for his current depressive symptoms and for determining what changes he needed to make. Such an approach would mirror George's values and fit with the image of a self-made man.

3. An Adlerian would show empathy for George's struggles, losing his father at a young age and dealing with the ups and downs in business. However, the counselor would not prefer staying with the feelings for too long and would not see emotional release as healing in and of itself. De-emphasizing emotional release would fit with George's use of language and way of thinking.

4. Individual counselors want the big picture of the whole of the client's life and would expect George to spend time describing his childhood and other life experiences. George, however, may be impatient with an approach that required a full lifestyle analysis.

5. George may appreciate the Adlerian counselor's expectation for change. The counselor may also expect George to change cognitive patterns that assume he deserved to be superior over others. George could be defensive when expected to admit mistaken views. However, such discomfort for George would be the crux of therapy and would create the change both George and the counselor expect.

6. The Adlerian counselor would have definitive ideas about George learning to operate according to the common good. Social interest may be a difficult concept for George, and his full change from hard core business for profit to a fully humanistic values base would not be demanded by the counselor who would also be accepting and patient.

Comparison with Other Approaches

The following describe and contrast preferences by counselors from other approaches. Note there may be some advantages for some clinical issues and some client styles in using different approaches. Can you see any advantage in combining the Adlerian approach with one of the following?

Psychodynamic: Counselors who favor transference relationships would interpret George's projections onto the counselor as reflective of his relationship with his mother rather than the more thematic approach of family patterns an Adlerian would use. Interpretations would be more abstract using terminology and concepts based on unconscious dynamics.

Person-centered and Gestalt: Counselors who prefer emotional expression would spend more time trying to draw out the feelings than would an Adlerian. George might find an emphasis on feelings uncomfortable and the pace difficult. However, in learning to express emotions, George might improve his interpersonal interactions, particularly in close relationships. Adlerians would undoubtedly adopt the core conditions of warm interactions but would not stress catharsis.

Existential and Transpersonal: An existential approach could explore meaning in a personally defined spiritual way. George could deepen his life experience through spiritual development. Adlerians might press social interest, but a personal journey of spiritual meaning could further enrich the client's life.

Cognitive-behavioral: Adlerians use cognitive restructuring, though they don't use the term. However, individual psychology reframes childhood themes into social interest concepts. Cognitive-behavioral counselors do not explore childhood history as a context for cognitive reframing nor is the standard of social benefit emphasized.

Example of a Published Research Article on Adlerian Therapy

Here is an example of Adlerian research. Remember, the commentary in the boxes to the left of the article will help you understand the research and the format of the piece.

The Effects of Adlerian Parent Study Groups Upon Mexican Mothers' Perception of Child Behavior[*]

Betty J. Newlon, Roman Borboa, and Miguel Arciniega

In the first paragraphs, the authors argue that a problem exists and summarize relevant research done so far in the problem area. This summary is called the *literature review*. The literature review here is very short, compared with literature reviews in other research articles.

Today's parents often find their role shrouded in confusion and bewilderment. This may result in parenting being left to chance when it becomes a process of trial and error, often mostly error. Parents who are dissatisfied with the results of their child-rearing efforts are seeking information on how to improve familial relationships.

The potential for helping parents by involving them in group experiences and providing them with child-training information has resulted in the development of parent education programs. Parent effectiveness training groups based on Gordon's work (Gordon, 1970), behavioral modification programs (Becker 1971; Krumboltz & Krumboltz 1972; Patterson & Gullion 1968), and transactional analysis groups (James, 1974) exist in many areas.

Adlerian parent study groups gained popularity through the works of Rudolf Dreikurs (Dreikurs & Soltz, 1964). These groups have been and continue to be organized in at least twenty countries worldwide. These parent study groups are based on a pattern of explication, study, reading, and group discussion of the Adlerian principles and practices which relate to parenting.

When studies have focused on one identifiable group (in this case, U. S. Anglos), it's not clear whether the results would be the same for other groups. Researchers experiment with other groups to investigate this. If results are similar for different cultural groups, there is support for *cross-cultural validity*.

Twenty-four studies examining parental attitudes and parents' perceptions of children's behavior have reported significant positive changes, following participation in an Adlerian parent study group (Smithells, 1983). In most of the studies, the parent study group skills were aimed toward the parenting skill in the majority culture (Anglo) of the United States. An exception is the study by Villegas (1977) which evaluated the Adlerian parent study group approach with Chicana mothers and found a positive change in the mothers' perception of their children's behavior. This study lends cross-cultural validity to the Adlerian model.

One area where the effectiveness of Adlerian parent study groups has not been studied is in Mexico. As the world

The Effects of Adlerian Parent Study Groups upon Mexican Mothers' Perception of Child Behavior, by Betty J. Newlon, Roman Borboa, and Miguel Arciniega from the *Journal of Individual Psychology* 42:1, pp. 107–113. Copyright © 1986 by the University of Texas Press. All rights reserved.

[*] Copies of the Spanish form of the Adlerian Parental Assessment of Child Behavior Scale (APACBS) may be obtained by writing the authors.

becomes smaller and portions of the United States are affected by immigration (both legal and illegal) from Mexico, effective parent education techniques need to be identified. Steps need to be taken to validate the Adlerian model with parent study groups in Mexico where the culture is uniquely different in terms of language, customs, values, and child socialization practices. *Children: The Challenge* (Dreikurs & Saltz, 1964) and *Systematic Training for Effective Parenting* (Dinkmeyer & McKay, 1976) have been translated into Spanish, which gives credence to the applicability of the Adlerian model to Mexico.

If American Chicana mothers found a positive change in their perception of children's behavior, will the same findings occur with Mexican mothers?

> The 1977 Villegas study involved American Chicana mothers, and these authors test the Adlerian study program with mothers in Mexico.

Purpose of the Study

The purpose of this study was to evaluate the effects of Adlerian parent study groups upon Mexican mothers' perception of child behavior.

Methods

> Under Methods, the authors summarize the content of Adlerian parent training. They describe the process of the study (Procedures), how the participants were found, and who the participants were (Sample).

Parent study groups are based on Adlerian principles as described by Dreikurs and Soltz (1964), Dinkmeyer and McKay (1973), Corsini and Painter (1975), Gould (1977), and Sonstegard, Shuck, and Beattie (1979). The basic aims of a parent study group include increasing awareness in the need to live together democratically as social equals within the family unit; understanding that behavior is contextual, purposeful, socially oriented and expresses movement toward a goal; and emphasizing and encouraging behavior which develops self-reliant, responsible, cooperative membership in the family group. Parents learn to guide their children by establishing firm, clear, and consistent limits applicable to all.

In order to determine the efficacy of the Adlerian model across the acculturation continuum of Mexican/Mexican American child-rearing practices, it was necessary to obtain information from Mexican nationals who had participated in similar Adlerian parent study group training.

Procedures. The parent study group met once a week for eight weeks with a counselor trained in Adlerian principles. The following topics were didactically presented and discussed:

1. Understanding behavior
2. Use of emotions
3. Encouragement
4. Communication
5. Developing responsibility
6. Decision making
7. Family meetings
8. Developing confidence

Each mother was asked to apply the Adlerian principles to her between sessions.

Sample. The Continuing Education Department of the Instituto Tecnologico de Sonora placed advertisements in the *Ciudad Obregon* newspaper announcing the availability of parent study groups. Interested parents were asked to contact the Institute for further information. Identified interested parents were then sent a personal invitation to attend.

Nineteen mothers participated in the parent study groups. They had a mean age of twenty-seven, had a high school education, considered themselves middle class, and had an average of three children,

Measurement

A pre-test and post-test group design was used in this study. The independent variable was the Adlerian parent training and the dependent variable was the mothers' perception regarding their target child's behavior as measured by the Adlerian Parental Assessment of Child Behavior Scale, The APACBS was administered prior to the first session and after the completion of the parent study group.

> Notice that the variable measured was the mothers' *perception* of the child's behavior. We don't know whether the mothers accurately rated the child's behavior, so the authors can't say that the child's behavior was being measured. However, we assume here that the mothers' perceptions are good reflections of the children's behavior.

Instrumentation

The Adlerian Parental Assessment of Child Behavior Scale (APACBS), consists of thirty-four seven-point Likert-type items. The scale was developed to assess parents' perceptions of typical child behaviors dealt with in Adlerian-based programs (McKay, 1976). The mothers were required first to identify a child they were most concerned about and then rate the behavior items on a continuum form "always" to "never" as it applied to the identified child. Both responsible and irresponsible child behaviors are represented in the items.

For the purposes of this study, the APACBS was translated into Spanish. The APACBS was judged for content validity by three judges familiar with Adlerian-based programs. A reliability test of the instrument was conducted in a pilot study with the results as follows: the Cronbach's alpha test for internal consistency ranged from .90 to .91; the Pearson *r* test for stability over time yielded a coefficient of .97.

> The APACBS rating scale was checked to make sure it measured what it was purported to measure by asking Adlerians to look at the item meanings (*content validity*). They also used a preliminary study to test whether the APACBS gives consistent results (*reliability*). The Cronbach's alpha reflects whether the items within the test are consistent with each other, and the Pearson's *r* reflects whether the test ratings stay consistent over a period of time. Both of these statistics range from 0 to 1, so the figures reported here (in the .90s) are very high.

Hypothesis

The following hypothesis was drawn: Mexican mothers who participate in a parent study group will positively change their perception regarding a target child's behavior.

Results. Using a *t*-test, the mother's perception of the behavior of her target child [before and after study group] was found to be statistically significant.

Because the questions on the APACBS represented a discrete behavioral measurement, it was analyzed using a separate t-test for dependent samples. For each item, a mother could mark a score from a range of one to seven. Table 1 presents mean, standard error, and overall t-value.

Table I

Overall t- Test of Mexican Mothers on the APACBS

Measure N	Pre-Test	Post-Test	t
Means 19	x = 145	y = 156.84	–2.00*
Std. Dev.	5.792	4.946	

*$p < .05$

Results of this study lend support to the effectiveness of Adlerian parent study groups upon Mexican mothers' perception of child behavior. Mexican mothers' perception of the child they were most concerned about improved after participation in the parent study group.

Discussion

This study provides confirmation of the validity of the Adlerian model in a cross-cultural setting. The following Adlerian assumptions were presented in the parent study group: (1) humanity is horizontal and people are seen as equally worthy of respect and consideration; (2) cooperation is an essential ingredient in developing social interest; (3) people need to feel a part of society, i.e., to belong; (4) behavior is purposive; and (5) individuals are responsible for their behavior. These theoretical tenets, when presented to Mexican mothers, were accepted and did not appear contradictory to the cultural values inherent in the Mexican life style.

One Mexican cultural value is the concept of *respeto* (respect). People are seen as worthy of respect and this value is included as an important part of child-rearing practices. Responsibility to the family is part of the children's socialization in Mexican families. The concept of pride and the responsibility of belonging to a special family provide significance to individual family members. Given these specific cultural values one can see how the Adlerian framework is consistent and in fact reinforces family values.

Evidently, in scoring the APACBS, all items are transformed so that a higher score means better behavior.

A *t* test compares the averages from two sets of scores and reflects whether the two sets are meaningfully different. In this study, the samples (the mothers' pre- and post-test ratings) were called *dependent* because the same people gave both sets of ratings. The samples would be *independent* if the study compared ratings of mothers who had been through the Adlerian program with mothers who had not been through the program (a *control group*).

The *p* value means that this study's difference in average scores would only be found by chance 5 times out of 100. So, the difference was probably due to the parent training.

In the Discussion section, the authors relate their findings to previous research and provide their reasoning on why they found what they did.

Researchers usually point out the limitations of their findings at the end of their articles. In this case, the limitation is that the participants all came from the middle class. More limitations are suggested in the last paragraph.

While the authors feel that the Adlerian model has validity when counseling all Mexican families, we cannot generalize to the total population. The mothers in this study were from middle-class backgrounds, and it remains to be confirmed whether this model is applicable to lower- and upper-class families.

The parent study group participants in this study were all mothers although the announcement letters were addressed to both parents. This appears to be consistent with other similar studies in the United States. This may indicate that Mexican families, like other cultures in the world, still leave the responsibility of child rearing to women.

The positive results of this study can be combined with the positive results of the Villegas study (1977), which included Chicana mothers from a metropolitan area in the Southwest who came from lower- and middle-class backgrounds. Much has been said of the difficulty in reaching Mexican American parents with meaningful child-rearing programs. It appears that Adlerian parent study groups are appropriate for Mexican American families ranging from traditional recent immigrants to the more acculturated. These studies indicate that this approach is applicable to a range of Mexican American families in the United States.

The authors return to their earlier questions about whether Adlerian study groups are effective for people from different cultures and levels of acculturation (that is, levels of identification with Mexican or mainstream American culture).

An interesting note is that both of these studies evolved from an educational institution. Given the value and respect that the Mexican culture has for education, parent study groups may be a viable vehicle in enlisting parents to work cooperatively with schools.

This study is a step toward the confirmation of the cross-cultural application of the Adlerian model with Mexican families. It must be noted that the use of the PECES kit in Spanish and the expertise of the group leader in Adlerian theory and Mexican culture contributed to the success of the parent group. Further study needs to be done with different leaders, different social classes, fathers, and rural-urban families.

References

Becker, W. C. (1971). *Parents are teachers: A child management program.* Champaign, IL: Research Press.

Corsini, R., & Painter, G. (1975). *The practical parent.* New York: Harper & Row.

Dinkmeyer, D., & McKay, G. D. (1976). *Systematic training for effective parenting.* Circle Pines, MN.: American Guidance Services.

Dinkmeyer, D. C., & McKay, G. D. (1973). *Raising a responsible child: Practical steps to successful family relationships.* New York: Simon and Schuster.

Dreikurs, R., & Soltz, V. (1964). *Children: The challenge.* New York: Duell, Sloan and Pearce.

The References list includes the works the authors cited in the article. This list is helpful to you in following up on topics within the article. For example, you might look at some of these sources to see what the Adlerian parent training course was like, in more detail.

Gordon, T. (1970). *Parent effectiveness training*. New York: Peter H. Wyden.

Gould, S. L. (1977). *Teenagers: The continuing challenge*. New York: Hawthorn Books Inc.

James, M. (1974). *Transactional analysis for moms and dads: What do you do with them now that you've got them?* Reading, MA: Addison-Wesley.

Krumboltz, J. D., & Krumboltz, H. B. (1972). *Changing children's behavior*. Englewood Cliffs, N.J.: Prentice-Hall.

McKay, G. D. (1976). Systematic training for effective parenting: Effects on behavior change of parents and children. Ph.D. dissertation, University of Arizona. *Dissertation Abstracts International, 37,* 342A.

Patterson, G. R., & Gullion, M. E. (1968). *Living with children*. Champaign, IL: Research Press.

Smithells, T. (1983). CO-PAS: An Adlerian-based program for preparing physically handicapped preschool children for mainstreaming. Ph.D. dissertation, University of Arizona.

Sonstegard, M, A., Shuck, A., & Beattie, N. C. (1979). *Living in harmony with our children*. Aylesbury, Bucks, England: Village Press.

Villegas, A. V. (1977). The efficacy of systematic training for effective parenting with Chicana mothers. Ph.D. dissertation, Arizona State University.

Discussion Ideas

1. From the article's brief description of the parent study group, what Adlerian essential concepts were emphasized?

2. Reread the section that explains how the participants were chosen. Do you think there was any meaningful difference between the mothers who participated and the mothers who did not?

3. Why do the authors believe that all the parents who signed up for the study group were mothers? In the last paragraph, they suggest that the experiment should be repeated with fathers as participants. Why? How might the results be different?

4. The authors say that in Mexico, "the culture is uniquely different [from the United States culture] in terms of language, customs, values, and child socialization practices." Do you agree with this statement? Why or why not?

Answer Key for Practice Test Questions

True/False	*Multiple Choice*	
1. F	1. e	11. a
2. T	2. e	12. e
3. T	3. d	13. a
4. T	4. b	14. c
5. T	5. c	15. e
6. F	6. d	
7. F	7. b	
8. F	8. a	
9. F	9. b	
10. F	10. d	

CHAPTER 6

Humanistic Approaches and Their Existential Roots

Chapter Review

Humanism and existential counseling share views of human experience based on existential philosophy. Both belief systems consider the development of an independent unique self as the goal of therapy. Both locate responsibility for the self with the individual, and both trust subjective experience as the vehicle for determining the meaning of life. Reality is seen from a phenomenological perspective, where the external world is interpreted by each individual's unique point of view.

Humanists stress the basic growth orientation of each individual and describe an innate *actualizing tendency* that presses individuals to express their innate potential. Person-centered counseling is designed to create conditions for the client to become more aware of his true self and to learn to trust his individual reactions to life's experiences. Carl Rogers, the creator of the Person-Centered approach, wrote that the natural inner process of the individual was corrupted by conditional love, a condition in which others set criteria for gaining approval and caring. In counseling, the client gains a safe environment to examine his inner world without judgment and renews an *organismic valuing* process where the inner expressions of self correspond with outward reactions. Such self-acceptance is shown when the client can confidently trust his internal reactions, reflecting an internal, rather than an external, *locus of evaluation*. The counselor models *congruence* by displaying genuineness in the counseling interactions. The counselor also shows *unconditional positive regard* for the client's self direction and efforts to find his way. The counselor focuses on the description of the client's inner world, reflecting the feelings and meanings expressed. Such reflections reveal *empathy*, an understanding of the client's experience. Rogers considered congruence, genuineness, and the communication of empathy as the necessary and sufficient conditions for therapeutic change. With such counseling, the client grows to accept and value his own internal process and becomes a *fully functioning person* open to experience but guided by his own sense of purpose.

Existential therapy is tied directly to philosophical concepts and has few techniques uniquely associated with it. Existentialism conceives all life as meaningless until the individual determines what meaning her life will express. The freedom to determine meaning is both liberating and an awesome task, liberating in that the individual defines herself despite external mandates, but awesome in that the individual becomes truly responsible for her life and her choices. Anxiety underlies all human experience with the need to create individual meaning. When the natural pull to face the meaning of existence is denied, a pervasive guilt is experienced.

Each person stands alone in an existential dilemma where relationships can be helpful but cannot erase fundamental isolation. An existential therapist listens to the meaning the client attaches to existence, exploring the efforts to express an inner self, personal values, and purpose. As existential dilemmas become apparent, therapy helps the client determine ways to be authentic in her experience. Often clients reveal *affect blocks* where the client is stuck, not knowing how she feels and unable to determine personal meanings. Dissolving an overlay of anxiety, the client comes to a point where choices, true to her values and existential awareness, become clear. Such insight regarding an authentic choice can be a *peak experience,* an awareness of being and becoming who one really is, experienced as real in the moment.

Both humanistic and existential counselors downplay the use of assessment and diagnosis since they focus on common factors of the human experience to foster client growth. Symptoms of depression and anxiety are described as denial of the natural process of becoming authentic, a true expression of the self. Both approaches are particularly effective for clients experiencing major life transitions and for clients who persistently repeat similar difficulties and block natural experiencing. Families can also get caught in persistently negative patterns of interaction.

Critiques of humanistic counseling approaches include a lack of recognition for biochemical determinants to mental illnesses. Current research has shown the effectiveness of medications that change neurotransmissions and provide relief for physiologically based symptoms. Since the goals for Person Centered and existential therapies involve internal process changes for the client, outcomes are difficult to quantify for research. However, the core conditions of empathy, genuineness, and positive regard have been rated and have shown an impact on the therapeutic relationship. Multicultural critics have suggested that some cultures have customs where nondirective methods are not appreciated and where value is placed on the counselor serving as an authority and an expert. A final criticism of existential and humanistic counseling is that the approaches require the clients to be articulate in describing their experience, and for some people such a process is an esoteric luxury outside of their experience.

Practice Test Questions

True or False: Consider each statement and try to explain in your own mind why it might not be fully true. Be sure to take into account any qualifying factors that might make the statement untrue. If you decide that the statement is fully true, circle **T**. Otherwise, circle **F**.

T F   1. Person-Centered counselors accept the client's behavior regardless of any violation of values.

T F   2. Person-Centered counselors do not hold theoretical ideas as the focal point of therapy.

T F   3. Existential therapists assign theological readings for clients to research in a quest to find the meaning of life.

T F   4. Freedom in existential thought relieves individuals from the burden of considering others or of societal rules.

T F   5. Accepting a loved one as responsible for creating his own meaning in life is a part of responsible relationships, according to existential ideals.

T F   6. The best defense for fearing death is to live a meaningful life.

T F   7. Severe anxiety is experienced only by people who have a chemical imbalance, according to existential therapists.

T F   8. A person experiencing existential guilt knows he has acted in a way that hurt another person.

T F   9. Rogers believed that counselors do not require extensive training to learn multiple strategies for dealing with psychological disorders.

T F   10. Rogerian therapists are careful to project a professional image of proficient competency to clients.

Multiple Choice: Circle the one letter next to the best answer to the following questions or to complete the sentence stem.

1. To be a fully functioning person, one would
    a. be open to life's experiences.
    b. trust one's own evaluation of what happens.
    c. be sure to find an authority's opinion to validate one's own.
    d. a and b
    e. a and c

2. Another characteristic of a fully functioning person is
    a. a unwillingness to accept changes as experiences differ.
    b. a trust in a personal sense of the meaning of life.
    c. a lack of acceptance and trust in other people.
    d. a and b
    e. all of the above

3. Rogers considered assessment and diagnosis
    a. a huge waste and an ineffective use of counseling time.
    b. a process benefiting clients.
    c. a necessary and sufficient component of therapy.
    d. a and c
    e. a and b

4. As described by existential therapists, an *affective block* is a
    a. point where the client considers life's meaning as apparent.
    b. place where the client is emotionally stuck and meaning is lost.
    c. point in therapy where the counselor explains moral issues.
    d. family situation where everyone disagrees with the therapist.

5. Rogers described the outcome of therapy as
    a. a client's experience of an internal loosening of feelings.
    b. a client becoming clear and absolutely firm in his attitudes.
    c. a client experiencing troubling feelings in the moment.
    d. a and c
    e. a and b

6. In existential and humanistic therapy sessions, *focused listening* refers to the
    a. client intensely concentrating on the therapist's explanations.
    b. use of tape recordings to induce progressive relation.
    c. therapist's instruction that the client hear what parents say.
    d. counselor listening for themes expressed by the client.

7. *Logotherapy* is
    a. a counseling approach that teaches proper speech.
    b. a technique used in counseling to reframe the client's words.
    c. a counseling approach that focuses on the meaning of life.
    d. none of the above

8. *Paradoxical intention* is a counseling intervention where the
    a. client is told to exaggerate a symptom rather than suppress it.
    b. client is given an explanation of the paradoxes in life.
    c. counselor's intentions sound very clear to the client.
    d. client's intentions are confusing to the therapist.

9. *Hyperreflection* is a term used in logotherapy to refer to the
    a. client's experience of breathing very fast when upset.
    b. goal of therapy as the client reflects on the meaning of life.
    c. client's behavior of excessively reflecting on himself.
    d. counselor's mistake of offering too many interpretations.

10. *Nondirective techniques* in Person-Centered therapy are designed to make
    a. certain counseling not extend for too many sessions.
    b. sure the client cannot sue the therapist for giving mistaken directions.
    c. sure the client sticks to the topic related to the presenting concern.
    d. sure the client feels a trust for his own ability to evaluate his experience.

11. *Nondirective techniques* include
    a. reflecting the content of what the client says.
    b. reflecting the feelings underlying what the client says.
    c. reflecting the meaning implied by what the client says.
    d. a and c
    e. all of the above

12. *Self-disclosure* is a term used to describe the
    a. client's inability to distance himself from negative feelings.
    b. counselor's sharing of personal thoughts, feelings, and experiences.
    c. counselor's ability to experience the client's inner feelings and thoughts.
    d. client's ability to find closure regarding memories of traumatic experiences.

13. A benefit of group therapy is that clients learn how their behavior
    a. is viewed by others.
    b. influences their self-esteem.
    c. changed from childhood.
    d. a and c
    e. a and b

14. Which of the following is described by existentialists as one the four dimensions of how people experience the world?
    a. the societal structure of the economy, religion, politics, and education
    b. the self, including awareness of feelings, thoughts, body, and individuality
    c. the psychological dynamics of the unconscious subparts, id, ego, and superego
    d. the roles people play to express their anger during social protests

15. Csikszentmihalyi describes the experience of flow as characterized by
    a. becoming so absorbed in an activity that time and distractions are not noticed.
    b. an activity that is challenging enough to hold attention.
    c. an activity that is not so challenging that it induces a feeling of incompetence.
    d. none of the above
    e. all of the above

Key Terms and Essential Concepts

Phenomenological stance: A number of psychological theories (existential, Person Centered, Adlerian and self psychology) approach human perspective as subjective and holistic. Each person interprets experience from a unique viewpoint, and that view is reflective of the person's overall approach to life. In contrast, psychoanalytically oriented counseling theories approach human nature as divisible with separate parts serving distinct functions that can be treated separately. To enter a client's inner world requires therapists to clear away their own perspective and to take on the overview of the client. From a phenomenological perspective, a person reflects in each moment the whole of his inner reality, and therefore, reviewing past experiences in therapy would only be needed if the past were carried into the present by the client's account.

Existentialism: In the mid to late 1800s, philosophers Kierkegaard and Nietzsche described the basic issues affecting the human condition. People exist in their awareness of themselves as unique beings, within the natural world, in relation to others, and alert to spiritual issues. Life has no predetermined universal meaning and yet people yearn to have purpose. Each individual has the freedom and responsibility to construct the meaning of his or her life and to choose values that determine important choices. To live without considering life's purpose, and to simply follow impulsive desires, denies personal responsibility and causes psychic pain. Ultimately each person is alone, though temporary meaning can be gained through transcendent intimacy with another person. Essential isolation requires each person to learn to depend on their own inner resources and to understand what cannot be gained from relationships. Life must also be understood as time limited. Anxiety related to death can be overcome through the meaning individuals create in the time they have. Rollo May and Yalom extended the philosophy into an existential therapy designed to support clients in making sense out of their lives through their own interpretations of life's meaning.

Existential anxiety: Given the existential requirement that each person defines life's meaning, anxiety represents the struggle to adhere to the person's subscribed values. A common experience for all people is a pervasive inner stressor forcing individuals to individually determine the meaning of their existence. The feeling of unease signals that the person needs to pay attention to life's requirements: that time for existence is finite; death is certain; and that we are responsible for creating meaning by choosing how we live. Psychological neurosis can be seen as behaviors that attempt to maintain important values in the face of life's conditions. For example, a workaholic may be preserving the only meaning a person has. Life involves unavoidable anxiety, since any subscribed meaning is limited and life events interfere.

Existential guilt: Existential guilt results when the anxiety indicators are ignored and no action is taken. The feeling of existential unease can develop into an overwhelming angst if the press toward meaning is ignored. Passively denying the press to create meaning shuts down the person's vitality, the natural innate quality to affirm the self and an inner drive to press forward. Guilt is the signal that change is needed and somehow the person needs to take charge of her life. To overcome the guilt, the person needs to determine those values that express personal meaning and to find ways to manage life accordingly.

Meaninglessness: A major concept of existential philosophy. Universal life is ever changing with no coherent design or purpose. Yet human beings have an innate need to determine the meaning of their lives and without meaning, they are subject to hopelessness and despair. Daily events must be managed, but people also need a larger context beyond the mandatory necessities and themselves. Mental health requires each individual to determine values that can provide standards for making choices. Meanings are held by people to make sense of their existence and to maintain patterns for living that meet higher goals.

Freedom: Another major existential concept. Endowed with freedom, every person is responsible for the choices he makes. Even attitudes toward negative experiences are chosen, and feelings are the individual's responsibility.

Wishing and willing: Rollo May, an existential counseling theorist, describes wishing as the force pressing human beings toward creating a life purpose. Willing is the movement toward action. Impulsive and compulsive behaviors stem from denying wishing, since the actions are taken without forethought regarding purpose. Behaving without a sense of responsibility to others or ourselves reflects a lack of purpose and the will to create meaning. Each individual has the freedom and responsibility to construct the meaning of his or her life and to choose values that determine important choices.

Isolation: Existentialists develop the concept of each person's aloneness as a part of the description of human life. Each person is alone in determining how she chooses to live and how she faces death. Although relationships can alleviate loneliness, ultimately even with friendships and family relationships, one is alone.

I/Thou relationship: An authentic relationship in which one listens to another without an overlay of expectations or presumptions. The listener experiences the other's described experience and transcends his own sense of self.

Fusion: A relationship where one person lives through another person, denying the meaning of his own separate existence by merging with the other. (In systems theory, fusion refers to a confusion of emotion and thought.)

Death anxiety: Existential thought emphasizes the finite nature of every person's life and describes the impact of this fact on the life's meaning. An awareness of death is warded off by avoidance and fantasies that somehow we'll be protected from losing our existence. Existentialists make the point that the best defense against anxiously facing our ultimate dying is to create a meaningful life.

Logotherapy: Logo derives from Greek, meaning words or speech. Victor Frankl chose the logo stem as indicating a counseling method emphasizing meaning. His approach maintains that the meaning individuals give to their experiences are self controlled and that under all circumstances, the person has the freedom, and responsibility, to choose how she will react to externals.

Affect blocks: When a person does not experience her own emotions with awareness, the flow of affect has been overcome by anxiety. Often such an impasse indicates that the person has not determined the meaning associated with the experience. Existential therapists describe affect blocks occurring in therapy as the person struggles to attain an understanding of what is happening in his life.

Confrontation: When an existential therapist perceives the client is avoiding deeper meanings or personal responsibility, the counselor will challenge the client to face the issue. An example is pointing out the common use of the phrase, "I can't," when actually the person means, "I won't." Another trigger for confrontation may be the counselor's becoming aware of his reaction to the client's manner of interacting. The counselor will share the effect the client's presentation had, offering feedback on how others may be reacting to the client.

Paradoxical intention: The counselor assigns to the client a task that is intended to create the opposite reaction of what the client expects. For example, the client may be told to exaggerate symptoms by trying to do the fearful reactions, such as fainting when afraid in a crowd. The consequence is that the client can't faint and then is able to recognize the fear with a new perspective.

Dereflection: A counseling technique used in logotherapy that is similar to an Adlerian technique. The therapist assigns the client the homework task of volunteering to do something for others, participate in a social activity, or take up a creative endeavor. The goal is for the client to take attention away from her own ruminations about herself and to focus on someone or something else.

Hyperreflection: Overdoing self-reflection. Logotherapy counselors describe clients who are so involved with their analysis of their own inner reactions that the self-absorption is unhealthy. Dereflection is the antidote.

Attitude adjustment: A counseling technique used in logotherapy to change the client's view of a situation. The therapist suggests different language to describe a situation. An example is changing the word *failure* linked to losing a job to an *opportunity* to try something new. In behavior therapy the same technique is called *cognitive reframing*.

Appealing: Victor Frankl used this term to describe his method of exhorting the client to change as he reassured the client of his ability to change and described the benefits of solving the difficulties.

Boundary situations: Changes that come with ending one phase of experience and the opening of new life events are termed boundary situations. When people experience a transition from one set of life circumstances to a new situation, often the change requires a reflection on personal meanings. A person's sense of what her life has meant may be called into question with new experiences. Such an *existential dilemma* is most prominent when death is vivid, either one's own death as with a terminal illness or injury, or the demise of a significant other. Beyond the grief felt in losing life or a relationship, are implications for how one lives his own life with questions such as, "Who am I?" or "How will I choose to live my life now?" Other major life events also involve losses when meanings are redefined, such as job loss, divorce, marriage, or unexpected defeats. The term *boundary situation* suggests coming to the edge of one phase of life before entering another era.

Humanism: Humanistic philosophy focuses on human beings and their positive attributes. Individuals are considered naturally capable of developing their innate potential, interests, and values. Humanists believe in an innate goodness to human nature. Fostering the natural core self will lead to self-worth and worthy lives benefiting all.

Authenticity: Living authentically is to be true to what one's self really is, without any pretenses. An authentic person lets go of false masks and roles and does not choose to be guided solely by what others think. The authentic self is fluid, in the moment, without rigid, predetermined reactions, but open to new experiences.

Actualizing tendency: A belief of humanistic philosophy that each person has the natural capacity to continually grow toward fulfilling all his inborn potential.

Self-actualization: To grow toward self-actualization is to reach for the fulfillment of the person's innate potential in all aspects of life (psychologically, spiritually, intellectually, physically, socially, etc.). Human nature requires progressive development of abilities, and blocking potential is a source of psychological difficulties. As each person accepts her true nature and realizes all she can be, there is movement toward greater personality integration.

The combination of beliefs that human nature is basically good and that people strive to become all they can be directs humanistic therapies to foster the development of the self. Such an approach views psychological problems as blocks to natural becoming rather than pathological diseases.

Organismic valuing process: An authentic person trusts her internal reactions to experience and sets personal priorities according to self-chosen values. Humanists use the phrase organismic valuing process to describe a natural way of being that leads to positive choices for the individual and for others.

Locus of evaluation: *Locus* refers to the source and *evaluation* indicates how judgments are made. An individual can measure her worthiness by looking for outside reinforcement or by depending on her own internal valuing system. External evaluations such as grades or paychecks provide concrete feedback that may or may not reflect the person's own estimate of what the experience meant. An internal locus of control indicates that the person is not driven solely by external standards but also gives considerable weight to personal assessments of events according to personal values.

Fully functioning person: A fully functioning person is simultaneously open to new experiences and aware of his own internal framework. He trusts his own ability to evaluate each life event according to his own values and to make responsible choices according to the meaning he attaches to life. He accepts and trusts others, offering the same respect to their struggle for self-actualization as he gives his own striving.

Peak experience: When a person feels a sense of becoming who one truly is, a holistic feeling of the self in the moment occurs.

Flow: Becoming so absorbed in an activity that all distractions and irrelevant inner reactions are not present in the moment. The person and the activity flow together as though one.

Person-Centered: Originally described by Carl Rogers, Person-Centered counseling involves a focus on the client's description of his experience and his internal self. As the client tells of his reactions, the counselor teases out the client's unique feelings and meanings and reflects back to the client what has been said. As the counselor maintains empathy and genuine positive regard, the client begins to trust his sense of life and self and discovers his own internal valuing system. Feelings rise to the surface more easily for the client, and the flow of experiencing becomes readily available to him. Carl Rogers believed that truly listening to the client and allowing the true self to emerge brought forth the person's basic goodness and his natural capacity to relate to others cooperatively. Carl Rogers first developed his approach in the late fifties, but since then his concepts have been extended to parent and teacher training as well as to business and industry management, health care, and cross-cultural communication. The approach focuses on creating authentic relationships that honor the person's self-expression, rather than theoretical interpretations.

Necessary and sufficient conditions of therapy: Rogers defined the qualities of the therapist and of counseling interactions that encouraged client change. The therapist is sincere, *congruent* in his presentation and his true inner reactions to the client (also called *genuineness* or *authenticity*). A false front mimicking honest caring, or a blank slate, would be antithetical to building a counseling relationship. The counselor feels *unconditional positive regard* or nonpossessive warmth for the client. Without judging the client, the counselor accepts the client's experience at face value from the client's perspective, placing no conditions for acceptance. The counselor shows respect for the client as a worthy human being who has seen and lived life in her unique way. Finally, the counselor feels and communicates to the client an understanding of the client's inner world. Such *empathy* reflected back to the client allows the client to explore her experience in an atmosphere of safety and compassion. These conditions, according to Rogers, are necessary for the client to feel free to change or capable of facing her existential situation. Under such conditions the client will naturally grow in a positive direction. Many therapy approaches consider Rogerian conditions as basic to establishing a relationship with the client and to setting a tone for therapeutic change. However, not all counseling approaches consider the core conditions as sufficient for helping clients change. Other approaches expect therapists to demonstrate additional knowledge and skills in counseling and regard client change as requiring further interventions.

Congruence and Incongruence: A person is said to be congruent when his inner world is reflected by his external presentation of self. Incongruence shows the person as wearing a mask or projecting a persona that is not truly representative of the self. Person-Centered therapy is designed to encourage the client to be open to honest internal reactions and to develop congruency. The counselor models congruency by entering therapy sessions with her inner space settled and prepared to focus on the client's description of his experience. The client experiences his own description of his inner world and realizes his true self and how the valuing process works.

Unconditional positive regard: In authentic interactions between people, each shows the other a congruent positive appreciation of the other's description of personal experiences. A listener does not evaluate the other from her own perspective but instead warmly accepts the other's attempt to understand the journey toward self-fulfillment.

Empathy: To understand another's experience from the other's felt perspective. Empathy requires divining the full meaning of the other's statements including underlying feelings and personal meanings. When full understanding is gained, the listener actually enters the other's experience and feels what the other is saying, without the listener losing his own sense of self.

Nondirective techniques: A Person-Centered counseling approach is designed to expose the client's inner experience and the client's valuing system. The client provides the content, or the material discussed in therapy; the counselor facilitates the process of the counseling interaction to consistently reflect how the client creates meaning from his experience. Any intervention on the part of the counselor that would move away from the client's focus on inner experiencing would discourage the client from trusting his own subjective capacity to live authentically. The client is encouraged to look inward and to allow feelings to inform his experience. Directive techniques, such as advice giving or interpretations, would reflect the counselor's expertise and would reinforce the client in trusting external influences, not his own internal valuing. The counselor's trust in the client's ability to direct his own life is modeled for the client, so the client can gradually trust his own reactions. Nondirective techniques are typically termed *reflecting*—feelings or content—to emphasize the process of giving back to the client what he or she has said. Person-Centered counselors also clarify client statements so the client's meaning is clear to both the counselor and the client. Open-ended questions are carefully framed by Rogerian counselors to allow the client to choose the direction of what is said. The Person-Centered therapist also takes care to time interventions so as to prevent interruptions as the client reflects on his experience. Nondirective techniques are also used in play therapy for children as originally described by Axline.

Focused listening: Existential and Person-Centered therapists pay attention to what the client says and to the underlying feelings expressed. From a full understanding of the client's experience, the counselor determines the client's unique personal meanings and how the content reflects the client's identity.

Self-disclosure: When the counselor reveals something about her own life in therapy, there is the risk of moving away from a focus on the client. However, a limited amount of counselor revelation could also be considered a display of genuine caring and joining. Person-Centered literature recommends brief disclosures directly tied to client content and carefully timed to keep the focus on the client. Research of client reactions to counselor talk showed clients appreciating counselors' sharing past experiences and current lifestyles as helpful, not at all what Person-Centered literature recommends.

Group work: Existential and Person-Centered counselors extend humanistic methods used in individual therapy to groups. Given beliefs in human goodness, psychological growth, and a common quest for meaning, groups of individuals interacting authentically are seen as therapeutic. Yalom, who wrote the most widely used and respected text for group counseling, is philosophically grounded in existentialism. In counseling groups, members gain feedback from others about how they come across and can see how others deal with their experiences. The value of focused listening and respecting the internal process of each individual has also fostered applications for parenting workshops (PET) and teacher training (TET). Indeed, Rogers applied the humanistic approach to a variety of groups located in political and work settings.

Representative Case: Person-Centered Approach: Jared

Representative cases are chosen to illustrate therapy that fits well with the approach under review. Questions and answers follow to encourage the development of clinical thinking within the paradigm.

Jared was referred to the high school counselor by a teacher. The teacher reported that Jared was very quiet, didn't seem to have any friends, and lately he appeared anxious. He checked his grades with the teacher several times during every class period. Such checking was unnecessary, since he most always turned in his work on time and his grades were above average. Though Jared declined to talk to the teacher, he did agree to see the counselor after he was assured everything he said would be confidential.

Jared was slow in opening up to the counselor during the first sessions. He said only that he was worried about his future and was afraid he wouldn't measure up. Jared had an older brother and a younger sister. He said he found it easiest to "fade into the background" at home, rather than "push himself into the limelight." The counselor asked a few open-ended questions designed to assess Jared's mood state and determined that he was not depressed or severely anxious. Though clearly self-conscious, Jared did want to talk. After the first few minutes of a session, he would offer a few comments and very gradually, reveal what he was experiencing.

The counselor gave Jared the space to explore his inner world. No problem was defined; no explicit goals were set. Jared made a few comparisons between himself and his older brother, who was outgoing and popular, but according to Jared, "a bit of a blow-hard." The counselor reflected, "It seems important to you that what you say is credible." Startled, Jared responded, "Exactly." The client's struggled to articulate his vague insecurities. One of his uncertainties included wondering how he could become "a real man". "How he could be sure that his preferences were truly expressive of who he really was, or were interests 'laid on him' by outside influences?" He wondered about his father, since Dad was very quiet, stayed in the background, and let Mom run everything. He described his sister as not very effective and too emotional; and he worried that the wrong crowd could influence her. The counselor noted to herself that family dynamics appeared unremarkable.

The one clearly defined issue Jared brought up was his decision not to get a driver's license. His brother had been injured in several car accidents, and Jared decided he could wait before committing to such tremendous responsibility. He feared his sister could also be harmed if she rode in a car with their brother, or other irresponsible teenagers. Jared did not admit his fears to anyone but the counselor and when others asked about driving, he said, "I'm not interested." Not driving was problematic when he became interested in dating a quiet young woman from his history class. The situation was resolved when the couple agreed to meet at the movies and she drove them home.

The counselor continued to paraphrase Jared's comments and to reflect his feelings and the meaning. She shared with Jared her impression that he was defining his identity in his own terms as was appropriate for his development. On occasion, she also shared her genuine appreciation for his sense of responsibility and his concern for others.

Thinking About Jared

1. How would you characterize Jared's counseling issues?

2. What was the impact of the counselor's statement that Jared needed to establish credibility?

3. From a Person-Centered point of view, would it have been maximally effective to ask Jared if his "staying in the background" worked well for him?

4. How would you analyze Jared's choice to forgo applying for a driver's license? Should the counselor have pursued this topic further, since not driving limited Jared?

5. What do you think of the counselor's reinforcement of Jared's sense of responsibility? Doesn't fear of negative consequences restrict Jared, and shouldn't the counselor confront him?

Check Your Thinking About Jared

1. Jared is experiencing profound psychological issues related to his identity and how he deals with the world.

2. Jared showed a recognition response to the counselor, saying it was important for him to be credible. Jared felt understood, recognizing the counselor "got it." Such support made it safe for Jared to continue exploring his internal experiences.

3. Jared's style of staying in the background is working to allow him the reflective space he needs to deal with his psychological issues. To challenge his coping mechanism would be to question his capacity to determine for himself how he wanted to be in the world.

4. Jared's choice to limit his mobility by not driving is representative of his over-all style. The counselor accepts his choice as legitimate and allows Jared the dignity of determining the time when he might change some of his choices.

5. The Person-Centered counselor assumes Jared's fears will lessen when Jared gains greater confidence in his natural experiencing. To confront Jared would be delivering a message that the counselor judged Jared's inner signals as negative. When Jared himself begins to question the limits of his style, he will be ready to change.

Core Case: Helen Lovelace

The case of Helen Lovelace is examined here from a humanistic/existential perspective The case will be revisited in Chapter 11. The format of this case follows a standard layout used by psychologists in writing case notes. **D** designates **Data,** where the client's presenting concerns and symptoms are described. **A** stands for **Assessment,** where the clinician describes diagnostic impressions and case conceptualization concepts. **P,** or **Plan,** tells the plan for future counseling interventions, and, where applicable, client homework assignments.

D: An attractive woman of 25 enters counseling saying her life is falling apart. She says she has made many mistakes in her life and she is afraid of repeating old patterns. Helen graduated from college with a double major in psychology and special education, receiving good grades. She teaches a class for emotionally disturbed children in an elementary school. She has never married. Helen has a two-year-old son. Recently she has discovered she is pregnant, and the father of her unborn child is married. He plans to leave his wife and two daughters and wants to marry. Helen is distraught, saying she has had many relationships with men and doesn't trust his vision of a loving marriage. Her alternative plan is to move to Utah where she could rent a cabin and live in the mountains alone with her two children. She is estranged from her parents, who disowned her when she had her first child. Helen lived in the mountains briefly after her son was born, receiving welfare benefits until she found a job. She found the mountains and the seclusion renewing. Though she had not planned to be in a situation where she needed to escape again, she now feels compelled to return to a lifestyle without men. Helen also describes a pattern of smoking marijuana and some experimentation with hallucinogens. She has also lived in a cooperative community where members followed the tenets of a little-known religion.

A: Helen's description of her life reflects back to her very strict authoritarian father who dominated the family, controlling the children and a passive mother. The youngest of three, an older brother and a sister in the middle, Helen was favored as the "china doll." From a young age she could smile sweetly and the father, who demanded absolute compliance from everyone else, would soften and allow her anything. Helen analyzes her childhood experience as learning to seduce men and to depend on her attractive appeal to gain advantages. She feels most comfortable with children who respond to her caring rather than her looks. Though she conceptualizes her pattern of easily relating to men as destructive, she also knows she sets herself up to be vulnerable, as she does when she is pregnant, and this is confusing to her.

P: Helen describes her experiences as though her attractiveness is objective, something she has to manage. She wavers between some insight into repetitive patterns and confusing feelings that are not integrated into a clear identity.

Thinking About Helen

1. How would a Person-Centered counselor approach therapy with Helen?

2. What would the course of therapy be like in terms of Helen's expression of feelings regarding her sense of her self?

3. As a counselor using the Person-Centered approach, would it be difficult for you to listen nonjudgmentally to her description of pregnancies outside marriage?

4. How would an existential counselor approach therapy with Helen? What techniques would the existentialist use that would be similar to a Person-Centered therapist; what would be different? Do you have an opinion as to which approach would be best, and can you describe why?

Check Your Thinking About Helen

1. A Person-Centered therapist would create core conditions of empathy, congruence, and positive regard while listening to Helen describe her situation. The counselor would not offer interpretations or suggest she describe her childhood.

2. Helen would feel warmly accepted and would be able to express her true feelings more and more openly, sometimes discovering feelings she had not fully admitted to herself. Her self-confidence would grow, and she would be better able to accept her self.

3. Helen's description of bearing a child without a husband is an action she has chosen. The counselor can accept Helen as a person of value without sharing the same moral attitude.

4. An existential counselor would approach Helen with the same core conditions. However, at some point, the counselor would raise the issue of what meaning Helen attached to her existence and to her decisions. Placing her concerns within the realm of values choices may be appropriate and helpful if Helen were open to such considerations. However, the timing of dealing with spiritual issues would be critical so as to not imply judgments against her value as a human being or to discount her own approach of dealing with the concerns she raises herself.

Representative Case—Existential Approach: Omar Hamid

A Malaysian college student comes to therapy extremely depressed. He has a cleft palate and describes growing up as extremely painful being treated as a freak by family members and people in the community. Most of his early life was spent in isolated withdrawal concentrating on academic studies. As a young man he begged an aunt to provide funds to come to the United States for graduate work. She readily agreed, thinking sending him abroad would spare the family the shame of his existence. Arriving in the States, he broke out of his previous restraints and spent his time drinking and socializing. He also discovered promiscuous behavior within the homosexual community. By the time he came to counseling, however, he renounced his cavorting lifestyle and returned to his previous pattern of withdrawing.

His depressive symptoms have progressed to the point where he has lost twenty pounds, having little appetite. He has difficulty getting to sleep and startles awake in the early morning. He cries frequently and experiences enormous guilt. He's unable to perform work tasks in a university laboratory, since his concentration is minimal and he has little interest in his academic work or social activities. He claims he has no suicidal ideation, no plan or intent to harm himself. He does have hostile thoughts for family members and particularly his aunt, though he has had no contact with anyone in his home country for over a year.

Antidepressant medication is prescribed. Monitor suicidality by enlisting assistance from roommates and resident hall advisors is recommended. HIV testing is done. Evaluation for surgery for cleft palate at university medical school facilities, when and if the client chooses, is investigated. Ongoing counseling for depression, identity concerns, and self-esteem is needed.

Thinking About Omar

1. Why was cleft palate surgery considered? Why was HIV testing ordered?

2. Can you predict what existential issues could be relevant for the client? How could the meaning of existence be connected to issues such as emotional abuse and a potential life-threatening illness?

Course of Therapy

The client responded to antidepressant medication, and his mood improved considerably. He elected to proceed with evaluation for cleft palate surgery, hoping a better appearance would improve his self-esteem. However, before the procedure took place, the HIV test came back positive. Though no longer depressed, he remains focused on his previous promiscuous behavior and feels great guilt. The history of emotionally abusive treatment by others does not balance out for him as an explanation for ignoring his moral prohibition against homosexuality and promiscuity. He prays and seeks forgiveness as his illness progresses and death approaches. He visits a campus church daily and comes to counseling weekly. Eventually both the counselor and the minister visit him at a hospice facility. Members of his family come to visit shortly before his death, but there is little conversation among them.

As he dealt with the meaning of his life, the client considered the moral prohibition against homosexuality and promiscuity. He felt he had handled his part in the family dynamics well, showing little rancor until he demanded the funds to go to the United States. He felt his rebellion in immoral behavior was unjustified, but he gradually accepted responsibility for his actions without damning himself. The consequent HIV illness was at first seen as a punishment, but eventually he let go of the view that retribution was God's will. The meaning of his life came through accepting responsibility for his actions without condemning his soul. He died in peace, and his friends, minister, and counselor admired his existential resolution.

Check Your Thinking About Omar

1. Omar demonstrated low self-esteem given the reactions of others to his facial characteristics. An operation that improved his appearance could allow him to see himself as a person without disfiguring characteristics. An HIV test was ordered to determine if the risk-taking behavior he described had resulted in acquiring the disease.

2. Omar felt guilty given his moral code that homosexuality and promiscuity were wrong. He did not excuse himself because he had been emotionally mistreated but instead came to accept responsibility for his actions. Through self-examination and facing his mortality he came to a point where he did not damn himself nor did he condemn those who had harmed him.

Finding a Balance

Most counselors choose several counseling approaches that suit their personalities and theoretical preferences. In this section, the characteristics that appeal to counselors are identified and tied to concepts and practices. Then a case is described. The next section shows how the counselor's preferences would play out in working with the case. Finally, a comparison is made, showing how other approaches with different preferences might deal with the case. Integrating several approaches might cover varying counselor preferences and differing client issues better than any singular approach.

Key Counselor Preferences

1. Person-Centered therapists typically are quite patient and will listen to clients as long as the clients need to explore internal ponderings. The patience stems from a belief that each person has an internalized self-striving to become a fully functioning human being, ready to contribute to society and to live a fulfilling life.

2. Person-Centered therapists typically have warm and understanding personalities and a knack for phrasing statements kindly rather than bluntly. They are temperamentally suited

to believe the purpose of counseling is to provide the conditions to encourage the client to fully become aware of his internal self.

3. Personal warmth and sincerity are preferred to such a degree that Person-Centered therapists show little interest in counseling techniques, theory, or client life histories. Core conditions for developing the client-counselor relationship are considered necessary AND sufficient for client change.

4. Person-Centered counselors develop the ability to follow client content while emphasizing the client's feelings and meaning underlying the content. The primary responsibility for bringing content to counseling is with the client; the counselor facilitates the therapy interaction process to reflect the client's internal world.

5. Person-Centered therapists have the capability for finding the good in almost every client. Positive regard, considered necessary for the counseling relationship, does not require fully liking the client or necessarily agreeing with the client's values. However understanding and caring are needed, and finding something likable is necessary.

6. The Person-Centered counselor is not deeply interested in the details of psychological assessment or diagnosis.

Case Example: Sam Salvo

Sam, a 19-year-old college sophomore, enters counseling, saying he doesn't know what to do with his life. An honor student, he is struggling to choose a major and is experiencing difficulty maintaining his own high standards for studying since he is unsure of his career direction. He is doing well in physics, but the route through a Ph.D. program seems endless and he enjoys many other subjects, such as dance and literature. He also reports a strained relationship with his mother, who has been a nurturing resource, but who is now seen as limited in her approach to life.

Sam spent several summers in several locations in Africa with a church-affiliated organization. Teenagers were brought to underdeveloped areas to work in projects helping villages build irrigation systems, establish sustainable agriculture, schools, weaving cooperatives and the like. Sam found the experiences very worthwhile, but he had become disillusioned with the agency organizing the trips. Students earn money to pay for travel expenses, and room and board through fund-raisers, selling magazines, obtaining donations from sponsors, bake sales, and walkathons. During the last trip several students received a refund from an airline after their plane had overbooked. Agency organizers demanded the students return the refund to the organization or they would be returned home from Africa. Sam thought this incident was handled poorly, taking advantage of the students. He also had lost respect for the proselytizing in the indigenous communities and felt the organizations' employees did not demonstrate the religious values they taught.

Sam's mother is a very religious woman and annoys him with her moral indignation for some of his choices. His earring has been interpreted as a violation of God's creation. His plan to room with several roommates next year, including two women, was interpreted as creating the impression of immoral sexual relations. Sam's father accepts his son's behavior and only comments that some choices are not what the father sees as best, but he makes no major judgmental reproaches. As a result, Sam and his mother argue regularly.

Sam has given up the religious tenets that defined his beliefs from his childhood, and he feels he has no standards left for making his decisions. He has done some minimal reading of Eastern philosophy but finds it vague and of little assistance. He is worried about his preoccupation with these "airy-fairy" thoughts that distract him from his academic work, though he's caught in a dilemma where he sees no purpose for his work.

Applying Counselor Preferences

Using the previously listed preferences, how would a counselor proceed with Sam Salvo?

1. The therapist would enjoy patiently listening to Sam as he relayed his story. Though Sam may be repetitive in his explanations and unfair in his judgments against his mother, the counselor would easily trust that Sam could work his way through ambivalent feelings. Sam would appreciate the projected belief that he has an internal ability to determine who he is and what he needs.

2. The counselor would warmly accept Sam at face value and offer comments in a very kindly way. Sam would feel accepted and be encouraged to open up to more and more thoughts and feelings reflective of his inner world.

3. The counselor would sincerely be interested in Sam and his story and have little need to ask probing questions regarding Sam's childhood or to apply theoretical concepts regarding his dynamics. Questions may be asked to clarify the meaning of what Sam said, but the counselor would not demonstrate a need to vary the interaction with a variety of counseling techniques. Although in the case description Sam sounds like a normal young man with developmental issues, some exploration of his childhood, career assessment, and an ear for potential diagnoses might be appropriate. Techniques that clarify Sam's thinking or self-management methods could become useful.

4. The counselor would have the ability to track the content plus Sam's implied feelings and special meanings. The counselor would also easily communicate to Sam multiple levels of understanding. Sam would experience the powerful feedback as facilitating deeper and deeper self-awareness.

5. The therapist would prefer not to assess or categorize Sam's symptoms. Instead, the counselor views Sam as capable of self-change within the context of core conditions. Sam's issues appear to be developmental, and the counselor's approach is fully appropriate. Sam would appreciate being treated as a human being experiencing normal concerns. However, there could be further issues that would not be examined by the Person-Centered counselor.

Comparison with Other Preferences

Existential: Sam's case could be conceptualized as an existential crisis. He has abandoned the belief system he learned from his upbringing, and he has no replacement. An existential approach could challenge him with his aloneness, mortality, and responsibility for creating meaning for his life. To only reflect his already stated dilemma of having no purpose without raising issues of meaning and spirituality could leave him stagnant.

Psychoanalytic and Psychodynamic/Adlerian: Exploring Sam's childhood could ferret out relevant issues that preceded Sam's current difficulties with his mother. His object relations prototypes could be a factor in his confusion regarding self-identity and in his interactions with others. The case study does not mention siblings nor would a Person-Centered counselor necessarily ask about his sibling array, but Sam's career confusion could stem from family of origin issues. The clash in his preferences between hard science and the arts is worth further exploration to encourage developmental growth.

Behavioral and Cognitive approaches: Sam might benefit from learning some behavioral self-management methods to maintain academic responsibilities while dealing with his personal and career issues. He may also have cognitive frames that block his consideration of a number of alternative career paths or presume unreasonably high achievement standards.

Example of a Published Research Article on an Existential/Humanist Experiment

This is an article on an existential/humanistic experiment. As in previous chapters, the commentary in the boxes to the left of the article will help you understand the research and the format of the piece.

The Effects of Choice and Enhanced Personal Responsibility for the Aged: A Field Experiment in an Institutional Setting

Ellen J. Langer and Judith Rodin

A field experiment was conducted to assess the effects of enhanced personal responsibility and choice on a group of nursing home residents. It was expected that the debilitated condition of many of the aged residing in institutional settings is, at least in part, a result of living in a virtually decision-free environment and consequently is potentially reversible. Residents who were in the experimental group were given a communication emphasizing their responsibility for themselves, whereas the communication given to a second group stressed the staff's responsibility for them. In addition, to bolster the communication, the former group was given the freedom to make choices and the responsibility of caring for a plant rather than having decisions made and the plant taken care of for them by the staff, as was the case for the latter group. Questionnaire ratings and behavioral measures showed a significant improvement for the experimental group over the comparison group on alertness, active participation, and a general sense of well-being.

The transition from adulthood to old age is often perceived as a process of loss, physiologically and psychologically (Birren, 1958; Gould, 1972). However, it is as yet unclear just how much of this change is biologically determined and how much is a function of the environment. The ability to sustain a sense of personal control in old age may be greatly influenced by societal factors, and this in turn may affect one's physical well-being.

> Questions of usefulness and purpose are existential themes. What meaning does our life have? Why is life worth living, and in particular, is *my* life worthwhile?

Typically the life situation does change in old age. There is some loss of roles, norms, and reference groups, events that negatively influence one's perceived competence and feeling of responsibility (Bengston, 1973). Perception of these changes in addition to actual physical decrements may enhance a sense of aging and lower self-esteem (Lehr & Puschner, Note 1). In response to internal developmental changes, the aging individual may come to see himself in a position of lessened mastery relative to the rest of the world, as a passive object manipulated by the environment (Neugarten & Gutman, 1958). Questioning whether these factors can be counteracted, some studies have suggested that more successful aging—measured by decreased mortality, morbidity, and psychological disability—occurs when an individual feels a sense of usefulness and purpose (Bengston, 1973; Butler, 1967; Leaf, 1973; Lieberman, 1965).

The notion of competence is indeed central to much of human behavior. Adler (1930) has described the need to control one's personal environment as "an intrinsic necessity of life itself" (p. 398). DeCharms (1968) has stated that "man's primary motivation propensity is to be effective in producing changes in his environment. Man strives to be a causal agent, to be the primary locus of, causation for, or the origin of, his behavior; he strives for personal causation" (p. 269).

Several laboratory studies have demonstrated that reduced control over aversive outcomes increases physiological distress and anxiety (Geer, Davison, & Gatchel, 1970; Pervin, 1963) and even a nonveridical perception of control over an impending event reduces the aversiveness of that event (Bowers, 1968; Glass & Singer, 1972; Kanfer & Seidner, 1973). Langer, Janis, and Wolfer (1975) found that by inducing the perception of control over stress in hospital patients by means of a communication that emphasized potential cognitive control, subjects requested fewer pain relievers and sedatives and were seen by nurses as evidencing less anxiety.

> Choice is an element of freedom and responsibility.

Choice is also a crucial variable in enhancing an induced sense of control. Stotland and Blumenthal (1964) studied the effects of choice on anxiety reduction. They told subjects that they were going to take a number of important ability tests. Half of the subjects were allowed to choose the order in which they wanted to take the tests, and half were told that the order was fixed. All subjects were informed that the order of the tests would have no bearing on their scores. They found that subjects not given the choice were more anxious, as measured by palmar sweating. In another study of the effects of choice, Corah and Boffa (1970) told their subjects that there were two conditions in the experiment, each of which would be signaled by a different light. In one condition they were given the choice of whether or not to press a button to escape from an aversive noise, and in the other one they were not given the option of escaping. They found that the choice instructions decreased the aversiveness of the threatening stimulus, apparently by increasing perceived control. Although using a very different paradigm, Langer (1975) also demonstrated the importance of choice. In that study it was found that the exercise of choice in a chance situation, where choice was objectively inconsequential, nevertheless had psychological consequences manifested in increased confidence and risk taking.

Lefcourt (1973) best summed up the essence of this research in a brief review article dealing with the perception of control in man and animals when he concluded that "the sense of control, the illusion that one can exercise personal choice, has a definite and a positive role in sustaining life" (p. 24). It is not surprising, then, that these important psychological factors should be linked to health and survival. In a series of retrospective studies, Schmale and his associates (Adamson & Schmale, 1965; Schmale, 1958; Schmale & Iker, 1966) found that ulcerative colitis, leukemia, cervical cancer, and heart disease were linked with a feeling of helplessness and loss of hope experienced by the patient prior to the onset of the disease. Seligman and his co-workers have systematically investigated the learning of helplessness and related it to the clinical syndrome of depression (see Seligman, 1975). Even death is apparently related to control-relevant variables. McMahon and Rhudick (1964) found a relationship between depression or hopelessness and death. The most graphic description of this association comes from Bettelheim (1943), who in his analysis of the "Muselmanner," the walking corpses in the concentration camps, described them as:

> Prisoners who came to believe the repeated statements of the guards—that there was no hope for them, that they would never leave the camp except as a corpse—who came to feel that their environment was one over which they could exercise no influence whatsoever. . . . Once his own life and the environment were viewed as totally beyond his ability to influence them, the only logical conclusion was to pay no attention to them whatsoever. Only then, all conscious awareness of stimuli coming from the outside was blocked out, and with it all response to anything but inner stimuli.

> Death swiftly followed and, according to Bettelheim, [survival] depended on one's ability to arrange to preserve some areas of independent action, to keep control of some important aspects of one's life despite an environment that seemed overwhelming and total.

Bettelheim's description reminds us of Richter's (1957) rats, who also "gave up hope" of controlling their environment and subsequently died.

The implications of these studies for research in the area of aging are clear. Objective helplessness as well as feelings of helplessness and hopelessness—both enhanced by the

---

Research indicates a psychological component to death and disease. This component involves existential issues.

The authors review literature about the psychological effect of control and lack of control. Then they relate the ideas to the problems of old age, their own research topic.

environment and by intrinsic changes that occur with increasing old age—may contribute to psychological withdrawal, physical disease, and death. In contrast, objective control and feelings of mastery may very well contribute to physical health and personal efficacy.

In a study conceived to explore the effects of dissonance, Ferrare (1962; cited in Seligman, 1975; Zimbardo & Ruch, 1975) presented data concerning the effects of the ability of geriatric patients to control their place of residence. Of 24 subjects who answered that they did not have "any" other alternative but to move to a specific old age home, 8 died after 4 weeks of residence and 16 after 10 weeks of residence. By comparison, among the residents who died during the initial period, only one person had answered that she had the freedom to choose other alternatives. All of these deaths were classified as unexpected because "not even insignificant disturbances had actually given warning of the impending disaster."

As Zimbardo (Zimbardo & Ruch, 1975) suggested, the implications of Ferrare's data are striking and merit further study of old age home settings. There is already evidence that perceived personal control in one's residential environment is important for younger and noninstitutional populations. Rodin (in press), using children as subjects, demonstrated that diminished feelings of control produced by chronic crowding at home led to fewer attempts to control self-reinforcement in the laboratory and to greater likelihood of giving up in the face of failure.

The present study attempted to assess directly the effects of enhanced personal responsibility and choice in a group of nursing home patients. In addition to examining previous results from the control-helplessness literature in a field setting, the present study extended the domain of this conception by considering new response variables. Specifically, if increased control has generalized beneficial effects, then physical and mental alertness, activity, general level of satisfaction, and sociability should all be affected. Also, the manipulation of the independent variables, assigning greater responsibility and decision freedom for relevant behavior, allowed subjects real choices that were not directed toward a single behavior or stimulus condition. This manipulation tested the ability of the subjects to generalize from specific choices enumerated for them to other aspects of their lives, and thus tested the generalizability of feelings of control over certain elements of the situation to more broadly based behavior and attitudes.

> The independent variables were enhanced responsibility and choice. The dependent variables were various indicators of improved quality of life.

Method

Subjects

This study was *quasi-experimental* because the researchers did not randomly assign participants to conditions. They used existing floor residents and attempted to make sure that the two existing groups were comparable. This type of arrangement is also seen in educational research when existing classrooms are used as experimental groups. Though it lowers experimental control, it protects against the bad effects of disruption.

The study was conducted in a nursing home, which was rated by the state of Connecticut as being among the finest care units and offering quality medical, recreational, and residential facilities. The home was large and modern in design, appearing cheerful and comfortable as well as clean and efficient. Of the four floors in the home, two were selected for study because of similarity in the residents' physical and psychological health and prior socioeconomic status, as determined from evaluations made by the home's director, head nurses, and social worker. Residents were assigned to a particular floor and room simply on the basis of availability, and on the average, residents on the two floors had been at the home about the same length of time. Rather than randomly assigning subjects to experimental treatment, a different floor was randomly selected for each treatment. Since there was not a great deal of communication between floors, this procedure was followed in order to decrease the likelihood that the treatment effects would be contaminated. There were 8 males and 39 females in the responsibility-induced condition (all fourth-floor residents) and 9 males and 35 females in the comparison group (all second-floor residents). Residents who were either completely bedridden or judged by the nursing home staff to be completely noncommunicative (11 on the experimental floor and 9 on the comparison floor) were omitted from the sample. Also omitted was one woman on each floor, one 40 years old and the other 26 years old, due to their age. Thus, 91 ambulatory adults, ranging in age from 65 to 90, served as subjects.

Procedure

As you read the nursing home administrator's communications, be sure to notice the differences in the messages. These are the main experimental manipulations.

To introduce the experimental treatment, the nursing home administrator, an outgoing and friendly 33-year-old male who interacts with the residents daily, called a meeting in the lounge of each floor. He delivered one of the following two communications at that time:

[Responsibility-induced group] I brought you together today to give you some information about Arden House. I was surprised to learn that many of you don't know about the things that are available to you and more important, that many of you don't realize the influence you have over your own lives here. Take a minute to think of the decisions you can and should be making.

For example, you have the responsibility of caring for yourselves, of deciding whether or not you want to make this a home you can be proud of and happy in. You should be deciding how you want your rooms to be arranged—whether you want it to be as it is or whether you want the staff to help you rearrange the furniture. You should be deciding how you want to spend your time, for example, whether you want to be visiting your friends who live on this floor or on other floors, whether you want to visit in your room or your friends' room, in the lounge, the dining room, etc., or whether you want to be watching television, listening to the radio, writing, reading, or planning social events. In other words, it's your life and you can make of it whatever you want.

This brings me to another point. If you are unsatisfied with anything here, you have the influence to change it. It's your responsibility to make your complaints known, to tell us what you would like to change, to tell us what you would like. These are just a few of the things you could and should be deciding and thinking about now and from time to time every day. You made these decisions before you came here and you can and should be making them now.

We're thinking of instituting some way for airing complaints, suggestions, etc. Let [nurse's name] know if you think this is a good idea and how you think we should go about doing it. In any case let her know what your complaints or suggestions are.

Also, I wanted to take this opportunity to give you each a present from the Arden House. [A box of small plants was passed around, and patients were given two decisions to make: first, whether or not they wanted a plant at all, and second, to choose which one they wanted. All residents did select a plant.] The plants are yours to keep and take care of as you'd like.

One last thing, I wanted to tell you that we're showing a movie two nights next week, Thursday and Friday. You should decide which night you'd like to go, if you choose to see it at all.

[Comparison group] I brought you together today to give you some information about the Arden House. I was surprised to learn that many of you don't know about the things that are available to you; that many of you don't realize all you're allowed to do here. Take a minute to think of all the options that we've provided for you in order for your life to be fuller and more interesting. For example, you're permitted to visit people on the other floors and to use the lounge on this floor for visiting as well as the dining room or your own rooms. We want your rooms to be as nice as they can be, and we've tried to make them that way for you. We want you to be happy here. We feel that it's our responsibility to make this a home you can be proud of and happy in, and we want to do all we can to help you.

This brings me to another point. If you have any complaints or suggestions about anything, let [nurse's name] know what they are. Let us know how we can best help you. You should feel that you have free access to anyone on the staff, and we

> The researchers manipulated choice and control in many different ways, and they also measured changes in quality of life in many different ways. This way, they were more likely to find changes if the treatment was effective.

will *do the best* we can to provide individualized attention and time for you.

Also, I wanted to take this opportunity to give you each a present from the Arden House. [The nurse walked around with a box of plants and each patient was handed one.] The plants are yours to keep. The nurses will water and care for them for you.

One last thing, I wanted to tell you that we're showing a movie next week on Thursday and Friday. We'll let you know later which day you're scheduled to see it.

The major difference between the two communications was that on one floor, the emphasis was on the residents' responsibility for themselves, whereas on the other floor, the communication stressed the staff's responsibility for them. In addition, several other differences bolstered this treatment: Residents in the responsibility-induced group were asked to give their opinion of the means by which complaints were handled rather than just being told that any complaints would be handled by staff members; they were given the opportunity to select their own plant and to care for it themselves, rather than being given a plant to be taken care of by someone else; and they were given their choice of a movie night, rather than being assigned a particular night, as was typically the case in the old age home. However, there was no difference in the amount of attention paid to the two groups.

Three days after these communications had been delivered, the director visited all of the residents in their rooms or in the corridor and reiterated part of the previous message. To those in the responsibility-induced group he said, "Remember what I said last Thursday. We want you to be happy. Treat this like your own home and make all the decisions you used to make. How's your plant coming along?" To the residents of the comparison floor, he said the same thing omitting the statement about decision making.

Dependent Variables

Questionnaires. Two types of questionnaires were designed to assess the effects of induced responsibility. Each was administered 1 week prior to and 3 weeks after the communication. The first was administered directly to the residents by a female research assistant who was unaware of the experimental hypotheses or of the specific experimental treatment. The questions dealt with how much control they felt over general events in their lives and how happy and active they felt. Questions were responded to along 8-point scales ranging from 0 (none) to 8 (total). After completing each interview, the research assistant rated the resident on an 8-point scale for alertness.

All the people who collected data were unaware of the details of the experiment. Thus, the data collection would be labeled a *blind procedure*. However, this is not a *double-blind experiment*, because the administrator who gave the communications knew which people were getting which treatment. In a *double-blind experiment*, even the people who give treatments don't know which is which; for example, they might hand out placebos and pharmaceuticals that look exactly alike.

The second questionnaire was responded to by the nurses, who staffed the experimental and comparison floors and who were unaware of the experimental treatments. Nurses on two different shifts completed the questionnaires in order to obtain two ratings for each subject. There were nine 10-point scales that asked for ratings of how happy, alert, dependent, sociable, and active the residents were as well as questions about their eating and sleeping habits. There were also questions evaluating the proportion of weekly time the patient spent engaged in a variety of activities. These included reading, watching television, visiting other patients, visiting outside guests, watching the staff, talking to the staff, sitting alone doing nothing, and others.

Behavioral measures. Since perceived personal control is enhanced by a sense of choice over relevant behaviors, the option to choose which night the experimental group wished to see the movie was expected to have measurable effects on active participation. Attendance records were kept by the occupational therapist, who was unaware that an experiment was being conducted.

Another measure of involvement was obtained by holding a competition in which all participants had to guess the number of jelly beans in a large jar. Each patient wishing to enter the contest simply wrote his or her name and estimate on a piece of paper and deposited it in a box that was next to the jar.[1]

Finally, an unobtrusive measure of activity was taken. The tenth night after the experimental treatment, the right wheels of the wheelchairs belonging to a randomly selected subsample of each patient group were covered with 2 inches (.05 m) of white adhesive tape. The following night, the tape was removed from the chairs and placed on index cards for later evaluation of amount of activity, as indicated by the amount of discoloration.

Results

Questionnaires. Before examining whether or not the experimental treatment was effective, the pre-test ratings made by the subjects, the nurses, and the interviewer were compared for both groups. None of the differences approached significance, which indicates comparability between groups prior to the start of the investigation.

The means for responses to the various questionnaires are summarized in Table 1. Statistical tests compared the post-test minus pre-test scores of the experimental and comparison groups.

> The comparison of pretests was done to make sure the nursing home residents were about the same before the experiment started, so pre-existing differences didn't affect the results.

Table 1

Mean Scores for Self-Report, Interviewer Ratings,
and Nurses' Ratings for Experimental and Comparison Groups

Questionnaire responses	Responsibility Induced (n=24)			Comparison (n=28)			Comparison of Change Scores
	Pre	Post	Change: Post-Pre	Pre	Post	Change: Post-Pre	(p<)
Self-report							
Happy	5.16	5.44	.28	4.90	4.78	−.12	.05
Active	4.07	4.27	.20	3.90	2.62	−1.28	.01
Perceived Control							
Have	3.26	3.42	.16	3.62	4.03	.41	—
Want	3.85	3.80	−.05	4.40	4.57	.17	—
Interviewer rating							
Alertness	5.02	5.31	.29	5.75	5.38	−.37	.025
Nurses' ratings							
General Improvement	41.67	45.64	3.97	42.69	40.32	−2.39	.005
Time Spent							
Visiting patients	13.03	19.81	6.78	7.94	4.65	−3.30	.005
Visiting others	11.50	13.75	2.14	12.38	8.21	−4.16	.05
Talking to staff	8.21	16.43	8.21	9.11	10.71	1.61	.01
Watching staff	6.78	4.64	−2.14	6.96	11.60	4.64	.05

The *t*-tests analyze the differences between mean scores of the two groups. The *p* values tell you how probable this *t* value is. For example, a *p* value of less than .05 means that this result would happen by chance fewer than 5 times in one hundred.

In asking about *control*, the experimenters used the word *control* in a way the patients did not understand. The results from the question were not meaningful.

In response to direct questions about how happy they currently were, residents in the responsibility-induced group reported significantly greater increases in happiness after the experimental treatment than did the comparison group, $t(43)$ = 1.96, $p < .05$.[2] Although the comparison group heard a communication that had specifically stressed the home's commitment to making them happy, only 25% of them reported feeling happier by the time of the second interview, whereas 48% of the experimental group did so.

The responsibility-induced group reported themselves to be significantly more active on the second interview than the comparison group, $t(43) = 2.67$, $p < .01$. The interviewer's ratings of alertness also showed significantly greater increase for the experimental group, $t(43) = 2.40$, $p < .025$. However, the questions that were relevant to perceived control showed no significant changes for the experimental group. Since over 20% of the patients indicated that they were unable to understand what we meant by control, these questions were obviously not adequate to discriminate between groups.

The second questionnaire measured nurses' ratings of each patient. The correlation between the two nurses' ratings of the same patient was .68 and .61 *(ps < .005)* on the comparison and responsibility-induced floors, respectively.[3] For each patient, a score was calculated by averaging the two nurses' ratings for each question, summing across questions, and subtracting the total pretreatment score from the total posttreatment score.[4] This yielded a positive average total change score of 3.97 for the responsibility-induced group as compared with an average negative total change of −2.37 for the comparison group. The difference between these means is highly significant, $t(50) = 5.18$, $p < .005$. If one looks at the percentage of people who were judged improved rather than at the amount of judged improvement, the same pattern emerges: 93% of the experimental group (all but one subject) were considered improved, whereas only 21% (six subjects) of the comparison group showed this positive change ($\chi^2 = 19.23$, $p < .005$).

The nurses' evaluation of the proportion of time subjects spent engaged in various interactive and noninteractive activities was analyzed by comparing the average change scores (post–precommunication) for all of the nurses for both groups of subjects on each activity. Several significant differences were found. The experimental group showed increases in the proportion of time spent visiting with other patients (for the experimental group, $\bar{X} = 12.86$ vs. −6.61 for the comparison group), $t(50) = 3.83$, $p < .005$; visiting people from outside of the nursing home (for the experimental group, $\bar{X} = 4.28$ vs. −7.61 for the comparison group, $t(50) = 2.30$, $p < .05$; and talking to the staff (for the experimental group, $\bar{X} = 8.21$ vs. 1.61 for the comparison group), $t(50) = 2.98$, $p < .05$.[5] In addition, they spent less time passively watching the staff (for the experimental group), $\bar{X} = -4.28$ vs. 9.68 for the comparison group), $t(50) = 2.60$, $p < .05$. Thus, it appears that the treatment increased active, interpersonal activity but not passive activity such as watching television or reading.

The jelly-bean contest was a good measure of how active the patients felt. But the wheelchair tires did not turn out to be a good measure because none of the tires got dirty. Evidently, the experimenters hoped that more dirt on the tires would show more activity. This is an example of why several different measures of the dependent variable were used.

Behavioral measures. As in the case of the questionnaires, the behavioral measures showed a pattern of differences between groups that was generally consistent with the predicted effects of increased responsibility. The movie attendance was significantly higher in the responsibility-induced group than in the control group after the experimental treatment *(z = 1.71, p < .05, one-tailed)*, although a similar attendance check taken one month before the communications revealed no group differences.

In the jelly-bean-guessing contest, 10 subjects (21%) in the responsibility-induced group and only 1 subject (2%) from the comparison group participated ($\chi^2 = 7.72$, $p < .01$). Finally, very little dirt was found on the tape taken from any of the patients' wheelchairs, and there was no significant difference between the two groups.

Discussion

It appears that inducing a greater sense of personal responsibility in people who may have virtually relinquished decision making, either by choice or necessity, produces improvement. In the present investigation, patients in the comparison group were given a communication stressing the staff's desire to make them happy and were otherwise treated in the sympathetic manner characteristic of this high-quality nursing home. Despite the care provided for these people, 11% were rated as having become more debilitated over a period of time as short as 3 weeks. In contrast with this group, 93 % of the people who were encouraged to make decisions for themselves, given decisions to make, and given responsibility for something outside of themselves, actually showed overall improvement. Based on their own judgments and by the judgments of the nurses with whom they interacted on a daily basis, they became more active and felt happier. Perhaps more important was the judged improvement in their mental alertness and increased behavioral involvement in many different kinds of activities.

The behavioral measures showed greater active participation and involvement for the experimental group. Whether this directly resulted from an increase in perceived choice and decision-making responsibility or from the increase in general activity and happiness occurring after the treatment cannot be assessed from the present results. It should also be clearly noted that although there were significant differences in active involvement, the overall level of participation in the activities that comprised the behavioral measures was low. Perhaps a much more powerful treatment would be one that is individually administered and repeated on several occasions. That so weak a manipulation had any effect suggests how important increased control is for these people, for whom decision making is virtually nonexistent.

The practical implications of this experimental demonstration are straightforward. Mechanisms can and should be established for changing situational factors that reduce real or perceived responsibility in the elderly. Furthermore, this study adds to the body of literature (Bengston, 1973; Butler, 1967; Leaf, 1973; Lieberman, 1965) suggesting that senility and diminished alertness are not an almost inevitable result of aging. In fact, it suggests that some of the negative consequences of aging may be retarded, reversed, or possibly prevented by returning to the aged the right to make decisions and a feeling of competence.

> Even a small encouragement of control and responsibility improved the treatment group markedly.

> Many research articles that apply psychological principles in a certain setting close with some remarks about the broader applications that are suggested by the results.

Reference Note

Lehr, K., & Puschner, I. *Studies in the awareness of aging.* Paper presented at the 6th International Congress on Gerontology, Copenhagen, 1963.

References

Don't stop at the end of the article! Always read through the Reference list and take note of items that interest you. Copy the references in your notebook or PDA.

Adamson, J., & Schmale, A. Object loss, giving up, and the onset of psychiatric disease. *Psychosomatic Medicine,* 1965, *27,* 557–576,

Adler, A. Individual psychology. In C. Murchinson (Ed.), *Psychologies of 1930.* Worcester, Mass.: Clark University Press, 1930.

Bengston, V. L. Self determination: A social and psychological perspective on helping the aged. *Geriatrics,* 1973.

Bettelheim, B. Individual and mass behavior in extreme situations. *Journal of Abnormal and Social Psychology,* 1943, *38,* 417–452.

Birren, J. Aging and psychological adjustment. *Review of Educational Research,* 1958, *28,* 475–490.

Bowers, K. Pain, anxiety, and perceived control. *Journal of Consulting and Clinical Psychology,* 1968, *32,* 596–602.

Butler, R. Aspects of survival and adaptation in human aging. *American Journal of Psychiatry,* 1967, *123,* 1233–1243.

Corah, N., & Boffa, J. Perceived control, self-observation, and response to aversive stimulation. *Journal of Personality and Social Psychology,* 1970, *16,* 1–4.

deCharms, R. *Personal causation.* New York: Academic Press, 1968.

Geer, J., Davison, G., & Gatchel, R. Reduction of stress in humans through nonveridical perceived control of aversive stimulation. *Journal of Personality and Social Psychology,* 1970, *16,* 731–738.

Glass, D., & Singer, J. *Urban stress.* New York: Academic Press, 1972.

Gould, R. The phases of adult life: A study in developmental psychology. *American Journal of Psychiatry,* 1972, *129,* 521–531.

Kanfer, F., & Seidner, M. Self-Control: Factors enhancing tolerance of noxious stimulation. *Journal of Personality and Social Psychology,* 1973, *25,* 381–389.

Langer, E. J. The illusion of control. *Journal of Personality and Social Psychology,* 1975, *32,* 311–328.

Langer, E. J., & Abelson, R. P. The semantics of asking a favor: How to succeed in getting help without really dying. *Journal of Personality and Social Psychology,* 1972, *24,* 26–32.

Langer, E. J., Janis, I. L., & Wolfer, J. A. Reduction of psychological stress in surgical patients, *Journal of Experimental Social Psychology,* 1975, *11,* 155–165.

Leaf, A. Threescore and forty. *Hospital Practice*, 1973, *34*, 70–71.

Lefcourt, H. The function of the illusion of control and freedom. *American Psychologist*, 1973, *28*, 417–425.

Lieberman, M. Psychological correlates of impending death: Some preliminary observations. *Journal of Gerontology*, 1965, *20*, 181–190.

McMahon, A., & Rhudick, P. Reminiscing, adaptational significance in the aged. *Archives of General Psychiatry*, 1964, *10*, 292–298.

Neugarten, B., & Gutman, D. Age-sex roles and personality in middle age: A thematic apperception study. *Psychological Monographs*, 1958, *72* (17, Whole No. 470).

Pervin, L. The need to predict and control under conditions of threat. *Journal of Personality*, 1963, *31*, 570–585.

Richter, C. On the phenomenon of sudden death in animals and man. *Psychosomatic Medicine*, 1957, *19*, 191–198.

Rodin, J. Crowding, perceived choice, and response to controllable and uncontrollable outcomes. *Journal of Experimental Social Psychology*, In press.

Schmale, A. Relationships of separation and depression to disease: A report on a hospitalized medical population. *Psychosomatic Medicine*, 1958, *20*, 259–277.

Schmale, A., & Iker, H. The psychological setting of uterine cervical cancer. *Annals of the New York Academy of Sciences*, 1966, *125*, 807–813.

Seligman, M. E. P. *Helplessness.* San Francisco; Freeman, 1975.

Stotland, E., & Blumenthal, A. The reduction of anxiety as a result of the expectation of making a choice. *Canadian Review of Psychology*, 1964, *18*, 139–145.

Zimbardo, P. G., & Ruch, F. L. *Psychology and life* (9th ed.). Glenview, Ill.: Scott, Foresman, 1975.

End Notes

[1]We also intended to measure the number of complaints that patients voiced. Since one often does not complain after becoming psychologically helpless, complaints in this context were expected to be a positive indication of perceived personal control. This measure was discarded, however, since the nurses failed to keep a systematic written record.

[2]All of the statistics for the self-report data and the interviewers' ratings are based on 45 subjects (25 in the responsibility-induced group and 20 in the comparison group), since these were the only subjects available at the time of the interview.

[3]There was also significant agreement between the interviewer's and nurses' ratings of alertness (r=.65).

[4]Since one nurse on the day shift and one nurse on the night shift gave the ratings, responses to the questions regarding sleeping and eating habits were not included in the

total score. Also, in order to reduce rater bias, patients for whom there were ratings by a nurse on only one shift were excluded from this calculation. This left 24 residents from the experimental group and 28 from the comparison group.

[5]This statistic is based only on the responses of nurse on duty in the evening.

Discussion Ideas

1. What existential dilemmas are addressed by research like Langer and Rodin's? In what sense was their experimental treatment a humanistic one?

2. Have you ever been in a situation, group, or institution that produced feelings of helplessness or hopelessness? What were some of the effects of these feelings?

2. Why were the two speeches delivered by the same "nursing home administrator, an outgoing and friendly 33-year-old male who interacts with the residents daily"? Why was this choice of message-giver important?

3. The results were measured by self-reports, nurse reports, and tallies of participation. What other measures might be good to collect in this experiment? Are there physical tests that could be meaningful?

4. According to the research findings, what changes should be made in nursing homes?

5. What other groups and institutions could be targets for experiments similar to this one? For example, how might the principles be applied to child-raising?

Answer Key for Practice Test Questions

True/False

1. F
2. T
3. F
4. F
5. T
6. T
7. F
8. F
9. T
10. F

Multiple Choice

1. d   11. e
2. b   12. b
3. a   13. a
4. b   14. b
5. d   15. e
6. d
7. c
8. a
9. c
10. d

CHAPTER 7

Gestalt Therapy

Chapter Review

Fritz Perls, the dominant figure in Gestalt therapy, drew terminology from Gestalt psychology and loosely applied research on perception to broader descriptions of human experience. As such, the Gestalt concept of figure/ground perception is explained as the person focusing on a figure in the forefront of a scene while the background is shapeless and less distinct. For Perls, our habits of interacting with our environment establish what elements we choose to fade into the background of our consciousness, and our needs organize what we pay attention to as the priorities shaping the foreground. Perls's definition of the figure/ground concept expands the original Gestalt psychologists' research and uses the concept as a description of awareness, the central principle of Gestalt therapy. The purpose of therapy for this approach is to increase the client's awareness of self, and the counselor's role is to facilitate the process of self-discovery. Continuing the figure/ground concept, the focus of the foreground and the faded background would be ever shifting for the fully aware person who maintains full consciousness of self and the world around him. The counselor would consistently encourage the client to describe inner awareness asking, "What are you doing?" "What are you feeling?" "What do you want?" Counseling also helps the client determine what she is avoiding and what expectations she brings to her experiences.

Full awareness of self allows fragmented pieces of experience to come together into a whole, whereas socialization requires people to suppress natural and spontaneous parts of themselves against the flow of an organismic internal process. The Gestalt approach seeks to heal the splitting of the human psyche that divides perceptions into false polarities. The person who has only learned to deny and disown internal conflicts is unable to resolve "unfinished business" from the past. To promote understanding of internal blocks, Gestalt terminology sometimes depicts easily understood scenes that imply the emotional struggle described. Top-dog is the social self who tries to control the resistant natural self, called the under-dog, in a dynamic similar to the conflicts between the superego and id from psychoanalytic thought. *Catastrophic expectations* is a Gestalt term that dramatizes the child's experience of natural wonderment, but then he learns to expect punishment and rejection. Instead of learning to navigate between personal and external pressures, adults retain the top/under-dog dynamic, always vacillating between extremes, or forever stuck in a limbo between choices. Gestalt therapy exaggerates the internal drama, bringing the polarities into awareness, so experiences can be owned by the person and integrated into a holistic sense of self.

The Gestalt approach emphasizes contact, an awareness of the moment, of the person connecting to the here and now. Counselors seek to facilitate client experiences in session rather than only talk about what life is like. Counseling also draws attention to boundaries, or the lines between one person and other human beings, believing that only the person herself can create an authentic experience and determine the course of her own life. Consequently a client may need to endure frustration and ambivalence before growth can occur, although therapeutic support may help. Clients' descriptions of their emotions may be drawn out to accentuate the experience as counselors ask questions such as, "Tell me what the pain is like," or clients are told, "Stay with the feeling." When clients reach an impasse, they must draw on their own inner resources to find their own unique experience. Counselors are true to their honest reactions to client behavior, modeling a mature and centered adult. So, counselors may act bored when clients deflect contact, project anger onto others, sound phony, or demonstrate introjection, expressing others' viewpoints.

The goal is for clients to experience ever deepening layers of the their true selves, to identify real-life choices and to manage external influences so that authenticity can be maintained. To facilitate self-awareness, counselors frequently note body language, and encourage clients to try something, anything, new to become newly aware. Language is consistently framed with the person as the responsible subject, rather than nebulous "shoulds," "have tos," or "can'ts." Role-plays are common Gestalt techniques, particularly the empty chair method. Two chairs are placed facing one another with each representing a side of a polarized issue, different people, or aspects of the self. The client takes the role of one side at a time, moving from one chair to the other and acting out the experience of the two sides. Themes from dreams can be experienced using the empty chairs. Psychodrama improvisations could be enacted with group members playing different parts and the client and counselor serving as the directors. In groups, another technique is the *hot seat*: one group member sits in a prominent place and works with the therapist, while others watch the work as spectators or participate by offering the hot seat client additional feedback.

Gestalt therapists share a common philosophy, but the techniques or format for counseling is not consistent among practitioners. Instead creative adaptations are seen as expressive of each therapist's style and of following the cues of the moment. All Gestaltists do intend to expand the client's awareness, to encourage the client to live in the moment, to overcome blocks to self-experiencing, and to assume self-responsibility for creating an authentic life. Gestalt techniques work particularly well with clients who are rigidly wedded to socialized messages regarding self-expression and behavior. Many women following a feminine stereotype can benefit by methods that encourage self-awareness. Family interaction patterns can be tied to Gestalt definitions of boundary problems. Although Gestalt conceptualizations do not assume that past traumas unconsciously control clients, the counselor could facilitate reexperiencing a disturbing event to integrate the unfinished business into a complete sense of self. Psychosomatic complaints are treated as a part of holistic experiencing and can be the focus for awareness techniques.

However, the goal of encouraging the true self's full expression makes many of the techniques inappropriate for sociopathic and narcissistically oriented clients. Indeed, the emphasis on a self-orientation is seen by some as denying the interconnections between people. Gestalt therapy is also criticized as anti-intellectual and philosophically sloppy. The loose creativity of adapting whatever technique for any client situation denies the professionalism of taking into account empirical validation for counseling practice. Consequently, few psychologists claim the Gestalt as their sole theoretical orientation, but many utilize some of the concepts and techniques within the context of other theoretical approaches.

Practice Test Questions

True or False: Consider each statement and try to explain in your own mind why it might not be fully true. Be sure to take into account any qualifying factors that might make the statement untrue. If you decide that the statement is fully true, circle **T**. Otherwise, circle **F**.

T   F   1.   Five questions from the therapist all preceded by Why? are the key therapy interventions.

T   F   2.   Self-responsibility must be tempered by understanding the person's past.

T   F   3.   The therapist can interpret client's speech by interpreting archetypal symbols.

T   F   4.   Nonverbal body language offers clues to the client's way of approaching the world.

T   F   5.   Clients who demonstrate an impasse are demanding too much from life.

T   F   6.   Perls wrote that therapists need a command of psychological theory to be competent to offer counseling.

T   F   7.   Perls described the therapist as expressing honest reactions to the client rather than showing positive regard.

T   F   8.   Gestalt therapists tend to use techniques that intensify the client's experience in the moment.

T   F   9.   Giving a voice to a physical symptom allows the client to experience the meaning of the symptom to the true natural self.

T   F   10.   The *hot seat* in Gestalt group work is a variation on the empty chair technique.

Multiple Choice: Circle the one letter next to the best answer to the following questions or to complete the sentence stems.

1.   Gestalts represent ways in which the brain organizes perceptions of sensory stimuli. Gestalts are based on what principle?
   a.   closure
   b.   figure/ground relationships
   c.   proximity
   d.   a and c
   e.   a, b, and c

2.   Clients may shut down awareness of parts of themselves and of their experience because they
   a.   learn that others disapprove of some aspect of themselves.
   b.   favor their natural reactions while dealing with daily responsibilities.
   c.   pay attention to the playful needs remembered from childhood.
   d.   a and b
   e.   a and c

3.   The goals of Gestalt therapy include
   a.   increasing the client's capacity to control their emotions with senses and feelings.
   b.   increasing the client's awareness of personal reactions to the environment and other people.
   c.   helping the client to work through feelings from childhood transferred to the therapist.
   d.   a and b
   e.   a and c

4.   Which of the following is NOT a Gestalt concept?
   a.   unfinished business
   b.   here-and-now awareness
   c.   impasse
   d.   social interest

5. Polarities are conflicts within the person's awareness that are resolved by
   a. becoming centered, accepting both extremes.
   b. becoming aware of which side requires expression in the moment.
   c. achieving homeostasis.
   d. organismic self-regulation.
   e. all of the above

6. Catastrophic expectations can be defined as
   a. believing life is full of traumas.
   b. learning that following natural impulses is punished.
   c. fearing that getting what you want is not possible.
   d. understanding that it is not a catastrophe to be disappointed.

7. In the top-dog and under-dog polarity, the
   a. under-dog wants to control the person.
   b. top-dog is righteous, telling the under-dog what to do.
   c. top-dog has many subtle, devious ways to get his way.
   d. under-dog is helpless and can never gain power.

8. What is the Gestalt concept of *contact*?
   a. paper used to line silverware drawers
   b. making a connection with past experiences
   c. connecting to the spiritual meaning of existence
   d. being aware of the flow of moment to moment experience

9. *Boundaries* are defined in Gestalt therapy as
   a. lines that separate people from each other.
   b. lines that connect people to each other.
   c. the spaces needed to maintain homeostasis.
   d. a and b
   e. a, b, and c

10. *Neurotic self-regulation* is characterized as
    a. paying attention to the organismic signals to gain homeostasis.
    b. "shoulds" carried to extremes, so that awareness in the here and now is lost.
    c. flexible awareness that allows a person to experience the natural self.
    d. a and b
    e. a and c

11. The *contact boundary disturbance* that assigns our own characteristics onto others is called
    a. introjection.
    b. retroflection.
    c. projection.
    d. deflection.
    e. confluence.

12. The *contact boundary disturbance* that connects to others where a person takes in another's values system without consideration of the natural self is called
    a. retroflection.
    b. deflection.
    c. confluence.
    d. introjection.
    e. projection.

13. The *contact boundary disturbance* where a person confuses the distinctions between self and another person is called
    a. deflection.
    b. projection.
    c. retroflection.
    d. introjection.
    e. confluence.

14. The *contact boundary disturbance*, in which a person directs feelings on to himself rather than admit his feelings about others, is a form of
    a. deflection.
    b. retroflection.
    c. introjection.
    d. confluence.
    e. projection.

15. Which of the following is NOT part of the *empty chair technique?*
    a. Each chair is assigned a character, emotion, attitude, or a personal quality.
    b. The client sits in each chair and speaks for the assigned characteristic.
    c. Moving back and forth, a dialogue between the characteristics takes place.
    d. The client writes a script to demonstrate the polarities to be enacted.
    e. Thoughts that criticize the self are softened through the dialogue.

Key Terms and Essential Concepts

Figure/Ground: Perls expanded this concept from Gestalt psychology research. The researchers demonstrated that perception focuses on the foreground of a scene, and the background fades into less distinct shapes and forms. Perls used this description to explain the self's perceptions in relation to personal needs. The individual focuses awareness on what is important according to her psychological world view, and disregards other elements of experience and the environment as less important. Shifts in perception occur as the person's awareness changes.

Awareness: Being fully aware is a consciousness of one's internal self and of the environment, including reactions to other people. Awareness is expressed as thoughts, feelings, behavior, and body sensations.

Polarities: Internal conflicts within an individual represent one aspect of the personality that is in direct opposition to another, keeping the individual stuck in the middle unable to make effective choices. Usually polarities can be described as themes such as the struggle between top-dog and under-dog—or tame versus wild.

Homeostasis: The ideal state of being in which the individual is centered, able to balance his or her energy within the context of what is best for the individual at the moment. In such a balanced state, there is an integration of polarities within the self, and the person can make choices in a state of equilibrium.

Top-dog/Under-dog: Conflicting polarized positions within the personality represent opposing drives within the self. Top-dog is the bullying force of the conscience that is righteous and attempts to dominate the under-dog, or the natural self, that resists social demands and attempts to express personal wishes.

Splitting: Pathological disorder in which an individual is unable to balance the positive and negative polarities within themselves and is unable to see others as simultaneously possessing both positive and negative sides.

Contact: An aware state of mind allows the person to be conscious of what is occurring in the here and now, both for external stimuli and for the self. Being in tune with the moment includes the ability to connect to another person through an empathic exchange of experiencing.

Support: Internal resources within the self, and external influences in the environment, allow the person to maintain balance in self. The individual is responsible for evaluating externals and creating the environment that is self-enhancing.

Impasse: When a person experiences the absence of necessary support systems and is unable to develop new influences, the individual is blocked, unable to move forward in life. At this time, a client often seeks therapy. Gestalt therapy will create interventions that expose how the person is emotionally stuck, and provide experiences for emotional release. Once the impasse is unblocked, the client can develop new venues of self-support.

Shoulds: Barriers that block the natural balance of the self are rigid self-censures that may not be in awareness but are internalized to the point that they hamper a person's ability to be freely adaptable in a given context.

Neurotic self-regulation: Unexamined learning within one's self enables the person to choose actions that seem natural and righteous, but are, in fact, personal rules that block the individual's organismic balance. Full awareness requires a natural shifting so the person can adapt in the moment to personal needs and external influences.

Disowning: When individuals do not make contact with others, through several methods called boundary disturbances, they are limiting conscious awareness. Separating one's self from natural reactions and experiences, denies fully living and can lead to self-restrictions and deprivation. In contrast, owning the self's natural way of being and staying open to the self's reactions to external influences as they really are, allow the self to live fully and authentically.

Introjection: One of the five types of boundary disturbance, which prevents accurate contact with the self as well as connections to others. In introjection, an individual is unable to define her own values but instead, wholly internalizes someone else's entire value system as her own without fully adapting the values to the self's unique way of being.

Projection: In another type of contact boundary disturbance, the individual transfers her own negative feelings and motives to other people, instead of owning the reactions as a part of herself. The individual thereby has an inaccurate perception of others, and consequently creates a block to real contact.

Retroflection: In yet another contact boundary disturbance the individual directs negative reactions to others or to external circumstance to the self. An example would be a person who is angry with someone else but directs the anger inward and becomes depressed.

Deflection: In another method for disturbing full awareness, the individual avoids contact by strategically not paying attention to painful subjects or feelings, and thereby turning aside the issues that are unpleasant or painful.

Confluence: Another contact barrier is erected when a person merges the emotions and perceptions of another person into her own, thereby ignoring the differences and distinctions between the self and another.

Unfinished business: When individuals play out experiences from their past, within their present life, they are living out experiences that were never resolved. This is a result of unexpressed emotions, or open-ended issues from the past, which continue to resurface until they are fully realized in the moment and completed. The resolution of this cycle is a primary goal within Gestalt therapy.

Layer: Perls described the human personality as expressed through ever deepening levels and used the layers of an onion as an analogy for peeling away tiers of the person's awareness. At the deepest level of self-awareness, the person is aware of external influences and able to constantly take in what is outside and still stay in touch with the real state of the self in the moment. Perls described therapy as following "layers of neuroses" to unveil all levels where the person comes in contact with the boundary, or line, between the self and the external world.

Phony layer: The personality level where the individual responds according to a superficial definition of self, reacting only in accordance with typically acceptable social behavior, and negating awareness of the natural self.

Phobic layer: The personality level where the person hides in fear of the reactions of others, spending more time covering up helpless feelings than dealing with the real issues.

Impasse layer: On this level, a person is confused as to what to do next. He may seek help from others, hoping someone else will tell him what to do.

Implosive layer: The personality level where the phony mask no longer works and the person questions the authenticity of his identity.

Explosive layer: An exciting, growthful personality stage when the person lets go of inauthentic defenses and is freed up to act in accordance with his natural, self-defining identity.

Organismic self-regulation: According to Perls, the self seeks to integrate personality polarities into a sense of wholeness. Such a process is natural and provides the means for the person to gain a balance within an ever changing life of multiple experiences and personal needs.

Experimentation: Gestalt therapists prefer to have clients actually do something rather than only talk about their experiences. New behaviors may be assigned as homework. Counseling sessions may focus on the client's awareness of what is happening in the moment. When clients describe a feeling, the counselor may encourage the client to, "Stay with that" to focus attention on the here and now. Imaginary scenes may be enacted within the client's mind while the client describes in detail what the experience is like. Techniques that bring out mind/body/feeling reactions are called experiments in living in the present.

Paradoxical theory of change: Gestalt therapists assign to clients experimental activities that are designed to heighten awareness. Often the experience is the opposite of what might be expected. So, the client could be told to do more of a symptom, rather than less; or to do the opposite of whatever was done before that wasn't working to see what happens. Doing something new brings new intensity to experience and may bring new insight.

Psychodrama: A client in a Gestalt group describes her experience, and group members act out assigned roles to reenact the client's description. The client and therapist direct the action so the scene is vividly portrayed as each actor displays a range of behaviors and feelings. The client could experiment with new ways of reacting or get in touch with the intensity of the drama. Instead of just talking about psychological issues, everyone involved is involved, actually living real experience.

Role playing: Clients may rehearse new behaviors or act in roles that depict personality polarities or parts that represent new perspectives. Role plays can resolve unfinished business or arouse awareness of unrecognized needs. The empty chair technique is where two empty seats are assigned a character, attitude, emotion, or personal quality. The client sits in one chair and gives voice to the perspective of that seat, then changes and speaks for the other chair. Such role playing intensifies experience to bring the client to a new awareness.

Hot seat: In a Gestalt group, one member may sit in specified place and do psychological work with the group leader.

Spectator learning: Those group members observing a client working with the therapist become aware of interaction and of their reactions to the experience. They may also offer comments regarding what they saw and felt.

Dream work: A Gestalt client may present a dream verbally and through dramatic reenactment. An empty chair technique may be used or other means are found to fully explicate the experience. Gaps in the scenes are explored to discover those areas that may be missing for the client. Themes or hidden meanings may be revealed.

Representative Case: Morticia Hassler

Morticia is a Black woman of 26 from an inner city located in an East coast metropolitan area. She is a graduate student attending a large midwestern university and has difficulties adjusting to the new environment. She has received feedback from professors that her speech and writing are "unprofessional" and she may lose her graduate assistantship given the poor quality of her work and her inability to complete assignments. Discouraged, she laments the loss of her original motivation to gain the expertise to help young people from her former neighborhood improve their situation. She admits that she has missed classes, often arriving late, and that she cannot understand some of the required readings and assignments. The only group of other young women she has been able to establish as a support system is an undergraduate sorority for minority students. The sorority activities take a great deal of time, another factor contributing to her spending too little time on her academic work and her assistantship duties. When she moved to the area she was accompanied by a partner, who now lives in an apartment with her and is not in school. He is unemployed and does not understand her time pressures or her motivation for upward mobility. They argue regularly, and Morticia finds it difficult to separate herself from his depressive inaction.

Morticia is alone in her environment without any community that reflects her particular situation. Her academic background is weak, though her former grades were high enough for her to be recruited to the university and given considerable financial assistance. Her significant social relationships add stress rather than support. As a graduate student she is required to understand expectations. Yet she needs more explicit directions than have been forthcoming, if she is to have any chance of approaching the standards she will be judged by. In her experience she has received mixed messages from the recruiting promises and the criticisms of her supervisors and instructors.

Thinking About Morticia

1. How would the psychotherapist conceptualize Morticia's situation from a Gestalt therapy perspective?

2. What Gestalt therapy techniques would be useful to help Morticia change?

3. Do you have an opinion regarding Morticia's academic preparedness and her participation in a sorority? How would your opinions affect your work as a counselor?

4. What impact does Morticia's partner have on her ability to meet demands? How can counseling help Morticia deal with the relationship?

5. Is it appropriate for the counselor to consult with Morticia's professors and supervisors?

Check Your Thinking About Morticia

1. Morticia's contact with her environment is disturbed. Her previous experiences have not prepared her for interacting with others who give her feedback. She is protecting herself through avoidance by lateness and neglecting her responsibility to ask for explanations for what she does not understand. She has polarized the interactions she has had with different professionals at the university—the admissions recruiters and her professors. She is also projecting her own confusion onto others by using the term "mixed messages" without considering her part in the communication failures. She is deflecting her awareness of her failure to achieve in her new environment and uses her original motivation as a means to justify her actions rather than considering the real problems that are blocking her. She has likely been at a phobic layer of awareness and may have moved to an impasse layer. She needs to gain enough self-discovery to move her self-awareness to an accommodation level.

2. Morticia could benefit by a full exploration of her real feelings. Her body language no doubt reveals the avoidance she is manifesting in her life. Role-playing her sense of how she feels when in the presence of her professors and her view of how professors experience her could be helpful. An empty chair enactment of Morticia before and after she came to the Midwest might be appropriate, as might another improvisation of the divisions Morticia might feel. Psychodrama and group work might be particularly effective with Morticia, particularly if other students could demonstrate an awareness of her experience.

3. Morticia had completed an undergraduate degree but had not learned the critical thinking and writing skills suitable to graduate school standards. Recruiting her, based on her previous grades was appropriate, and expecting her to perform according to established standards is also appropriate. The sorority is an unfortunate choice for a graduate student who needs to devote time to academics, but it is understandable that Morticia sought out a support group in an environment with few people of her race and cultural background. Morticia's experience is the focus of counseling, and opinions regarding her performance and social group are not relevant, though offering Morticia feedback regarding what she can expect might be.

4. Morticia's partner allows her to maintain a connection to her previous environment, but his view of the future seems at odds with hers. Within this conflict Morticia demonstrates confluence. His depression may connect to her own denied depression, but she clearly becomes unable to separate his feelings from her own.

5. Contacting Morticia's professors would be out of keeping with supporting her self-responsibility. The counselor can assist Morticia in determining how to approach them herself.

Core Case: Marianna Chavez

Marianna is also described in the Chapters 1 and 8 for Behavioral Approaches. Here the case is conceptualized from a Gestalt therapy perspective. The format follows the standard DAP layout in which **D** designates **Data**, **A** designates **Assessment**, and **P** designates **Plan**.

D: The client is a 22-year-old refugee from Colombia. She and her mother escaped their home country and fled to Costa Rica when she was three and came to the United States several years later. She is attractive and lively in her conversation, and she is a well informed, enthusiastic activist for social causes and diversity on campus. When Marianna is calm and less animated, however, her facial expression looks strained. She has a high grade point average and is majoring in economics. Recently, she has been experiencing flashbacks of warlike scenes, of her own brutal rape and of watching her mother being physically abused and raped. She cries, saying there are days when she cannot leave her room.

Marianna's flashbacks began several months ago when she tried to date or to dance with men. Whenever she is sensually aroused or there is any hint of sexuality, she becomes numb and cannot focus her attention. Her appetite has decreased; she has trouble getting to sleep, and when she does her sleep is troubled, fearing flashback memories will be in her dreams. She has tried to talk to her mother, but the mother remains stoic, saying she cannot discuss the past and they must move on. Although the client understands her mother's abusive experiences are also painful, she longs for mutual support that is not forthcoming.

The client also reports an aversion to gold. During her escape, she wore many pieces of jewelry under her clothing. Her mother is now an importer, selling jewelry wholesale. In high school Marianna served as a model for merchandise showings until severe body rashes made it necessary for her to stop. The medical diagnosis assumed allergic reactions, but now she feels dizzy at the sight of any jewelry with the look of gold, even when it is another person wearing the piece.

Marianna's father was a drug dealer who was killed by Colombian government soldiers advised by American special forces. Her parents separated when she was one because her maternal grandparents disapproved of her father's illegal activities. She and her mother lived on the grandparents' estate for two years until the wealthy landowners, associated with government leaders, were killed by the drug cartel. Marianna is tearful when she talks about her father and sobs when she tells of her grandparents' deaths. Another flashback is a scene where men arrive at her home with guns and drag her grandparents away.

The two coping mechanisms that offer Marianna some relief are journaling and drawing. Her roommate discovered some drawings and became upset with their violent content, so the client hides her work and is careful to draw only when her roommate is absent. The client has been to the campus health services complaining of fatigue and stomach cramps, but after extensive tests no medical condition has been diagnosed.

A: Marianna has lost contact with her true self, showing a social persona of animation and activism for social causes. She is attempting to forestall fully dealing with her childhood trauma by pushing memories out of consciousness. She cowers from the flashbacks that signal it is time to reexperience traumatic scenes and avoids her life further by confining herself in her room. One attempt to face her trauma is trying to discuss her shared experiences with her mother, who is even more closed off from her own experiencing. Another attempt to face her trauma is her journaling and drawings, symbolic efforts and maybe truly self-expressive. Another factor that points to the need to integrate the trauma is her stage of adolescent development, where she faces the task of opening up to her sensuality. Finally, there are the psychosomatic symptoms in reaction to gold, which symbolizes her escape from her grandparents' estate and her childhood home.

Marianna's facial expressions evoke a childlike appeal while her body language suggests a growing awareness of the seductiveness of a woman. She holds onto an image of helplessness and that of being a victim. To face her trauma would be to show the courage of growing up and taking responsibility for her budding sexuality as well as dealing with the horrific memories from her past. She has reached an impasse and is stuck betwixt and between. She retains images of men as dangerous and recoils at the sound of loud male voices even when heard as rock music. She can describe the horrors of poverty as well as war, demonizing the U.S. government as if the political leaders were villains in a tragedy and she was the innocent hero. Her passionate appeals at social protest meetings can sound strident in inappropriate ways.

Although Marianna speaks words of affection regarding her grandparents, her voice does not sound warm and loving; it sounds cold. She admits she works hard to prevent full memories of the happy times with her grandparents for fear of summoning up the fearful scenes of their death. Marianna needs to gain the full range of her voice with the nuances her emotions lack. She can cover her coldness with intellectual words and she demonstrates an incisive thinking process, but her words and tone are limited to the safe areas she has chosen, not true self-expression.

P: There are any number of techniques to encourage self-awareness. Her voice tone and language can be pointed to as lacking credible self-expression and personal responsibility. Telling her what the flat voice is really saying or having her own her articulation by saying, "I choose" or "I won't" might be a start. Certainly drawing attention to her body language would begin to peel away the layers covering her real self. She could act out how her memories feel as she avoids them or she could play the voice of her memories telling her why they are pressing to come out. Marianna could do an improvisation of a generic man and how he responds to her recoiling, or she could dramatize the dangerous man and feel his power. Her drawings need to be encouraged. She could bring her pictures to sessions and give voices to the depictions. Ultimately she needs to face the role of victim she depicts. Possibly empty chairs could seat her child self in one and her woman adult in another chair, and they could converse back and forth. A group enacting her actual memories might be effective with Marianna directing. Her experience of being in charge of the action could help her see the scene as a part of her but under her control. An alter ego might follow her around during the enactment and could speak up with an honest voice saying how she feels. She could be instructed to give a voice to the strength she feels inside as she directs and designs the ending. The counselor would have these and other techniques in mind but would create the actual intervention in the moment in response to Marianna's impact in the relationship. Marianna would be encouraged to fully express her experience in the moment to deepen her awareness.

Finding a Balance

Most counselors choose several counseling approaches that suit their personalities and theoretical preferences. In this section, the counselor personality characteristics are identified and tied to concepts and practices. Then a case is described. Then, another section shows how the counselor's preferences would play out in working with the case. Finally, a comparison is made showing how other approaches with different preferences might deal with the case. Integrating several approaches might cover varying counselor preferences and differing client issues better than any singular approach.

Key Counselor Preferences

1. Gestalt therapists value the connection with the client and believe that intensifying the contact between human beings is more curative than interpretations.

2. Gestalt therapists enjoy mind-body exercises and usually are aware of their own bodies as well as the nonverbal signals they see clients display.

3. Gestalt therapists often enjoy dramatic role plays and psychological enactments and usually do not shy away from confrontations and pressing the client to maximum emotion. Here and now awareness is considered vital to a satisfying life and usually Gestaltists express this value in their own lives.

4. Gestalt therapists often have exquisite timing and intuitively know when to introduce techniques, how to phrase simple, clear instructions, and when to press emotions to full expression.

5. Gestalt therapists can be impatient with client's own psychological interpretations and other conceptually based explanations for feelings and behavior. Theoretical conceptions

detract from here and now experience from a Gestalt's point of view. Instead, a tone is set for full client self-responsibility in the present time, regardless of past experiences.

Case Example: Sam Tanglewood

Sam is a 30-something White male who recently moved to a small town outside a metropolitan area in western United States. He is starting his first professional job after completing graduate school. He is unmarried and knew no one in the area before he moved. He appears confident, articulate, and reasonably attractive. Recently a colleague of his called the counseling agency to report that Sam had threatened suicide and had said he would kill the colleague's children. Sam refused to come to the counseling center unless his colleague, Tom, would come with him. Tom agreed and both came into the session.

The two told about their friendship. They work together and Sam spends much time with Tom's family, a wife and two young children. Sam baby-sits regularly. Tom and Sam play racquetball daily and speak on the phone every evening. Tom's wife has been complaining that Sam has been spending too much time with the family and that his intrusions are affecting the marriage. Tom told Sam that they would have to limit their contact to work and racquetball twice a week. Tom was exceedingly patient explaining the situation, saying he valued the friendship, but he had to respect his wife's wishes. Sam was distraught and very excited. He interrupted Tom's explanation and began accusing the wife of trying to control everyone, and Tom as refusing to stand up to her. Tom patiently listened and returned to his message that some restraints on their relationship were needed. The counselor thanked Tom and said that he would see Sam alone, saying if Tom wanted further counseling, arrangements could be made for him to see another therapist.

In individual counseling Sam was confronted with the manipulative quality of his suicidal/homicidal gesture. A no harm contract was written and Sam was scheduled for another appointment.

In the next appointment Sam described his family. He said he had resisted his mother's objections to his friendship with Tom. Sam's parents were divorced and both have been treated for alcoholism. Sam and his older brother (1 year older) and sister (3 years older) were placed in foster care for two years when Sam was 10. Mother regained custody after treatment. Mother and father still see each other regularly and if both drink, they have loud arguments and physical fights. Sam described himself as his mother's protector, helping her when she passed out, and calling the police when "things got too rough." Moving to a new area limited his interactions with his mother to several phone calls a day. When his mother is sober, she is anxiously aware of everything in Sam's life, and even though they now live some distance apart, she becomes upset when she doesn't know where he is. Sam's siblings have left home and their whereabouts are unknown. Sam wavered between resenting the pressure his mother brought to his life and feeling overly responsible for her.

Sam cried when he considered the fact that he would no longer be a part of Tom's family life. The relative calm of his friend's life had been a respite he had never known before. He could see that he had made demands on Tom that were similar to his mother's excessiveness. Yet he felt he needed something that would counter the pressure his mother caused.

The Gestalt counselor first addressed boundary issues. Tom faced an open chair and described his mother as though she were sitting there. The counselor then sat in the chair and spoke to Sam as if the counselor was the Mother, "Where have you been?" Do you know how long I have been calling?" "What did you do today?" "Have you seen that Tom guy?" Sam was encouraged to tell his mother what he felt as he was bombarded with questions and expected to account for all of his time. The counselor, playing Mom, overrode all of Sam's statements and continued to implode the conversation. Finally, Sam put both arms over his face and curled his hands over the back of his head, shutting out his view of his "mother" and said nothing. The counselor changed chairs and gently asked the "curled-up-Sam" to talk. Sam cried, saying he couldn't listen to his mother anymore and he wished he could escape her. As he was encouraged to stay with the feeling, he cried, saying he was afraid and all alone. He was overwhelmed by his mother's demands, but he was afraid to be without anyone. Sam came to realize his mother's voice, always in his consciousness, trapped him with her needs and her unreasonable expectations.

Therapy continued over time using various experiences to develop Sam's strong voice that could set limits for Mom rather than be silenced into "curled-up-Sam." He learned to say, "I have decided not to confront my mother" rather than "I am not able to," "I choose not to leave her" rather than " I can't," and even "I want to have my mother in my life" instead of "I have to." Finally, he was able to say to his mother that he cared about her, but he could not be responsible for her, and he would not be responsive to her when she demanded too much. He limited her calls to once or twice a week, only in the evenings, and only as long as conversations were respectful. He would not account for his time but learned to say, "I have this time for you."

Sam participated in a group where he enacted a number of psychodramas dealing with his polarized views of himself. The most prevalent polarity was his responsible self versus his worthless self. He received much support from group members and was able to reciprocate with sensitivity to the strains others described. As he separated from his mother's demands, he began to feel free to spend time in new pursuits, further developing the new Sam. The counselor encouraged Sam to imagine a new life filled with his own interests. Sam created a fantasy of an amusement park filled with new rides and seemingly risky experiences; but actually, the new experiences could be lots of fun. He and other group members created enactments that included pairs twirling one another around as fast as they could, imagining the roller coaster climbing high and speeding downward, and other physical "rides." As each person described the sensations they felt, they described excitement, fear, and joy. Sam felt ready to leave counseling after he introduced his fantasy to the group. He said he now saw his feelings as normal, and he knew how to make his own choices for how he wanted to live his life.

Applying Counselor Preferences

Using the previously listed psychodynamic preferences, how did the therapist manage therapy with Sam Tanglewood?

1. A Gestalt therapist would enjoy working with Sam because he presented very emotional relationships, both with Tom and with his mother. Capitalizing on the drama, the therapist could quickly identify boundary issues and the pull of polarities where Sam felt both a desperate need to connect to others and a need for self-consolidation.

2. The Gestalt therapist would appreciate Sam's enactment of his feeling with a curled-up position. The body position nicely creates an image that depicts how Sam feels internally. Rather than only labeling the curled-up position, the Gestalt counselor encouraged Sam to verbalize the experience of tightly drawing in his body. The intervention worked well in identifying Sam's sense of feeling overwhelmed and his difficulty with an intrusive mother.

3. The counselor did not shy away from immediately confronting Sam with the suicidal manipulation gesture. Using the Gestalt open chair technique to dramatize Sam's conflict with his mother allowed the counselor to use his theatrical flair as well as serving to intensify Sam's here-and-now experience. The Gestalt counselor also appreciates Sam's image of the roller coaster ride in group. Serving as a behind-the-scenes director for psychological enactments is a Gestalt skill.

4. The use of experiential techniques and the skill of timing interventions is a well developed talent for Sam's Gestalt therapist. The counselor provided emotional releases through role plays and the like, helping Sam gain full here and now experience. The therapist was

encouraging Sam to own his direct experience and to develop a full sense of self. With clearer boundaries and greater identity development, Sam was ready for the counselor's direction to use a strong voice to set limits for the mother.

5. The Gestalt therapist did not demonstrate a preference for conceptual explanations. Although the concepts of boundaries and polarities are seen in the case description, the counselor emphasized experiential interventions rather than psychoeducational explanations.

Comparison with Other Approaches

Psychodynamic: Interpretations regarding Sam's relationship with his mother would be considered primary. The reliving of the dysfunctional interactions would occur through the transference relations. An Adlerian approach would also examine the lifestyle established in childhood. Individual psychology would be critical of Perls's omissions of a social interest point of view.

Person-Centered: Encouraging the expression of feeling would occur through the dialogue between the therapist and the client without the dramatic enactments. Here-and-now emphasis is shared with the Gestalt approach. Adding Gestalt techniques, such as the open chair exercise, is compatible with the Person-Centered approach.

Behavioral/Cognitive-Behavioral: Feelings associated with behavioral patterns are considered but not intensified as with the Gestalt approach. Learning patterns are seen as the basis for behavior, and changing the problematic behaviors occurs through establishing new learning. For example, a behaviorist might change Sam's phone call behavior through a stimulus control/contingency management plan. A counselor using a cognitive approach might help Sam reframe his thoughts in reaction to his mother's behaviors in addition to changing his own actions.

Existential and Transpersonal: The Gestalt approach places the person as the valuing base without much reference to spirituality, although some Gestalt practitioners make references to humans as beings in the universe. Existentialists are more tied to philosophy than the Gestalt approach, though both approaches emphasize self-responsibility. Sam's overattachment to his mother might be interpreted as his means of escaping his own responsibility for creating meaning in his life.

Example of a Published Researched Article, a Gestalt Program Report

This article describes a psychoeducational program using the Gestalt counseling approach. The commentary in the boxes to the left of the article will help you understand the research and the format of the piece.

This article is a program report rather than an empirical study. The focus is on a complex experience in a natural setting, an already existing day-care center. The results are reported in a narrative rather than through quantitative analysis of scores on standard measures.

Staff Training for a Day-Care Center*

Katherine Ennis and Sandra Mitchell

*So shall we
sit upon our lovely hands?
Or shall we reach
and touch, and speak across
the long fields?*

E.I. VanBuren

We believe that a good day-care center is alive; that it vibrates with noise, feelings, and curiosity; that it offers an opportunity for growth and learning; and that it enriches the lives of the children who attend and of the adults who care for them. Unlike a kindergarten or a nursery school, which operate for a few hours in the morning and/or afternoon, our center is open from 7:00 A.M. until 12:00 midnight, seven days a week, and each child is with us about nine hours a day. We believe that much that happens with that child during those nine hours is directly related to the growing edge of the adults who care for him and to the relationships between those adults.

After establishing why adults' growth and relationships are important to the children they care for, the authors list the problems they saw in their day-care center. Most psychoeducational programs in institutions seek to solve existing problems.

About a year ago, as we looked at the relationship between ourselves and other staff members and at the way they were relating with each other and with the children, we saw much behavior that, if not actually destructive, certainly was not growth facilitating. We saw our difficulties in accepting the limitations of staff members and our reluctance in expressing anger toward them. We saw them sulking when their feelings were hurt, gossiping about each other, displacing their angry feelings onto the children, and competing for the children's affection. In many instances, we were all relating with the children and with each other from

---

Reprinted with permission of Science and Behavior Books, Inc.

* The St. Joseph Infirmary Day-Care Center provides care for the children of women employees of the hospital. The Center is licensed by the Georgia Department of Family and Children Services to care for fifty children during each of two hospital shifts. The children range in age from six weeks to six years. The staff is composed of a director, a program director, twelve teachers, and a housekeeping aide.

introjected *shoulds* rather than from a realistic acceptance of ourselves or the children.

As the directors, we felt frustrated. We had tried involving the rest of the staff in program planning for the children and in decisions about equipment purchases for their rooms. We had encouraged them to take additional day-care vocational courses to increase their understanding of children's growth and development, and we had made specific reading requirements in areas where we felt they needed more knowledge. We had observed their growth in many ways, but the area which we felt was most important—that of relationships—seemed relatively unchanged.

We had to accept the fact that "learning" was not going to solve our communications problems. The clue seemed to lie in staff members' having the opportunity to experience the kind of open, honest communication that we had seen occur in Gestalt groups and in Art and Movement Workshops devoted primarily to nonverbal communications process. Our staff members have varied cultural, educational, and experiential backgrounds, and we realized that the help of a professional therapist was needed to provide opportunities to effect significant changes in our interactions as a staff. We realized also that each staff member would have to recognize a need for better communication, be willing to risk change, and understand the importance of professional help to facilitate that changing. We told them our concern about the center and the kinds of behavior we saw. We also shared with them our excitement about the growth that had occurred with us individually and in our relationship with each other as a result of our experiences with direct verbal and nonverbal communication in Gestalt workshops. We let them know of our belief that similar experiences with them might improve and clarify our relationships as a staff. We acknowledged our limitations—the relative newness of our own growth and our lack of experience in leading a group—and explained our need for professional help. We found that they shared many of our dissatisfactions, felt the need for change, and were willing to try working with a consultant. Following this meeting, we asked the hospital administration for financial assistance to help us secure the services of a psychologist for consultation. Our request for six visits was made with the understanding that the administration would pay approximately two-thirds of the consultant's fee, and that we, as a staff, would pay approximately one-third.

Our experiences with the rest of the staff in the above decision-making process had brought us all closer together. We had been honest with them about our concern for the center and about our helplessness in making any change without their involvement. We felt they had responded honestly and were willing to take some new interpersonal risks. Since we knew that it would take time to implement our request for funds, we asked ourselves how we could encourage

---

Previous efforts to solve the problems are reviewed. The authors suggest that these efforts did not focus on the crucial area of relationships.

Notice that the psychologist in this setting is labeled a *consultant*. This label avoids the stigma attached to psychological treatment.

Principles of Gestalt psychology are meant to be used outside of the therapy session. These authors began to use Gestalt ways of speaking and thinking before the formal program began.

more of the openness we had just experienced with them. The experiences we had assimilated during and as a result of the Gestalt groups we had attended provided the answer.

We shared a belief in the tenets of Gestalt therapy and the conviction that these tenets were not confined to the therapeutic encounter. We began slowly to try some of the techniques that seemed especially relevant to us. In staff meetings, in individual conferences, and in our daily encounters, we struggled to come across straight with them and encouraged them to do the same with us, with each other, and with the children. As we met with them, we tried to "stay in the here and now" and began to try the "How do you feel?" and "What's going on now?" kinds of questions instead of "What do you think?" or "Why?" We did not introduce any of the nonverbal art and movement techniques at this time because we were not sure we could handle the depth of feeling they might evoke. We continued working on our relationship with each other and took advantage of every workshop, marathon, institute, short course, and lecture that was offered to enrich our individual growth. We were striving for congruence in our own lives, and we wanted to have the kind of center that would nourish in others the capacity to experience intellectually, emotionally, and sensorially.

In the months that followed, we found that our Gestalt-oriented approach did break down some of the communications barriers we had been experiencing with the rest of the staff. They were being more honest, but they still had trouble expressing many of their feelings directly, and we, although somewhat more free, were not as honest or as spontaneous with them as we wanted to be. Frequently, we could see some of the projections and defensive maneuvers that were going on, but we did not have the knowledge or experience to help them or ourselves solve these deeper conflicts. We felt keenly our need for professional guidance and were anxious for the administrative *yes* that would make it possible.

> In terms like "projections" and "defensive maneuvers," you can see Gestalt's roots in psychoanalytic theory.

The excitement we all felt when we finally received approval for a consultant was accompanied by a sense of relief. The therapist chosen was a clinical psychologist who was essentially existential in his therapeutic orientation. He had evolved his own style of therapy and moved comfortably between the approaches of Gestalt therapy, transactional analysis, and theme-centered therapy. He had worked with children, adults, families, and groups—and in addition, he had some experience as a consultant for a day-care center.

On the day of our first session, all of us were excited and/or scared. Our consultant began by making a "contract" with each of us for the first meeting. These contracts involved our stating one thing that we wanted from that meeting for ourselves (for example, better understanding of a co-worker, the opportunity to deal with unresolved conflicts and/or unexpressed feelings) and his agreeing to help us get

> Awareness of needs is essential to Gestalt therapy. The acknowledgment of something each member of the group wanted for himself or herself was a step toward awareness of unfulfilled or cut-off needs.

it. "Getting something for ourselves" remained the theme of our first six sessions. We now had a time when we could explore the feelings that made us uncomfortable, clarify our communications, and risk new ways of relating. Our consultant gave us his support and knowledge as we struggled to express our anger, hurt, tenderness, and love. He also had the courage to shatter our fantasies and to confront us with our manipulations and projections. We discovered that growth is sometimes painful, sometimes joyful, and always rewarding.

Our sixth session was devoted to saying good-by to our experiences with each other during the past five sessions and deciding whether we would continue meeting. Saying "good-by" made us aware of how much we had gotten for ourselves. It also made us aware that we wanted more of these experiences together. We knew that we would have to submit an evaluation of these sessions to the hospital administration along with a request for additional funds if we were to continue meeting. However, we did not want to stop meeting while our request was being processed, so we decided to pay the entire fee ourselves until we received a reply from the administration or until we decided we wanted to stop.

We met three times over a period of six weeks before our request for twelve additional sessions was granted. After our request was approved, we proceeded in basically the same manner as in our initial meetings. We continued our confrontations with each other—we examined experientially our modes of relating and the defenses we used to keep from relating. There were times when a seeming lack of involvement during our meetings led us to question the value of our continuing. Simply raising the question seemed to help us reevaluate what we did want. It also made us aware that we were taking risks with each other daily that in the beginning we could take only in the safety of the sessions. Each time we questioned the value of our meetings, we decided to continue.

At approximately the same time that our consultant started coming to the center, we began leading the teachers in the art-and-movement experiences we had been reluctant to risk without the support of a therapist. These once-a-week sessions were designed to help them "lose their minds and come to their senses." They had opportunities to become more aware of their bodies by localizing sensations in the various parts and by becoming more aware of breathing, muscular tensions, and posture. Touching, lifting, and holding provided opportunities to experience interacting with each other on a bodily level. Blindfold walks allowed them to examine their ability to trust each other and to experience their other senses. The directed fantasies of creative-imagery games helped them to restore the balance between imagination and reality. They used various art media, such as clay, chalk, and paint, to explore and communicate their feelings in an unstructured manner. At the completion of each of these experiences, we encouraged them to talk about what they had

---

Gestaltists believe that the mind versus body polarity is one of the most misleading. The body encodes messages about one's psychological state.

Creative expression is a cornerstone of Gestalt therapy. A person's self concept evolves as a result of experiential learning (as opposed to intellectual learning).

been aware of during the experience and what they were aware of then.

At the time of writing, we have met with our consultant for ten of our twelve sessions, and we have continued leading the art-and-movement experiences. We have found that our verbal group encounters and the art-and-movement experiences are complementary. Used together, they have facilitated our growth as a staff more effectively than either experience would have if used alone. The following comments from the other staff members support our perceptions of the growth that is occurring:

> This type of program report frequently includes quotations from participants, whereas empirical research reports rarely include such data.

I feel very good about myself ... I feel that I am human ... I feel more alive.

I have a great struggle in saying what's on my mind ... I want to tell a person off so bad I cry on the inside ... with [the consultant's] help, I have learned to deal with this much better ... the center is now a place I am proud of ... When I watch some of the older children that were once infants which I [cared for], I find that I am very pleased with myself.

I had difficulty showing my true feelings with [the rest of the staff].... Especially angry feelings and tenderness.... After only two of the sessions, I was beginning to express my true feelings.... We began to work more as a team.... [As a result of the art-and-movement sessions] I became very aware of my body and senses, and the bodies and senses of my fellow staff members. They suddenly came alive for me— three-dimensional, flesh-and-blood human beings—people with whom I could laugh, love, argue, and cry.... I began to burst the bonds which made me a prisoner within myself.... I have begun to find new ways of doing things.

Children are children and not adults and that they should be treated with all the understanding and kindness that one has ... I wish that everyone could see and feel what we are doing.

[The consultant] has helped me to understand myself ... I feel better about the center and about myself.

I feel that I belong here.

I feel his continued services will mean a great deal to the staff.

We have made gains in many other areas. As we look at the relationships in the center now, we are aware that we are all being more direct. We hear these questions: "How do you feel about that?" "What's happening?" "What do you mean?" or we hear: "That makes me mad." "If you want something from me, ask me directly. I can't read your mind." "I like you." "I

Results are reported in a summary of experimenters' perceptions of changes they attribute to the Gestalt program.

appreciate your saying that to me." We are all more openly affectionate with each other and with the children. We see the teachers encouraging the children to be aware of their bodies by calling attention to their breathing, or the way they are sitting, or how their skin feels. We see them helping the children to become aware of their feelings by acknowledging their anger, hurt, loneliness, or joy. We see them encouraging the children's creativity by providing unstructured art experiences, by listening to them attentively, and by valuing them as unique individuals. We have moved somewhat closer to our goal of having a center that will nourish in the children who come and in the adults who are there for them the capacity to experience and develop their intellectual, emotional, and sensory capacities.

Discussion Ideas

1. What words or phrases in the article reflect essential concepts and key terms of Gestalt therapy?

2. The experimenters in this study are also participants in the program they report on. Does this make a difference in the way you interpret the article?

3. The experimenters were directors of the day-care center, while the other participants were staff members, and the two groups are referred to as "we" and "they" early in the article. What problems lie in a Gestalt intervention that involves two such groups?

4. List five differences you perceive between this program report and an empirical research report. What are the advantages and disadvantages of the program report?

5. Name one or two ways that the Gestalt intervention for day-care center personnel could have been tested in a more empirical manner.

6. Have you been in any work situations that would benefit from the Gestalt program described in this report? What benefits do you think would be derived from such a program?

Answer Key for Practice Test Questions

True/False

1. F
2. F
3. F
4. T
5. F
6. F
7. T
8. T
9. T
10. F

Multiple Choice

1. e
2. a
3. b
4. d
5. e
6. b
7. b
8. d
9. d
10. b
11. c
12. d
13. e
14. b
15. d

CHAPTER 8

Behavioral Therapies

Chapter Review

Behavioral therapies are based on learning theory and empirical research rather than personality theory and abstract views of underlying human motivations. Behavioral counselors translate scientific findings into modes for helping clients change. Such methods allow clients to improve their lives by establishing desired behaviors, getting rid of bad habits, and by dealing with major negative behaviors such as alcoholism. The focus for behavioral treatments is not global personality change but specific behaviors that interfere with life functioning.

B. F. Skinner translated the learning experiments from laboratory trials with animals to human behaviors. He defined stimulus as a distinct condition, either internal, such as hunger, or external, such as cold air, and he defined a response as what observable behavior the person does. Skinner defined reinforcers as stimuli that increased the frequency of behaviors and punishment as stimuli that decreased the frequency of responses.

Dollard and Miller described counterconditioning, when original associations are unlearned by changing conditions. For example, a fear of snakes can be countered by pleasant experiences with snakes. Learning is also generalized, when similar stimuli become associated with the same response. Discrimination in learning occurs when stimuli become more distinct and responses more specific to certain stimuli. Dollard and Miller also redefined the psychoanalytic term *repression* as an avoidance response, when thoughts are so aversive they are expelled from consciousness.

Wolpe developed a technique called *reciprocal inhibition* that is widely used in behavioral therapy. To change a response the client learns a new response that contradicts an undesirable response. Then the client uses the new response to approach the conditions that originally produced the negative reaction. Examples are relaxation or assertiveness responses that are practiced in response to threatening cues associated with anxiety.

Mary Cover Jones developed another behavioral technique using the social learning concept of modeling. A client, Peter, was afraid of furry things, and his treatment included watching other children having fun playing with rabbits. The models provided by other children experiencing no harm helped Peter overcome his fears and enabled him to learn to deal with rabbits. Bandura's description of social learning included internal thoughts as responsive to the application of learning methods. Behavior therapies may apply learning techniques to the client's natural circumstances, by enlisting the cooperation of others to change conditions, or by planning reinforcements for the targeted behavior.

Behaviorists insist on defining client concerns as observable, measurable, and testable through research. Such characteristics can be defined in clinical manuals that describe symptoms and appropriate clinical treatments. Some therapists object to the manualization of counseling, saying such procedures limit the breadth and depth of the psychological work.

Behavioral counselors do use core conditions, as outlined by Rogers, to create a warm relationship so clients gain trust in the process and a willingness to participate in the treatment. With a warm relationship established, the counselor becomes a consultant that collaborates with the client to set clear goals and to define target behaviors for change. Assessing current behavior and determining effective rewards can take considerable time and effort for positive results. It must be ascertained when and how frequently the targeted behavior occurs. The preconditions, post conditions, associated thoughts, feelings, and previous attempts for change must be defined. Prochaska and Norcross categorized behavioral goals: an excess of the behavior, a deficit in performing the behavior, or inappropriateness of behavior in the circumstances. To assist assessment efforts, clients are often required to record behaviors, to imagine targeted behaviors for a detailed rendering, to take inventories or questionnaires defining behavior. However, the very act of completing assessment records could change the client's behavior, and counselors need to take into account such reactivity to measurement. Evaluating reinforcements is important, too. It has been found that rewards that are unrelated to the reinforced task may not increase the frequency of the task behavior since the job is done only for the external reward, and there is no reinforcement through the intrinsic enjoyment of completing the task or the natural consequences of completing it.

Once a full assessment is accomplished, behavioral counselors apply techniques designed to change behavior. Acting as psychoeducational teachers, counselors could use contingency methods by making rewards contingent upon the appropriate behavior, using operant conditioning procedures. A behaviorist could recommend to parents or teachers a technique called *shaping* where a child is rewarded for behaviors that approach the desired behavior. Or, differential reinforcement could be applied when clients are rewarded for alternative behaviors. Rewards could be defined as the reactions gained for behaviors, so it could be recommended that reaction rewards are withdrawn as in extinction trials in a laboratory.

To reinforce client change, counselors may introduce self-management techniques including: public commitment, stimulus control, and positive reinforcement. Systematic desensitization uses reciprocal inhibition techniques by gradually pairing items in an anxiety hierarchy with progressive relaxation. Assertiveness training is used to help clients change social interactions. Behavioral techniques fit well with brief treatment models since changes can be created in shorter periods of time than those therapies that emphasize overall personality change. The very nature of behavioral therapy is an active approach where clients participate both in choosing what to change and in the activities that create change.

For some behavioral change, punishments for behavior may be included in treatments. Recalling Skinner's definition of *punishment* as methods that decrease the frequency of behavior, aversive methods require controlled conditions to meet the purpose of limiting behavior without inducing unintended side effects. Punishment must be immediate so the negative consequence is directly connected to the undesired behavior. Punishment has to be intense enough to be meaningful but not so overwhelming that the punishment outweighs the behavior. Punishment must be consistent, calmly delivered, and should be accompanied by reinforcers for alternative behaviors. Imaginal techniques utilize the client's picturing appropriate behaviors, whereas *in vivo* techniques involve exposure to actual conditions—either gradually or by flooding. In flooding the client is exposed to intense conditions from which there is no escape, teaching the client that major consequences he fears do not occur. Aversion methods could increase the response cost to undesired behaviors, as when Anabuse is taken to create major physical distress if alcohol is consumed. Implosion methods intensify the aversion experience with fearful symbols related to aggression or sex.

Social learning concepts such as modeling can be used by behavioral therapists to facilitate client's imagining (covert modeling) an admired figure or by using other clients more well-versed in a behavior to serve as participant models. Group counseling is an application of social learning where clients learn from each other. Couples can alter small behaviors to demonstrate commitment to each other. Token economies are used in milieu treatments to reward some behaviors, to fine other behaviors, and to pay for privileges.

Evaluation of treatment throughout a counseling sequence can test client progress in changing behavior and can determine the effectiveness of rewards. Termination sessions also include reviewing methods to prevent relapses or a return to old behavioral patterns. Booster sessions are offered in which clients return to review previous treatment learning and report how maintenance of behavioral change is going.

Critics of behavioral methods express concern that counselors could enforce socially acceptable behaviors, reducing the client's freedom of choice. Behaviorist counselors would emphasize their practice of encouraging clients to choose what behaviors they want to change using the counselor's expertise. Some clients, like the severely mentally ill, are unable to articulate what behaviors they want, and to them the counselor's choice of treatment leads to improved functioning and relief from distress.

Practice Test Questions

True or False: Consider each statement and try to explain in your own mind why it might not be fully true. Be sure to take into account any qualifying factors that might make the statement untrue. If you decide that the statement is fully true, circle **T**. Otherwise, circle **F**.

T F   1. It is always vitally important in behavioral therapy to explore the clients' childhood.

T F   2. Behaviorists consider the relationship with the client as irrelevant to the effectiveness of therapy.

T F   3. The counselor determines the goals for behavioral therapy.

T F   4. Behaviorists are active in counseling, directing the course of treatment.

T F   5. Assessment in behavioral therapy includes an extensive examination of conditions and behaviors associated with the client's presenting problem.

T F   6. Manuals describing treatments for specific problems are not considered valid for use by professional behaviorists.

T F   7. Social learning theory is intended to describe how to organize a successful celebratory function.

T F   8. Behaviorists believe emotional insight is important for clients to change their lives.

T F   9. The client in behavioral therapy is expected to remain in the mode of a student who listens to instructions.

T F 10. Behavioral therapy is characterized as a phenomenological approach.

Multiple Choice: Circle the one letter next to the best answer to the following questions or to complete the sentence stems.

1. Which of the following did Skinner suggest as a way to encourage writing behavior?
    a. Start writing for a short time and don't demand quality standards at first.
    b. A regime of healthy diet, rest, and exercise is considered a lower priority than writing.
    c. Write whenever, ignoring a consistent schedule.
    d. Arrange a writing area that can be cluttered with writing materials.
    e. Collect experiences by carrying a notebook and taking regular notes.
    f. a and e

2. *Classical conditioning* can be characterized as a
   a. stimulus, or a condition, that is paired with a response, or what a person does.
   b. stimulus-response pattern that can be unlearned by a process called *extinction*.
   c. stimulus, or ego pattern, that controls behavior by responding to the superego.
   d. a and b
   e. a and c

3. *Operant conditioning* can be characterized as
   a. manipulating conditions before a behavior is performed.
   b. providing rewards for specific behaviors.
   c. manipulating conditions after a behavior is performed.
   d. a and c
   e. b and c

4. Thorndike developed which of the following, the law of
   a. repetition.
   b. exercise.
   c. consistency.
   d. effect.
   e. b and c
   f. b and d

5. *Positive reinforcers* as defined by Skinner are
   a. anything that increases a behavior.
   b. conditions that create approval.
   c. anything that results in a positive outcome.
   d. conditions that will reoccur repeatedly.

6. *Negative reinforcers* as defined by Skinner are
   a. behavior that causes negative feedback.
   b. behavior that creates disapproval.
   c. relief from pain or distress.
   d. conditions that are catastrophic.

7. *Continuous reinforcement* versus *intermittent reinforcement* is
   a. rewarding behavior every time versus always rewarding behavior.
   b. rewarding behavior every time versus sometimes rewarding behavior.
   c. reinforcing behavior each time versus not rewarding behavior.
   d. a, and c
   e. b, and c

8. *Counterconditioning* is changing
   a. the conditions or stimuli so established behavior changes.
   b. behavior in order to change the conditions.
   c. the conditioning by following the original stimuli pattern.
   d. established behavior by changing developmental patterns.

9. Which of the following is NOT an example of client activities in behavioral therapy?
   a. describing behaviors and conditions that need change with the counselor
   b. learning concepts and methods to make changes as taught by the counselor
   c. planning the implementation of changes without the counselor present
   d. doing homework outside therapy sessions without the counselor present

10. According to Prochaska and Norcross, most behavior problems fall into what categories?
    a. too much, too little, and unsuitable
    b. difficult, easy, and appropriate
    c. excess, deficit, and inappropriate
    d. a and b
    e. a and c

11. Which of the following is a characteristic of *effective reinforcers?*
    a. Value is high enough that the client will work for the reward.
    b. The reward is individualized according to the client's preferences.
    c. The reward is related to the contingent behavior.
    d. a and b
    e. a, b, and c

12. *Aversive* methods in behavioral therapy follow certain empirically-based conditions including which of the following?
    a. Punishment is given only after a period of time has passed since the behavior occurred.
    b. Negative consequence is not too intense, just enough for the person to notice.
    c. As long as the punishment meets a standard, the meaning to the person is not important.
    d. Punishment should be given early in the course of the behavior so the behavior isn't seen as too beneficial.
    e. a and b

13. Which of the following is NOT an activity in *systematic desensitization?*
    a. The client enacts the fearful situation and cannot escape from it.
    b. The client imagines a situation that arouses the existing fear structure.
    c. The client learns progressive relaxation.
    d. The client and counselor create an anxiety hierarchy.
    e. The client imagines scenes that are progressively more anxiety provoking while relaxing.

14. *Assertiveness training* teaches clients to
    a. express annoyances and anger every time these feelings occur.
    b. share only positive feelings of caring and respect.
    c. state opinions that may differ from what others think.
    d. a and b
    e. a and c

15. Modeling is used in behavioral therapy in all the following ways EXCEPT that
    a. the counselor models the behavior for the client to observe.
    b. participant models in a group demonstrate a behavior for others.
    c. archetypal models from the collective unconscious are hypnotized.
    d. negative models of behavior are described to show the client the consequences.
    e. the client imagines a covert model so he can imitate the positive representation.

Key Terms and Essential Concepts

Learning theory: Conceptual framework for how animals and people learn through the systematic reinforcement of behavior in the presence of specific conditions.

Classical conditioning: Classical conditioning experiments demonstrated how learning occurs by repeated associations. A stimulus, such as illuminating a light, paired with a response, such as Pavlov's dogs salivating for food, established a connection between the behavior and the stimulus. After repeated trials, the dogs would salivate when they saw the light, even when food was not present. The dogs learned to salivate to the light.

Stimulus: An internal or external condition that is associated with a specific response.

Response: A definable behavior associated with specific conditions.

Discrimination: Making distinctions between different stimuli.

Generalization: A conditioned response occurs when a new stimulus that is similar to the original cue is introduced.

Counterconditioning: Reversing previous learning by changing the response set. For example, an aversive situation will no longer stimulate anxiety if the negative responses are replaced with pleasant ones.

Extinction: When a learned response occurs and the stimulus is withdrawn, eventually the behavior will cease. For example, with Pavlov's dogs, no longer ringing a bell when the dogs were fed would eliminate the dogs' salivating to the sound. The dogs no longer associated the bell's sound with eating.

Response burst: An increase in behaviors when reinforcement is withdrawn. The increase is an attempt to bring back the reinforcement, expecting that the intermittent nature of reinforcement be in play. Response bursts discontinue when it is clear the reinforcement will not reoccur.

Operant/ Instrumental conditioning: The conditions following a specific response or behavior are manipulated. Such conditioning makes the doing of the behavior instrumental in gaining the reward or reinforcement. Rewards are given only when the targeted behavior occurs. The subject does the behavior to gain the reward. The reward or reinforcer is contingent upon the response.

Law of exercise: Thorndike demonstrated the law of exercise showing the connection between the response and stimulus becomes stronger the more often the pairing of the stimulus and response sequence is repeated. For example, a person who awakens every morning at the same time to an alarm would become more likely to respond to the alarm daily. Conversely, the more often the consequence does not follow the behavior, the weaker the connection between the two. That is, the more often a person ignores the alarm, the less likely they will awaken when the alarm rings.

Law of effect: Thorndike also demonstrated the law of effect stating that the level of satisfaction determines the strength of the connection between the stimulus and response. For example, if a person enjoys conversations with a friend, seeing the friend would elicit the behavior of talking whereas if conversing with another person is annoying to the person, seeing that person might elicit less conversation. If the consequence of a particular behavior is satisfying, the connection of the behavior and the consequence is strengthened. Conversely, if the consequence is not satisfying the weaker the connection.

Reinforcement: An occurrence that increases the tendency to repeat a response.

Schedule of reinforcement: The rate and frequency with which rewards are given for specific behavior.

Intermittent reinforcement: Experimentation has shown that if the reinforcement occurs every time a behavior occurs, the person will learn the behavior quickly but will also cease the behavior quickly when the reinforcers are withdrawn. If the reinforcement is intermittent, occurring only some of the times when the behavior occurs, the learning will be slower, but giving up the behavior will also be slower. The timing and frequency of delivering rewards is called a *schedule of reinforcement.*

Positive reinforcement: Using desirable consequences or rewards to increase behaviors.

Negative reinforcement: Using undesirable consequences of not performing a behavior in order to increase the behavior. For example, a person will use his or her hearing aid when not hearing things becomes bothersome enough.

Punishment: Negative consequences applied to reduce the frequency of response.

Immediate consequences: Punishment or reward that follows a behavior directly after the action is formed is more effective because the connection between the behavior and the resulting consequence is obvious to the learner. For punishment, immediacy is particularly important because the side effects of aversive penalties, such as discouragement, risk teaching unwanted lessons.

Contingency management: Manipulating the circumstances (stimuli) before a behavior or the responses (consequences) after a behavior.

Stimulus control: Managing the conditions that encourage the desired behavior. Manipulating the situation that precedes the behavior can make the conditions more conducive for the behavior to occur.

Shaping: Rewarding behaviors that approach the desired behavior in successive approximations. Used to develop behaviors that would not occur naturally, such as teaching children self-control.

Successive approximation: Part of shaping: rewarding any behavior that is in the direction of the desired response. Then rewarding behaviors that come even closer to the desired response in a progression until the desired behavior occurs.

Differential reinforcement: Rewards are given when the client does not do undesirable behavior and performs an alternative behavior instead.

Response withdrawal: Withdrawing rewards to reduce the frequency of behaviors. Time Outs for children who misbehave removes attention from them, which is why Time Outs eliminate misbehavior faster than paying attention to it.

Token economies: Clients can earn tokens or vouchers to gain rewards for behaviors, to pay for misbehaviors, and to pay for privileges.

Social Learning Theory: The recognition on the part of behaviorists that social cues and interactions serve as reinforcements for learning. Obviously children learn by imitating adults, and Social Learning Theory posits concepts that describe how such learning occurs throughout life. The most well-known author of Social Learning Theory is Bandura who extended behaviorism to human internal reactions; emphasizing this, he revised the name of the theory to *Social Cognitive Theory* in 1986.

Modeling: A major factor in Social Learning Theory is the concept of modeling, when a person observes another person and imitates the behavior observed. People who are admired and those who share similar characteristics to the learner serve as the most effective models

Covert modeling occurs when the person imagines a model to remind him of the behavior.

Participant modeling uses group members who are most skilled to demonstrate behavior for others who are not as adept.

Negative, contrast, and stressful modeling demonstrate consequences of behaviors that are to be avoided. Contrast modeling shows behavior that is the opposite of socially desirable behavior to demonstrate negative consequences. Stressful modeling shows the stress that can be eliminated through more considered behavior.

Therapy goals: Behavioral therapists require clear, well-defined goals for counseling. Typically, goals called *targeted behaviors* are explicit behaviors that will change. Preferably goals are observable and measurable so progress can be easily determined. In a behavioral model considerable effort is spent determining goals before therapeutic interventions are implemented. Goals can change as the clients grapple with the implications of what they want to change.

Reactivity of measurement: To determine the specific conditions and responses for behavioral change and to track progress, accurate measurement is needed. Clients are often assigned tasks of keeping records of their behavior or filling out questionnaires summarizing behaviors. However, the measurement tasks may create change in the client's actions. Behavioral therapists define such initial change and take that into account as therapy proceeds.

Baseline: A record of behavior before treatment begins is used as a measure of the client's starting point. The record serves as a comparison for behavior after treatment interventions to indicate if improvement has taken place.

Excess, deficit, inappropriateness: Categories for classifying behavioral difficulties: Too much of the behavior (excess); not enough of the behavior (deficit) or a behavior that is out of place in the circumstances (inappropriateness).

Transfer of training: As with the concept of generalization, new behaviors learned in treatment are applied to other situations not directly addressed in therapy.

Reciprocal inhibition: A client is taught nonanxious responses to threatening cues. Wolpe developed the therapeutic treatment where anxiety responses to fearful stimuli are replaced with positive responses. Clients learn to relax or to use assertive statements and then practice using these behaviors under anxiety-provoking circumstances. The new behaviors reduce anxious reactions because relaxation and assertion are not compatible with anxiety or social inhibition.

Progressive relaxation: A technique where muscles are tightened and then relaxed in a progression throughout the body. This is used in reciprocal inhibition training.

Anxiety hierarchy: A list of anxiety-provoking situations organized in descending order from those that create a little fear to those that create the most. Used during desensitization treatment where each item on the list is imagined while the client is relaxed until the client can experience the most threatening item without anxiety.

Systematic desensitization: Using the reasoning of reciprocal inhibition, relaxation is paired with clearly defined fearful cues. The client describes his internal fear structure specifying what makes him most anxious and what is least anxiety provoking. The therapist creates an anxiety hierarchy starting with the least troubling situation and progressing to the most disturbing. The client then practices relaxation techniques in the presence of the least difficult circumstances and proceeds through the sequence until the relaxation response can be summoned in the most difficult situation.

Imaginal treatment: Learning methods can be applied in the client's imagination. The client can imagine himself doing the targeted behavior, or a model can be pictured for observation. The client can imagine fearful situations while using relaxation methods. Using images to establish responses can then be transferred to real-life situations.

In vivo treatment: Rather than using imaginary methods, clients can be coached to use behaviors in real-life circumstances. Exposing clients to approach fearful situations or to practice new behaviors with therapeutic support reduces negative reactions and can assist in behavioral changes.

Manualization: The use of written, standard procedures by therapists to treat particular client concerns.

Self-management therapy: Therapists teach the concepts and methods of learning theory to help individuals establish or change their own behavior. Clients may need assistance in defining the targeted behaviors, in recognizing the cues that elicit negative behaviors, and in determining effective rewards as well as learning procedures that will be helpful in creating and maintaining changes.

Reality therapy: A counseling approach that stresses the consequences of behavior and self responsibility.

Psychoeducational: A behavioral approach implies the necessity for clients to learn and for counselors to teach psychological concepts and methods that will improve the clients' lives. A collaborative rather than a didactic process is most common, though behaviorists are typically efficient in offering information and techniques as they are needed rather than depending on an internal change process fostered by humanistic approaches. Use of psycho-educational groups where a number of clients are taught basic concepts and can assist each other in learning new behaviors is also a natural extension of a behavioral approach.

Assertiveness training: A common difficulty for clients is the ability to determine and openly express their legitimate needs in social interactions. Satisfying relationships require communication open enough to meet the needs of the parties involved. When a person is unable to relay important messages that will improve mutual understanding, relationships become unsatisfying to all involved. Assertiveness training starts with educating the client about the necessity for articulating needs and then helps the client determine legitimate requests, requirements, and desires. Finally, the client learns effective phrases that are spoken with respectful clarity, which is neither too hostile nor too passive, so another can hear the messages.

Aversive therapy: Methods of treatment providing a negative impact are sometimes effective in eliminating unwanted responses or behavior. Flooding is a technique that forces a person to endure anxiety-provoking conditions so she will learn that the consequences are not as destructive as imagined. Imploding is another aversive technique in which the client imagines a fearful scene that is intensified by the counselor adding anxiety-provoking images such as symbols with sexual and hostile implications.

Response cost: A term in aversion therapy indicating the price paid for negative behavior. For example, in forced smoking to the point of nausea the sick feeling is the response cost.

Avoidance repression: Avoiding the thought of aversive conditions so anxiety is not felt.

Exposure and response prevention: Exposing a client to feared events and preventing the client from escaping or withdrawing. Such a technique is used when the client's imagined fears are greater than the actual reality. By exposure to the fearful situation, the client learns his or her fears are exaggerated.

Flooding: Intense and prolonged exposure to anxiety-provoking events until the fearful response dissipates. The treatment is predicated on the fact that when fear subsides, the client learns that she can face the fear without dire consequences. This treatment contrasts with systematic desensitization in which the threat is introduced in tiny steps.

Implosive therapy: A variant on the flooding technique, this therapy uses inner stimuli associated with aggression, sex, and threatening events. The exposure scenes called forth with great intensity are in the imagination rather than reality.

Biofeedback: Instruments signal bodily states giving the participant information regarding physical reactions. When a person gains control of the physical reaction, a mind state will also change, given the mind-body connection.

Representative Case: Terry Terror

A 5-year-old boy was referred to the psychologist for inappropriate classroom behavior at nursery school. Recently he refused to display his crayon drawing on the bulletin board during the school open house and instead tore up his drawing. The teacher reprimanded him and he proceeded to tear down the drawings posted by other children. He also interfered with the other children doing their seatwork by poking them, whispering, cracking jokes, and making noise. He frequently interrupted the teacher when she was explaining lessons and the other children were giving answers.

Terry is being raised by his grandparents who are, of course, older than the other children's parents. They do not attend school functions but are willing to come to the school for conferences and to bring Terry to the counseling appointments. Terry's parents were killed in an automobile accident when he was 6 months old. His grandparents report he is respectful and well behaved at home and he doesn't question his parents' absence. He plays well with neighborhood children without aggressive or other inappropriate behavior.

Terry's teacher speculates that he may be held to rigid behavioral standards at home since his grandparents are very traditional and conservative. The teacher also requests an evaluation for attention deficit disorder or a learning disability. The teacher did note that Terry's behavior was appropriate on the playground and during classroom learning activities that entailed moving around such as singing, playacting, writing on the board or doing things at play stations. He also enjoyed story times and did not interrupt as a plot developed or characters were described; he only interrupted during times when questions were asked, and he grabbed at the book when pictures were held up for the children to see. Terry also loved treat time and was very polite, saying please and thank-you when children passed out cake or cookies or ice cream. Terry's most favorite activity was passing out treats to all the children, and during sharing time he would fully describe recipes, ingredients, and how his grandmother cooked or baked.

Thinking About Terry

1. How would the counselor conceptualize Terry's inappropriate actions in nursery school?
2. What behavioral techniques would be useful to help Terry change?
3. How would the counselor deal with the deaths of Terry's parents?
4. How would the counselor utilize the adults in Terry's life to help him change?

Check Your Thinking About Terry

1. A behaviorist would consider Terry's behavior as conditioned by the attention he is receiving from teachers who probably react every time he misbehaves. The psychologist would interview the grandparents to determine their responses to Terry's behavior at home. He would observe and may administer tests for learning disabilities and ADHD if needed and would integrate these diagnoses into his recommendations according to results.

2. A behavioral program would eliminate rewards for misbehavior so the psychologist would probably recommend to the teachers that they try to ignore misbehavior unless he or someone

else was about to come to harm. Teachers would also be instructed to react positively to any affirmative social interactions Terry showed. A system to punish misbehavior could be designed along with rewards for not misbehaving. Terry could be told if he spoke out or behaved inappropriately three times he would be put in Time Out during singing, plays, or play station times. If he misbehaved five times he would not receive treats for the day. If he did not misbehave for an entire morning, he could pass out treats or help another student pass out treats. The grandparents could also be included by displaying an award certificate Terry could receive after several days of no misbehavior and/or letting Terry assist in making treats for the class when he behaved well.

3. The counselor using a behavioral approach might ask Terry about his parents' death, but unless Terry seemed to be currently thinking about his parents, the counselor would drop the subject. If Terry thinks of the parents often in distressing ways, the counselor might consider teaching him distraction techniques and self-talk methods, borrowing from Cognitive-Behavioral approaches (Chapter 9).

4. Since Terry is well-behaved at home, the grandparents could learn not only to praise his behavior but to point out what it is that he's doing right. They may be currently giving him globally positive feedback without specific references. From more specific praise, Terry can learn exactly what behaviors are praiseworthy. We hope that he transfers this learning to school.

Core Case: Marianna Chavez

The core case of Marianna Chavez appeared in Chapters 1 and 7. Now we will see a conceptualization of her case from a behavioral perspective. As in previous cases, **D** designates **Data**, **A** designates **Assessment**, and **P** designates **Plan**.

D: The client is a 22-year-old refugee from Colombia. She and her mother escaped their home country and fled to Costa Rica when she was 3 and came to the United States several years later. She is attractive and lively in her conversation, and she is a well-informed, enthusiastic activist for social causes and diversity on campus. When Marianna is calm and less animated, however, her facial expression looy for them, imposese point average and is majoring in economics. Recently, she has been experiencing flashbacks of warlike scenes, of her own brutal rape, and of watching her mother being physically abused and raped. She cries, saying there are days when she cannot leave her room.

Marianna's flashbacks began several months ago when she tried to date or to dance with men. Whenever she is sensually aroused or there is any hint of sexuality she becomes numb and cannot focus her attention. Her appetite has decreased; she has trouble getting to sleep, and when she does her sleep is troubled. She fears flashback memories will be in her dreams. She has tried to talk to her mother, but the mother remains stoic saying she cannot discuss the past and they must move on. Although the client understands her mother's abusive experiences are also painful, she longs for mutual support that is not forthcoming.

The client also reports an aversion to gold. During her escape, she wore many pieces of jewelry under her clothing. Her mother is now an importer, selling jewelry wholesale. In high school Marianna served as a model for merchandise showings until severe body rashes made it necessary for her to stop. The medical diagnosis assumed allergic reactions, but now she feels dizzy at the sight of any jewelry with the look of gold, even when it is another person wearing the piece.

Marianna's father was a drug dealer who was killed by Colombian government soldiers advised by American Special Forces. Her parents separated when she was 1 because her maternal grandparents disapproved of her father's illegal activities. She and her mother lived on the grandparents' estate for two years until the wealthy landowners, associated with government leaders, were killed by the drug cartel. Marianna is tearful when she talks about her father and sobs when she tells of her grandparents' deaths. Another flashback is a scene where men arrive at her home with guns and drag her grandparents away.

The two coping mechanisms that offer Marianna some relief are journaling and drawing. Her roommate discovered some drawings and became upset with their violent content, so the client hides her work and is careful to draw only when her roommate is absent. The client has been to the campus health services complaining of fatigue and stomach cramps, but after extensive tests no medical condition has been diagnosed.

A: The client demonstrates PTSD, Post Traumatic Stress Disorder. She and all the members of her family experienced traumatic events. Assessment showed she considers the aversive reaction to gold to be the least threatening and her own rape as the most disturbing memory. Her greatest hope is for a better relationship with her mother and to make her proud. She also sees her social activism as a way to work for a better world that could prevent conditions like those in the country of her birth. Although Marianna is suffering flashbacks she is highly functional, doing well academically with high grades and socially, with friends, with the exception of dating. Somatization may be the first symptom to treat.

P: Continue to establish a relationship with the client. Educate her regarding the etiology of PTSD, of conditioned anxiety, and the generalization of anxiety, such as the aversion to gold. Monitor the number of flashbacks experienced daily and teach SUD (subjective units of distress) scale for the client to use in reporting. (SUD scale begins with zero as when asleep, moves up to 3, normal attention without tension, and progresses to 10 representing extreme distress). Describe relaxation response training and exposure strategies.

The process of therapy will be determined by what symptoms Marianna considers most crucial to eliminate. With Marianna, determine what symptoms might respond most easily to relaxation response for a starting point, maybe targeting cramps, then gold, before determining hierarchy for trauma scenes. Depending on which goals are chosen, counseling can go in several directions. Treatment can integrate journaling with SUD reports and drawings can be framed as Marianna's own attempt at exposure therapy for her memories. Invite Marianna to bring her drawings to counseling. Possible suggestions to Marianna may be to draw jewelry for now and to invite mother to therapy. Assistance with counselor can help mother and daughter determine how to support each other with assertive expressions and respect the other's needs in individual choices for dealing with past trauma. Discuss with Marianna a plan for what dating contact she wants to experience while in therapy.

Finding a Balance

Key Counselor Preferences

1. Behaviorists prefer and skillfully elicit fully detailed descriptions of current conditions and client behaviors related to the presenting concern. Time spent thoroughly assessing and defining the problem in detail contributes to determining effective interventions for change. Historical antecedents are examined only as needed to determine if the past experiences are readily influencing current behavior.

2. Behaviorists pay attention to the quality of the relationship with the client, demonstrating warmth and understanding, believing they can be positive reinforcers for the client's efforts

in changing behavior. Feelings may be reflected to show understanding, but they are not the focus of the interactions. Teaching collaboratively and encouraging the client is appropriate.

3. Behaviorists trust clients to choose what specific behaviors they want to change. Counselors depend on their own expertise to determine effective methods as to how the change will come about in collaboration with the client.

4. Behaviorists believe in clients' actively doing something about their problems both in the counseling room and in real-life situations. Once the assessment is complete, talking about the problem is not forbidden if the client needs to briefly discuss issues, but too much time spent talking reinforces old behavior and conditions rather than creating hopeful change.

5. Behaviorists evaluate progress toward client goals regularly. Counselors are obligated to stay up to date with empirical research describing treatments.

Case Example: Diane Timorous

Client is a 42-year-old slightly overweight secretary, married to a construction engineer, with two teenage children: a boy aged 16 and a daughter aged 10. She speaks very quietly, saying she is afraid of being in public and around a number of people. Her son has recently received an award for a science project, and in six months he is expected to go to a state convention where he will describe his experiment. The client's fears of being in the public eye where attention could be on her are mounting, yet she does want to support her son and show him she is proud of him. During the session she never maintains eye contact. She describes her life as going to work where she sits at an isolated desk typing and entering computer data, interacting only with the head secretary who delivers her tasks. She becomes very anxious when she has questions regarding her work assignments and has been known to spend days trying to approach the head secretary. Usually her boss perceives her anxious demeanor and asks if she has any questions, and the situation is resolved after much trepidation for Diane. Otherwise she spends most of her time inside at home or outside in her garden. Her husband is often out of town on construction sites. Diane and her daughter do the grocery shopping during early morning hours on Sunday. She has suffered from chronic depression over the years and has been in therapy several times for several months at a time. She reports counseling has helped her feel better, and she has learned to monitor and combat negative thoughts. With medication Diane feels she is able to manage depression. She also was introduced to assertiveness training, but she was unable to follow the counselor's instructions.

The client agrees that her life satisfaction would improve if she were able to speak to other people. She notes that her fear of people stems from her inability to talk and that talking when more than one person was around would be impossible.

Applying Counselor Preferences

Using the previously listed behaviorist preferences, how would a counselor proceed with Diane?

1. The behaviorist would continue to assess the client's behavior and her deficits in terms of social interactions. It would be important to determine what connection there is between her description of fears related to being in public and her inability to speak up. When the behavior began could be important if the historical conditions or images are currently active for her; otherwise previous experiences need not be elaborated.

2. The counselor would attend to Diane with warmth and understanding, knowing that eliciting her cooperation would be needed for her to do new behaviors. The counselor would also serve as a reinforcement agent, praising and encouraging her in her efforts.

3. Given Diane's learned distrust of assertiveness training, a different approach toward the same end might be appropriate. It would be important for Diane to understand and fully agree to the behavioral change method chosen by the therapist.

4. Diane would need to gain confidence in her ability to do new behaviors. Role-playing practice in session might be needed before she would attempt to try behaviors in her own environment.

5. It would be important to continually discuss Diane's progress, pointing out that she can do the behaviors she thinks she cannot do. It would be inadvisable to continue talking about her behavioral deficits once the assessment is completed.

Course of Therapy

An understanding, warm relationship developed with the therapist as Diane described her life. The counselor suggested they create an anxiety hierarchy and role-play situations together. Although Diane said she enjoyed the counseling sessions and appreciated the time with the counselor, she expressed some doubt that she could learn to speak up. With encouragement and the assurance that the counselor would not be disappointed if she faltered, Diane agreed to try. A twenty-item hierarchy was developed, starting with Diane maintaining eye contact with herself in the mirror and then silently with the therapist for several minutes. Middle hierarchy items included saying something to the therapist with eye contact during a role play of common interactions with one other person. The counselor demonstrated speaking up behaviors in role rehearsals for such things as asking a waiter for a menu or asking a sales clerk for directions. After the counselor's demonstration, Diane enacted the speaker role herself. Higher hierarchy items included openly stating an opinion to another person such as her husband or offering a suggestion to her supervisor. Some items were repeated with difficulty, but the entire progression of role plays was completed to Diane's satisfaction in fourteen sessions. Diane reported speaking up at home more and some positive interactions at work.

Another phase of therapy included a second hierarchy of ten items where Diane enlisted the help of co-workers and her supervisor. Diane and the therapist would design the interaction she wanted to practice and she would enact the role play in real life the next day. Diane reported others appreciating her competency and her suggestions, and some said they enjoyed talking with her. She described her excitement at work and the greater satisfaction she felt in her marriage. Finally, Diane came to counseling with a written description of what she expected when she attended the science fair with her son. She imagined herself smiling at strangers who viewed his work and beaming when he would say a few words accepting his award. The crowd would only be people who were admiring her son as she did. She could even see herself saying, "This is my son who makes me very proud." Diane reported her son told her he was proud of her willingness to attend his event.

Comparison with Other Approaches

Psychodynamic: Counselors who prefer to work through issues from an historical perspective would spend time examining Diane's past and how her childhood contributed to her interactive style. Diane would gain an understanding that her behavior may have worked well given the family dynamics she experienced as a child, but that now, as an adult, the behaviors were not working for her. In the transference relationship she could also work through the latent pain she carries.

Person-Centered and Gestalt: With a Person-Centered counselor Diane could gradually discover her deeper feelings that make interactions so fearful. She could, on her own, determine what she has to say, which may be particularly relevant in dialogues with her husband. With a Gestalt therapist she might unearth polarities that bind her up, such as simultaneously fearing others and wanting to gain connections with others.

Existential and Transpersonal: The meaning of her withdrawn silence may become clear to Diane with an existential or transpersonal therapist, in terms of grappling with mortality, meaninglessness, freedom, and isolation. She could learn to accept her own responsibility for making connections to others and discover the contributions she could add to the lives of others. Finally, she might reflect on her own behavior in relation to her sense of spirituality.

Example of a Published Research Article on Behavior Therapy

Here is an article on behavioral research. The commentary in the boxes to the left of the article will help you understand the research and the format of the piece.

Effect of Length of Treatment on Weight Loss

Michael G. Perri
Department of Psychology, Fairleigh Dickinson University

Arthur M. Nezu
Franklin Delano Roosevelt Veterans Administration Hospital

Eugene T. Patti
Department of Psychology, Fairleigh Dickinson University

Karen L. McCann
Department of Psychology, Fairleigh Dickinson University

> The authors begin by explaining why a problem exists.

Behavior therapy is generally recognized as the treatment of choice for mild obesity, but its effectiveness for moderate and severe forms of obesity is limited by the modest amount of weight loss that is typically accomplished during treatment (Foreyt, 1987). Behavioral programs usually span 15–20 weekly sessions and produce weight losses of approximately 1.1 lb. per week (Brownell & Wadden, 1986). Because moderately obese people need to lose more than 20 lb., treatment programs of 20 or fewer weeks duration may not allow such clients sufficient opportunity to achieve clinically significant weight losses.

> Now, they suggest a possible solution to the problem, and this is the solution they tested in their study. This type of study is a treatment comparison study, even though the only difference in the two treatments is length of time.

In a recent quantitative review of 105 obesity treatment studies, Bennett (1986) found that duration of treatment was the single most important factor positively correlated with weight loss. Bennett speculated that the longer a treatment continues, the longer its participants adhere to the behaviors necessary for weight loss. These correlational findings suggest that lengthening the course of treatment offers promise as a method to enhance the efficacy of behavior therapy for obesity. In the present study, we conducted a prospective, experimental investigation to test the effect of treatment length on weight loss. We compared the effectiveness of a standard 20-session obesity treatment program with an extended program consisting of 40 weekly treatment sessions.

Method

Random assignment, or random sampling, means that each person had an equal chance of being assigned to either group. The descriptions show that the groups turned out fairly equivalent in several ways.

Newspaper advertisements were used to recruit clients who were 21–60 years of age, were 25%–100% overweight, were free of obesity-related medical disorders, and had obtained physicians' approval to participate in a weight reduction program. Forty-eight clients who met these criteria were randomly assigned to either a standard treatment program of 20 weekly sessions n = 24, 4 men, 20 women; M = 96.61 kg [53.6% overweight] or to an extended treatment regimen of 40 weekly sessions n = 24, 6 men, 18 women; M = 100.36 kg [52.4% overweight] . The typical subject reported previous participation in two or three commercial or professionally led weight loss programs in which he or she lost an average of 10 kg. (22 lb.) but regained an equivalent or greater amount during the year following treatment.

Counterbalancing means that the researchers rotated the therapist teams so that each team did both short and long versions. Therefore, therapists' abilities were evenly distributed between versions. This kept a particularly excellent team from affecting which version came out ahead.

Treatment was conducted in four groups of 12 clients by one of two teams of clinical psychology graduate students. Therapist teams were counterbalanced by treatment condition in such a way that each team conducted one 20-session group and one 40-session group. Therapists were provided with a manual detailing session-by-session treatment procedures. In addition, all therapists participated in weekly training sessions to help ensure uniformity of treatment procedures across therapists.

The behavioral treatment techniques taught in the 20- and 40-session programs were identical, but the procedures were introduced in a more gradual manner in the extended treatment condition. The treatment procedures included training in self-monitoring, stimulus control, self-reinforcement, cognitive modification, problem solving, and programmed aerobic exercise (see Perri, McAdoo, McAllister, Lauer, & Yancey, 1986 , for details).

Three weight-related dependent measures were included in the data analyses: body weight, body weight lost, and percentage over ideal body weight. Changes in weight were assessed at Weeks 20, 40, and 72. At each assessment meeting, clients also completed questionnaires rating the degree to which they adhered to nine treatment strategies on a 7-point Likert-type scale (i.e., 1 = nonadherence ; 7 = full adherence). The following weight-control techniques were included in the adherence questionnaire: daily self-monitoring of eating and exercise behavior; calorie counting; eliminating second portions; limiting between-meal eatings to one per day; eating only in appropriate food areas (e.g., kitchen or

The behavior therapy techniques used are listed.

cafeteria); slowing the pace of eating; maintaining appropriate stimulus control over food cues; refraining from nonsocial behaviors (e.g., reading) while eating; and completing prescribed number of minutes of exercise per day.

Results

A MANOVA compares the two groups' original average scores on more than one variable at once (in this case, body weight and percentage overweight). A *p* value of over .20 means that the differences in the groups' scores are probably due to chance. That is, this difference would be found over 20 times in 100 by chance.

An overall multivariate analysis of variance (MANOVA) indicated initially that there were no significant pretreatment group differences in body weight or percentage over ideal body weight ($p > .20$). Rates of attrition were identical for both the standard and extended length programs; over the course of 72 weeks, 8 clients dropped out of each condition. Subjects who dropped out did not differ from participants who completed treatment with respect to pretreatment body weight or percentage over ideal weight ($ps > .20$). Individuals who dropped out attended an average of 9.38 sessions and had a mean weight loss of 4.59 kg (10.09 lb).

The *main effect of time* means that the total amount of weight lost differed significantly between weeks 20, 40, and 72. The *main effect of condition* means that the amount of weight lost differed significantly between the two groups (the *conditions* are the short and long versions). The *interaction effect* means that the two groups had different patterns of weight loss over time. The *F* statistic indicates the magnitude of differences (in this case, across time, between groups, and in groups' patterns). You can tell whether an *F* statistic is big by its *p* value: the smaller the *p* value, the bigger the magnitude of difference.

Table 1 presents means and standard deviations for body weight lost (kg.) for each condition at Weeks 20, 40, and 72. A repeated measures multivariate profile analysis was used to examine the differential effects of conditions over time. This analysis initially indicated the following overall effects: (a) a significant main effect for time, $F_{2, 29} = 8.46$, $p < .001$; (b) a significant main effect for condition, $F_{1, 30} = 4.87$, $p < .03$; and (c) a significant interaction effect for Condition x Time, $F_{2, 29} = 7.77$, $p < .002$.

Table 1

Means and Standard Deviations for Weight Loss (kg.) by Condition Across Assessments

Assessment	Treatment condition	
	Extended ($n = 16$)	Standard ($n = 16$)
Week 20		
M	$10.09_{a,A}$	$8.89_{a,A}$
SD	5.53	4.75
Week 40		
M	$13.64_{a,B}$	$6.41_{b,A,B}$
SD	9.00	5.99
Week 72		
M	$9.85_{a,A}$	$4.61_{b,B}$
SD	8.21	5.16

Note. Dissimilar lowercase subscripts (across rows) indicate significant differences between conditions within a time period, and dissimilar uppercase subscripts (down columns) indicate significant differences within a condition across time periods ($ps < .05$).

The follow-up tests show what the differences in pattern between groups were: for example, the long version group lost weight between Weeks 20 and 40 while the short version group gained a little.

Another way to look at the results is to survey how many participants in each group lost 10 lb. between Week 20 and Week 40, since the second twenty weeks was hypothesized to boost effectiveness. The c^2 (chi square) statistic reflects the magnitude of differences in proportions between groups.

The overall significant interaction effect was examined further by means of univariate F tests (pooled error variances) and individual contrasts using the Newman-Keuls procedure. From pretreatment to 20 weeks, the interaction effect was not significant; both conditions showed comparable weight losses (M = 8.89 kg., or 19.60 lb., for the standard treatment; M = 10.09 kg., or 22.20 lb., for the extended treatment). Over the period from Week 20 to Week 40, however, there was a significant interaction effect for Condition x Time, $F_{1,30} = 16.03$, $p < .001$. Individual contrasts indicated further that the extended treatment group lost a significant additional amount of weight between Weeks 20 and 40 M = 3.55 kg., or 7.81 lb., lost, $p < .05$ and that the standard treatment gained a nonsignificant amount during this period M = 2.48 kg., or 5.46 lb., gained . By the time of the 40-week assessment, participants in the extended treatment had an average net weight loss of 13.64 kg. (30.01 lb.) compared with 6.41 kg. (14.10 lb.) for clients in the standard 20-session program. From Week 40 to Week 72, there was a significant effect for time, $F_{1,30} = 17.23$, $p < .001$, and a significant effect for condition, $F_{1,30} = 7.10$, $p < .01$. The interaction effect for Condition x Time, however, did not reach significance. Although both conditions showed weight gains during this period, at Week 72 the extended treatment maintained a significantly greater mean net loss than did the standard treatment ($ps < .05$; see Table 1).

An examination of the proportion of subjects who demonstrated weight losses of 10 lb. (4.55 kg.) or more from Week 20 to Week 40 showed that 10 of the 16 participants (62.50%) in the extended treatment achieved this degree of additional progress compared with only 1 of 16 subjects (6.25%) in the standard condition, c^2_{1}, N = 32 = 11.22, $p < .001$. This finding indicates that the majority of participants benefited significantly from the additional 20 sessions of the extended treatment condition. From Week 40 to Week 72, no one in the extended condition sustained an additional loss of 10 lb. (4.55 kg.) or more, but one participant in the standard condition achieved a further weight loss of this magnitude.

The analyses of body weight and percentage over ideal body weight showed similar patterns of significant effects as the weight loss measure. For example, at Week 20, the groups were equivalent in terms of percentage over ideal weight (M s = 37.05% vs. 37.87% overweight, for the extended and standard conditions, respectively). At Weeks 40 and 72, however, the extended treatment condition showed significantly greater improvement on this measure compared with the standard treatment (M s = 31.28% vs. 41.90 % overweight at Week 40, and 37.40% vs. 44.80% overweight at Week 72, for the extended and standard conditions, respectively; $ps < .05$).

Analyses of the data from the adherence questionnaires were conducted in the same manner as the weight-related

Participants rated how well they stuck to the behavioral strategies they learned (*adherence ratings*). Differences in adherence between groups were analyzed to see whether the longer version encouraged greater adherence, which it did between Weeks 20 and 40.

measures. Table 2 presents means and standard deviations for the sum of self-ratings of adherence to nine weight loss strategies. Initial MANOVA results revealed a significant main effect for time, $F_{2, 29} = 85.89$, $p < .001$, and a significant Condition x Time interaction effect, $F_{2, 29} = 9.26$, $p < .001$. At Week 20, each condition showed equivalent degrees of adherence to treatment strategies. At Week 40, however, the extended treatment group reported significantly greater program adherence than did the standard treatment group $p < .01$. At Week 72, the between groups difference in adherence was no longer significant (see Table 2). A correlational analysis was calculated to determine the relation between self-reported adherence and weight loss. A significant positive relation between subjects' ratings of adherence to self-management strategies and weight loss was observed, $r = .43$, $p < .05$.[1]

Discussion

The major finding in this study was that extending the length of treatment from 20 to 40 weekly sessions significantly improved weight loss. Clients in the extended treatment condition on average increased their weight losses by 35% during the period from Week 20 to Week 40. Moreover, both the weight loss and adherence data support the hypothesis

Table 2
Means and Standard Deviations for
Adherence by Condition Across Assessments

	Treatment condition	
Assessment	Extended ($n = 16$)	Standard ($n = 16$)
Week 20		
M	50.44$_{a,A}$	54.06$_{a,A}$
SD	6.63	7.43
Week 40		
M	48.06$_{a,A}$	37.75$_{b,B}$
SD	7.48	14.80
Week 72		
M	30.13$_{a,B}$	30.81$_{a,C}$
SD	7.35	12.03

Note. Dissimilar lowercase subscripts (across rows) indicate significant differences between conditions within a time period, and dissimilar uppercase subscripts (down columns) indicate significant differences within a condition across time periods ($ps < .05$).

that the longer clients are in treatment, the longer they adhere to the behaviors necessary for weight loss (cf. Bennett, 1986 ; Brownell & Wadden, 1986 ; Foreyt, 1987). Thus, extending the length of treatment may provide clients with a continued opportunity to maintain habit changes and to sustain additional weight reductions.

The significance of the additional progress achieved in the extended treatment is tempered by the slowing in average rate of weight loss from 1.17 lb. per week over the first 20 sessions to 0.39 lb. per week over the second 20 sessions. The impact of the extended treatment during the second 20-week period, although modest M = 3.55 kg., or 7.81 lb., was significant when compared with the mean weight gain experienced in the standard-length treatment. These findings, together with the 72-week data showing deterioration in adherence and weight loss progress for both groups, indicate that after clients conclude their active involvement in obesity treatment, they typically abandon weight loss strategies and begin to regain weight. Such findings suggest that obesity should be conceptualized and treated as a chronic condition requiring ongoing long-term care (Jeffery, 1987). Therefore, initial treatments may need to be longer, spanning perhaps a year or more for moderate and severe cases of obesity. In addition, such treatments may need to be supplemented by maintenance phases that provide ongoing therapeutic contacts to help clients deal with the various obstacles inherent in the long-term management of obesity (Perri et al., 1988).

> Given the results of the study, the authors suggest further solutions to the problem they introduced at the beginning of the article.

References

Bennett, G. A. (1986). Behavior therapy for obesity: A quantitative review of the effects of selected treatment characteristics on outcome. *Behavior Therapy, 17,* 554–562.

Brownell, K.D. & Wadden, T.A. (1986). Behavior therapy for obesity: Modern approaches and better results. In K. D. Brownell & J. P. Foreyt (Eds.), *The handbook of eating disorders: Physiology, psychology, and treatment of obesity, anorexia nervosa, and bulimia* (pp. 180—197). New York: Basic Books.

Foreyt, J. P. (1987). Issues in the assessment and treatment of obesity. *Journal of Consulting and Clinical Psychology, 55,* 677–684.

Jeffery, R.W. (1987). Behavioral treatment of obesity. *Annals of Behavioral Medicine, 9,* 20–24.

Perri, M.G., McAdoo, W.G., McAllister, D.A., Lauer, J.B. & Yancey, D.Z. (1986). Enhancing the efficacy of behavior therapy for obesity: Effects of aerobic exercise and a multicomponent maintenance program. *Journal of Consulting and Clinical Psychology, 54,* 670–675.

> From the References list, you can tell that the first author Perri often does research on the problem of obesity. If you are interested in the topic, you should jot his name down for future purposes.

Perri, M.G., McAllister, D.A., Gange, J.J., Jordan, R.C., McAdoo, W.G. & Nezu, A.M. (1988). Effects of four maintenance programs on the long-term management of obesity. *Journal of Consulting and Clinical Psychology, 56*, 529–534.

Stalonas, P.M. & Kirschenbaum, D.S. (1985). Behavioral treatments for obesity: Eating habits revisited. *Behavior Therapy, 16*, 1–14.

[1] The significant positive correlation between adherence and weight loss observed in this and other studies (e.g., Perri et al., 1988 ; Stalonas & Kirschenbaum, 1985) supports the external validity of the questionnaire assessment of adherence. Nonetheless, these data should be interpreted with caution because they are based on self-reports without corroboration by independent observers.

Discussion Ideas

1. What was the problem with 15 to 20-week behavior therapy for moderate and severe forms of obesity? Why did the authors believe that lengthening the treatment might solve this problem? Did the researchers change the behavior therapy in any way?

2. The researchers recruited participants through newspaper ads. Do you think this gave them a sample of obese people that represents obese people in general?

3. From your knowledge of behavior therapy, elaborate on the behavioral strategies of this weight loss program. Are the strategies familiar to you? Would you expect such a program to work? Can you explain the strategies in terms of learning theory?

4. The researchers looked at three time periods, 1 to 20 weeks, 20 to 40 weeks, and 40 to 72 weeks, for all the participants. What period showed the most promising differences between groups? What period would you say showed disappointing results?

5. Suggest a design for an experiment that would test one of the potential treatments discussed in the last paragraph of the article.

Answer Key for Practice Test Questions

True/False

1. F
2. F
3. F
4. T
5. T
6. F
7. F
8. F
9. F
10. F

Multiple Choice

1. a		11. e	
2. d		12. d	
3. c		13. a	
4. f		14. c	
5. a		15. c	
6. c			
7. b			
8. a			
9. c			
10. c			

CHAPTER 9

Cognitive-Behavioral Therapies

Chapter Review

Cognitive therapies describe the inner speech that takes place inside each person's mind. As events occur, our thoughts mediate between the external input and our outward responses. This mediation process subjectively interprets outside events according to an individual's experience. Personal constructs form the lens through which we view the world and create our own phenomenological reality. From this perspective, emotions can be changed by changing thought patterns. Rather than emotional processing as other therapies describe, cognitive counselors search for patterns of thinking that underlie mental health difficulties. Chronic and severe disorders reveal common thought patterns. However, the thinking behind more neurotic and less severe emotional distress may not be as obvious given the automatic, spontaneous nature of habitual thoughts a client may have.

Cognitive therapists share common practices with behavioral therapists; hence the title, Cognitive-Behavioral therapy. Both behaviorists and cognitive counselors know emotional factors influence client cooperation, and both use behavioral methods to establish and reinforce learning patterns. The therapy process for the cognitive approach creates a problem solving tone, collaborating with clients to develop coping skills for dealing with stressful situations. Some client crises are so stressful that automatic thinking patterns are unable to meet the demands of the circumstances. Other clients struggle to meet daily responsibilities, feeling life has become unmanageable. They process experience through a negative cognitive screen that induces ineffective responses. Therapists infer the negative schema that has led clients to emotional distress. Identifying ineffective beliefs, the counselor serves as a persuasive teacher, a trusted guide, who can help the client change thoughts that are no longer working to generate a satisfying life. The therapist creates a warm, understanding atmosphere for the cognitive work, providing a model of effective coping, but also as an example of another flawed human being who has to meet similar life demands. The goal of counseling is to change client thought patterns, to assist the client in determining realistic considerations, and to help the client learn how to establish effective responses.

In the early stages of counseling, therapist and client engage in a dialogue designed to determine the client's thinking patterns, encouraging specific descriptions, not only general descriptions of experiences. The therapist teaches the client the mechanics of completing a thought record as homework between sessions. Often the counselor and client will make a prioritized list of problems, and the counselor will offer suggestions for one of the simplest concerns to create an early success for the client. Over time, in the middle working stage of counseling, the client's belief system and how it works is thoroughly examined. Clients consider the evidence for a belief, brainstorm alternative interpretations, and examine the implications. For homework, clients try out new cognitions or participate in experiences designed to expose thoughts to reality testing. Counselors may use Socratic questioning to lead clients into rational examination, or therapists may create experiences constructed so the client will discover new ways of looking at issues. In the final counseling sessions, clients' new schemas are reinforced, and relapse prevention interventions prepare clients to meet the demands of future difficult situations.

Ellis provides one cognitive approach called Rational Emotive Behavior Therapy (REBT). This method teaches clients a mnemonic of A, B, C, D, E, F. A stands for the activating event, B represents the client's beliefs, and C is consequential reaction. According to Ellis, people assume A, the event, happens and C, the reaction, results automatically, not realizing that the reaction has been influenced by B, the associated beliefs. Ellis presents eleven common irrational thoughts that create many negative reactions. Incorrect beliefs include assumptions that one has to be loved or perfectly competent; that experiences must conform to the person's expectations; that others are bad and should be punished. If events vary from such prescriptions, people say in their minds, "Life is awful!" and they feel burdened. To overcome faulty assumptions, REBT counselors go to D which is disputing the irrationality. The therapist, and eventually the client, refute the negative assumptions and come to more reasonable conclusions. When the disputing takes hold, E occurs and the client is effecting a new philosophy so that F, new feelings will also occur. According to Ellis the eleven irrational thoughts underlie most emotional difficulties.

Beck provides a number of errors in informational processing that lead to negative emotions and faulty responses to life events. His work with depression suggests a cognitive triad in which afflicted clients report self-concepts of being ineffectual and worthless, interpret experiences as overwhelming, and see the future as without hope. For diagnosis, the Beck Depression Inventory assembles the triad's descriptors to measure the severity of the problem. Beck's therapeutic approach is collaborative, and his interventions engage the client in an empirical search to find evidence for negative thoughts or for more balanced, rational conclusions.

Meichenbaum devised a cognitive treatment called *stress inoculation* (SIT), a sequence of self-talk strategies designed to help clients cope with very difficult situations such as intense memories of trauma. Psychologically damaging memories trigger a sequence of emotions, and treatments require extensive cognitive restructuring. Other clients can be prepared for intermittent stressful experiences or for chronic, continual stress. Automatic thought responses may not be adequate for dealing with unusual stress, so Michenbaum's methods prepare clients before they face the difficult circumstances. The therapy sequence begins with the conceptual phase, where clients report in detail what distressing signals can be expected and what their typical responses have been. The next phase of treatment entails the clients' gaining the appropriate skills needed, and the final phase involves applying skills in real situations. Necessary follow-up sessions help maintain new learning. Michenbaum's SIT methods have been used for a wide variety of people from surgical and cancer patients to psychiatric patients adjusting to post hospitalization to PTSD patients and their families.

Glasser designed an approach called *reality therapy*. His major clientele, juvenile delinquents, are described as denying realistic constraints, making excuses, and ignoring the natural consequences of their behavior. Glasser encourages empathy for client emotions, but his counseling does not emphasize affect. Instead, he teaches self-regulation using the metaphor of cybernetics, the study of how mechanical systems are designed to automatically adjust to changing conditions. Clients learn to identify what they want and how their behavior can either lead to gaining their goals or to negative consequences. The approach popularized by Glasser's colleague Wubbolding uses the letters WDEP to indicate: Wants, Direction and Doing, (self) Evaluation, and Planning. The theory also considers universal needs: survival, belonging, power or achievement, independence, and fun. Finally, much time in counseling is spent recognizing the effects of behavior on other people and emphasizing responsibility for oneself.

Lazarus created a counseling approach called *multimodal therapy*. As the name suggests, Lazarus describes client difficulties as affecting multiple dimensions of human personality. He devised the acronym BASIC ID, or basic identity, to indicate the different modalities requiring assessment and appropriate treatment interventions. B stands for behavior, A for affect, S for sensation, I for imagery, C for cognition, I for interpersonal relationships, and D for drugs or biological components. The client describes her personality, rating the strength of each dimension for a structural protocol. The therapist then creates a modality protocol, a plan for interventions. Treatment starts with interventions affecting the strongest personality factors and utilizing gains made in the strength modality to influence changes in other dimensions. Thus, the therapist is able to determine the sequence of interventions and to track client change across modalities. The approach utilizes techniques from many different therapy approaches and is known for its technical eclecticism.

Linehan developed another many faceted treatment approach for borderline personality disorders called *dialectical behavior therapy* (DBT). Linehan recognized that clients face conflicting pressures such as the need to both accept the self and to change, to let go of negative behavior but not to lose the behaviors that have worked, to validate personal experience and yet to redefine what has happened. In treating chronically distressed personalities, considerable effort is needed to help clients acquire skills in emotional self-regulation. DBT methodically educates clients in approaching many different situations with new perspectives and problem-solving methods. Linehan also has designed interventions based on Zen mindfulness methods that encourage the acceptance of life events just as they are, without demanding that reality be any different than it is.

EMDR or Eye Movement Desensitization and Reprocessing is a technique that is said to change the neurological storage of traumatic memories. The desensitization treatment essentially has the client remember difficult scenes from the past while the therapist passes two fingers back and forth to guide the client's eye movements. Before the eye movement intervention, the counselor listens to the client's history, targets the memory scenes, and prepares the client for the procedures. During each set of eye movement treatments, the client views the scene as in a movie, at a distance, and utilizes relaxation methods. Between eye movement sets, the therapist assists the client in developing positive cognitions to counter negative ones. Once the client's distress ratings have lessened, the client holds both the memory and positive cognitions together at the same time to install the new reaction. As a check for stress level, a body scan is done before final closure of the session. Between sessions the client records flashbacks, and in the next session, a reevaluation is done to determine if the memory has been reprocessed. If the ratings for stress and cognitions have not shown progress, the therapist does what is called a *cognitive interweave* where the positive cognitions are discussed. A controversy among practitioners exists, with some skeptical reactions conflicting with some research showing the treatment as effective as other exposure methods.

Critiques for the cognitive-behavioral approach say that it is too prescriptive, that it overemphasizes rationality and de-emphasizes dependency needs, that it can leave the client with unfinished business, and that the methods are similar to brainwashing procedures. However, cognitive therapists value empirical validation for their methods and pay attention to what works according to the research. The field will continually evolve as scientific investigations offer new results. The methods also have the advantage of working within a short term model that is becoming both acceptable and necessary for counseling practice.

Practice Test Questions

True or False: Consider each statement and try to explain in your own mind why it might not be fully true. Be sure to take into account any qualifying factors that might make the statement untrue. If you decide that the statement is fully true, circle **T**. Otherwise, circle **F**.

T F   1. Researchers focusing on cognitive learning patterns and those investigating behavioral responses have a common view of collecting empirical evidence.

T F   2. Cognitive-behavioral counselors discount emotions in counseling.

T F   3. Cybernetics studies how human systems such as organizations make adaptations to changing conditions, thereby regulating controls.

T F   4. Attitudes involve thoughts, emotions, and behavior expressed holistically.

T F   5. Phenomenology is the study of the configuration of the human head.

T F   6. Reflexive reactions are caused by the automaticity of thought.

T F   7. To change thoughts and consequent feelings is an easy task.

T F   8. Cognitive-behavioral therapy requires a long-term commitment.

T F   9. Cognitive-behavioral counselors depend on their intuitive creativity to design therapy interventions.

T F   10. According to Albert Ellis, societal messages influence people to believe ideas that cause unhappiness.

Multiple Choice: Circle the one letter next to the best answer to the following questions or to complete the sentence stems.

1. Which of the following is NOT one of Ellis's *eleven irrational beliefs*?
   a. It is essential for a person to be loved by everyone they know.
   b. There will not always be a perfect solution to problems and that's O.K.
   c. A person must accept that outside forces create conditions causing unhappiness.
   d. It is easier to avoid some difficulties rather than face them.
   e. All human beings need someone stronger to rely on and to protect them.

2. Which of the following represents part of Ellis's *eleven irrational beliefs*?
   a. A person needs to become upset when other people have major problems.
   b. A person need not be thoroughly competent to be considered worthwhile.
   c. The past determines present behavior and the influence cannot be overcome.
   d. a and c
   e. b and c

3. In the ABCDEF of REBT therapy
   a. A is the activating event.
   b. B is the boundaries needed.
   c. C is the contact with others.
   d. D is disputing.
   e. a and d

4. In the ABCDEF of REBT therapy
   a. A is the activating event; B is the belief; and C is the consequence.
   b. D is disputing; E is effecting a new philosophy; and F is new feelings.
   c. A is the activating event; B is burying feelings; and C is conclusion.
   d. a and b
   e. b and c

5. *Arbitrary inference* is an error in informational processing defined as
   a. coming to a conclusion without enough evidence.
   b. drawing a deduction by carefully examining the evidence.
   c. failing to draw a conclusion from some evidence when there are contradictory facts.
   d. a and b
   e. a and c

6. *Selective abstraction* is a thinking error characterized by
   a. selecting inappropriate minor evidence out of the context.
   b. taking some evidence and weighing it in comparison to other facts.
   c. taking into account meaningful features of the situation.
   d. labeling the whole experience on the basis of an early impression.
   e. a and d

7. *Overgeneralization* is a thinking error defined as
   a. coming to a conclusion by considering all the related incidents.
   b. applying general conclusions to other similar situations.
   c. drawing a general rule from one isolated incident.
   d. applying a concept to those situations that show the same characteristics.
   e. coming to a conclusion by researching what has been empirically validated.

8. Which of the following statements best characterizes Beck's *cognitive triad* for depressed people?
   a. The self is better than others; the future is full of possibilities; experience is good.
   b. The self is defective; experience is overwhelming; the future is bleak.
   c. The self is inadequate; experience helps overcome obstacles; the future is happy.
   d. The self is adequate; experience doesn't help; the future presents problems.
   e. The self is competent; experience has been positive; the future will be hard.

9. Michenbaum created a treatment for *stress inoculation* (SIT) to
   a. help people endure negative cognitions.
   b. train people to use healthy internal talk when facing difficulties.
   c. deal with a sense that life cannot be seen as positive enough.
   d. prepare people to understand confusing but good times.
   e. help people remember to get a vaccination.

10. Glasser's *reality therapy* is characterized by
    a. encouraging clients to express their emotions and gain new levels of insight.
    b. helping clients recognize the demands of reality and self-responsibility.
    c. determining the influences of negative experiences in childhood.
    d. a and b
    e. a and c

11. The WDEP (an acronym) helps clients remember how to evaluate choices. What do the letters signify?
    a. W is what; D is designing; E is testing; P is putting forward.
    b. W is wants; D is direction; E is ego; P is planning
    c. W is wants; D is doing; E is self-evaluation; P is planning.
    d. W is what; D is desire; E is self-evaluation; P is proposing solutions.
    e. W is wants; D is doing; E is environment; P is planning.

12. Lazarus's multimodal therapy is characterized by the use of many techniques
    a. based on the therapist's intuitive inferences.
    b. used after careful assessment of the client's personality.
    c. in a sequential treatment plan.
    d. to guarantee at least one technique will work.
    e. b and c

13. Linehan's dialectical behavior therapy is designed to
    a. meet the treatment needs of interrelated facets of the client's personality.
    b. teach therapists the methods of Socratic questioning.
    c. help clients deal with severe pathology in a brief therapy mode.
    d. allow creative interventions that tap into the client's unconscious.
    e. limit treatment to one therapist without expensive consultations with others.

14. EMDR is a treatment that includes which of the following?
    a. The counselor moves fingers in front of the client's face, and the client's eyes follow the movement.
    b. The client rates sensible cognitions according to a SUD scale.
    c. The client rates variations in feeling reactions according to a VOC scale.
    d. A body scan determines the client's level of inoculation.
    e. The counselor interweaves the imagery of a happy place.

15. Which of the following is a critique of cognitive-behavioral therapy?
    a. The approach is too dependent on the counselor's creativity.
    b. C-B counselors follow a prescriptive regime.
    c. Empirical validation of treatment results determines C-B practice.
    d. Cognitive reframing allows clients to gain new perspectives.
    e. Careful sequencing of treatments engages multiple personality dimensions.

Key Terms and Essential Concepts

Mediational position: Cognitive theory describes how external influences are interpreted inside our minds. Thoughts add our own idiosyncratic meaning to events and influence our emotional reactions. To change feelings, thoughts can be reinterpreted, intervening (mediating) in the cycle of personal reactions.

Rational-Emotive Behavior therapy: REBT is a counseling theory, founded by Albert Ellis, that stresses the impact of negative thinking pattern on emotions and behavior. How a person perceives a problem shapes the person's reaction and the outcome of the situation. According to Ellis, it is not negative events that create emotional reactions but the thinking that occurs between the event and the feelings. Change negative thinking and negative feelings will dissipate.

A-B-C-D-E-F: Ellis's simple method to illustrate the mediational process, or the conversations in our heads. A indicates the activating event; B is the belief in our minds related to the event; C stands for the consequence or the reactions, either emotional or behavioral, that follow B. Since B happens instantaneously and automatically, it can seem like the sequence occurs from A, event, to C, consequent reaction, not recognizing that B, the thoughts in between, have enormous influence. To change emotions and ineffective behaviors, D can be used. D stands for disputing, questioning the automatic thought. E is effecting a new philosophy or developing new automatic thoughts in reaction to what happens. Over time, the disputing teaches new thinking that is more reasonable and effective. F stands for the new feelings that are automatically associated with new beliefs and that will replace old reaction to events.

Automaticity: Thinking reactions are spontaneous, occurring quickly and without effort (automatically), making the thoughts seem inevitable. However, habitual thoughts that happen involuntarily are subject to change when the thoughts are drawn out and repeatedly challenged.

Personal constructs: Kelly explained that each individual develops thought patterns that attribute idiosyncratic meanings to what happens in life. The thinking structure creates the world view characteristic of the person.

Core schemas: Beck described the network of beliefs that become a part of the individual's personality and characteristic of the individual's reactions to some events. The beliefs are learned from experience, often during childhood, and are embedded to the degree that the thoughts may never be completely unlearned. The basic, core nature of the schema indicates that the thoughts are built in to the cognitive structure even when a person establishes new thought patterns. Such thoughts reoccur when events trigger associations to past events, so cognitive therapists prepare clients for dealing with potential relapses.

Irrational beliefs: Ellis's theory says people who are not happy and/or have emotional difficulties share a common set of beliefs. Some of the eleven beliefs involve assumptions about the self as someone who must be loved and competent and can never overcome past experience. Other irrational thoughts involve outside circumstances, perceiving that unwanted events are terrible and require worry as well as implying that all externals are out of the person's control. Still other irrational beliefs consist of reactions to others, suggesting that other's approval and assistance is necessary; or that others should be blamed as bad and in need of punishment; or that the problems of others require one to become upset. Finally, beliefs about methods for dealing with difficulties can be irrational, suggesting that problems have perfect solutions or that avoiding problems and personal responsibility is wise.

Cognitive therapy: Cognitive therapists identify clients' dysfunctional thought patterns and lead clients to challenge negative constructs. Automatic thoughts are tested through behavioral experiments and are logically assessed. Clients learn to analyze their own thinking so even difficult life events are seen in perspective and the positive aspects of life are remembered.

Errors in information processing: Beck devised a list of common mistakes people make in interpreting or perceiving what is happening. The next six terms refer to such errors that are identified by cognitive therapists to help clients change ineffective thinking patterns.

Arbitrary inference: Coming to a conclusion that is not supported by the evidence. An example could be the lion in the Wizard of Oz who claims to be a coward but demonstrates courage in protecting Dorothy against danger.

Selective abstraction: Ignoring some aspects of a situation and characterizing the circumstances on the basis of some details but not others. Blame is often the focus of some aspects of a person's behavior, while other behaviors that would contradict the negative assumptions are ignored.

Overgeneralization: Assumes that one or two facts tell the whole story about a situation and presumes that the characterization is an accurate prediction for what will happen in the future.

Magnification and Minimization: Assumes an event is either more important than it is or less important than it is. Magnifying something may unreasonably characterize the whole situation, and minimizing may lead to ignoring something that has true significance.

Personalization: An individual makes personal assumptions about external events, when in reality whatever happened may not be at all related to the person. For example, an earthquake could be seen as "my bad luck" when the event had nothing to do with the person or his luck.

Absolutistic: The person thinks in absolutes, that everything is black or white without any shades of gray. The thinking is dichotomous in that everything fits into clear distinct categories, and usually each division is the direct opposite of the other. The person's speech patterns suggest judgments that place other people, or events, in good or bad, positive or negative groupings.

Cognitive triad: Beck's empirical research showed that depressed people demonstrated negative thoughts in three categories: the self, current experience, and the future. The self is characterized as defective, inadequate, unhealthy, or disadvantaged. Experience is interpreted as consistently negative, showing a world view that life is overwhelming in its demands, with impossible obstacles and unreasonable daily expectations. Finally, the future is predicted to be more of the same, painting a picture of inevitable failure and unhappiness.

Learned helplessness: Term coined by Seligman describing a pattern of reacting helplessly when negative consequences allow no escape and are repeated consistently. For example, a victim of childhood abuse may accept abuse even as an adult, given the assumption that she has no control over current circumstances. The cognitive pattern presuming no personal control and accepting negative circumstances often leads to depression.

Collaborative empiricism: In cognitive therapy, the client is encouraged to identify thoughts and determine whether the thinking is accurate or not. Logical analysis may show if thoughts are realistic; or experiments, such as trying out a behavior or asking others for feedback, may reveal how rational a thought may be. Stimulating an active problem solving approach to evaluating experiences helps clients resist automatic conclusions that may not work very well. The client learns to examine his own life in a manner similar to a scientific researcher, evaluating evidence and trying things out, rather than accepting suppositions without scrutiny.

Socratic dialogue: Cognitive therapists use a method of questioning that leads the client to come to a conclusion or shows previous conclusions to be inaccurate. This form of questioning was used by Socrates in teaching his students critical thinking.

Guided discovery: Cognitive therapists may use Socratic questioning or assign behavioral tasks that will lead a client to realize the usefulness of particular ways of thinking or the truth of some conclusions. When clients discover alternative thoughts or approaches, the learning has a more powerful initial impact compared to simply being told something.

Choice theory: Glasser developed an approach for helping clients, often juvenile delinquents, recognize the impact of realistic choices. Basic needs are universal: survival, belonging, power and achievement, independence, and fun. Within the context of such needs, individuals make choices to satisfy both needs and wants. The quality of everyone's life is based on the choices they make and the effectiveness of their thinking and behavior to reach individual goals. The theory suggests that negative, ineffective behavior often occurs when the person does not take into account realistic considerations. Therapists have clients name what they *want* and then to consider whether their behavior leads them in a *direction* toward their goals or not. The impact of behavior on the client's satisfaction and the resulting effect on other people are *evaluated*. Finally, the client is assisted in *planning* future behavior that may realistically gain the goals. The counseling approach uses Wubbolding's WDEP acronym as a learning tool to help clients remember how to think clearly in making realistic choices. The counseling system stemming from choice theory is reality therapy.

Time projection: Reality therapists underscore long term negative consequences by asking clients to vividly describe future life circumstances if negative behaviors are continued. An example would be, "Where will you and your family be in one year, or five years, if you continue to act in this manner?"

Natural consequences: In Glasser's choice theory and other parenting systems, such as Adler's, there is a concept of what naturally occurs after a behavior. For example, if a person is rude to other people, the natural expectation of what would happen is that others will respond negatively or not at all. People learn to moderate their behavior to create the outcomes they want to live with. So, therapists teach clients to predict what would likely happen when certain actions are taken. Understanding natural consequences can be an effective inducement for clients to behave in ways that will bring about positive, not negative, effects.

Control theory: Also called *cybernetics*, control theory describes how systems regulate themselves to maintain desirable conditions. A heating system contains a thermostat to indicate when the furnace needs to emit more heat and when the temperature signals the furnace to stop. The temperature set on the thermostat would be defined in cybernetics as a reference point. For our own self-regulation, we define what state we want and check our behavior to see if the results conform to our desired reference point or not.

Dialectics: Linehan developed a sequence of multiple treatment methods to assist clients diagnosed with borderline personality disorder. The methods recognize that competing demands pull clients in divergent directions. Clients need to change but also accept themselves as worthwhile just as they are. Clients' symptoms may be serving the clients' needs in some ways, but they also have to learn to give up symptoms to improve their lives. Clients also have to feel as though their experiences are valid, but at the same time they need to learn new interpretations of their experience.

Stress: A sense of anxiety a person feels when he perceives that the situation is beyond his capacity to cope with the demands. Stressors can be the intense reaction to an important life event; multiple strong emotional reactions associated with trauma or negative experience; or ongoing pressure induced by dealing with difficult situations over time. Even positive experiences cause stress, such as hoping to live up to high expectations.

Stress inoculation: Meichenbaum conceptualized methods to help individuals deal with stressful situations through healthy self talk. Clients are encouraged to face and describe the fears they expect to experience for future situations and are then taught skills and thinking patterns that will make coping easier. Clients then use new skills in situations that are increasingly more difficult until they gain a sense of efficacy in meeting situational demands.

Multimodal therapy: Lazarus developed a therapy approach that recognizes that client issues may need a number of interventions to deal with multiple effects. Rather than assuming client needs can be summarized by a diagnosis, counselors assess seven dimensions of the client's personality.

Basic ID: An acronym designed by Lazarus to indicate the client dimensions requiring assessment. Behavior, affect, sensation, imagery, cognition, interpersonal relationships, and drug/biological factors compose the assessment protocol.

Modality profile: A compilation of symptoms arranged by the Basic ID system.

Structural profile: The rating system used to designate the strength of personality characteristics indicated in each category on the modality profile. Clients rate their tendencies on a scale from 1 to 10.

Technical eclecticism: Most counselors utilize interventions from multiple sources. Techniques are drawn from several theoretical bases, as long as they work well together toward client goals. Multimodal therapy is an example of technical eclecticism.

Tracking: In multimodal therapy, the sequence of introducing treatment interventions is based on the ratings the client has given to dimensions on the structural profile. As therapy progresses, the therapist keeps track of changes made in each dimension. However, therapists from other approaches use the term *tracking* to indicate following the client's content or progress in therapy.

Bridging: In multimodal therapy, the therapist notes which modalities the client rated highest and the order of ratings for all the other dimensions. The order of counseling interventions is based on utilizing the strongest tendencies first and using the skills learned in these area to influence change for other modalities. Bridging is the term that means creating client change between modalities.

EMDR: Eye movement desensitization and reprocessing system is termed by the letters for the previously listed treatment method. The technique developed by Shapiro has the counselor move two fingers in front of the client's face while the client's eyes follow the fingers' movement. According to Shapiro, traumatic memories held in the client's consciousness during the eye movements are neurologically reprocessed. Negative thoughts associated with memories are identified, and more positive cognitions are developed. After a set of eye movement sequences the client rates her reaction to the memory using a SUD (subjective units of distress) scale(0–10) to indicate the intensity of negative feelings. Positive thoughts are also rated using a VOC (validity of cognition) scale (0–7). The treatment is controversial, with some practitioners skeptical and with some empirical evidence showing it works as well as other techniques, such as exposure treatments.

Cognitive Interweave: If the client's distress is not lessened with eye movement treatments, the counselor introduces adaptive thoughts during rest periods between eye movement treatments.

Phenomenological: Many therapy approaches agree that the individual's perceptions are determined by the person's unique way of viewing the world. For cognitive therapies, the world view is contained within the person's cognitive structure and the thoughts the person uses to interpret events. Each person adds subjective meanings to external occurrences.

Problem-solving: Cognitive counseling defines problems as situations that cannot be resolved with the client's naturally occurring automatic reactions. Nonadaptive cognitions make it difficult for clients to develop effective responses to stressful situations. In addition negative thought patterns make dealing with everyday situations more stressful. Cognitive restructuring can allow clients to see many problems as normal and can prepare clients for dealing with difficult circumstances.

Representative Case: Axel Tainer

Client presented as a carefully spoken young man of 17. Axel's intelligence was shown by his articulate speech and his history of achievement. With a high school grade point average of 4.0, he was taking college courses before high school graduation. He received a nearly perfect score on the math section of the SAT and a score in the ninetieth percentile for the verbal section. He had received a number of awards for science projects, computer program innovations, and essay writing. The client had been accepted to an honors program at a prestigious east coast university. During the last six months of his senior year, Axel had become increasingly depressed. He had isolated himself and had been studying constantly, spending all of his time after his classes alone in his room. After graduation he did not leave his room at all for three weeks. Then, his mood deteriorated to such a degree that he was finding it difficult to get out of bed. Finally, his parents brought him to counseling. They described him as usually quite social, enjoying family time and peer activities. They did not understand why he changed to isolating himself in his room. Axel said he stayed in his room to get work done. His most pressing complaint was that he was no longer able to work on the computer projects he wanted to finish before attending college in the fall. When he did get out of bed, he played computer games or read magazines. Axel reported no thoughts of suicide or of harm to others.

The counselor's first recommendation was that Axel's parents make arrangements for Axel to be evaluated for antidepressant medication. Social isolation appeared to be the first problem amenable to change. A dialogue with Axel created a plan to spend at least ten minutes a day talking with any member of his family, and any amount of time exchanging with friends over e-mail or the phone. The counselor also noted the number of "shoulds" Axel expressed, and the client agreed to bring a list of his internal demands for himself to the next session.

As Axel continued therapy he was a ruthless self-critic, saying that he was worthless and intellectually capable but not as productive as he needed to be to live up to his potential. When his work fell behind his self-created time line, he would continue to berate himself saying the tasks should have been done months before. Axel's report suggested a dysthymic condition spanning several years. To meet the demanding productivity requirement he gradually created a sparse lifestyle, assuming a variety of activities would be too much for him to manage. When he experienced depressive moods, he would create another project so he could avoid feeling pain. He envisioned more of the same for the future, himself isolated, trying to work enough, but never measuring up to the standards he expected, and always feeling pain and loneliness.

Axel was assigned the task of finding a chat room where he could discuss how people defined the worth of human beings. Although many others on-line did offer achievement criteria, many said a person's worthiness could be seen in their interactions with others. Axel pondered the responses and decided kindness to others and positive human connections made a person worthwhile—but such values could never apply to him. His intelligence defined him. If he did not achieve great things with his intellectual efforts, he would disappoint his teachers and parents and family members. Socratic questioning examined why Axel held different standards for his self-worth than he would apply to others. The therapist asked Axel to consider if he would treat his younger brother as he treated himself, always demanding maximum achievement and calling him worthless if he did not produce quality work each and every day. Axel could understand the negative impact of such demands and understood the rationale that his internal critic was sapping his internal strength. Still, Axel felt everyone saw him as "a brain" and that behaving outside this self-concept would not be possible.

Axel was assigned the task of collecting evidence as to how others valued him as a human being. He found others enjoyed his wealth of information, and although they knew he was smart, they appreciated his calm, thoughtful manner as much as the knowledge he brought forth. His quietness was presumed to be part of his thinking process, and no one assumed he had self-doubts. People trusted his carefulness and knew that when he considered an issue he weighed many factors with sensitivity. Axel was very moved by the comments of others and his rigid self-concept loosened. He was able to make a list of "shoulds" and began to see none were absolutely necessary all of the time and that a "good enough" standard was often reasonable.

Axel showed a renewed sense of energy as he began to use his careful thoughtfulness to evaluate his own self-concept and punitive thoughts. His "to do" lists began to show more prioritizing. Axel found one method most useful. When he reverted to previous self-denunciations criticizing his work efforts, he would ask himself, "Would I talk to my brother in this same way?" After challenging self-recriminations, he could consider what efforts would be reasonable by thinking how he would help his brother plan activities. Eventually, Axel was able to express his new view of a balanced life for himself that included achievement activities, leisure time, and social interactions. By the time he was preparing to leave for college, he looked forward to both challenging academics and extracurricular activities.

Thinking About Axel

1. How would you describe Axel's original self-concept and the quality of life his sense of self created for him?

2. What combination of cognitive and behavioral interventions were used in Axel's therapy?

3. How did the social isolation Axel imposed on himself affect his depressive symptoms?

4. Which of the information processing errors described by Beck did Axel demonstrate? What were the specifics of the depressive triad for Axel?

5. Which of Ellis's eleven assumptions was Axel demonstrating?

Check Your Thinking about Axel

1. Axel's narrow self-concept reduced his worth to only the criteria of intellectual achievement and, in its extreme, reduced his world to isolating himself in his room. Alone, he attempted to work but became increasingly unable to focus his attention on the tasks so crucial to his sense of well-being.

2. The therapist identified the limited self-concept and used Socratic questioning to expose the beliefs that only intellectual achievement gave Axel self-worth. The contradiction between valuing human interaction and using isolation to meet demanding productivity criteria was brought out. Axel also recognized that using different criteria for himself than others showed inconsistency. Behavioral interventions included asking others the basis for a person's worth and how they viewed Axel's worth. Collecting evidence through such questioning revealed the imbalanced critiques Axel was using to judge himself.

3. Without human contact, Axel was alone with his thoughts, and there was no other input to contradict or soften the exaggerated internal demands he had imposed. Intervening with easy social interaction assignments broke the isolation and gave Axel some support early in therapy.

4. Axel clearly used selective abstraction, assuming that his reputation as a "brain" was the only personal trait that others held as his value, and then he overgeneralized by believing that living up to his maximum potential would only come through achievement products. He magnified the disappointment of others and the amount of productivity required for him to demonstrate his value. He also showed dichotomous and absolute thinking when he judged himself as either productive or not, and when the consequences of not producing the maximum amount was seen as disastrous. His core schema built one assumption that followed another, starting with a limited self-concept and building to unreasonable requirements and an overestimation of the consequences. The depressive triad shown was his sense of worthlessness, an assumption that too many activities would be overwhelming, and a prediction that the future would hold more of the same.

5. Axel believed, a person must be perfectly competent to be considered worthwhile. He feared he would lose the approval and caring of others if he did not demonstrate intellectual achievement. He thought it would be a terrible catastrophe if his productivity schedule was not as he wanted it to be. He also assumed that there would always be a right or perfect solution to the computer programming problems in his work and believed it would be catastrophic if the solution was not found within the time frame he designated.

Core Case: Marianna Chavez

We have seen the core case of Marianna Chavez in Chapters 1, 7, and 8. Now we revisit the case from a cognitive-behavioral perspective. Again **D** designates **Data, A** designates **Assessment,** and **P** designates **Plan**.

D: Marianna's data appear in Chapter 7.

A: Much of the assessment in the behavior approach would be the same for cognitive therapy. However, cognitive therapies would also assess Marianna's thinking structure. Marianna showed dichotomous, absolutistic thinking by setting up idealistic requirements for governments and for significant relationships. Marianna believed all governments function to control the citizenry and that each person must be ever vigilant in determining the latest abuse of power that endangered the people. Her activism and her constant research regarding government activities represented only part of the cognitive activity spent worrying about political action and policy. Marianna also believed she was vulnerable in all relationships and that hypervigilance was necessary to protect herself. She was particularly fearful of relationships with men. Her schema began with an idealized vision of the perfect man, one who was scholarly, politically active, and most interested in relating to others through ideas. She attributed the idealized characteristics to any man who could come close to her image, but she was, of course, consistently disappointed when the man did not measure up. If any sexualized gestures were made in her contacts with a man, her fears of potential brutalizing were reinforced in her mind. Marianna also had idealized thoughts regarding her relationship with her mother who she believed should be all loving and supportive. In reality, her mother had high expectations, insisting Marianna achieve high grades and plan for a successful career to bring honor to the family. Marianna sought her mother's approval and had many thoughts of fear that she would shame her family.

P: Desensitization for gold aversion is accompanied by examination of cognitive schema. When the client is ready and has gained full trust with the therapist, EMDR treatment for rape scenes and escaping from her home country can occur. Adaptive cognitions such as "I am capable of making myself safe" can be interweaved to replace "I am helpless." When trauma has been reprocessed, Marianna can fully examine thoughts regarding her political obsessions and her relationships. Although her ideals can be retained, her vigilance and her constant reinforcement of negative disappointments can be lightened and can become more realistic. Marianna could describe her reactions to young men and brainstorm alternative interpretations to her automatic judgments. Reasonable expectations for her relationship with her mother would be worked out in individual sessions before any joint sessions would be planned. Assertiveness training would follow Marianna's cognitive reframing of her own sensible needs. Relapse prevention would include dealing with triggers to flashbacks, possible fears that could arise when Marianna faces difficult political news and natural struggles that occur in her relationships.

Finding a Balance

Most counselors choose several counseling approaches that suit their personalities and theoretical preferences. In this section, the counselor's personality characteristics are identified and tied to concepts and practices. A case is described, and then the next section shows how the counselor's preferences would play out in working with the case. Finally, a comparison with other approaches is made showing how different preferences might deal with the case. Integrating several approaches might cover varying counselor preferences and differing client issues better than any singular approach.

Key Counselor Preferences

1. Cognitive-Behaviorists (C-B) prefer a warm, careful modulated tone to therapy that models a rational approach to life.

2. C-B counselors approach issues as problems to be solved, kindly understand emotions, but focus on the clients' thinking processes to determine problems and to indicate solutions.

3. C-B counselors enjoy teasing out underlying cognitive patterns and teaching new thinking approaches.

4. C-B counselors prefer to focus on detailed, carefully planned interventions that consider the sequence of interventions.

5. C-B therapists are skilled in persuasive dialogues designed to convince clients to change thinking patterns.

Case Example: Barbara Scheman

Barbara is a middle-aged woman who is struggling with a decision as to whether to end her marriage. She is a competent researcher in an agricultural lab developing methods for sustainable food production and is in charge of home schooling her children. She has two teenage children, both boys. She is convinced her husband is an alcoholic like her father and has spent much time for the last two years attending AlAnon and, with her sister siblings, analyzing her current life and her childhood. She experiences much anxiety that her children will blame her for destroying the family and describes previously experienced major depressive episodes. She has gained medication from a psychiatrist, though she is ambivalent about taking any substance to help her cope.

During initial sessions she spends much time describing her evidence for her husband's addiction: he doesn't express emotions because he is numbed with alcohol; she found hidden caches of liquor; she has discovered money was spent without explanation; he is aligned with her alcoholic brother. She describes herself as an enabler, not questioning her husband's behavior in order to avoid family crises for the sake of the children. Her own emotional difficulties are described as codependency with her husband's alcohol abuse, not recognizing difficulties because she could not face issues that are similar to her childhood issues.

Barbara describes her family of origin as each member playing a role learned in AlAnon: her one sister was a substitute wife, sexually abused by the father; another sister acted the part of the responsible child; she herself was the scapegoat. Her father worked as a salesperson and was out of town much of the time. When he was at home he drank constantly and terrorized the family, criticizing the food, the laundry, and every aspect of the family's activities. Barbara was criticized as ugly, stupid, clumsy, and incompetent. Her mother was a quiet woman who said little and worked hard. Barbara served as her mother's confidant, hearing horror stories that painted the father as the tyrant and the mother as a victim like her children.

Barbara says she chose her husband as a man who would never be as oppressive as her father, but later she began to see her spouse as ineffectual. She notes her home schooling parallels her mother's method of gathering the children against her father.

Applying Counselor Preferences

Using the previously listed C-B preferences, how would a counselor proceed with Barbara?

1. Cognitive-Behaviorists (C-B) prefer a warm interaction with clients and would maintain a careful rational tone to therapy. The counselor listened to the story portrayed and sorted out the primary issues: deciding to leave the marriage; determining how to deal with her husband and children; and making arrangements for how she would live if a separation took place.

2. The C-B counselor would prefer to align with Barbara collaboratively by focusing on her thinking processes to indicate solutions. The complaints regarding her husband's alcohol abuse could be seen as interfering with Barbara's movement. The counselor might confront Barbara, asking if it was more important to prove her spouse was an alcoholic or to decide if she would enact a separation. Barbara admitted that a constant stream of thoughts diagnosing her husband's behavior dominated her thoughts.

3. A C-B counselor would enjoy discovering underlying cognitive patterns and teaching new thinking approaches. The counselor inferred a number of thoughts corroborated by Barbara including, "He's an alcoholic, making me codependent"; "I'm helpless to end the addiction cycle"; "I'm trapped." Each thought was examined and held to the scrutiny of its relevance for her decision regarding the marriage. Eventually, Barbara realized her focus on the alcoholism kept her recycling her fears, and she could not move forward unless she gave up the continual blaming. She assessed the quality of her marriage as sterile regardless of her husband's substance use. The decision to separate came more easily once Barbara dispassionately viewed her thinking process.

4. A C-B therapist would be inclined to carefully plan interventions and consider the sequence of behavior change. Dealing with the stress of carrying out Barbara's decision required preplanning. Barbara practiced her announcement to her husband, stating her decision without accusations. She also thought through what she would say aloud to her children, and what she would say internally to herself if the boys objected. She made a plan to find a place to live and to come home during the day to supervise home schooling. Facing the possibility of her children choosing to live with their father and how she would talk to herself in such a difficult situation was the most laborious stress inoculation.

5. A C-B counselor would skillfully persuade Barbara to change her thinking patterns. Barbara was a strong woman who benefited from a problem-solving approach without reexamining her childhood. Initially, she was caught up in an emotional recycling of the family of origin dynamics. Although she gained some understanding from the support group, AlAnon, when she came to counseling she was ready to act and not stay "stuck" in analyzing her husband's presumed diagnosis. The counselor's confrontation and persuasive argument was that she could let go of the husband's behavior and focus on her own thinking and her responses. She also was better able to deal with her issues by considering her own thought process, changing her emotional reactions, and planning her methods to deal with her situation.

Comparison with Other Approaches

Psychodynamic/Adlerian: Psychoanalytical, ego psychology, object relations, and Adlerian therapists would find it necessary to spend more time focusing on Barbara's childhood memories and the emotional picture she carries regarding significant relationships. Developing a transference relationship and analyzing her ego defenses would allow her to approach her current situation without renewing the patterns from her past.

Person-Centered and Gestalt: Person centered counselors would allow Barbara time to tell her story with understanding and support. She would be able to gain perspective through her own inner resources in an accepting atmosphere. Gestalt therapists might utilize interventions dramatizing the polarities of her inner world such as the blaming side that accuses her husband and the fearful side that is afraid of losing her children.

Existential and Transpersonal: The meaning of Barbara's life would gain more attention with counselors using these approaches. Leaving her husband could have moral implications as could her willingness to stay in a relationship she found lacking. What meaning she would be modeling to her children could be an ethical issue. Meditation training could help Barbara loosen her tightly held belief that her husband was an alcoholic.

Family Systems/Feminist: A family systems counselor could help Barbara gain insight into family of origin dynamics and her projections onto her current family. Barbara, her husband, and her sons could enter a family session and each describe their experience of living in their system. Family members could gain insight regarding the functionality of each parent relating separately to the children. A feminist therapist would help Barbara understand how the social demands of femininity, wifehood, and motherhood have affected her self-evaluations and her decisions.

Example of a Published Research Article on Cognitive-Behavioral Research

Here is an example of a cognitive-behavioral research article. The commentary in the boxes to the left of the article will help you understand the research and the format of the piece.

Treatment of Acute Stress Disorder:
A Comparison of Cognitive-Behavioral Therapy
and Supportive Counseling

Richard A. Bryant, Allison G. Harvey, Suzanne T. Dang,
Tanya Sackville, and Chris Basten

Abstract

When you see a lot of abbreviations in the abstract, pay attention to what they stand for. Later, the authors will probably use the abbreviations (like CBT for Cognitive-Behavioral therapy) without repeating the whole words, which can become confusing if you haven't looked closely at them earlier.

Acute stress disorder (ASD) is a precursor of chronic posttraumatic stress disorder (PTSD). Twenty-four participants with ASD following civilian trauma were given 5 sessions of either cognitive-behavioral therapy (CBT) or supportive counseling (SC) within 2 weeks of their trauma. Fewer participants in CBT (8%) than in SC (83%) met criteria for PTSD at posttreatment. There were also fewer cases of PTSD in the CBT condition (17%) than in the SC condition (67%) 6 months posttrauma. There were greater statistically and clinically significant reductions in intrusive, avoidance, and depressive symptomatology among the CBT participants than among the SC participants. This study represents the 1st demonstration of successful treatment of ASD with CBT and its efficacy in preventing chronic PTSD.

The recent introduction of acute stress disorder (ASD) in the fourth edition of the Diagnostic and Statistical Manual of Mental Disorders (DSM-IV; American Psychiatric Association, 1994) describes posttraumatic stress reactions that occur between 2 days and 4 weeks following the trauma. Although ASD is conceptually similar to posttraumatic stress disorder (PTSD), in that it includes reexperiencing, avoidance, and arousal symptoms, it differs from PTSD because of its stronger emphasis on dissociative symptoms (Bryant & Harvey, 1997). A major rationale for the introduction of this diagnosis was to identify those individuals who are at risk of developing longer term PTSD (Koopman, Classen, & Spiegel, 1994). Recent work indicated that, whereas 78% of motor vehicle accident (MVA) victims who initially satisfied criteria for ASD suffered PTSD 6 months after the trauma, only 4% of those with no ASD subsequently met criteria for PTSD (Harvey & Bryant, 1998). This pattern indicates that the ASD diagnosis identifies individuals who will suffer chronic PTSD and who may benefit from early treatment.

Several studies have investigated the early intervention of posttraumatic stress. Kilpatrick and Veronen (1984) provided recent rape victims with behavioral intervention, repeated assessment, or delayed assessment. Although they reported symptom reduction for all groups 3 months posttrauma, there were no significant differences between groups. Foa, Hearst-Ikeda, and Perry (1995) provided recent sexual and nonsexual assault victims with four sessions of either cognitive-behavioral therapy (CBT) or repeated assessments. The CBT program involved trauma education, relaxation training, imaginal exposure, in vivo exposure, and cognitive restructuring. Two months posttrauma, 10% of the CBT group met criteria for PTSD compared with 70% of the repeated-assessments groups. Foa et al. (1995) suggested that the benefits of their brief CBT resulted from the activation of fear structures by their exposure treatments and the consequent modification of fear-related beliefs. Although this interpretation is consistent with current theorizing about trauma resolution (Foa & Kozak, 1986), Foa et al.'s (1995) study lacked a comparison group that received equivalent therapeutic attention as the CBT group.

Our study attempted to extend Foa et al.'s (1995) findings in two ways. First, we compared the efficacy of a brief CBT program with nondirective supportive counseling (SC) to provide an index of the benefits of CBT relative to nonspecific therapeutic support. Second, we selected participants who met criteria for ASD. On the basis that these participants are most likely to develop chronic PTSD, we considered that they represent a more stringent test of the efficacy of brief early intervention of posttraumatic stress. We predicted that

Dissociative symptoms involve disruptions in consciousness, memory, identity, or perception.

The authors explain the evidence that Acute Stress Disorder leads to longer term Post Traumatic Stress Disorder. Thus, PTSD may be prevented by early interventions for people with ASD. The introduction sets forth the importance of the research topic.

In Foa et al., one group received CBT and the other group received assessments (measurement) only. So CBT was basically compared to no treatment. The question of whether CBT was better than another psychotherapy was not addressed.

Here is the hypothesis of the research study.

CBT would result in fewer PTSD symptoms both at posttreatment and at the 6 month follow-up.

Method

Participants

Think about why the researchers chose the inclusion and exclusion criteria they did. Consider how using these criteria made the sample of participants different from people in general.

Participants in both groups were survivors of either MVAs or industrial accidents who were referred to the PTSD Unit at Westmead Hospital in Westmead, New South Wales, Australia. The referral sources included hospital staff and local community mental health centers. Inclusion criteria included (a) having been involved in either an MVA or an industrial accident within the past 2 weeks, (b) satisfying criteria for ASD, (c) proficiency in English, and (d) between 18 and 60 years of age. Exclusion criteria included (a) current suicidal ideation; (b) diagnosis of psychosis, organic mental disorder, or substance abuse; and (c) evidence of brain injury sustained in the trauma.

This material is provided so that the comparability of the two groups (cognitive-behavior therapy, or CBT, and supportive counseling, or ST) can be judged. If the two groups were meaningfully different from the start, the research findings would not be convincing.

The CBT group comprised 12 (7 women and 5 men) participants with a mean age of 32.25 years (SD = 12.61), and the SC group comprised 12 (7 women and 5 men) participants with a mean age of 33.00 years (SD = 11.41). The trauma-assessment interval was 9.92 days (SD = 4.23) for the CBT participants and 10.33 days (SD = 4.99) for the SC participants. The perceived severity of the trauma was 6.62 for the CBT participants (SD = 2.47) and 7.33 (SD = 1.75) for the SC participants. Mean Dissociative Experiences Scale (DES) scores were 23.50 (SD = 17.92) for the CBT group and 22.42 (SD = 12.34) for the SC group. Each group comprised 7 MVA and 5 industrial accident victims. Each group included 2 participants who did not fully satisfy criteria for a diagnosis of ASD because they reported only two, rather than three, dissociative symptoms.

Measures

Sensitivity is the test's rate of correctly identifying who has the disorder; *specificity* is the test's rate of correctly identifying who does not have the disorder.

We assessed ASD using the Acute Stress Disorder Interview (ASDI; Bryant, Harvey, Dang, & Sackville, in press). This structured clinical interview is based on DSM—IV criteria for ASD, contains 19 dichotomously scored items that relate to ASD symptoms, and provides a total score of acute stress severity (range = 1—19). The ASDI possesses sound test—retest reliability (r = .95), sensitivity (92%), and specificity (93%) in a sample of MVA and nonsexual assault survivors. Participants were also administered the Impact of Event Scale (IES; Horowitz, Wilner, & Alvarez, 1979), the Beck Depression Inventory (BDI; Beck, Ward, Mendelsohn, Mock, & Erbaugh, 1961), the State-Trait Anxiety Inventory (STAI; Spielberger, Gorsuch, Lushene, Vagg, & Jacobs, 1983), and the DES (Bernstein & Putnam, 1986). Participants were also asked to estimate the degree to which they were "badly hurt

The DES is a scale of dissociative symptoms.

in the accident" on a 10-point Likert scale ranging from 1 (not at all) to 10 (extremely). We assessed PTSD using the Composite International Diagnostic Interview (CIDI) PTSD Module (Peters et al., 1996).

Procedure

Participants were assessed at pretreatment (Time 1), posttreatment (Time 2), and 6 months posttrauma (Time 3). The mean pretreatment–posttreatment interval was 41.50 days (SD = 7.00), and the mean posttreatment—follow-up interval was 179.50 days (SD = 7.96). All assessments were conducted by a clinical psychologist who was unaware of treatment group status. All measures were administered at each assessment, except that the ASDI and the DES were administered at Time 1, and the CIDI PTSD Module was administered at Times 2 and 3. Participants who met criteria for ASD were randomly allocated to one treatment program. Each group received five 1.5-hr individually administered sessions conducted by clinical psychologists. Sessions occurred once weekly. Treatment adherence was monitored by Richard A. Bryant, who reviewed case notes and monitoring records of each participant.

The CBT program comprised (a) education about trauma reactions, (b) progressive muscle relaxation training, (c) imaginal exposure to traumatic memories, (d) cognitive restructuring of fear-related beliefs, and (e) graded in vivo exposure to avoided situations. Forty minutes of each of the final four sessions were devoted to participants reliving their trauma by focusing attention on their memories and engaging with their affective responses. These narratives were not audiotaped, but participants were instructed to complete this exposure in the same manner as in therapy as daily homework. The SC program comprised education about trauma and general problem-solving skills and provided an unconditionally supportive role. Homework included diary keeping of current problems and mood states. SC specifically avoided exposure or anxiety-management techniques.

Results and Discussion

Participant Characteristics

Table 1 presents the mean psychopathology scores. Planned comparisons indicated that the two groups did not differ in terms of age, trauma-assessment interval; perceived severity of trauma; DES; or pretreatment IES, STAI, or BDI scores.

Treatment adherence means how closely the clinical psychologists followed the researchers' plans in treating the clients. If the psychologists didn't deliver the CBT and SC properly, the results of the experiment would be hard to interpret.

The two treatment plans are described.

Table 1 is not reprinted here, to save space. It shows the pretreatment equality between the two groups.

The χ^2 statistic reflects how strongly percentages differ. For example, here 83% of the SC group had PTSD at posttreatment, while 8% of the CBT group did. The difference in percentages would happen by chance fewer than one in a thousand times.

The *2 x 3* design means 2 groups (CBT and SC) measured 3 times (pretreatment, posttreatment and 6 month follow-up). Once the ANOVAs found that there were differences among groups, among time points, and among group patterns over time, the Tukey follow-up comparisons show between *which* groups and times the significant differences lie. The same procedure, using ANOVAs followed by Tukey tests, was done for Posttraumatic Stress Severity, Anxiety, and Depression.

Diagnostic Status

At posttreatment, fewer participants in the CBT group (8%) met criteria for PTSD than in the SC group (83%), χ^2 (1, N = 24) = 13.59, p < .001. Similarly, at the 6-month follow-up, fewer participants in the CBT group (17%) met criteria for PTSD than in the SC group (67%), χ^2 (1, N = 24) = 6.17, p < .05.

Posttraumatic Stress Severity

A series of 2 (group) x 3 (assessment) repeated measures analyses of variance (ANOVAs) were conducted on posttraumatic stress symptoms, anxiety, and depression (see Table 1). A 2 x 3 ANOVA on IES Intrusion scores indicated significant main effects for group and time and a significant Group x Time interaction effect. Post hoc Tukey comparisons indicated significant differences in both groups between Time 1 and both Time 2 and Time 3 assessments. Post hoc comparisons indicated that IES Intrusion scores were less for the CBT participants than for the SC participants at both Time 2, t (22) = 9.38, p < .01, and Time 3, t (22) = 6.69, p < .02. A 2 x 3 ANOVA on IES Avoidance scores indicated significant main effects for group and time and a significant Group x Time interaction effect. Post hoc Tukey comparisons indicated significant differences in both groups between Time 1 and Time 3 assessments and between Time 1 and Time 2 for the CBT group. Post hoc comparisons indicated that IES Avoidance scores were less for the CBT participants than for the SC participants at both Time 2, t (22) = 21.37, p < .001, and Time 3, t (22) = 10.32, p < .005.

Anxiety

A 2 x 3 ANOVA on STAI State scores indicated significant main effects for group and time and a significant Group x Time interaction effect. Post hoc Tukey comparisons indicated significant differences in both groups between Time 1 and both Time 2 and Time 3 assessments. Post hoc comparisons indicated that STAI State scores were less for the CBT participants than for the SC participants at both Time 2, t (22) = 7.95, p < .01, and Time 3, t (22) = 7.13, p < .025. A 2 x 3 ANOVA on STAI Trait scores indicated a significant main effect for time. Post hoc Tukey comparisons indicated a significant difference in the CBT group between Time 1 and Time 2 assessments.

Depression

A 2 x 3 ANOVA on BDI scores indicated a significant main effect for time and a significant Group x Time interaction effect. Post hoc Tukey comparisons indicated significant differences in the CBT group between Time 1 and both Time 2 and Time 3 assessments. Post hoc comparisons indicated that BDI scores were less for the CBT participants than for the SC participants only at Time 3, t (22) = 3.09, p < .01.

Treatment Effects

To index the clinical significance of therapy gains, we followed Jacobson and Truax's (1991) suggested technique for when population norms are unavailable. That is, because of the lack of normative data on ASD populations, we defined clinical improvement as a reduction of at least 2 standard deviations below the pretreatment mean of our sample. Table 2 presents the summary data of treatment effects. At posttreatment, more CBT than SC participants improved in terms of IES Intrusion scores, IES Avoidance scores, and BDI scores. The groups did not differ on either STAI State scores or STAI Trait scores. At follow-up assessment, more CBT than SC participants improved in terms of IES Intrusion scores, IES Avoidance scores, and BDI scores. The groups did not differ on either STAI State scores or STAI Trait scores.

Whereas previous work indicates that 78% of ASD participants following MVAs will continue to suffer PTSD 6 months posttrauma (Harvey & Bryant, 1998), this brief CBT program resulted in only 17% of ASD participants receiving a PTSD diagnosis at this time. These findings are generally

> Since most people never get ASD, norms from large groups have never been established. So improvement has to be defined by change within the treated group rather than by comparison with a big population average. The researchers decided to define improvement as a reduction of 2 standard deviations from the pretreatment means of their own sample. This is something like a 48% reduction in distress for an individual classified as improved.

> The researchers compare their own findings with other research findings and speculate on similarities and differences.

Table 2

Treatment Effects

Time and measure	% improvement		χ^2 (1, N = 24)	p
	CBT	SC		
Posttreatment:				
IES Intrusion	75	25	6.00	.05
IES Avoidance	50	0	8.00	.01
STAI State	42	17	1.82	ns
STAI Trait	0	0	0.00	ns
BDI	50	0	8.00	.01
Follow-up:				
IES Intrusion	75	25	6.00	.05
IES Avoidance	58	17	8.06	.01
STAI State	25	25	0.00	ns
STAI Trait	0	0	0.00	ns
BDI	58	17	6.94	.05

Note. CBT = cognitive-behavioral therapy; SC = supportive counseling; IES = Impact of Event Scale; STAI = State-Trait Anxiety Inventory; BDI = Beck Depression Inventory consistent with the results of Foa et al. (1995). In contrast to our study, however, Foa et al. did not find a significant difference between treatment and wait-list control groups 5.5 months posttrauma. This lack of difference was apparently due to the remission of PTSD in 78% of their control sample. In contrast, it seems that our stricter inclusion of only participants who met criteria for ASD resulted in selection of participants who suffered a more severe posttraumatic stress reaction and were more likely to experience chronic PTSD. In this sense, treating ASD participants may represent a more rigorous test of CBT because these individuals are more prone to long-term psychopathology. Comparisons between our findings and previous studies that have treated assault victims are limited, however, because assault is often associated with higher rates of PTSD than MVAs (Foa & Riggs, 1995).

Our design differed from Foa et al.'s (1995) study in that it compared CBT with SC. The greater gains achieved by CBT suggest that nonspecific therapeutic factors were not critical in achieving success. The relative ineffectiveness of SC suggests that early intervention that attempts to provide support and problem-solving advice will not substantially reduce PTSD. The similarities between SC and debriefing programs that are frequently provided to trauma survivors during the acute trauma phase (Mitchell & Bray, 1989) may indicate that such interventions may not prevent PTSD in individuals who suffer more severe acute reactions.

Although the primary goal of our treatment program was to reduce PTSD symptomatology, the CBT group also displayed lower BDI scores 6 months posttrauma than did the SC group. Recent commentaries have noted that posttraumatic depression is often secondary to the distress of PTSD symptoms and that depression may remit after successful treatment of PTSD (Nishith, Hearst, Mueser, & Foa, 1995). We recognize that the CBT group received cognitive restructuring, which has the potential for reducing depressive responses. It is difficult to identify the exact mechanism that may have mediated the greater reduction of depression in the CBT group. Interestingly, the BDI scores of the two groups did not differ at posttreatment. Similarly, Foa et al. (1995) found that their treatment group displayed greater reduction in depression at 5.5 months than at the 2-month follow-up. This pattern may be explained in terms of depression developing over time as a response to the distressing problems associated with PTSD. The successful treatment of these core symptoms in the acute stage may have assisted adjustment and promoted remission of depression.

Although our design demonstrated the superiority of CBT over nonspecific therapy factors, we can only speculate concerning the mechanisms that mediated successful treatment. Imaginal exposure is based primarily on

The authors argue that since they compared CBT to another therapy, they have shown that other therapies will not have the same positive results. Current programs may not be preventing PTSD as well as CBT would.

The relation between PTSD and depression is explored, since CBT lowered depression as well as PTSD symptoms.

This experiment didn't show which elements of the CBT caused the improvements.

information-processing theories that propose that resolution of a trauma requires (a) activation of fear structures and (b) modification of threat-based beliefs (Foa & Kozak, 1986). One possibility is that the imaginal exposure promoted habituation to the anxiety elicited by the traumatic memories and that the cognitive therapy facilitated alterations to views of the world as a threatening and uncontrollable place. Alternately, the instruction of anxiety management may have led to decreased anxiety and enhanced perceptions of self-mastery. Further, the in vivo exposure component may have been instrumental in decreasing avoidance behaviors, which are critical in prolonging PTSD (Bryant & Harvey, 1995). Future studies need to compare the efficacies of different components of CBT in treating ASD.

> Some CBT participants developed PTSD between posttreatment and follow-up. The authors consider why this might happen.

The incidence of PTSD in the CBT group increased from 8% at posttreatment to 17% at follow-up. This pattern suggests that immediate treatment effects may not be long lasting. Further, this finding is consistent with the proposal that posttraumatic adjustment is dependent on a range of factors that occur in the months following a trauma (Solomon, Mikulincer, & Flum, 1988) and that future treatment studies of ASD need to index the role of posttrauma stressors on relapse following treatment. Future work also needs to address the finding that CBT did not reduce anxiety more than did SC. According to cognitive theory, anxiety should subside as the fear network is modified. Although Foa et al. (1995) found a difference in arousal symptoms between their CBT and control groups at posttreatment, no difference was observed at follow-up. One possible explanation for these findings is that acute arousal symptoms may remit in the ensuing months in a way that minimizes the likelihood of group differences. The mean STAI scores for the CBT group at follow-up were comparable with normative means; accordingly, our sample may have reached a level of anxiety that was consistent with their pretrauma levels.

> Authors customarily point out the shortcomings (limitations) of their research, near the end of their article.

We recognize that our conclusions are limited by our small sample size. Replication with larger samples would support our conclusions and permit analysis of predictors of successful outcome. Second, our study included only MVAs and industrial accidents. It is possible that individuals who have suffered different types of traumas may not respond similarly to this brief program. We also note that our procedure did not include interrater reliability checks of the ASD diagnosis. Our conclusions could also have been strengthened by indexing expectancy factors by means of credibility ratings from participants in the respective treatments. We also recognize that acute stress reactions may be complicated by comorbidity issues, including major depression and substance abuse. Future studies need to index the effect of brief interventions on these coexisting disorders. Despite these limitations, our findings indicate that the treatment of individuals with ASD can be effectively achieved with brief CBT intervention during the initial month after a trauma. Further research is required that delineates the optimal components of CBT to treat ASD, specifies the contraindications of early intervention, and identifies the complications of treating this potentially fragile population.

References

American Psychiatric Association (1994). Diagnostic and statistical manual of mental disorders (4th ed.). Washington, DC: Author.

Beck, A. T., Ward, C. H., Mendelsohn, M., Mock, J. & Erbaugh, J. (1961). An inventory for measuring depression. *Archives of General Psychiatry, 4*, 561–571.

Bernstein, E. M. & Putnam, F. W. (1986). Development, reliability, and validity of a dissociation scale. *Journal of Nervous and Mental Disease, 174*, 727–735.

Bryant, R. A. & Harvey, A. G. (1995). Avoidant coping style and post-traumatic stress following motor vehicle accidents. *Behaviour Research and Therapy, 33*, 631–635.

Bryant, R. A. & Harvey, A. G. (1997). Acute stress disorder: A critical review of diagnostic issues. *Clinical Psychology Review, 17*, 757–773.

Bryant, R. A., Harvey, A. G., Dang, S. T. & Sackville, T. (in press). Assessing acute stress disorder: Psychometric properties of structured clinical interview. (*Psychological Assessment.*)

Foa, E. B., Hearst-Ikeda, D. & Perry, K. J. (1995). Evaluation of a brief cognitive-behavioral program for the prevention of chronic PTSD in recent assault victims. *Journal of Consulting and Clinical Psychology, 63*, 948–955.

Foa, E. B. & Kozak, M. J. (1986). Emotional processing of fear: Exposure to corrective information. *Psychological Bulletin, 99*, 20–35.

Foa, E. B. & Riggs, D. S. (1995). Posttraumatic stress disorder following assault: Theoretical considerations and empirical findings. *Current Directions in Psychological Science, 4*, 61–65.

Harvey, A. G. & Bryant, R. A. (1998). The relationship between acute stress disorder and posttraumatic stress disorder: A prospective evaluation of motor vehicle accident survivors. *Journal of Consulting and Clinical Psychology, 66*, 507–512.

Horowitz, M. J., Wilner, N. & Alvarez, W. (1979). The Impact of Event Scale: A measure of subjective stress. *Psychosomatic Medicine, 41*, 209–218.

Jacobson, N. S. & Truax, P. (1991). Clinical significance: A statistical approach to defining meaningful change in

When you see several articles by one author in the References, you can note this name as one to look for when you study the topic of the article further.

psychotherapy research. *Journal of Consulting and Clinical Psychology, 59,* 12–19.

Kilpatrick, D. G. & Veronen, L. J. (1984). Treatment for rape-related problems: Crisis intervention is not enough.(In L. H. Cohen, W. Claiborn, & C. A. Specter (Eds.), *Crisis intervention* (2nd ed., pp. 165–185). New York: Human Services Press.)

Koopman, C., Classen, C. & Spiegel, D. (1994). Predictors of posttraumatic stress symptoms among survivors of the Oakland/Berkeley, Calif., firestorm. *American Journal of Psychiatry, 151,* 888–894.

Mitchell, J. T. & Bray, G. P. (1989). *Emergency services stress.* (Englewood Cliffs, NJ: Prentice Hall.)

Nishith, P., Hearst, D. E., Mueser, K. T. & Foa, E. B. (1995). PTSD and major depression: Methodological and treatment considerations in single case design. *Behavior Therapy, 26,* 319–335.

Peters, L., Andrews, G., Cottler, L. B., Chatterji, S., Janca, A. & Smeets, R. (1996). The composite international diagnostic interview post-traumatic stress disorder module: Preliminary data. *International Journal of Methods in Psychiatric Research, 6,* 167–174.

Solomon, Z., Mikulincer, M. & Flum, H. (1988). Negative life events, coping responses, and combat-related psychopathology: A prospective study. *Journal of Abnormal Psychology, 97,* 302–307.

Spielberger, C. D., Gorsuch, R. L., Lushene, R., Vagg, P. R. & Jacobs, G. A. (1983). *Manual for the state-trait anxiety inventory.* (Palo Alto, CA: Consulting Psychologists Press.)

Discussion Ideas

1. Name two ways that this study improved on the Foa et al. (1995) C-BT study. Explain why the authors chose to extend the study in these ways.

2. What were the three exclusion criteria in selection of participants? Why did the researchers exclude participants who met these criteria?

3. What is a dichotomously scored item? What other types of items are there in psychological testing?

4. Why were the participants subjected to so many tests? How many tests did they take at each assessment point?

5. What elements of cognitive-behavioral therapy were included in the treatment?

6. What elements were included in the supportive counseling (SC) treatment? Why did the SC treatment avoid exposure or anxiety-management techniques? Did SC do the participants any good? In what situations do you think SC is an effective form of therapy?

7. The authors speculate on how the different components of the C-BT worked to prevent PTSD. Explain their reasoning in your own words.

Answer Key for Practice Test Questions

True/False	*Multiple Choice*

True/False

1. T
2. F
3. T
4. T
5. F
6. T
7. F
8. F
9. F
10. T

Multiple Choice

1. b   11. c
2. c   12. e
3. e   13. a
4. d   14. a
5. a   15. b
6. e
7. c
8. b
9. b
10. b

CHAPTER 10

Systemic Approaches: Family Therapy

Chapter Review

Family therapies are characterized by viewing the client as a group, rather than treating the individuals within the system separately. Even when individual clients are seen alone, a major focus of counseling is the influence of the family. Systemic thinking explores the impact of group as an organism functioning as a whole with interrelated parts. The most basic grouping is the family of origin, the group in which a person is born, a nuclear family consisting of parents and children. The basic family group has an extended family consisting of relatives and very close friends. Each family is unique, characterized by its history across generations and by establishing its own way of doing things, or its own rules that can be explicitly stated or implicitly enforced. The family, like individuals, has different experiences across the life cycle, starting with a couple's early-marriage period; changing to parenting of first young children, then older ones, until the children become adults and leave home. Children are an important factor in the system, and they behave in ways that meet their own goals, though systemic mechanisms regulate their behavior and development.

An important systemic concept is the balancing of the needs of individual members and the needs of the group, stabilizing group functioning, in an effort to maintain homeostasis. Each family has interaction patterns that govern the communication between members and alignments between individuals and between subgroups within the system. Boundaries separate the family group from outside influences and can be either permeable, allowing a flow of information, or impermeable, permitting only minor input.

When families present themselves for counseling, often there is an identified patient—the person said to have a problem. From a systemic perspective, the "problem," though attached to one person, is actually a group issue; and the individual member's difficulties may serve a function for the group as a whole (symptom functionality). A family may be a problem-determined system, meaning that the focus on difficulties allows the family to deal with the group's anxiety regarding less obvious issues. A common example would be parents bringing to counseling a rebellious teenager whose behavior may actually hide marital difficulties in the parents. A problem-determined system includes everyone who considers themselves affected by the problem, so sometimes a family member may not be included, and sometimes a nonfamily member is included.

A number of family therapy approaches have different explanations for how families work and what goes wrong when groups become dysfunctional. The systemic approach emphasizes group anxiety and what functions a symptom serves. Bowen describes how families come together to worry about one member's difficulties in a process called *family projection*. Cross-generational transmission can carry problems from one generation to the next. Families may establish interaction patterns where emotions and thinking are so undifferentiated that the feelings and thoughts are said to be fused. Where fusion dominates, family members operate on the basis of pseudoselves, where thoughtful consideration is denied in favor of doing whatever it takes to maintain emotional connections. To tease out the pervasive themes that may induce families to act out historically reinforced emotions, genograms may be used by counselors. A genogram is a diagram showing the family in an historical sequence. Exploring stories about the family depicted on the genogram helps therapists and clients determine multigenerational influences. Another systemic concept is triangulation: two people in conflict involve a third member and avoid direct confrontation. The triangle interaction is meant to reduce anxiety for the triad and for the system as a whole. However, it doesn't always work and often produces more problems.

The structural therapy approach emphasizes the construction of the family organization. What are the openly spoken rules and the unspoken ones? What subgroups exist where two or more family members align themselves and interact with other subsystems? Often parents are one subsystem with its own purposes and relationship, and siblings, or some combination of the children, form other coalitions. How tight knit is the family? How close are family members? The family structure maintains boundaries around the group and dictates how much outside influence is allowed in. When the flow of communication and emotional connections are disrupted, some members may disengage or cut off direct exchanges. Or, the degree of closeness may be too intertwined, with family members enmeshed, suggesting that they have difficulty separating their individual needs from each other.

The strategic therapy approach pays attention to the circular causality within families: what happens to any part of the system affects the rest of the system. Therapists use a technique called *circular questioning*, asking each and every member the same question to reveal the interrelationships and expose differing points of view. Strategic therapists use calculated interventions to create systemic changes, and they may choose not to reveal the purpose of the therapeutic techniques. One such method is paradoxical intention where clients are told to do more of a symptom. Other techniques help clients gain new interpretations of family events or problems. The counselor may use a new word to reframe a single client perception, or new interpretations may fully restructure broad cognitive patterns used by family members.

Experiential family therapists share techniques and counseling goals with Gestaltists. The purpose of many counseling activities is to induce full emotional experiences so everyone in the group will be more congruent in communicating and will gain empathy for what others are going through. Techniques include the parts party, where family members act out one person's personality parts; and sculpting, where one person directs others in a pantomime of a family scene. Experiential counselors attempt to create change for primary, underlying emotions, rather than fixing surface feelings, or secondary emotions. Some dysfunctional families may exhibit emotional deadness: awareness of feelings and spontaneity is lacking. Experiential counselors themselves may join the empathic sharing among family members as everyone shares in the experiencing of the moment.

The narrative approach stresses the impact of family stories that depict how families characterize themselves and relay values through shared lore. The social constructions each person carries from the family narrative may include unexamined meanings. By telling the stories, old interpretations can be examined and changed or held with respect. Family social constructionists also assign letter writing so clients can express what they might want to say to another family member, even though the client may choose not to send the letter. Reflecting teams observe family sessions and then share their thoughts with the family so differing viewpoints can be noted.

Although different family therapy approaches may vary in their emphasis, all share the broad ideas of systemwide influences. Some approaches prefer the counselor to take a neutral stance and objectively observe families interacting. Other approaches may prefer participating in the family experience. Some family counselors may accommodate family language and emotional tone to join the system. Common techniques include the miracle question, asking clients how their lives would be different if problems magically disappeared. Or, clients may be asked to recall a time when they did *not* experience the problem, a technique called *unique outcome*, or asked to rate the problem's severity on a scale to gain perspective. Family drawings are commonly used as a visual depiction of family members or family activities, as with kinetic drawings. Yet another technique is family mapping, where clients label characteristics of each family member and identify interaction patterns between dyads. Sometimes counseling can offer the means for families to reduce surface level anxieties and create what is termed *first-order change.* At other times, second order changes are achieved where the basic structure of the family is transformed.

Practice Test Questions

True or False: Consider each statement and try to explain in your own mind why it might not be fully true. Be sure to take into account any qualifying factors that might make the statement untrue. If you decide that the statement is fully true, circle **T**. Otherwise, circle **F**.

T F 1. Family therapists stress the psychology of the individual more than group dynamics.

T F 2. The experience of previous generations has no influence in modern families.

T F 3. The identified patient in a family may have problems that allow the system to avoid other issues.

T F 4. When an individual experiences change, other family members may also change.

T F 5. Rules, whether spoken or unspoken, are not needed for functional families.

T F 6. It would be difficult for a person enmeshed with a parent to gain an individual, separate identity.

T F 7. The culture associated with a family may influence the system.

T F 8. A *parts party* is a technique where family members take apart an object and then play a game to see who can name the most parts.

T F 9. A problem-determined system is a highly functional family that is exceptionally adept at resolving the troubles that sometimes occur.

T F 10. Family scapegoats are the members who take the blame for difficulties.

Multiple Choice: Circle the one letter next to the best answer to the following questions or to complete the sentence stems.

1. A young woman consistently chooses partners who try to control her every move. What explanation might a family therapist give for this behavior?
   a. Her early childhood training created weak ego strength.
   b. She is unattractive and cannot expect to find a considerate partner.
   c. She cannot differentiate between her thinking and feeling processes.
   d. She is so attractive men need to control her so she won't find another relationship.

2. Members of families with fused, enmeshed relationships are very close to each other. How do these families deal with influences from outside the system?
   a. Very close, fused families love to participate in community events because the shared activities help them become closer and share with other families.
   b. Outside influences are shunned in fused, closed families who are threatened when their system is affected by nonmembers or new information.
   c. Enmeshed relationships in families are relieved when outsiders visit.
   d. Boundaries for fused relationships are so open to outside influence, the lines between the family systems are said to be permeable.

3. Change in family systems can occur on two levels. Which of the following correctly describes the levels of change according to family systems approaches?
   a. First-order change reorganizes the structure of the family and second-order change makes the minor adaptations needed after overall changes are made.
   b. Second-order change deals with the underlying major dysfunctions while first change entails taking the family history.
   c. First-order changes are done at the suggestion of the therapist and second-order changes are decided by the majority of family members.
   d. First-order changes relieve basic system anxiety without changes in family structure while second-order changes involve altering the family organization.

4. Which of the following is NOT a style of interacting with a family according to the therapist roles described by Ferber and Ranz (1972)?
   a. mediator
   b. diplomat
   c. lone ranger
   d. conspirator

5. When Dattillo (1994) observes and listens to family discussions, several categories of cognitions are most relevant for understanding the dynamics. Which of the following would be considered relevant?
   a. Who is noticed?
   b. What do family members expect in the future?
   c. How do family members think the world should be?
   d. a and b
   e. a, b, and c

6. A *family dance* is defined in a particular way in family therapy. Which description best fits a systemic approach?
   a. Family structure is shown by who is asked to dance first and who is asked last.
   b. Families talk in predictable ways that are often repeated, like formal dancing.
   c. Families that encourage members to go to dances are open to outside influences.
   d. Family dance events celebrate important occasions like weddings and bar mitzvahs.

7. Family therapy is considered inappropriate for which of the following counseling issues?
   a. alcoholism
   b. anorexia
   c. archetypal imaging
   d. expulsion from school
   e. c and d

8. The termination stage of therapy is characterized by certain counseling activities and topics. Which of the following are appropriate for the closing stage?
   a. The counselor starts the joining process to accommodate the family's style of interacting.
   b. The counselor explains who are the appropriate family members for counseling.
   c. Children give a recognition reflex that tells the therapist the goals described are true.
   d. Families review the progress they have made and brainstorm how they can prevent going back to old habits.

9. When individual family members share their timelines, what are they telling each other?
   a. They are sharing their descriptions of major events across a period of time.
   b. Noting any differences between timelines helps members understand each other's experiences.
   c. People gain perspective on how world affairs have affected society and social groups.
   d. a and b
   e. b and c

10. *Triangles* in family relationships are described as
    a. relieving system anxiety by circumventing direct communication.
    b. a way that family members use to disengage emotionally.
    c. a mechanism that induces enmeshment among people.
    d. two people in conflict talking to each with a third person present.
    e. a and d

11. *Experiential* family therapists do which of the following?
    a. They strategically plan to solve system difficulties.
    b. They encourage family members to become more aware of emotions.
    c. They participate in the family interactions, spontaneously sharing reactions.
    d. a and c
    e. b and c

12. Which of the following is NOT a goal for children's behavior or misbehavior?
    a. attention getting
    b. self-evaluation
    c. withdrawal
    d. power
    e. getting

13. Which of the following are found on family maps?
    a. boxes with men's names
    b. circles with women's names
    c. adjectives describing individuals
    d. descriptors of relationships
    e. all of the above

14. What do *kinetic* family drawings show?
    a. several generations of the family members
    b. all the members of the nuclear family
    c. family members doing something together
    d. all the members of the extended family

15. Which of the following is an example of *marking boundaries?*
    a. Children are assigned helping partners.
    b. The parents are told to spend the weekend together.
    c. Enmeshed pairs are ordered to disengage for some time.
    d. a and b
    e. a, b, and c

Key Terms and Essential Concepts

Nuclear and extended family: Nuclear family is the basic group consisting of parents and children. Extended family branches out to include grandparents and other close relatives or friends that have consistent or powerful impact on the basic group.

Family life cycle: Family relationships naturally and inevitably change as the nature of the system changes with births, deaths, children growing up, children leaving, job changes, retirements, and so on. Young children who are dependent on parents eventually grow up and establish independence. Marriages change as career efforts dominate for periods of time and gradually recede in priority. Separateness and connectedness may be helpful and harmful depending on the context of the family's place in the cycle.

Family of origin: In an intergenerational view of an extended family, the family of origin is the unit where a particular person is born.

Homeostasis: A system, or a family, operates in ways that will move toward an equilibrium of all of the factors that influence the group. Needed adaptations are made in a fluidity that allows for change. A basic stability is retained so the system can continue functioning. Homeostasis is disrupted by family conflict and tension within the system, and the system will create mechanisms to keep the group together.

Child goals: Dreikurs, an Adlerian author, proposed four purposes of children's behavior: getting attention, power, revenge, and withdrawal. Bitter described three more goals: getting, self-elevation, and avoidance of tasks. Children in counseling will show a verbal or nonverbal recognition of these goals as reasons for their behavior or misbehavior. Parents and counselors can teach children more effective means to meet their psychological needs.

Symptom functionality: A major tenet of family systems thinking is the concept that the symptoms shown by a family member serve a purpose to maintain the group's interaction and cohesion. When the family focuses on one member's difficulties, other anxieties in the system are ignored or reduced.

Parentification: A family dynamic that requires a child to take on the role of a parent may mean the child becomes one spouse's confidant, or one sibling becomes the caretaker for other children, or the child does adult responsibilities such as cooking for the entire family or bill paying. In essence the child is no longer treated as a child and the level of responsibility impairs the child's experiencing childhood activities. Depending on the degree of parentification, natural psychological development can be impeded and interactions between family members can be affected.

Problem-determined system: When family dynamics revolve around an identified problem, solving the problem could disrupt the family's sense of belonging. Discussing the problem is a family activity, rarely including outsiders, so the conversation increases cohesion among members only. A problem-determined system includes everyone who is concerned with the problem, including nonfamily members and sometimes excluding a family member.

Identified patient: The family member who demonstrates problems that upset the family is usually named as "the problem" to the counselor. From a family system perspective, the identified patient could be acting in ways that serve a family function. For example, a child's difficulties could be a means to force the parents to cooperate and draw attention away from marital difficulties.

Scapegoat: The behavior of a person in the family is blamed for the system's difficulties. Scapegoats can be acting inappropriately according to societal expectations or not. The "misbehavior" could be violations of unreasonable family rules.

Systemic: This approach to family therapy is characterized by multigenerational concepts, genograms, and the family projection process. The systemic approach describes how families manage chronic systemwide anxiety and the effects of differentiation and fusion. Interaction patterns are explained, particularly how three members form a triangle of communication to defuse the conflict between two members.

Differentiation: The person who has the ability to separate emotions from rational thought is able to distinguish between automatic feelings stemming from current and historical systemic influences. Differentiation as to internal workings within the person allows the person to separate his or her own identity and assessment of situations from the group's.

Fusion: When individuals do not distinguish between thoughts and emotions, they react according to emotional patterns of alignments and unconscious acting out of historical experiences. Unhealthy fusion patterns within families create rigid, dysfunctional boundaries closed to outside influences. Passing down low differentiation from one generation to the next can develop into mental health difficulties characterized by fusion, such as schizophrenia, where the person cannot effectively discern reality from inner projections.

Triangle, triangulation: A specific type of coalition is a subgroup of three people, where two of the people are in conflict and a third person relieves some of the tension between the two. Such an arrangement can be positive with the relief provided; but at other times and if the pattern is maintained over time, communication becomes triangulated—an unhealthy dynamic. When direct communication between the two people in conflict is thwarted, suspicions or other negative emotions are increased and the system's functioning becomes rigid, and unable to make necessary adaptations to changes to the family life cycle.

Pseudoselves: When a person's identity is designed to conform to group norms whether or not the social expectations have a rational basis, the person is seeking only to belong. Such an identity is labeled as an example of fusion where emotionality overtakes thoughtful considerations.

Family projection process: Family members share an emotional common ground and difficulties with one member, or with a subgroup, are felt by all members. Likewise difficulties in the system's structure create problems for individuals. An individual person's concerns may be reflecting problems related to the system as a whole or with any part of the group. Problems are projected onto individuals and onto the system.

Chronic anxiety: A general fear that has no specific object, or has so many objects that it reoccurs consistently, affects a person's ability to function. In family systems approaches, anxiety can be a characteristic of the group as a whole. Methods to stabilize the family dynamics control systemwide anxiety, and when the tension is continually repetitive, the controlling mechanisms are built into the patterns of interactions.

Multigenerational transmission process: Some patterns of past generations are carried into the next generation's families through conscious and unconscious processes. Each adult who carries responsibility for the functioning of a family has experienced the effects of previous modeling by older family members. Many attitudes such as time orientation, spending patterns, parental disciplining and teaching of children, values, and behavioral standards are transmitted from one generation to the next. Cultural influences are embedded within the expectations that have been developed throughout family history.

Genogram: A diagram using boxes (for men) and circles (for women) and other symbols depicts family members across generations. Ages and sex are noted. Themes, values, disorders like alcoholism, or occupations may be noted to show influences across time.

Structural: This approach to family therapy describes the system's set of rules—explicit and implicit. The boundaries between the family and outside influences, as well as subsystems and coalitions, create the basic group structure. Also, the interactions between members are described on a continuum from too close to too distant.

Rules: Systems, like families, develop expectations for members to follow to maintain the functioning and homeostasis of the group. Communication patterns, appropriateness of activities, the power to make decisions in different areas, and so forth are understood and maintained by individual members to create a stable atmosphere.

Subsystems: Within the larger group, smaller groups support the interests of their members. Interactions between subgroups form patterns that are a part of the complexity of the system as a whole.

Coalition: Alignments of some portion of a family create coalitions or subsystems. The children are often a coalition divided from the parents who are another subgroup. Within the subsystems there may be further coalitions as in sibling groupings. Sometimes an ad hoc coalition forms for a specific short-term goal.

Boundaries: The psychological division between people, or between a system and outside influences, creates the degree of separation needed for individual identities or distinct systems.

Closed systems: A family or another group that is impervious, or resistant to, outside information or influences is labeled as closed. An open system allows interactions and influences from the outside and with other systems. Closed systems are less adaptable and open systems more able to change. Families with secrets such as home violence and alcoholism are likely to be closed systems.

Permeable and Impermeable: Boundaries can be permeable, allowing for connections between people and opening up to outside stimulation. Boundaries can also be impermeable, forbidding human contact and staying closed to outside pressures.

Disengagement: On a genogram too much distance between family members is indicated by two parallel lines with a slash across the lines. The symbol indicates that the people are not engaged emotionally and may communicate infrequently.

Emotional cutoff: As a simile for disengagement, people are emotionally cut off from each other when they are separated without emotional exchanges. With no feeling connection to other family members, emotional cutoff allows the person to figuratively run away.

Enmeshment: When family members, or people in relationships, are so close emotionally that it is difficult for them to separate their individual thoughts and feelings, distinct identities are not fully maintained. The blending of feelings and identities is labeled *enmeshment.* Family system approaches define enmeshment as too much closeness and indicate the unhealthy pattern by three parallel lines on a genogram.

Strategic: An approach to family therapy where therapists are known for tactical interventions that disarm clients into changing their perceptions. Clever techniques include circular causality, paradoxical intention, the miracle question, and reframing. Therapist directives are designed to target particular attitudes and behaviors without necessarily explaining the purpose to clients.

Circular causality: A change in any part of a system affects all other parts of the system. In families, one individual's changing will affect all the others and all the interacting subsystems.

Circular questioning: The counselor asks the same question to each and every member of the family, bringing out the circular causality in the system and helping people realize the interrelatedness of their emotional lives.

Miracle question: Clients are asked how their lives would be different if a miracle occurred and their problems were solved. Such a technique induces a new mind-set in that clients' answers create a vision of living without the difficulties that often dominate their views.

Cognitive restructuring: The counselor reinterprets the client's thinking patterns or supports a more positive view of a situation. With a new structure, the family or individual client may be able to gain a new way of perceiving even though the basic facts of an event are not changed. However, the implications of the situation are changed.

Reframing: The counselor attaches a new frame on the meaning given to particular situations or interactions. Similar to cognitive restructuring but usually used for more specific verbal restructuring, a word or phrase is changed.

Intellectualization: Although intellectual functioning is held to be a major coping skill to manage emotions and stress, intellectualizations are verbal defenses to hide feelings or to justify bad behavior.

Paradoxical intervention: As with individual clients, the counselor may ask the family to exaggerate a symptom with the hidden agenda to demonstrate that doing the system deliberately gives the client control. Also exaggerating the symptom brings new perspectives for clients who may discover the symptom does not bring the results expected.

Experiential: Another family system approach is noted for its use of techniques that are designed to create evocative emotional experiences, rather than simply talking about issues. Experiential family counselors join in family experiences, becoming participants in the family interactions. This approach emphasizes the need for families to be aware of current here-and-now emotions and the unhealthy effects of alienation and emotional deadness. Therapy is designed to create congruent communication and growth experiences.

Congruent communication: When a person's verbal content matches the nonverbal presentation of the message, the communication is said to be *congruent.* In contrast, when a person's words say one thing, but the emotional tone or body language relays a different message, the communication does not match, or is *incongruent.* In families, incongruent communication confuses interactions and/or lets a member conform just enough to not be too disruptive.

Emotional deadness: When a family rarely, if ever, expresses emotion and lacks spontaneity, the lack of animation is striking, without a sense of aliveness. Some families may be typically emotionally responsive but demonstrate emotional deadness around one issue or topic.

Reprocessing: Experiential family therapists encourage family members to become aware of deep underlying feelings and for all family members to recognize the powerfully felt emotions faced by others in the group. By empathically noting the full emotions of each family member, people gain a sense of the full experience of themselves and others. Reprocessing assumes that experience has been processed in an incomplete or flawed way the first time or habitually.

Primary and secondary emotions: Surface emotions easily shown to others are considered secondary feelings with primary emotions defined as deeper, underlying feelings. Experiential therapies are designed to uncover deeper feelings and to encourage family members to understand one another's primary emotion.

Parts party: An experiential technique also used in Gestalt therapy where one family member directs the others to enact parts of the director's self. Everyone is able to experience the focus person's issues.

Narrative: The stories that families tell about common experiences of the members or about previous generations communicate meanings that characterize the group. Client narratives attach meaning and values to plots and characterizations. Therapists from this approach encourage storytelling to externalize the influences on clients, making the meanings explicit. Therapeutic letters may be assigned. Or, clients may be asked to note occasions when problems seem to disappear. Reflecting teams may observe family sessions and share their thoughts with clients. Counselors may also suggest new meanings for client problems, encouraging new perceptions.

Externalization: A well-known technique of narrative therapy where problems are labeled and given personal characteristics. So the "crappy attitude" invading a family suggests that the people have other attributes that are not encompassed by a labeled problem. The external term can be handled with new enthusiasm even if change was resisted in the past.

Social constructionist: The concept that people define meanings based on family patterns or stories suggests that motivating values are socially learned. The social constructions are held internally by individuals and may be unconscious. Individuals may try to force situations to conform to internal views. The underlying connotations of narratives or the applicability of stories to new situations can be reanalyzed by individuals or families in therapy to create change.

Reflecting team: For some systems counseling, the counselor and clients are observed by other therapists behind a screen. At some point in the counseling session, the reflecting team discusses what has occurred in the session and the clients gain multiple perspectives.

Unique outcome: Clients are asked to describe the times when they were able to react differently than the typical times when problematic reactions occur. Such a description offers hope that difficulties are not unsolvable and that the client does have the capacity to behave differently.

Neutrality: Some schools of thought expect the counselor to remain neutral in relating to members of the family, suggesting that alignments with any one member or subgroup harm objectivity. The counselor's stance is one of curiosity, maintaining communication and understanding, but not becoming a family participant. Interventions may induce change in the system by introducing something new.

Joining: When the counselor enters the family system by participating in the family interactions and conforming to the family rules, the therapist is said to be joining. Such participation allows the counselor to assess the dynamics and determine what changes and interventions are needed.

First-order and second-order change: When families make a change that reduces conflict, or anxiety, it is called a *first-order change*. When change entails a deeper transformation that alters the actual structure of the system permanently, it is called a *second-order change*.

Accommodation: The counselor adapts her use of specific language, phrases, and emotional tone to the style of the client or the family. Accommodation is the means for the counselor to insert herself into the family system. This is called *joining*.

Curiosity: Bowen's style of family therapy includes a neutral stance where the counselor observes the family as a curious onlooker who wonders how the different interactional patterns work to keep the system operating. Curious inquiries may influence the system to reflect on itself and open the door to new patterns.

Family drawing technique: A visual technique to show how the client views the family. A kinetic drawing specifically shows family members doing something together.

Family mapping: Using boxes and circles as in a genogram, each family member is named and given three descriptive adjectives. Then a descriptor is given to depict the nature of the relationship between each pair of individuals within the family. The result is a picture of how the client views each person and the interrelationships. Family members can exchange maps and discuss similarities and differences in their views.

Family sculpting: An experiential technique has all family members creating a pantomime to show a meaningful scene from their lives together. One member directs the others to place themselves in specific ways and to do specific things; then everyone discusses the meaning of the act.

Letters: Clients are asked to express what they would want to say to someone in letter form. In writing a letter, the client does not have to face the person directly but still has the opportunity to collect his thoughts and communicate them. The letter may very well never be sent, but the experience of communicating in this form can offer relief.

Goals: Dreikurs, an Adlerian therapist and author, proposed children reveal four major purposes for misbehavior: attention getting, power struggle, revenge, and withdrawal. Other goals include: getting, self-elevation, and avoidance. Children will typically acknowledge why they behaved as they did by openly agreeing to a counselor suggesting such goals or by displaying a "recognition reflex" in their facial expression. Since children are not fully conscious of the reason behind their behavior, acknowledging the motivation and discussing other behaviors to gain goals is helpful.

Representative Case: Ruth Lear

Ruth came to counseling presenting with depressive symptoms associated with grief after several family members died over the last several years. She is 33, unmarried, and the youngest of four children in a farm family from the Midwest. Physically she is a large woman, stocky in build, with a square-shaped, stoic face. Her eyes show deep pain, though only a few tears break through as she describes her family.

Ruth's father, Henry, was the older son of two children. He inherited the family farm and became the patriarch who took care of his aging parents, his younger brother, and his wife's parents. Ruth's maternal grandparents were farm laborers and Ruth's mother, Jean, was an only child. The paternal uncle, Sam, was not interested in farming and started several businesses that failed. Henry finally financed a successful antique-selling business for his brother and built a home on the farm for Sam, his wife, and two children. Henry expanded the original acreage considerably and made enough money that the entire extended family lived well.

Ruth's early memories included family stories about her paternal grandfather emigrating from Germany. Although he had little means for himself and his family, he sent money back to poor relatives abroad. As she grew up, Ruth watched her older siblings and cousins, wishing she could participate in more grown-up activities. Everyone had chores doing farm work, caring for animals or restoring and transporting antiques. Ruth remembers school as another place where her two brothers, sister, and cousins were active participants on sports teams and school plays. By the time Ruth entered high school, the older children were in college and or starting families. One older brother moved away to another state and returned home only on occasion.

As the sole child left on the large farm, Ruth became her father's assistant. She thoroughly enjoyed helping him in the barn, riding in the tractor beside him, and going with him to livestock shows. The only disruption in her world came when her oldest sister divorced and came home briefly, left and remarried, and divorced again. Ruth knew her father worried about her sister, though her parents never discussed the situation in front of her. She only knew the sister was sent to an private hospital to receive treatment for emotional difficulties. Then the farm economic crisis hit, and the family's financial situation diminished. There were no funds for Ruth to enter one of the state universities that the older children had attended, so she went to a local community college and continued helping her father on the farm. Uncle Sam died, and Henry became the executor of his estate. Ruth's cousins inherited the antique business, sold it, and moved away. Both sets of grandparents also died in the next several years, and finally her father died last year. Ruth was named the executor of his estate.

One night before her father's funeral, Ruth's oldest sister came home. Ruth was alone in the house since her mother was gone. Carol, now divorcing her third husband, had been living in a distant city and had not been in contact with the family for a number of years. Carol marched into the home and proceeded to collect items she wanted and expected to inherit, including some jewelry Henry had given his mother. Ruth was quite upset, feeling responsible for guarding the family belongings, and she called the police. Carol left before the police arrived.

Ruth's oldest brother, Ted, and his family returned home to run the family farm. Ruth was uncomfortable trying to help her brother on the farm. Besides, her mother needed her assistance, so the two of them moved to a small home in the local village. At this time, Ruth's oldest sister, Carol, filed a lawsuit against the father's estate. The suit charged that her father had illegally mismanaged the estates for the uncle and both sets of grandparents and that Carol had not been fairly considered in the father's will.

Ruth told her story in a moderate tone without expressing any emotion except for a few tears, until she described the sister's accusations against her father. And then her voice cracked and she cried. The counselor tentatively reflected that it was upsetting for her to know her father's reputation was brought into question. Ruth answered with a loud resounding, "Yes!" and continued to say, "How could Carol do this to the family?"

Thinking About Ruth

1. Often when clients tell about their families, it is difficult to keep the names straight for all the family members. Draw a genogram of Ruth's family and fill in the names contained in the above description.

2. What values are apparent in Ruth's family? How do these values relate to Ruth's self-concept and her psychological issues?

3. Ruth's father died almost a year ago. Why does she still seem to be in the throes of grief over his death?

4. Ruth's depressive symptoms relate to numerous losses. List all of her losses, not only naming specific people but also other significant losses in her life.

5. Ruth's emotional expressiveness is limited. What specific techniques would encourage her opening up?

Check Your Thinking About Ruth

1. Exchange your genogram with at least one of your classmates' versions and discuss discrepancies until you can agree on an accurate version.

2. Ruth's family values hard work, stoic acceptance of whatever life circumstances exist, helping family members who have difficulties, male privilege and patriarchy, education, and family reputation. Ruth inculcates all the family values. She's a hard worker who enjoyed gaining more responsibility as she grew up and particularly when her older siblings

left home. She sees herself as nonemotional and offered no complaints when family finances required her to attend junior college and to stay home working with her father. She values education, gaining the schooling she could. As a woman, she accepted the role of her father's assistant, her mother's caretaker, and her brother's inheritance of the family farm. She relates to other family members according to assigned roles and is most upset by her sister maligning her father and the family reputation. Ruth clearly admired her father and sees any criticism of him as a major betrayal. Ruth sees herself as someone who upholds the family values and protects family property even if she does not gain materially herself. Would it be helpful to her to become more aware of her emotions?

3. Ruth's connection to her father became her most significant relationship after the older children left home and after financial restrictions limited her access to a wider world. She may have become so enmeshed with him that she completely succumbed to honoring his role as patriarch and all the values he established. She doesn't describe any deviation from her father's tenets, and it is difficult to see a separate identity she has created for herself. She has even taken on the role of taking care of her mother in replacement of her father. Her father's loss leaves her without his presence and with only a rigid memory to uphold. Letting go of her father and her grief would require her to separate from him in a way she was unable to do when he was alive.

4. Ruth has lost both sets of grandparents and an uncle as well as her father. In high school she lost any place she may have had in the children's subsystem. She lost any expectations she may have had to leave home and gain a four year degree, including any career role that may have been associated with a B.A. She does not mention any expectation of meeting a potential spouse, but such a vision may have existed at some point. In addition she has effectively lost her place as her father's assistant and her participation in farming activities. She is also in danger of losing her idealized vision of her father and the image of a stable family all under her father's patriarchal control. Since her identity is so inextricably bound with her father and her family, her losses reveal the sparseness of her separate sense of self.

5. It may be useful to Ruth to do a family map depicting her view of relationships and individual characteristics of family members during several points in time across her lifespan. Such an activity could help her see how her world has progressively diminished and may reveal earlier hopes and dreams envisioned as a young girl before she was swallowed up into her relationship with her father. She might also benefit from writing a letter to her sister telling Carol what the lawsuit signifies in Ruth's view—the loss of family honor, the dissolution of the family unit, the betrayal of her father's memory. The letter might also explain Ruth's sense that Carol violated family values by taking the jewelry. With the counselor's encouragement, a letter to Carol may allow Ruth to express her feelings.

The danger of bringing out Ruth's feelings is that she is likely to discover her lack of self-definition and her despair may be difficult. However, she is stuck in a place where she cannot move on unless she comes to terms with her psychological situation. Core conditions for counseling can provide a safe place for Ruth to explore emotions, and sensitive timing of feeling reflections can allow the process of a healing experience.

Ruth might be able to identify times when she was less sad, through the unique outcomes question. The magic question of how Ruth would see her life without the problems of the lawsuit or grief could also tease out her sense of life that does not have to be tied up with family relationships. Her father's death could be reframed as his permission for her to establish her own life, and cognitive restructuring could build a view of Ruth as deserving of a life she could create for herself.

Core Case: Mrs. A

The core case of Mrs. A was first presented in Chapter 4 and was also reviewed in Chapter 5. Here we view the case from a family systems perspective. Again **D** designates **Data,** **A** designates **Assessment,** and **P** designates **Plan.**

D: Mrs. A's data was presented in Chapter 4.

A: Mrs. A came from a dysfunctional family and in eight years of marriage has created her own family difficulties. The couple subsystem is clearly not supportive, as the husband and wife have separated several times and do not seem to parent together, only separately. Indeed, Mrs. A's obsessiveness with cleanliness, phobic fears of knives and death, and suicidal thoughts cause the family to remain preoccupied with her difficulties rather than examining the quality of the marriage and the effectiveness of the parenting. The children, with the knowledge that their mother has thoughts of harming them, are at risk of emotional difficulties and developmental blocks. Mrs. A has also been functionally absent for periods of time. The father seems unable to offer compensating strength and nurturing for the children to experience stability. Mrs. A's thoughts of harm may be a functional way, however extreme, of expressing the family's inability to deal with the task of parenting. Her husband's career disappointments may be hidden as he is required to take on childcare responsibilities, and the need to watch his wife may be the only way he can offer protection to his children.

From a transgenerational perspective, Mrs. A's alcoholic abusive father left her without a model for finding a suitable marital partner, a functioning marriage, or parenting examples. She chose a husband who did not represent the threat her father did but ended up with an ineffective partner who left her with much of the family responsibility. Her mother sounds more competent in nurturing and running a household, so Mrs. A did learn homemaking basics. Focusing on cleaning, even to the point of obsessiveness, she may serve the family in the one way she knows how.

Coalitions among the siblings requires further assessment. The children undoubtedly have acquired some implicit rules to maintain behavior that will keep them safe from their mother's threats. In all likelihood the system's repetitive anxiety has also created unhealthy, impermeable boundaries so that the children have not been open to outside influences. At least one or two of the children might be disengaged. Unless first-order change for the system can be accomplished, placing the children in other homes may be necessary.

P: In the beginning, the subsystems of the parents and of the children need separate treatment. The parents need training in communication skills and methods to negotiate who takes care of family responsibilities. By building some strength in the marriage, the couple might become ready for parenting training. The children can be seen as a group to provide the means for them to gain empathy for each other and methods to help each other. Family drawings could offer each of the children the means to express how each sees the family dynamics. Circular questioning could encourage the group to generate ideas about how they can cooperate for the benefit of all.

If the parents can begin to function as a couple and can learn parenting skills, bringing the children and parents together for full family sessions would become possible. The therapists, including a reflecting team, could encourage family members to become aware of deep underlying feelings and help all family members to recognize the powerfully felt emotions faced by others in the group. New family rules and communication patterns could be established in family meetings.

Finding a Balance

Most counselors choose several counseling approaches that suit their personalities and theoretical preferences. In this section, the counselor personality characteristics are identified and tied to concepts and practices, then a case is described. The next section shows how the counselor's preferences would play out in working with the case. Finally, a comparison with other approaches is made showing how different preferences might deal with the case. Integrating several approaches might cover varying counselor preferences and differing client issues better than any singular approach.

Key Counselor Preferences

1. Family therapists tend to be socially skilled and comfortable with most any combination of clients, individuals, dyads, and with both sociable and more aloof groups.

2. Systems counselors enjoy working with other therapists in conjoint therapy or with others observing therapy sessions. They appreciate consulting with colleagues.

3. Often family therapists are happily married and actively involved parents, although some may have had negative experiences with their family of origins or previous marriages. They may or may not share personal experiences with clients depending on their style and the needs of the clients.

4. Family counselors think holistically and are skilled in considering the contexts surrounding individual issues. Contextual thinking also leads to determining strategies for change for the groups as a whole, and some family practitioners emphasize implicit tactical manipulation more than others do.

5. Family counselors tend to be quite articulate in expressing complicated issues in ways family members understand.

6. Even those family therapists who do not join in the family interactions tend to be directive, orchestrating system change, and most prefer short-term counseling rather than lengthy reprocessing.

Comparison with Other Approaches

Cognitive-behavioral: With continual ideas about impending doom, Mrs. A. suffers from several of Ellis's irrational beliefs about disastrous consequences of her action or inaction. A cognitive-behaviorist would help her identify and dispute these beliefs and design experiments to prove their falsity.

Gestalt: A Gestaltist would identify the lack of genuine identity in Mrs. A.'s story. She is constantly in reaction to others around her. She might benefit from two-chair dialogue with some of the significant others in her life, like her father, husband, and mother.

Existentialist: Mrs. A. is driven by an extreme fear of death. An existentialist would perceive this fear as a normal condition of life. The existentialist therapist would encourage deep discussion of death and the meaning of life. Mrs. A. might review her life history, exploring what she has found meaningful, and work on expressing her own value system.

Case Example: The Sharp Family

Danielle and Steven Sharp came to the family counselor requesting help with her youngest daughter, Katherine, who is 13. Katherine had become disrespectful with a smart-aleck comment for everything. Danielle, age 39, is married to Steven, 43; they have been married for twenty-one years. The couple also has a son, David, who is 17.

Danielle was the Director of Technical Support at the headquarters for a national computer manufacturing company. She spoke crisply with a matter-of-fact tone and was dressed in an expensive suit softened by a ruffled blouse. She described the past year as a difficult one with her father dying and her mother requiring extra care given a diagnosis of dementia or possible Alzheimer's. She admitted she was so frustrated with her daughter that she screamed at her often, but she didn't understand why Katherine had become so difficult. Katherine was preparing for a bat mitzvah, but her grudging attitude made Danielle wonder if the important family celebration would be ruined by Kathy's attitude. Danielle said her marriage was fine, no problems.

Steve, husband and father, was the sales manager for a local manufacturer of party goods. Also well dressed, he wore a suit and turtleneck. He spoke casually, smiling often and holding his wife's hand. He added to the description of the family by saying that Danielle has been harried of late making arrangements to help her mother and preparing for the bat mitzvah. He also noted that Danielle was close to her father and his death had been difficult for her. It was Steven's opinion that Danielle's standards for the children's grades and behavior were too strict, though David had always measured up. He said, "Kathy just wants to have a little fun." Steven said the marriage had had some difficult times when he had mismanaged money and when he had done "something stupid." Extended family included Danielle's younger sister, Katrina, a beautiful woman, married but with no children. Katrina and her husband owned several homes, traveled a great deal, and were home for holidays. Kat contributed money for the mother's care but visited only on occasion. Danielle worried that Kat's "overly social" lifestyle is not a good influence for Kathy. Danielle's brother, the oldest, was gay, living with his partner across town. Heinrich was a banker and art collector and was close to David. When family papers were reviewed after the father's funeral, it was discovered that Heinrich was born prior to the father's marriage to the mother and was adopted by the father when he was 2 years old. Danielle explained that learning about this family secret had put many of her memories in perspective. When she was a teenager, her parents were exceptionally overprotective. She was not allowed to be alone with a boy ever, and when she even accepted a ride home from school with a boy, there was a family crisis with her parents overreacting. Danielle had realized that the parents were concerned that she or her sister would become pregnant out of wedlock as her mother had. Danielle had complied with the no dating rule until she went to college. Kat had rebelled, partied, took drugs, and had an abortion.

Danielle's parents had emigrated from Poland where their parents had been killed in the holocaust. The mother had been warm but "flighty" according to Danielle. Her mother, she noted, had one skill: laying guilt on everyone. Danielle's father was a lawyer and a legal scholar. He had once argued a case before the Supreme Court and was greatly admired for his incisive intelligence and his skill as a public speaker. Danielle was close to her father and was his confidant. He shared with her his disappointments with his other siblings and his wife.

Steven's family was working class, Irish Catholic. His parents ran a tavern and had died in a car accident ten years ago. Steven was an only child and had pleasant memories of being the center of attention not only for his parents, but also for tavern patrons from the neighborhood.

Applying Counselor Preferences

Using the previously listed preferences for family system approaches, how would a counselor proceed with the Sharps?

1. Family therapists tend to be socially skilled and comfortable with most any combination of clients. The Sharps were seen as a couple initially by two therapists: a woman and a man. Danielle's crisp style was respected without comment, though the difference between her matter-of-fact description and Steven's more casual expression is noted in the case documentation.

2. Family counselors appreciate input from colleagues. A reflecting team also met the Sharps near the end of the session. One team member shared his observation that all family names given were quite formal except Kat's and once when Steven referred to Kathy. The couple was given instructions to use only formal names at home for the next week, including Katrina and Katherine. Another observer suggested the couple may need to discuss the "something stupid" Steven had mentioned. The next week's session was scheduled to include the parents and the children, but the parents could request a couple's time just before the nuclear family being seen.

3. Family counselors typically have analyzed their own backgrounds and have well functioning families themselves. Before the first session ended, the woman therapist shared her experience that a longstanding secret in her family, like Heinrich's birth history, had major implications for family communications and feelings. Like Danielle, the therapist understood that much of what had taken place in her growing up made much more sense once the secret was known.

4. Family therapists are skilled contextual thinkers, and they determine strategies for change for the groups as a whole. The instructions for the Sharp couple were to discuss whatever Steven referred to as "something stupid" and were designed to build communication between the parental subsystem. Though the couple did not show a strain in their relationship, they did disagree about how to handle Katherine, and the reflecting team felt that opening communication between them would affect the interactions between the parenting subsystem and the children for the next session. Likewise using formal names supported a family pattern rather than splintering Kat and Kathy as separate.

5. Family counselors are gifted in articulating complicated interactions and devising strategies that help clients understand the impact of family dynamics. The Sharps did request a private session before the full family session the next week. Steven reported his "something stupid" had been an affair ten years earlier that had resulted in a child by another woman. He had never seen the child but had paid support over the years. Danielle knew of the situation and had forgiven Steven and had written the support checks every month. The couple had not spoken about the situation since it happened. In discussing the incident now, Danielle reported she felt Steve was being irresponsible in not taking part in the life of the child. The news of her brother's birth history and her memories of her father's sense of justice made her realize that she and Steven had a family secret too. Like her parents they had hidden the birth of a child, but unlike her parents they had contributed only money. The couple had agreed Steve would contact the child's mother and inquire about what other needs the child might have. The explanation of the effect of a family secret by the woman therapist was a simple intervention that allowed the couple to engage in problem-solving.

6. Family counselors enjoy directly or indirectly orchestrating system change, and most prefer short-term therapy. During the family session, the male therapist opened by asking David first to describe what he saw happening in the family. David was asked because his position was the least expressed in the sessions. David described his mother as doing too

much and his father as letting her. He described his sister and father as joking around a lot and having fun. Finally, he said he felt left out by everyone. He said he liked calling Katherine by her real name and Kathy sounded too much like Aunt Kat who he said was a "flake." Katherine spoke up without being asked her opinion by the therapist. Katherine defended Aunt Kat and liked being called Kathy. She said she enjoyed joking around with her father and doesn't want to be as serious as her mother, brother, and uncle. The intervention assignment of using formal names brought out the split in the family regarding seriousness versus fun.

Course of Therapy

Danielle realized from the family session that her daughter was rebelling against her as a model of the serious, responsible woman. For herself, Danielle realized, she had spent her life earning her father's approval and not being like her mother or her sister. She said in session she was tired of being so serious and responsible for everything, so she now wanted to be called Danny by her husband and she would call him Steve, her daughter Kathy, and her son Dave. She also requested another parenting session. In the couple's session, she turned over the bill paying to her husband and said she wanted to plan the bat mitzvah as a family.

The reflecting team and co-counselors also helped the parents brainstorm ideas for dealing with David's disengagement, including his helping his sister prepare her Hebrew memorization for the ceremony. They mentioned the transgenerational effect of keeping the secrets and of conflict avoidance in general. The children, both Kathy and David, had demonstrated symptom functionality. The children's behavior relayed discomfort regarding the imbalance of responsibilities between the parents and the simplistic differences assigning some family members as fun lovers and others as serious.

Three more family sessions were held to work on communication patterns between all the members of the family. The children's subsystem was strengthened as David and Kathy worked together preparing for the bat mitzvah. Danny was encouraged to tell family stories regarding her father, communicating his values of education and justice. Steve's family stories relayed fun-loving episodes and the enjoyment he and Danny had experienced in the family tavern. Family sharing of chores was hashed out, but the children were allowed to complain. Steve joined his wife in insisting that work be shared. The final session included the family discussing their aunt and uncle. They all agreed that Kat was fun and that Heinrich was serious, like Mom and Dad used to be. When the issue of the uncle's gayness was broached by the therapist, each family member said that his sexual orientation was not an issue. Danielle agreed that it was not an issue, but that it was also not something they had to keep out of conversation and not talk about. David said he appreciated his uncle's ability to manage his lifestyle and to be a family member to them all and observed that he could be a good friend when you needed someone. The triangular relationship David had with his uncle had given him a person to consult when he felt excluded from other family members.

Example of a Published Research Article on Family Psychology

Here is an example of published research on family psychology. Commentary in boxes to the left of the article will help you understand the research and the format of the piece.

Mother-Blaming in Major Clinical Journals

Paula J. Caplan, Ph.D., and Ian Hall-McCorquodale, B.Sc.

The incidence of mother-blaming in major clinical journals was investigated for the years 1970, 1976, and 1982 to determine whether reductions have resulted from the efforts of the women's movement. Very few changes were found across the target years, and mother-blaming was only slightly affected by type of journal and by sex of author.

The authors begin by surveying the history of mother-blaming among psychologists, citing famous theories that focus on the mother's failings as a source of psychological distress in other family members.

Since early in this century, mental health professionals have legitimized the tendency of both lay-people and professionals to blame mothers for whatever goes wrong with their offspring. There are trends in this direction in some of Freud's work. More recently, Brodkin [4] pointed out that some later writers provided substantial impetus along the same lines:

In 1943, an influential report on maternal over-protection by David Levy set the scene for dyadic-based intervention in the family. In 1948, Fromm-Reichman coined the term "schizophrenogenic mother"; four years later, Mahler described the "state of symbiosis" between the mother and the child schizophrenic. There followed a spate of dyadic-style studies of schizophrenics emerging from a psychoanalytic framework and implicating the mother-child relationship. (p. 8)

Chess and Thomas [9] noted that this trend was climaxed by Bowlby's work [3] on "maternal deprivation," and they said that such

. . . reports did have a salutary influence in highlighting the psychological needs of the young child, and in emphasizing the importance of a humane nurturant environment for the infant's healthy development. But such considerations are different from the professional ideology that crystallized by the 1950s, in which the causation of all psychopathology, from simple behavior problems to juvenile delinquency to schizophrenia itself, was laid at the doorstep of the mother. The guilt and anxiety created in mothers whose children had even minor behavior deviations were enormous. (pp. 213–214)

Chesler [6] has observed that clinician-theorists claim that children need "intensive and exclusive female mothering" (p. 73) and are quick to talk about their patients' "terrible and damaging" mothers (p. 248). Indeed, as Chodorow [10] explained, the mother is expected to provide total physical and psychological care, "total environmental provision" (p. 83) for her infant; as the infant grows, she has the responsibility for bringing about, in perfectly timed and graduated sequence, the healthy degrees of her child's separation and independence from her. She is to do all of this without either providing too much care (the "smothering, overprotective mother" image) or too little (the "cold, hostile, rejecting mother" image). [5]

These theoretical and clinical claims, when added to society's tendency to have women do most child rearing, have provided powerful support for the belief that women's physiology and hormones—but not men's—naturally suit them for child rearing. What has not been pointed out is that, if women come by child-rearing skills naturally, it is curious that they create emotional disturbances in so many of their children. The attribution of offspring's problems to the mother is, of course, profoundly misogynist. Pogrebin [24] has written that the mother-blaming attitude pervades everyday life and language as well:

> A nasty woman is a "bitch," but a nasty man isn't nasty in his own right: he's a "son of a bitch" or a "bastard," both words reflecting badly on his mother. (p. 540)

One way of dealing with discomfort about the current feminist movement is to claim that the problems feminists have identified have now been largely solved; indeed it seemed possible that the movement might have brought about a decrease in mother-blaming. It seemed, important, therefore, to investigate the extent to which mother-blaming persists and to assess the warning of Chess [7] that:

> The specific examples of this kind of "blame the mother" attitude that were common in 1964 would not be entirely applicable today, but the focus would be unchanged. (p. 96)

Like most research articles, this one explains why the issue under study is worth exploring. In this case, the authors assert that mother-blaming creates negative attitudes toward women in everyday life.

The purpose of the study is to investigate whether feminist (pro-woman) thinking has reduced the amount of blame psychologists attribute to mothers.

Method

This type of research is called *archival*, because it uses data collected from existing print sources like files, public records, or in this case published journals. The researchers explain which journals they surveyed and how they chose the years to examine. They looked at three separate years of nine major journals, and read all articles concerning the sources of a person's emotional problem.

The authors decided exactly what to look for by examining 50 articles that were *not* going to be used as research data. From these, they made up 63 questions to answer about each target article.

The *Union List of Scientific Serials* was inspected for its listing of psychiatric and psychological journals. An initial list was made of 71 journals which showed promise of including articles with discussion of etiology of psychopathology. Most of those were eliminated because they included *too few* articles in which the etiology of psychopathology was discussed or because they were not available in Toronto, where the authors were doing the research. Volumes from three years were selected for study: 1970, because it would presumably include articles that were conceived just at the beginning of the new feminist movement; 1982, because it was the last full year for which journals were available; and 1976, because it was midway between the other two years. In the following nine journals, all articles in which etiology of someone's emotional problem was discussed were read and classified: *American Journal of Orthopsychiatry, American Journal of Psychoanalysis, Canadian Journal of Psychiatry, Journal of Consulting and Clinical Psychology, Family Process, International Journal of Psychoanalysis, Journal of Child Psychology and Psychiatry, Journal of Clinical Psychology,* and *The Journal of Psychology.*

The number of articles read and classified was 125: 31 from 1970, 38 from 1976, and 56 from 1982. On the basis of approximately 50 clinical articles from nontarget years, the authors developed 63 items to use to evaluate articles from the target years. These fell into five categories (a complete listing of items by category is available from the authors on request): 1) *general*—14 items (such as the number of words used to describe the mother, compared to number used to describe the father); 2) *information-gathering*—8 items (i.e., was the history taken only from the mother or only from the father?); 3) *attribution of blame*— 26 items (i.e., does the mother's pathology—or the father's—affect the family?) 4) *treatment*—6 items (i.e., was only the mother or only the father involved in treatment?); and 5) *previous literature*—9 items (i.e., was there uncritical citation of previous literature in which mothers are blamed?).

When the sex of the authors was clear from the names given, it was recorded. Of the 125 articles, 69 had only male authors, 20 had only females, and 17 had at least one of each; in 19 articles authors used only initials or had names that could represent either sex.

Percentages were calculated for the number of "yes" and "no" answers called for by 57 of the 63 items; totals were computed for the five items calling for a numerical response (*e.g.,* number of times "mother" is cited); a ratio was computed for one item (number of times mother/father was cited in specific illustrations). In addition, percentages were calculated to determine whether mother-blaming varied with type of article (general psychiatric, psychological, psychoanalytic, family therapy), year of publication, or type of article *and* year. Interrater reliabilities for the two raters ranged from .87 to .92.

Results

The authors of the 125 articles read for this study attributed to mothers a total of 72 different kinds of psychopathology; these are listed in Table 1. In 2% of the articles the mother was not mentioned at all, compared to 14% in which the father was not mentioned at all, even as "parent." In all 125 articles put together, 37,492 words were used to describe the mothers and 14,406 to describe the fathers.

The word "mother" was used a total of 2,151 times in the 125 articles, in contrast to the word "father," which was used 946 times. The word "parents" was used 1,177 times. Thus, mothers were by far the most likely to be discussed, followed by parents as a couple, and fathers individually were the least likely. Specific examples of problems in which the mother or the father was mentioned were noted, and a mother: father ratio was computed. That ratio was 346:73—or almost 5:1—in the 125 articles. In other words, when authors wanted to illustrate some problem or other, and when they used only mother or father for this purpose, they chose father only 17% of the time.

In 77% of the articles, some research or therapy was done on the mother-child interaction. In 49% of articles some research or therapy was done on the father-child interaction. This is a generous interpretation of articles in which father-child interaction was discussed, for articles in which "parent-child," but not specifically father-child, interaction was a focus were also classified as including some work on the "father-child" interaction. In 89% of articles, some information was given about the mother, compared to 69% for the father. It must be noted, however, that in many of the articles all that was said about the father was that he was absent or dead; in several cases, it was something complimentary, such as that "he helped the child and was upset that his wife had trouble with the child and asked him to 'bail her out' " and that he did well in therapy [21] (p. 681). In one case, [26] the authors wrote:

> The mother was nurturant and overprotective. The boy's relationship with his father appears to have been ideal in virtually every respect. (pp. 239–240)

In no article was the mother's relationship with the child described as simply healthy, nor was she ever described only in positive terms. In another article, [20] the following information was given:

> These researchers report most of their findings in the form of percentages—for example, 77% mother versus 49% father. The reader is left to decide whether this difference in percentages is meaningful. In other studies, percentages are compared statistically through the chi square test, which provides a *p* value (how often the situation would occur by chance).

<table>
<tr><td>

The listing in this table is of items considered to be problems by the authors of the various articles reviewed.

</td></tr>
</table>

Table 1

Problems Identified
in the Literature
as Attributable to Mothers

Absence of genitality	Koro (feeling of penile
Aggressiveness	shrinkage and fear of
Agitation	death)
Agoraphobia	Loneliness
Anal obsession	Loss of control
Anorexia nervosa	Marijuana use
Anxiety, fear	Minimal brain damage
Arson	Moodiness
Avoidance of peers	Narcissism
Bad dreams	Need to be anally
Behavior problems	penetrated
Bizarre behavior	Need to become
Chronic vomiting	pregnant/abort
Creation of rigidly sex-role	Neonaticide
stereotypic daughter	Pathological reaction to
Delinquency/criminality	sexual stimuli
Delusions	Phobias
Denial of	Poor concentration
pregnancy/childbirth	Poor language development
Dependency	Premature mourning
Depression	Problems in emotional well-
Disturbance in Klinefelter's	being
syndrome children	Pseudoneurosis
Encopresis	Pseudosociopathic
Enuresis	neurosis
Failure to mourn	Psychiatric disorder
Fear of separation	Scapegoating
Fetishism	Schizophrenia
Frigidity	School dropout
Gaslighting	School phobia
Homosexuality	Self-induced television
Hyperactivity	epilepsy
Hysterical character	Severe mental handicap
Inability to separate from	Sexual dysfunction
mother	Sibling jealousy
Inability to deal with color	Sleepwalking
blindness	Success conflict
Inability to establish a	Suicidal behavior
transference	Tantrums
Incontinence	Timidity/withdrawal
Incest	Transsexualism (regular
Ineducabililty (intellectual)	and homicidal)
Isolation	Truancy
	Ulcerative colitis

Their father, a carpenter, was 33 years old when they were born. He was described as patient and easy-going. Their mother was 31 years old at the time of their births and she was described as wearing the pants and hardheaded. (p. 145)

That is all that was said about the parents of twin homosexual men who had an incestuous relationship with each other and could not form attachments with other people.

In 10% of articles, most or all of the history had been taken from the mother, in contrast to only 1% in which the father was the prime source. In 28% of articles, the mother was the only parent investigated for psychopathology or a contribution to the child's problem, in stark contrast to the total absence of articles in which only the father was investigated in this way. Related to this is that 82% of articles included information about the mother's psychological functioning. Information was given about the father's psychological functioning in 54%. Problems were said to be found in the mother, with no description given of how these conclusions were reached, in 62% of articles; similar reports with respect to the father were found in only 26%.

The father's absence or lack of involvement with the family was noted but not said to contribute to the child's problem in 24% of articles, but in only 2% was the mother's absence or uninvolvement noted but not said to be contributory. Separation of child from mother was considered a trauma in 54% of articles. Separation of child from father was considered a trauma in 33% of cases. The child's pathology was attributed at least in part to the mother's activity in 82% of articles, to the mother's inactivity in 43%, to the father's activity in 43%, and to the father's inactivity in 39%. Thus, the mother's activity was regarded as harmful more than four-fifths of the time, but the father's activity and either parent's inactivity were implicated less than half the time.

In 64% of articles, the mother's pathology was said to disturb the family, compared to only 34% in which the father's pathology was so described. The child's pathology was said to affect the mother in 43% of articles, compared to 19% in which it was said to affect the father.

Twenty percent of the articles included discussion of the etiology of the mother's problems, compared to only 7% for etiology of the father's problems. In 16% of articles the psychological problems of at least one parent were attributed to *their* mothers, in contrast to only 7% in which they were attributed to their fathers. The mother's pathology was regarded as chronic and intractable in 25% of articles, the father's in 12%. In 40% of articles, the mother was said to blame, scapegoat, or reject the child, whereas in only 17% was the father so described. Judgmental terms were used by the

> The evidence for mother-blaming in the journals is plentiful. The authors survey all the different ways in which this attitude could be manifested: for example, comparing separation from mother with separation from father, and comparing mother's absence with father's absence.

authors to describe the mothers in 74% of articles and the fathers in only 41%.

In 18% of articles, the mother's behavior was specifically discussed, with no reference to the father's or the "parents'" behavior being made; this is in contrast to only 2% in which this was done for fathers' behavior. In 27% of articles the mother's interaction with the child was specifically discussed, in contrast to 2% in which the father's interaction with the child was discussed. Treatment, in 18% of the articles, was undertaken *only* with the mother and in 2% *only* with the father. In 19% of articles, the mother was said to have profited from treatment, and in 10% of cases the father was said to have profited from treatment (including cases in which both parents received treatment). Treatment of the child was seen as the mother's responsibility in 10% of articles and the father's in 2%. Moving to reviews of the literature in the articles studied, in 28% a traditional division of labor was explicitly regarded as normal and healthy, and deviation from it was assumed to be pathogenic. Nontraditional division of labor was never regarded as normal and healthy. Traditional sex roles (in terms of behavior) and traditional family structures (two-parent, heterosexual) were regarded as normal and healthy, and any deviation from this as pathogenic in 43% of articles; in no article was the converse true.

In 42% of articles, claims were made based on theory from earlier literature that the mother is linked to the child's pathology. Uncritical citations of previous literature in which mothers were blamed appeared in 44% of articles; in 53%, the unquestioned assumption that mother was the problem appeared. Fifty-seven percent of articles included speculation about how the mother-child interaction could lead to the child's psychopathology. In 41% of articles, there were uncritical citations of previous literature suggesting that a child can only develop normally if its mother does the right things.

The frequency of mother-blaming varied only slightly depending on the type of article, the year of its publication, and the item in question. The sex of the authors did not affect the mother-blaming tendency for any of the 63 items.

Discussion

The most striking pattern reflected in our results is that, in every category, the mothers emerged in a far less favorable, more blameworthy light. As illustrated in Table I, mothers are blamed for a wide variety of problems and forms of psychopathology.

Mother-blaming is a very common practice in clinical journals. In some ways, the most distressing pattern on individual items was that mothers' activity is highly likely to be blamed for children's problems, whereas mothers' inactivity and fathers' activity are so blamed only at chance level, and

> The Discussion section first brings
> together the findings of the Results
> section and interprets them. Then it
> introduces new material, not
> included in the research, that relates
> the topic to the future.

fathers' inactivity or lack of involvement with their children is even *less* likely than chance to be so blamed.

Although there is slight variability according to the type of article for some items, the overwhelming picture in all journals for more than two-thirds of the 63 items was one of mother-blaming. This practice was not affected either by sex of author or by year of publication for any of the 63 items. Caplan [5] has examined some of the ways that females are socialized to judge each other as harshly at times as males judge females; the evidence from the present study is that female clinicians are as likely as male clinicians to indulge in blaming mothers for their children's problems.

Recently, some signs of improvement have appeared, primarily in the form of writings aimed specifically at taking the blame off mothers and pointing out the pervasiveness and the harm of mother-blaming. Examples come from such diverse sources as the excellent, popular-distribution *Homemaker's Magazine,* in which Maynard's well-researched, well-documented article, "Let's Stop Blaming Mum" [19] appeared; Badinter's book, *Mother Love: Myth and Reality;* [1] a paper called "Mothers of Autistic Children: Are They The 'Unacknowledged Victims'?" by Clarke Institute of Psychiatry researchers; [16] and Chess's illuminating article, "The 'Blame the Mother' Ideology." [7] In a publication distributed with a daily newspaper, physician Howard Seiden in his weekly medical column [25] cited a comment by two other physicians that mothers are more likely to teach their little boys to wash behind their ears than beneath their foreskins and added his own comment: "Why this responsibility has been given to mothers is a puzzle to me" (p. 18).

The 1980 volume *of Annual Progress in Child Psychiatry and Child Development* [8] included the observation that Jerome Kagan believes that the crucial importance of the so-called "mother-infant bond" is "society's folk theory" and still remains largely unproven. Along similar lines, Chess and Thomas [9] have argued convincingly and with detailed evidence that the mother-infant interaction does not predict very well the infant's subsequent functioning (except in cases of extreme deprivation by everyone). Chess and Thomas [9] pointed out that, recently, Klaus and Kennell's formulation about the importance of "bonding" between mother and infant during the first year, and even during the first hour, of the infant's life [15] has been the subject of a great deal of attention. Both Chess and Thomas [9] and Herbert, Sluckin and Sluckin [13] rejected this notion after thoroughly reviewing the relevant literature, with the latter group summarizing the situation as follows:

> It is said that foolish or reprehensible child-rearing practices, particularly on the part of the mother, and distortions in the formation of the mother's attachment to her offspring are responsible for the

various unsatisfactory aspects of the child's physical and psychological development. . . .

Some conjectures about the unidimensionality of attachment behaviour, the existence of a critical period in infant-to-mother attachment, an exclusive role for the mother in the formation of a bond and the dangers of separation have been modified in the face of growing empirical evidence. . . . [13] (p. 205)

Specifically related to the issue of the "schizophrenogenic mother" is Parker's recent paper, [23] in which he concluded that

> . . . case-control studies raise doubt as to whether such a maternal style is over-represented at all in the families of schizophrenics. (p. 452)

Reviewing the pertinent literature, he stressed that a dominant, overprotective, but basically rejecting *parental* style is relevant to neurotic disorders in offspring but not particularly to the development of schizophrenia. Similarly, Hirsh and Leff [14] concluded that

> . . . the characterization of these mothers as showing a combination of overprotection and hostile rejection cannot be sustained. (p. 95)

However, despite such improvements, in the citation of previous literature and the application of it to current work, social changes are rarely being taken into account. As fewer mothers are assuming exclusive responsibility for child care and as more take on work outside the home, one might expect that clinicians' interpretations of such phenomena as school phobia would be modified, and blame no longer placed on the mother for wanting to keep her child at home with her. As fewer mothers are at home during school hours in particular, such circumstances need to be taken into consideration. But in the articles on school phobia reviewed for the present study, [2, 26] this simply was not done. Nor has it been done in very recent work on school phobia. [11] Although fewer mothers are at home all day now than formerly, child rearing is still primarily considered the mother's responsibility. The increasing number of single mothers—whether due to separation and divorce or due to young, single mothers' decisions to raise their babies themselves—means that, above all, the mothers are *there*. They are there for the professionals who assess and treat their children; they are there to be identified, studied, and questioned by these professionals; and they are there for the general public to see, raising their children. Thus, they, more than the absent fathers, are easy targets for blame. It is easier to attribute a child's problems to the behavior of a parent who is present than to the imagined or suspected behavior of a parent who is no longer on the scene.

Chodorow [10] has poignantly summarized the position of the mother who knows she is likely to be blamed:

> Until the contemporary feminist movement, social and psychological commentators put the burden of solution for these problems onto the individual and did not recognize that anything was systematically wrong. They described both the potential contradictions in mothering and their actual expression—mothers on a balancing wire of separation and connection. . . . To overcome these difficulties, mothers were to learn their balancing act better . . . (p. 214)

The present study has demonstrated that mother-blaming is a significant and serious problem that continues in the current clinical literature. For mothers' sakes, clinicians' tendency to blame mothers must be curbed. In the meantime, mothers recognize as echoes of their persistent thoughts these words from the play, *'night, Mother,* [22] as the mother says desperately to her suicidal daughter:

> *I don't know what I did, but I did it, I know.*
>
> and
>
> *Everything you do has something to do with me.*

References

In this journal's citation system, the sources are alphabetized and also numbered. In the text of the articles, the numbers are used to reference the sources.

1. Badinter, E. 1981. *Mother love: myth and reality.* Macmillan, New York.

2. Berg, I. 1970. A follow-up study of school phobic adolescents admitted to an inpatient unit. *J. Child Psychol. Psychiat.* 11:37–47.

3. Bowlby, J. 1951. *Maternal care and mental health.* World Health Organization, Geneva.

4. Brodkin, A. 1980. Family therapy: the making of a mental health movement. *Amer. J. Orthopsychiat.* 50(1):4–17.

5. Caplan, P. 1981. *Between women: lowering the barriers.* Personal Library, Toronto.

6. Chesler, P. 1973. *Women and madness.* Avon Books, New York.

7. Chess, S. 1982. The "blame the mother" ideology. *Inter. J. Ment. Hlth* 11:95–107.

8. Chess, S. and Thomas, A. eds. 1980. *Annual progress in child psychiatry and child development.* Brunner/Mazel, New York.

9. Chess, S. and Thomas, A. 1982. Infant bonding: mystique and reality. *Amer. J. Orthopsychiat.* 52(2):213–222.

10. Chodorow, N. 1978. *The reproduction of mothering: psychoanalysis and the sociology of gender.* University of California Press, Berkeley.

11. Desousa, A. and Desousa, F. 1980. School phobia. *Child Psychiat. Quart. 13*(4):98–103.

12. Fromm-Reichman, F. 1948. Notes on the development of treatment of schizophrenics by psychoanalytic psychotherapy. *Psychiatry 11:*263–274.

13. Herbert, M., Sluckin, W. and Sluckin, A. 1982. Mother-to-infant bonding. J. *Child Psychol. Psychiat. 23*(3):205–221.

14. Hirsh, S. and Leff, J. 1975. *Abnormalities in parents of schizophrenics.* Oxford University Press, London.

15. Klaus, M. and Kennell, J. 1976. *Maternal-infant Bonding.* C. V. Mosby, St. Louis.

16. Konstantareas, M. et al. 1983. Mothers of autistic children: are they the "unacknowledged victims"? Presented to the Canadian Psychological Association, Winnipeg.

17. Levy, D. 1943. *Maternal overprotection.* Columbia University Press, New York.

18. Mahler, M. 1952. On childhood psychoses and schizophrenia: autistic and symbiotic infantile psychosis. *In The psychoanalytic study of the child.* R. Eissler et al, eds. International Universities Press, New York.

19. Maynard, R. 1983. Let's stop blaming Mum. *Homemaker's Mag,* (May):8–26.

20. Myers, M. 1982. Homosexuality, sexual dysfunction, and incest in male identical twins. *Canad. J. Psychiat. 27*(2): 144–147.

21. Naylor, A. 1982. Premature mourning and failure to mourn: their relationship to conflict between mothers and intellectually normal children. *Amer. J. Orthopsychiat. 52*(4):679–687.

22. Norman, M. 1983. *'night, mother.* Hill and Wang, New York.

23. Parker, G. 1982. Researching the schizophrenogenic mother. *J. Nerv. Ment. Dis. 170:*452–462.

24. Pogrebin, L. 1981. *Growing up free: raising your child in the 80s.* Bantam, Toronto.

25. Seiden, H. 1982. Circumspection. *Today Mag.* (July 11): 18–19.

26. Smith, R. and Sharpe, T. 1970. Treatment of a school phobia with implosive therapy. *J. Consult. Clin. Psychol. 35*(2):239–242.

The Reference list includes some of the classic theoretical writings that pathologized mothers, like Levy and Mahler.

Discussion Ideas

1. What is the problem with attributing people's psychological distress to the actions or inactions of their mothers? Do you consider this a problem in your own practice or future practice settings?

2. Why did the researchers use fifty articles outside the study's data base to make up the questions for their survey?

3. Why are the sexes of the article writers in the database reported?

4. If you studied psychologists' attitudes toward mothers today, twenty years or more after this research, do you think you would find the same pattern? Why or why not?

5. The founders of family systems therapies were raised in the atmosphere described in this study. Do you think that mother-blaming affected the theory of family systems? Do you think that family therapy blames the mother more often than other factors?

6. This study is an example of archival research using psychological journals to argue that a certain theme existed (or exists). Think of one or two other topics that could be explored through this kind of research.

Answer Key for Practice Test Questions

True/False

1. F
2. F
3. T
4. T
5. F
6. T
7. T
8. F
9. F
10. T

Multiple Choice

1. a
2. b
3. d
4. d
5. e
6. b
7. c
8. d
9. d
10. a
11. e
12. b
13. e
14. c
15. e

CHAPTER **11**

Systemic Approaches: Culture and Gender Bases

Chapter Review

Cultural systems thinking takes into account the influences of subgroups within the larger culture. Human beings are social in nature, and as such form communal groups. Societal structures determine how the groups relate to one another. People within groups take on characteristics that reflect the interactions between subgroups and the distribution of power or influence. To a large degree, the groups we belong to affect who we are in our own minds and in the minds of others. Focusing attention on the interaction of societal groups can reveal important influences on individual human beings.

The social context each person grew up in, and lives in, creates a values orientation, such as valuing individual independence rather than social belongingness. Contextual influences are so basic; it is difficult to think outside the defining confines of what we are taught and what is reinforced. Each person has internalized expectations originating from the mainstream culture and relevant subcultures to which he or she belongs. Some mental health disorders show global uniformity regardless of the specific society, but culture affects the impact of a disorder in terms of clients' behavior, prognosis, and symptom improvement. Research also demonstrates that counseling professionals show inconsistencies in diagnosing clinical disorders based on societal expectations of people in specific groups.

Training and education alert helping professionals to cultural differences and encourage ethnographic attitudes. As counselors clarify the contextual conditions, clients can better understand themselves and the origins of psychological issues. Gender expectations create an image of what defines masculinity and femininity and are the most salient of all social mandates based on subgroup classification. Mirror image stereotypes prescribe characteristics for men that are the opposite of what is considered appropriate for women, though scientific research has not shown a genetic basis for broad behavioral differences between sexes. Counselors help clients recognize the prescribed quality of gender expectations and facilitate an awareness of resulting inner experiences. As societal messages for gender roles have changed across generations, role strains and conflicts have also created psychological reactions and issues relevant for counseling. Feminist therapists stress the sex differences in power, status, and economic equity. To encourage a therapeutic experience of empowerment rather than submissive acceptance, feminists also emphasize a collaborative counseling process and encourage social activism. Consciousness-raising groups examine personal experiences in the context of societal sexism. Men's groups and individual counseling deal with the restrictive nature of male gender roles.

Minority groups have subcultural differences as well as experiences stemming from their minority status. The majority culture has the influential power to set not only major expectations for participating in the society at large, but also to characterize minority groups from the majority culture's point of view. Discrimination and bias demand that minority members acquire the social habits of paying attention to differing expectations as well as deferent behaviors acceding to the power of members of the ruling group. Economic status, also controlled to a great extent by the majority, often overlaps with minority status and adds external pressure as well as social psychological difficulties. Respect for cultural differences and sensitivity to the implications of differing economic and power positioning includes acceptance of healing traditions that are not certified by mainstream professionalism. Indeed, the profession itself is a subgroup with its own biases that need to be adapted according to Person-Centered preferences.

However, training that explicates cultural differences runs the risk of amplifying generalities to the point of stereotyping, assuming that general observations about the group as a whole apply to individuals. Examining client characteristics and counseling issues from various perspectives, cultural as well as family dynamics and individual preferences, avoids stereotypic assumptions. There is considerable similarity between humanistic and other counseling approaches and cultural orientations, and in fact, most counselors integrate diversity awareness with other theoretical conceptualizations.

One particular concept is worth noting. The psychological costs of negative social conditions do not suggest individuals lose an ability to make independent choices or to overcome obstacles that inhibit psychological health and contentment. Although recognizing external influences can reduce shame and self-blame, healing entails taking personal responsibility for the course of one's life. Living from a victim's stance over time diminishes a person's capacity for self-expression and his very humanity. The goal of sorting out cultural and gendered precedents from individual preferences is to enhance personal identity.

Practice Test Questions

True or False: Consider each statement and try to explain in your own mind why it might not be fully true. Be sure to take into account any qualifying factors that might make the statement untrue. If you decide that the statement is fully true, circle **T**. Otherwise, circle **F**.

T   F   1. Cultural and gendered approaches are more concerned with social activism than individual development.

T   F   2. Consciousness-raising brings into awareness the conflicts between the id and the superego.

T   F   3. Minority status allows people of diverse groups to gain the privileges of the majority.

T   F   4. Self-defeating personality disorder is a DSM diagnosis applied only to women.

T   F   5. The problems that are more characteristic of men are typically related to an innate male psychology.

T   F   6. Asian cultures set a priority on individual independence and self-expression.

T   F   7. "Cognitively available schema" are mental structures basic to our identities such as sex-role expectations.

T   F   8. Sex is a biological description whereas gender is a societal image defining the characteristics designated as masculine or feminine.

T F   9. How we see ourselves mirrored every day by other's reactions does not impact our own view of ourselves.

T F   10. Scientific research validates innate differences in ways women and men process, understand, express, and feel emotion.

Multiple Choice: Circle the one letter next to the best answer to the following questions or to complete the sentence stems.

1. The phrase "the personal is political" implies which of the following?
   a. Personal feelings are rarely related to social structures and practices.
   b. Psychological issues sometimes originate in social-role expectations.
   c. To overcome the impact of some psychological difficulties, social activism must be avoided.
   d. a and b
   e. a, b, and c

2. In the practice of facilitating therapy for people with diverse backgrounds, counselors should
   a. learn all the characteristics of various cultural groups and make sure to apply such knowledge to clients from the respective groups.
   b. be sensitive to cultural differences for clients who come from groups with minority status.
   c. consider client issues from multiple perspectives, not always assuming cultural group characteristics apply to individuals.
   d. a and b
   e. b and c

3. *Personality* includes fundamental ingredients that are commonly shared by different cultures. Which of the following are among such attributes?
   a. introversion vs. extraversion
   b. an openness vs. a closed attitude toward experience
   c. conscientiousness vs. imprecision
   d. a and b
   e. a, b, and c

4. Which of the following defines *gender* as distinct from *sex*?
   a. Sex is a biological categorization, and gender is a synonym.
   b. Gender is the social characterization of male and female, and sex is biological.
   c. Sex is the appropriate term for intercourse, and gender is used for the biological categorization of male and female.
   d. Gender is the summary of social role expectations, and sex refers to Freudian unconscious drives.

5. A common feature that does NOT define healthy functioning, regardless of cultural history or setting, is
   a. accurate understanding of social expectations.
   b. reasonable assessment of personal interests, capabilities, and limitations.
   c. consistent political activism.
   d. cognitive and behavioral flexibility.
   e. self-control of behavior.
   f. hope for the future.

6. Which of the following are typically seen as gender stereotypes and differences?
    a. Women are kind, socially skilled, manipulative, and have more learning disabilities.
    b. Men are tough, self-reliant, and more likely to attempt suicide.
    c. Women are nurturing, dependent, bitchy, and less likely to attend graduate school.
    d. Men are oriented toward success, status, risk-taking, and hyperactivity.

7. Which of the following is an accurate description of *mirror image stereotypes?*
    a. Stereotypes that define two groups as the opposite of each other.
    b. Mirror images label men as self-expressive and women as instrumental.
    c. Mirror images label women as rational and men as relational.
    d. a, c
    e. a, b

8. The statement, "We seek to explain differences (among groups) instead of explaining domination," would see diversity as most representative of what domain?
    a. infant-mother dynamics
    b. cultural background
    c. economic conditions
    d. social role conditioning
    e. a and b
    f. b, c, d

9. *Role strain* and *role conflict* are defined by which of the following?
    a. *Role strain* is having too many roles to fulfill and *role conflict* is hostile interactions with someone in a higher role.
    b. *Role conflict* refers to confusing demands for different roles and *role strain* to many demands from too many roles.
    c. *Role strain* is having too many taxing demands from different roles and *role conflict* is the pressure of external demands for a role.
    d. *Role conflict* is juggling demands from a hierarchical system and *role strain* is the pressure of having too many roles.

10. The values of global culture do not include which of the following?
    a. individual rights
    b. choice
    c. intolerance to diversity
    d. openness to change

11. *Complex hybrid identity* refers to
    a. retaining cultural identity for the region in which you grew up.
    b. adapting to the mainstream culture after immigration.
    c. a combination of characteristics representative of many cultures.
    d. an identity rooted in cultural expectations.

12. Many victims of domestic violence do not take action against their attackers because they
    a. feel shame and do not want to bring the issue to the attention of others.
    b. are afraid others will blame them for instigating the violence.
    c. are confused as to whether aggression is acceptable for men.
    d. are loyal to their attackers.
    e. are afraid they will suffer reprisals if they speak out.
    f. all of the above

13. Counselors who are aware of gender and cultural issues emphasize financial independence or security for clients because
    a. without economic resources, people are more likely to face physical danger.
    b. without money for basic necessities, health problems are avoided.
    c. financial strains often include personal shame.
    d. changing the distribution of wealth is an important political issue for fairness between subgroups.

14. An *ethnographic* perspective would include all of the following EXCEPT
    a. What can I learn about how specific groups define the world, right and wrong, and establish goals for life?
    b. How can I modify my thinking and interactions to facilitate creating a relationship of trust and mutual respect?
    c. How can I make sure the client will follow the way procedures are administered?
    d. How can I negotiate treatment and prevention plans so both the client and the counselor agree as to how to proceed even if priorities and beliefs differ?

15. Which of the following is an issue that a gender-aware counselor would pay attention to for male clients?
    a. shame and confusion regarding male sex-role expectations
    b. impulsiveness and risk-taking behaviors
    c. relationship dysfunction and loneliness
    d. consequences of cutting off aspects of the self
    e. none of the above
    f. all of the above

Key Terms and Essential Concepts

Expectations: External sources set criteria for the behavior and characteristics that are considered appropriate for different groups of people. Social institutions typically teach what is regarded as suitable for men and women, for people in particular roles or professions, for people in different racial groups, or for people with specific religious affiliations. The external expectations, once taught, become internal to individuals who learn to live up to what is customary and who are surprised by others who do not. People learn to respond to what has been defined as normative according to situational demands that require expected behaviors.

Gender expectations: Positive and negative qualities set as societal standards for femininity and masculinity. Stereotypes of femininity include being nice to others, polite, sociable, nurturing, aesthetically pleasing, creative, and neat, as well as being neurotic, hysterical, weak, devious, manipulative, dependent, bitchy, unreasonable, and flighty. Masculine stereotypes include being strong, silent, successful, tough, confident, independent, and self-reliant, as well as being aggressive, violent, and a daredevil. Gender characteristics are internalized and become part of identity, fusing a sense of self with external expectations.

Gender role socialization: The developmental process whereby human beings are taught gender role differences is called *gender role socialization*. People are taught how to appear and behave within the expectations of society for men and women. The process starts early with embryos defined by sex even before birth and as children read stories and play adult roles. Gender expectations are particularly salient during puberty as teens begin to relate romantically and sexually, and then roles solidify in adulthood with family role expectations.

Mirror image stereotypes: When two groups are defined as being characterized by opposite traits, the pairs reflect each other. The image of a typical male, for example, is supposed to be strong, while the typical female would then be weak. Slave owners could be said to be responsible, taking care of the plantation and its inhabitants, while slaves would then be careless and in need of supervision. Such complementarity gives an impression of inevitability, as people in different groups seem deserving of privilege while other groups are assigned lower status.

Instrumental versus expressive: According to mirror image stereotyping for men and women, men actively exert their influence to manage their lives while women are sensitive to situational demands and passively accept what is happening to them and around them. Their orientation is expressive, meaning that they are emotional rather than functional.

Rationality versus relationality: Feminist authors redefined the mirror image stereotypes of men and women to change the bias of instrumentality versus expressiveness. Instead, women are said to possess a gift for relationships, intuitively reading emotions and human needs, while men are said to be analytical, logically dealing with all matters through intellectual reasoning while insensitive to emotions and others' needs.

Externalize: When people "act out" internal feelings, they are said to externalize the emotions. An example is when someone is depressed and she drives recklessly. When dealing with psychological issues, the focus for an individual is outside the self. So, when a client describes unhappiness, the description emphasizes external factors that create pressures without recognizing how internal attitudes contribute to dealing with the situation.

Internalize: A person's experiences are turned inward without referring to the external factors involved. For example, Sally is teased as "silly" and feels hurt. She focuses on her hurt and her silliness, rather than recognizing the teasers could simply be wrong or mean. She "owns" the problem rather than considering factors other than herself. Internalizing also refers to a person taking into his internal sense of self such external influences as societal messages or others' opinions.

Minimizing bias: When diagnostic criteria are reduced in importance so the client is seen as having fewer or less severe difficulties than other similar clients, there is a minimizing effect. The danger is that the client does not receive the help needed or is given inappropriate treatment because problems were de-emphasized. For example, depression may be minimized among mentally retarded people.

Overdiagnosis bias: When clients from a particular group are consistently labeled with the same disorder, the diagnosis is being overutilized. The clients may be receiving the diagnosis because they are members of the same group, rather than from an objective analysis of symptoms.

Overpathologizing bias: When counselors demonstrate a consistent pattern of characterizing client issues as examples of mental illness when other more normal explanations might describe the client's difficulties equally well, they are said to be overpathologizing. Research has shown that clinicians consistently perceive some groups as showing severe disturbances where other groups could present similar symptoms and be perceived as less disturbed.

Underdiagnosis bias: When people from a particular group are less likely to be diagnosed with a particular disorder, regardless of symptoms, there is a bias suggesting such people don't have such disorders. A medical example is overlooking heart disease in women because the diagnosis is considered more likely for men.

Role conflict: The expectations considered appropriate for one role may be incompatible with the demands of other roles. For example, a woman business leader is required to be assertive and decisive on the job, but when she goes home to her children, she needs to be nurturing and responsive. Sometimes the differences in expectations create confusion, and balancing a stable identity with situational demands becomes difficult.

Role strain: A person who serves a number of demanding roles experiences the stress of trying to meet multiple demands. Each position may require a great deal of effort, and juggling several roles taxes energy and an ability to keep track of the responsibilities for each function. Leisure and relaxation become impossible, so the person is drained without much time for rejuvenation. Unlike role conflict, a role strain can come from consistent role demands such as being nurturant on the job, in the family, and in volunteer duties.

Nonsexist therapy: Counselors attempt to avoid the influence of society's definitions of what is proper and healthy for men and women. For example, a nonsexist career counselor would encourage clients to consider careers that are unusual choices for their sex, as well as traditional ones.

Feminist therapy: Counselors, who avoid traditional stereotyping of men and women, work to raise client awareness of the personal impact of gender roles and the influence of power in relationships. Societal influences, such as economic inequalities and media representation of ideal body images, are raised in therapy as sources of psychological difficulties. To promote a sense of personal power, clients are encouraged to explore their own evaluations of societal messages and to possibly take political action to change attitudes and practices.

Empowerment: The goal of gender- and culture-based counseling is to raise awareness of societal influences for personal development and for problematic psychological issues. Once awareness of outside pressures is evident, however, the movement for counseling and for clients is to regain personal power and to determine self-direction despite social restrictiveness. Empowerment is considered the opposite of victimization.

Self-disclosure: When the counselor shares personal experiences with the client, she is self-disclosing. Since therapy focuses on the client and is designed to facilitate change for the client, too much counselor content would change counseling into a conversation between friends. Feminist therapists, however, note that counselors who never self-disclose enhance their position of power and reduce mutuality.

Shared power: Collaborative methods in counseling give a message to the client that both the client and the counselor share influence in the relationship. Feminist therapists emphasize collaboration by bringing counseling decisions into the open for mutual input. When techniques for change are introduced, the purpose is explained and the client is asked if such methods seem reasonable.

Consciousness-raising: Bringing into awareness the impact of gender bias and the inequalities of sexism in society allows the person to explore embedded social psychological issues. When women realize that most women share some personally painful issues, they feel less alone and self-blaming. Clients can better deal with those difficulties originating in a society that prescribes gender identity in narrow terms and endorses a subordinate position for all women.

Gender intensification: During preadolescence, peer pressures encourage young girls to subscribe to feminine stereotyping by being social and submissive and to expect males to be independent and aggressive. Young girls can lose touch with an earlier sense of self, become overly self-conscious, and lack self-efficacy. Many turn away from interests in traditionally male fields such as math and science. Others become depressed. Boys of the same age are distressed if they do not fit masculine stereotypes. Feminist-oriented counseling can offer psychological education regarding male-female equity and can encourage identity development and social skills that are not stereotypical.

Racial identity: A part of an individual's identity that involves an inner sense of what it means to be of a specific race, such as Chinese, Latino, or Caucasian. Awareness of personal racial implications may occur in stages, according to some psychological studies. Racial awareness also includes attitudes toward races other than one's own.

Minority status: A group who share visible physical characteristics located in a region where the group is fewer in number than the majority group or who are underrepresented in leadership roles or higher economic levels are considered to have minority status. Minority group members may have cultural backgrounds different from the majority's and additional distinctive experiences stemming from their minority status. Generations of prejudicial treatment required defensive behaviors of caution, mistrust, caginess, and secretiveness to survive. Minority status may also induce biases against the majority values and a cynicism for values that have not been universally applied to all groups.

Stereotyping: Beliefs about the similarities of everyone within an identifiable group. Stereotyping often leads to ignoring individuals for who they are as human beings and breeds distrust among groups.

Prejudice: A bias or opinion attributing a set of predetermined characteristics (usually negative) to people belonging to a particular group.

Backlash effect: When matters of diversity are emphasized, sometimes the highlighting of cultural differences itself creates a reaction against the values intended. In drawing attention to different cultural practices, stereotypes are reinforced. Furthermore, people rebel against preachiness.

Globalization: Media and communication technologies present throughout the world spread information to every local area and create shared experiences for everyone. Differences among people may become less prominent, particularly for young people who develop with a global awareness of multiple points of view rather than restricted regional views.

Complex hybrid identity: A sense of self develops within a social context. Identity that is formed with the influences of television and the Internet is not confined to the culture of the neighborhood, nation, or region. Instead, combinations of geographical and social stimuli are experienced, creating a hybrid identity with multiple connections to outside influences.

Native healers: Different cultures have a variety of healing practices and practitioners that provide solace and change for those who subscribe to them. Appropriate respect for other healing traditions is a part of cultural sensitivity, so counselors ask clients about cultural practices and support the use of helpful modalities.

Normalization: When a person feels intense emotion and experiences difficulties, he or she may conclude, "There is something wrong with me." Sometimes, regardless of the intensity of the feelings, problems are a part of typical psychological development, change, or the reactions anyone would feel under the circumstances. The sheer recognition that others have similar experiences helps a person feel better, without minimizing what the person is going through.

Social action: Taking part in social activities designed to create social change can be therapeutic to those who have suffered under social inequities. Social involvement can be seen as a responsibility of professionals who seek to help others overcome the difficulties induced by social unfairness.

Value systems: A collection of beliefs and priorities held by individuals and shared by groups of people as culture or as subcultures. Such concepts provide a moral compass, guides for personal choices, behavior, and social interactions.

Victimization: When a group has been restrained or mistreated through societal structures and pressures, they are the victims of forces outside themselves. Analyzing the impact of unequal treatment explains the root cause and development of psychological issues so the victim is not blamed.

Victimhood: Though becoming a victim is not within a person's control, it does not mandate a preoccupation with deficits in privileges nor does unequal treatment excuse unacceptable behavior. To take on a mantle of being a victim as though the word defines a person's identity is self-defeating. Instead, understanding social influences is intended to lead to an insight that personal limits may have been set by external sources, and the individual can make choices to negate restrictive thinking.

Representative Case: Mahatma Uli

At 21, Mahatma attends a competitive university with a national reputation for excellence in engineering. He is from Pakistan and came to the United States on a student visa. He came to counseling through a referral from a physician who is treating him for debilitating migraine headaches. Several roommates from his country accompany him, and they express an agitated concern saying that, "He may be going mad." Mahatma screams out in shrieking cries late at night, sometimes in pain but at other times in pure frustration. His friends have insisted he seek help, though Mahatma is reluctant to describe his issues.

The first topic Mahatma will explain is his academic situation. He failed two courses several semesters ago and has been trying to make up the deficiencies. Each semester he registers for twenty-one credits, repeating the failures and taking the next courses in the sequence. Though he can achieve B's and a few C's for the majority of his credits, usually sixteen, he cannot seem to fulfill all the required courses at an acceptable level and he gets D's or F's for one or two courses each semester. Consequently, he registers for additional credits the next semester, trying to catch up in quality points, but he has not been able to complete all the requirements three semesters in a row. He strains to make the counselor understand that he is willing to suffer any amount of pain and will work any amount of time, but it is absolutely mandatory that he finish his degree on time. Suggestions that he balance his schedule by taking breaks, enjoying some leisure activities, or that he seek supportive friends are dismissed as impossible. Instead, he describes a grueling schedule of waking up at 5 A.M. to study, attending class, working a part-time job, and studying until 1 or 2 A.M. He observes the Muslim religion and prays a number of times a day but says his practice does not offer relief but is a rote activity his duty requires.

The counselor does not try to persuade Mahatma to change his behavior immediately but asks him to pay attention to his fatigue level, noting degrees of tiredness several times a day. In the next session, Mahatma shares a neat record of his fatigue level for fifteen hours a day. Always tired, he notes that he is not really sleepy until after 11 P.M. when he forces himself to stay awake for at least two more hours. The counselor offers Mahatma some literature regarding sleep deprivation and discusses how his fatigue affects his concentration and contributes to developing migraines. With some resistance Mahatma agrees to follow the prompting of his body and try sleeping at 11 P.M.

With prompting, Mahatma also reveals his self-punishing thoughts: he is a disgrace, he must succeed, others will find out he is unworthy, lazy, or stupid. The counselor gently explains that his negative self-criticism also contributes to his fatigue and anxiety and blocks his concentration. Mahatma finds the prospect of less severe attitudes toward himself very difficult, but he agreed to say "STOP" out loud when he berates himself. In the next session, Mahatma shows his record of how often he has said "STOP," showing he started with six times an hour and gradually only needed to say the word once an hour. Over the course of the next several weeks, he reduced the litany of self-criticisms to once or twice a day and reported feeling somewhat better. With medication, he also reduced his migraines to once a week. These occurred when he did not comply with the protocol of taking the medicine because he felt better.

A crisis occurred when he failed a midterm for one course. The counselor suggested he drop the course and concentrate on the other subjects to gain eighteen instead of twenty-one credits.

Mahatma was reluctant to reduce his course load but succumbed to the reasoning that completing the other courses would improve his record. Mahatma was able to finish the semester with all B's and was very pleased. However, he registered for another twenty-one credits for the next semester.

Finally, he explained his family situation. He was the youngest sibling of four children, all of whom had advanced degrees and were successfully contributing to the extended family finances. Studying abroad was a major drain on the family resources and was preventing one other brother from pursuing advanced studies. He had not informed his family of his academic situation since it could require an extra semester of expense and would demonstrate his ingratitude for the privilege. Exploring the possibility of telling his parents created extreme anxiety for Mahatma, and he insisted he simply must continue to press himself into completing an excessive number of credits within the time frame previously set. For the next semester, Mahatma checked in with the counselor and agreed to report his grades following midterms and in time to drop a course. Again, he was unable to achieve acceptable grades in every course but dropping a course again was completely impossible for him since it would guarantee he would have to stay an extra semester.

The counselor tried to describe the pressure of keeping a secret from his family as adding to the anxiety, but Mahatma insisted that asking his parents to provide money to extend his time in the United States would be disrespectful. Finally, the counselor suggested she call Pakistan and talk to his parents to explain that his physical condition required his dropping a course or his health would be jeopardized. Mahatma considered saying his health was in danger to be a lie until he accepted a definition of mental health and the operation of brain circuitry as legitimately a part of his physical condition. He also felt his parents would not accept a nonmedical doctor as a legitimate authority to make recommendations. When arrangements were made for the physician to make a call to his parents, Mahatma agreed to the action. Though typically a counselor would expect a client to take responsibility for informing parents of an academic situation, in this circumstance, the intervention worked to relieve the client.

Thinking About Mahatma

1. What was the source of Mahatma's anxiety?

2. What cultural expectations and attitudes were associated with Mahatma's thinking and behavior?

3. Why do you think the counselor chose cognitive and behavioral interventions rather than using other counseling approaches?

4. Do you agree that contacting Mahatma's parents was appropriate?

Check Your Thinking About Mahatma

1. Mahatma's boxed himself in with excessive demands of constant study, little sleep, and punishing thoughts. Though his attempts were not working for several semesters, he continued to repeat the same patterns. His anxiety represents his fear that he will not be able to succeed, that he will shame himself and his family, and that others will discover his unworthiness.

2. Mahatma viewed himself as a part of a collective family identity rather than as an individual identity. The question regarding his interest in the field of engineering was not open for examination. He was expected to perform in an academic field chosen by his father and to gain credentials to quality for a job that would contribute to family finances. A wife would be chosen for him when he returned to Pakistan and could be presented as ready to earn

a living appropriate to his station. Views toward mental health were clouded with issues of character, self-discipline, and performance of duty. Only with a legitimate physical condition was there any leeway in adapting the plans for his degree completion.

3. Other orientations that depend on reflecting feelings, or examining childhood experiences, would not have been acceptable for Mahatma. He expected himself to set feelings aside and to focus his attention on the goals set before him. To tell stories about his family would have been considered disrespectful and inappropriate. The concrete data gained in his fatigue record presented evidence that he needed to change his sleep habits. The thought record indicated thinking he did not question. From his perspective, self-punishing thoughts were accurate statements because he had not performed as expected. Only the suggestion that self-criticism created anxiety and interfered with his concentration made it acceptable for him to reduce the pressure.

4. Mahatma worked within the collective context of his family and the authority of his father. Within the confines of his thinking and the expectations imposed on him, his pattern of suffering would continue as he failed more courses and ran out of time. Informing his parents offered the means for the family to deal with the problem. A report by a physician regarding a physical condition was considered a valid means of giving information to the parents, whereas Mahatma's own report would be considered disrespectful according to his thinking. This was not excuse-making since he was willing to suffer until the conclusion of the course of events and had indeed suffered over time.

Core Case: Helen Lovelace

The Helen Lovelace case was first described in Chapter 6, Existential and Humanistic Approaches. Here we see it from a culture- and gender-based approach. Again **D** designates **Data, A** designates **Assessment,** and **P** designates **Plan**.

D: Although Helen's relationship with her authoritarian father and passive mother offers some clues to difficulties in her relationships with men, other relevant data regarding the cultural background of the family adds further insight. Helen's father emigrated from Germany just before World War II. He retained "old world" patriarchal gender roles that prescribed his duty as a breadwinner, head of the family, and protector of his wife and daughter; these set up an expectation of submission to his orders. Once in the United States for several86, Laws, 1847, ecame a master sergeant. Within the subculture of his work environment, he submitted to and gave orders without question according to the hierarchy's structure. For him, his background and his work subculture reinforced maintaining the hierarchy of the family. Also, he maintained social and religious images of femininity as either the innocent virgin or the seductive temptress; and he was determined that his daughter would live up to the "good" model.

Helen's mother was a second generation immigrant who upheld her husband's authority in accord with her experience in her family of origin. To her, women stayed in their role as a reflection of religious and social expectations, though she found manipulative methods to enhance her freedom of movement. Helen's mother encouraged her daughter to "get an education, so she would never have to submit to a man." Helen's mother also taught her how to use her "female appeal" to get the father to agree to what the mother and daughter wanted. Both mother and daughter learned to cry on demand and to act hurt when the father made demands they wanted changed. Helen's brothers also accepted her as a fragile feminine object, and she learned to appeal to their protection when she wanted them to do something for her. The mother aligned with Helen when it was useful in dealing with her husband and with her sons when she needed their assistance. The mother would describe her sacrifices for the children and her pain in dealing with their father, in essence playing the victim and extracting guilt from the children.

A: Helen's embedded image of femininity and masculinity are particularly stereotypic, leaving her without healthy models for male or female identities or for egalitarian relationships. She has automatic behavioral patterns of manipulation that are successful enough to reinforce her core schemata, though she recognizes her inability to establish a stable lifestyle. Her insight is limited to some understanding of the family dynamics without fully taking into account both past and present societal influences. She has been estranged from her parents since the birth of her first child out of wedlock. Her brothers, who had been supportive, have lost patience with her because she is again pregnant. Helen is acting out her image of femininity, using her beauty to attract men and to appeal to her brothers for help as the victim who was used by men. At the same time, she has chosen men who are clearly not in a position to develop a stable relationship with her, so she doesn't have to live in submission to them. She has some understanding of her self-destructive patterns but little insight as to alternatives except living a bare subsistence lifestyle in the mountains.

P: Helen is ready to examine the influences of gender roles her parents played out and to determine alternative partnership relationships or her desire to retain independent status. Exploring the roles played by her parents and their interaction patterns can help Helen understand the power dynamics underneath. Gaining insight that her mother did have subversive power can loosen the pure victim image Helen retains. Challenging Helen to "own" her power of choice rather than repeating the manipulative interactions she learned from her mother could expose the quality of relationships she gains. She may also benefit from viewing the role her body image plays for her identity and in her relationships and may recognize the societal influences regarding her appearance. It is not clear how motherhood fits into her cognitive schema, and this area may also deserve scrutinizing. It is also not clear what sort of relationships Helen has had with other women, and she may benefit from a group where consciousness-raising could offer insight regarding sexism and support from others who share similar concerns. The goal of recognizing the influences of external gender expectations and her own choices in reactions to such influences could free Helen to consider alternative choices and empower her to feel able to manage her life with full awareness.

Finding a Balance

Fitting a counseling approach to the counselor's personality and preferences is an ongoing challenge. In this section, we describe some characteristics of counselors who employ gendered and cultural points of view.

Key Counselor Preferences

1. Gender- and culture-aware therapists are often people who themselves have been exposed to prejudice and stereotyping due to their membership in a visibly identifiable group. For example, most feminist counselors are women.

2. Gender- and culture-aware counselors look at the world in more political terms than many others do. They may be involved in community or national politics and enjoy the study of history and geography. How sociological factors influence individual lives seems continually relevant in their case conceptualizations.

3. Wherever gender- and culture-aware counselors are often found working, in community mental health centers or other sites, they enjoy seeing clients from many cultures and economic strata. Their sensitivity to gender and cultural issues is useful since all clients will have schema from their background and often counseling issues will be related. Systemic

thinking, recognizing the influence of the group on the individual, becomes natural to counselors whether they see clients individually, in pairs, or in groups.

4. All counselors need to develop gender and cultural awareness as part of their approach. Any theoretical stance is enriched by this awareness.

Applying Counselor Preferences

1. Regardless of the sex or cultural background of the counselor, awareness of the gender-assigned role characteristics in a client's family of origin can be related to client issues. Helen's parents modeled stereotypic roles with strong emotional overlays. Clearly her ambivalence regarding intimate relationships is related to her experience in her family.

2. The religious and cultural background of Helen's family demonstrates power issues that are a part of social activism's agenda. Helen's mother appears to accept a subordinate position and then finds manipulative ways to assert her influence. She teaches Helen the same methods of acting helpless with strategic purposes. Analyzing such power dynamics might be helpful for Helen.

3. Helen apparently has moved a number of times to distance herself from community and family influence. The counselor helps Helen become aware of the social constructs she carries in her mind whether she is living in the same community or not.

4. The counselor may subscribe to any number of theories. A person-centered orientation would allow Helen to explore her personal experience of gender role issues. A Gestalt counselor might use any number of techniques to intensify Helen's feelings in the moment as she describes her situation. A cognitive-behavioralist could analyze the social constructs and help Helen tease out what concepts and behaviors she wants to retain. Obviously systems oriented therapists and Adlerians can work through family issues and gender issues together.

Example of a Published Research Article, a Cultural Attitude Study

Here is an article on a cultural attitude study. Commentary in boxes to the left of the article will help you understand the research and the format of the piece.

Sex-Role Stereotypes and Clinical Judgments
of Mental Health

Inge K. Broverman, Donald M. Broverman,
Frank E. Clarkson, Paul S. Rosenkrantz, and Susan R. Vogel

A sex-role Stereotype Questionnaire consisting of 122 bipolar items was given to actively functioning clinicians with one of three sets of instructions: To describe a healthy, mature, socially competent (a) adult, sex unspecified, (b) a man, or (c) a woman. It was hypothesized that clinical judgments about the characteristics of healthy individuals would differ as a function of sex of person judged, and furthermore, that these differences in clinical judgments would parallel stereotypic sex-role differences. A second hypothesis predicted that behaviors and characteristics judged healthy for an adult, sex unspecified, which are presumed to reflect an ideal standard of health, will resemble behaviors judged healthy for men, but differ from behaviors judged healthy for women. Both hypotheses were confirmed. Possible reasons for and the effects of this double standard of health are discussed.

The importance of the research topic is developed. Do counselors see stereotypical male qualities as healthy and mature, while they see stereotypical female qualities as pathological?

Evidence of the existence of sex-role stereotypes, that is, highly consensual norms and beliefs about the differing characteristics of men and women, is abundantly present in the literature (Anastasi & Foley, 1949; Fernberger, 1948; Komarovsky, 1950; McKee & Sherriffs, 1957; Seward, 1946; Seward & Larson, 1968; Wylie, 1961; Rosenkrantz, Voget, Bee, Broverman, & Broverman, 1968). Similarly, the differential valuations of behaviors and characteristics stereotypically ascribed to men and women are well established (Kitay, 1940; Lynn, 1959; McKee & Sherriffs, 1959; Rosenkrantz et al., 1968; White, 1950), that is, stereotypically masculine traits are more often perceived as socially desirable than are attributes which are stereotypically feminine. The literature also indicates that the social desirabilities of behaviors are positively related to the clinical ratings of these same behaviors in terms of "normality-abnormality" (Cowen, 1961), "adjustment" (Wiener, Blumberg, Segman, & Cooper, 1959), and "health-sickness" (Kogan, Quinn, Ax, & Ripley, 1957).

Given the relationships existing between masculine versus feminine characteristics and social desirability, on the one hand, and between mental health and social desirability on the other, it seems reasonable to expect that clinicians will maintain parallel distinctions as their concepts of what, behaviorally, is healthy or pathological when considering men versus women. More specifically, particular behaviors and characteristics may be thought indicative of pathology in members of one sex, but not pathological in members of the opposite sex.

The present paper, then, tests the hypothesis that clinical judgments about the traits characterizing healthy, mature individuals will differ as a function of the sex of the person judged. Furthermore, these differences in clinical judgments are expected to parallel the stereotypic sex-role differences previously reported (Rosenkrantz et al., 1968).

Finally, the present paper hypothesizes that behavioral attributes which are regarded as healthy for an adult, sex unspecified, and thus presumably viewed from an ideal, absolute standpoint, will more often be considered by clinicians as healthy or appropriate for men than for women. This hypothesis derives from the assumption that abstract notions of health will tend to be more influenced by the greater social value of masculine stereotypic characteristics than by the lesser valued feminine stereotypic characteristics.

The authors are suggesting, then, that a double standard of health exists wherein ideal concepts of health for a mature adult, sex unspecified, are meant primarily for men, less so for women.

Method

Subjects

Ss is the abbreviation for *subjects*. Today, most authors refer instead to *participants*. The word *subject* suggests that the people in the experiment were passive and not fully human.

Seventy-nine clinically-trained psychologists, psychiatrists, or social workers (46 men, 33 women) served as Ss. Of these, 31 men and 18 women had PhD or MD degrees. The Ss were all actively functioning in clinical settings. The ages varied between 23 and 55 years and experience ranged from internship to extensive professional experience.

Instrument

The questionnaire has 122 items, but only 38 of them are sex-typed. The other items exist in order to disguise the fact that the study concerns sex stereotyping. If only the 38 relevant items were used, it would be clear to participants that their attitudes on sex-typed qualities were being tested, and this awareness might change the way they answer.

The authors have developed a Stereotype Questionnaire which is described in detail elsewhere (Rosenkrantz et al., 1968). Briefly, the questionnaire consists of 122 bipolar items each of which describes, with an adjective or a short phrase, a particular behavior trait or characteristic such as:

Very aggressive	Not at all aggressive
Doesn't hide emotions at all	Always hides emotions

One pole of each item can be characterized as typically masculine, the other as typically feminine (Rosenkrantz et al., 1968). On 41 items, 70% or better agreement occurred as to which pole characterizes men or women, respectively, in both a sample of college men and in a sample of college women (Rosenkrantz et al., 1968). These items have been classified as "stereotype."

The questionnaire used in the present study differs slightly from the original questionnaire. Seven original items seemed to reflect adolescent concerns with sex, for example, "very proud of sexual ability . . . not at all concerned with sexual ability." These items were replaced by seven more general items. Since three of the discarded items were stereotypic, the present questionnaire contains only 38 stereotypic items. These items are shown in Table 1.

Finally, in a prior study, judgments have been obtained from samples of Ss as to which pole of each item represents the more socially desirable behavior or trait for an adult individual in general, regardless of sex. On 27 of the 38 stereotypic items, the masculine pole is more socially desirable (male-valued items), and on the remaining 11 stereotypic items, the feminine pole is the more socially desirable one (female-valued items).

Table 1

Male-Valued and Female-Valued Stereotypic Items

Male-valued items [Masculine pole is socially desirable.]

Feminine pole	*Masculine pole*
Not at all aggressive	Very aggressive
Not at all independent	Very independent
Very emotional	Not at all emotional
Does not hide emotions at all	Almost always hides emotions
Very subjective	Very objective
Very easily influenced	Not at all easily influenced
Very submissive	Very dominant
Dislikes math and science very much	Likes math and science very much
Very excitable in a minor crisis	Not at all excitable in a minor crisis
Very passive	Very active
Not at all competitive	Very competitive
Very illogical	Very logical
Very home oriented	Very worldly
Not at all skilled in business	Very skilled in business
Very sneaky	Very direct
Does not know the way of the world	Knows the way of the world
Feelings easily hurt	Feelings not easily hurt
Not at all adventurous	Very adventurous
Has difficulty making decisions	Can make decisions easily
Cries very easily	Never cries
Almost never acts as a leader	Almost always acts as a leader
Not at all self-confident	Very self-confident
Very uncomfortable about being aggressive	Not at all uncomfortable about being aggressive
Not at all ambitious	Very ambitious
Unable to separate feelings from ideas	Easily able to separate feelings from ideas
Very dependent	Not at all dependent
Very conceited about appearance	Never conceited about appearance

Female-valued items [Feminine pole is socially desirable.]

Feminine pole	*Masculine pole*
Very talkative	Not at all talkative
Very tactful	Very blunt
Very gentle	Very rough
Very aware of feelings of others	Not at all aware of feelings of others
Very religious	Not at all religious
Very interested in own appearance	Not at all interested in own appearance
Very neat in habits	Very sloppy in habits
Very quiet	Very loud
Very strong need for security	Very little need for security
Enjoys art and literature very much	Does not enjoy art and literature at all
Easily expresses tender feelings	Does not express tender feelings at all

Instructions

Each participant only received one questionnaire and one set of instructions. This design disguises the fact that the study will compare results from different instructions (male, female, and adult). Each participant thinks that his or her questionnaire is the only form given. Like the extra items on the questionnaire, the design is intended to keep the participants' answers from being influenced by their ideas about the experimental goals.

The clinicians were given the 122-item questionnaire with one of three sets of instructions, "male," "female," or "adult." Seventeen men and 10 women were given the "male" instructions which stated "think of normal, adult men and then indicate on each item the pole to which a mature, healthy, socially competent adult man would be closer." The Ss were asked to look at the opposing poles of each item in terms of directions rather than extremes of behavior. Another 14 men and 12 women were given "female" instructions, that is, they were asked to describe a "mature, healthy, socially competent adult woman." Finally, 15 men and 11 women were given "adult" instructions. These Ss were asked to describe a "healthy, mature, socially competent adult person" (sex unspecified). Responses to these "adult" instructions may be considered indicative of "ideal" health patterns, without respect to sex.

Scores

Although Ss responded to all 122 items, only the stereotypic items which reflect highly consensual, clear distinctions between men and women, as perceived by lay people were analyzed. The questionnaires were scored by counting the number of Ss that marked each pole of each stereotypic item, within each set of instructions. Since some Ss occasionally left an item blank, the proportion of Ss marking each pole was computed for each item. Two types of scores were developed: "agreement" scores and "health" scores.

The agreement scores consisted of the proportion of Ss on that pole of each item which was marked by the majority of the Ss. Three agreement scores for each item were computed; namely, a "masculinity agreement score" based on Ss receiving the "male" instructions, a "femininity agreement score," and an "adult agreement score" derived from the Ss receiving the "female" and "adult" instructions, respectively.

The health scores are based on the assumption that the pole which the majority of the clinicians consider to be healthy for an adult, independent of sex, reflects an ideal standard of health. Hence, the proportion of Ss with either male or female instructions who marked that pole of an item which was most often designated as healthy for an adult was taken as a "health" score. Thus, two health scores were computed for each of the stereotypic items: a "masculinity health score" from Ss with "male" instructions, and a "femininity health score" from Ss with "female" instructions.

Male and female participants (clinicians who filled out questionnaires) did not differ in their responses. Thus, they could be lumped together for the analysis. If they *had* differed, separate analyses would be done. The difference would be a matter for the Discussion section.

Sigmas are standard deviations.

---

z is a standardized score, with a mean of 0 and a standard deviation of 1.

Qualities that are socially desirable are also considered signs of good mental health.

Results

Sex Differences in Subject Responses

The masculinity, femininity, and adult health and agreement scores of the male clinicians were first compared to the comparable scores of the female clinicians via *t* tests. None of these *t* tests were significant (the probability levels ranged from .25 to .90). Since the male and female *S*s did not differ significantly in any way, all further analyses were performed with the samples of men and women combined.

Agreement Scores

The means and sigmas of the adult, masculinity, and femininity agreement scores across the 38 stereotypic items are shown in Table 2. For each of these three scores, the average proportion of *S*s agreeing as to which pole reflects the more healthy behavior or trait is significantly greater than the .50 agreement one would expect by chance. Thus, the average masculinity agreement score is .831 (z = 3.15, *p* < .001), the average femininity agreement score is .763 (z = 2.68, *p* < .005), and the average adult agreement score is .866 (z = 3.73, *p* < .001).

These means indicate that on the stereotypic items clinicians strongly agree on the behaviors and attributes which characterize a healthy man, a healthy woman, or a healthy adult independent of sex, respectively.

Relationship Between Clinical Judgments of Health and Student Judgments of Social Desirability

Other studies indicate that social desirability is related to clinical judgments of mental health (Cowen, 1961; Kogan et al., 1957; Wiener et al., 1959). The relation between social desirability and clinical judgment was tested in the present data by comparing the previously established socially desirable poles of the stereotypic items (Rosenkrantz et al., 1968) to the poles of those items which the clinicians judged to be the healthier and more mature for an *adult*. Table 3 shows that

Table 2

Means and Standard Deviations for Adult, Masculinity, and Femininity Agreement Scores on 38 Stereotypic Items

Agreement score	M	SD	Deviation from chance	
			Z	p
Adult	.866	.116	3.73	< .001
Masculinity	.831	.122	3.15	< .001
Femininity	.763	.164	2.68	< .005

the relationship is, as predicted, highly significant (x^2=23.64, p<.001). The present data, then, confirm the previously reported relationships that social desirability, as perceived by nonprofessional Ss, is strongly related to professional concepts of mental health.

The four items on which there is disagreement between health and social desirability ratings are: to be emotional; not to hide emotions; to be religious; to have a very strong need for security. The first two items are considered to be healthy for adults by clinicians but not by students; the second two items have the reverse pattern of ratings.

Sex-Role Stereotype and Masculinity Versus Health Scores

On 27 of the 38 stereotypic items, the male pole is perceived as more socially desirable by a sample of college students (male-valued items); while on 11 items, the feminine pole is seen as more socially desirable (female-valued items). A hypothesis of this paper is that the masculinity health scores will tend to be greater than the femininity health scores on the male-valued items, while the femininity health scores will tend to be greater than the masculinity health scores on the female-valued items. In other words, the relationship of the clinicians' judgments of health for men and women are expected to parallel the relationship between stereotypic sex-role behaviors and social desirability. The data support the hypothesis. Thus, on 25 of the 27 male-valued items, the masculinity health score exceeds the femininity health score; while 7 of the 11 female-valued items have higher femininity health scores than masculinity health scores. On four of the female-valued items, the masculinity health score exceeds the femininity health score. The chi-square derived from these data is 10.73 *(df* = 1, *p* < .001). This result indicates that clinicians tend to consider socially desirable masculine characteristics more often as healthy for men than for women. On the other hand, only about half of the socially desirable feminine characteristics are considered more often as healthy for women rather than for men.

On the face of it, the finding that clinicians tend to ascribe male-valued stereotypic traits more often to healthy men than to healthy women may seem trite. However, an examination of the content of these items suggests that this trite-seeming phenomenon conceals a powerful, negative assessment of women. For instance, among these items, clinicians are more likely to suggest that healthy women differ from healthy men by being more submissive, less independent, less adventurous, more easily influenced, less aggressive, less competitive, more excitable in minor crises, having their feelings more easily hurt, being more emotional, more conceited about their appearance, less objective, and disliking math and science. This constellation seems a most unusual way of describing any mature, healthy individual.

Table 3

Chi-Square Analysis for Social Desirability
Versus Adult Health Scores on
38 Stereotypic Items

Item	Pole elected by majority of clinicians for healthy adults
Socially desirable pole	34
Socially undesirable pole	4

Note. chi^2 = 23.64, *p* < .001.

Mean Differences between Masculinity Health Scores and Femininity Health Scores

The *health scores* indicate the proportion of "healthy adult" qualities marked for each sex. Men were considered to have 83% and women to have 75% of these qualities. The mean "healthy adult" scores for men and women differed significantly, as shown by the *p* value of the *t* test, which compared the two groups' means.

The above chi-square analysis reports a significant pattern of differences between masculine and feminine health scores in relationship to the stereotypic items. It is possible, however, that the differences, while in a consistent, predictable direction, actually are trivial in magnitude. A *t* test, performed between the means of the masculinity and femininity health scores, yielded a *t* of 2.16 (*p* < .05), indicating that the mean masculinity health score (.827) differed significantly from the mean femininity health score (.747). Thus, despite massive agreement about the health dimension per se, men and women appear to be located at significantly different points along this well-defined dimension of health.

Concepts of the Healthy Adult Versus Concepts of Healthy Men and Healthy Women

Another hypothesis of this paper is that the concepts of health for a sex-unspecified adult, and for a man, will not differ, but that the concepts of health for women will differ significantly from those of the adult.

This hypothesis was tested by performing *t* tests between the adult agreement scores versus the masculinity and femininity health scores. Table 4 indicates, as predicted, that the adult and masculine concepts of health do not differ significantly (*t* = 1.38, *p* > .10), whereas, a significant difference does exist between the concepts of health for adults versus females (*t* = 3.33, *p* < .01).

These results, then, confirm the hypothesis that a double standard of health exists for men and women, that is, the general standard of health is actually applied only to men, while healthy women are perceived as significantly less healthy by adult standards.

The first *t* test compared the masculinity score with the healthy adult score, and the second *t* test compared the femininity score with the healthy adult score. The *p* values show that the masculinity and healthy adult scores did not differ, while the femininity scores and healthy adult scores differed significantly.

Table 4

Relation of Adult Health Scores to Masculinity Health Scores and to Femininity Health Scores on 38 Stereotypic Items

Health Score	M	SD
Masculinity	.827	.130
		$t = 1.38$[*]
Adult	.866	.115
		$t = 3.33$[**]
Femininity	.747	.187

[*] $df = 74$, $p > .05$
[**] $df = 74$, $p < .01$

Discussion

The results of the present study indicate that high agreement exists among clinicians as to the attributes characterizing healthy adult men, healthy adult women, and healthy adults, sex unspecified. This agreement, furthermore, holds for both men and women clinicians. The results of this study also support the hypotheses that *(a)* clinicians have different concepts of health for men and women and *(b)* these differences parallel the sex-role stereotypes prevalent in our society.

Although no control for the theoretical orientation of the clinicians was attempted, it is unlikely that a particular theoretical orientation was disproportionately represented in the sample. A counterindication is that the clinicians' concepts of health for a mature adult are strongly related to the concepts of social desirability held by college students. This positive relationship between social desirability and concepts of health replicates findings by a number of other investigators (Cowen, 1961; Kogan et al., 1957; Wiener et al., 1959).

The clinicians' concepts of a healthy, mature man do not differ significantly from their concepts of a healthy adult; However, the clinicians' concepts of a mature healthy woman do differ significantly from their adult health concepts. Clinicians are significantly less likely to attribute traits which characterize healthy adults to a woman than they are likely to attribute these traits to a healthy man.

Speculation about the reasons for and the effects of this double standard of health and its ramifications seems appropriate. In the first place, men and women do differ biologically, and these biological differences appear to be reflected behaviorally, with each sex being more effective in certain behaviors (Broverman, Klaiber, Kobayashi, & Vogel, 1968). However, we know of no evidence indicating that these

Because many people believe that biology determines psychological differences between the sexes, these authors must present their point of view on the topic.

biologically-based behaviors are the basis of the attributes stereotypically attributed to men and to women. Even if biological factors did contribute to the formation of the sex-role stereotypes, enormous overlap undoubtedly exists between the sexes with respect to such traits as logical ability, objectivity, independence, etc., that is, a great many women undoubtedly possess these characteristics to a greater degree than do many men. In addition, variation in these traits within each sex is certainly great. In view of the within-sex variability, and the overlap between sexes, it seems inappropriate to apply different standards of health to men compared to women on purely biological grounds.

More likely, the double standard of health for men and women stems from the clinicians' acceptance of an "adjustment" notion of health, for example, health consists of a good adjustment to one's environment. In our society, men and women are systematically trained, practically from birth on, to fulfill different social roles. An adjustment notion of health, plus the existence of differential norms of male and female behavior in our society, automatically lead to a double standard of health. Thus, for a woman to be healthy, from an adjustment viewpoint, she must adjust to and accept the behavioral norms for her sex, even though these behaviors are generally less socially desirable and considered to be less healthy for the generalized competent, mature adult.

By way of analogy, one could argue that a black person who conformed to the "pre-civil rights" southern Negro stereotype, that is, a docile, unambitious, childlike, etc., person, was well adjusted to his environment and, therefore, a healthy and mature adult. Our recent history testifies to the bankruptcy of this concept. Alternative definitions of mental health and maturity are implied by concepts of innate drives toward self-actualization, toward mastery of the environment, and toward fulfillment of one's potential (Allport, 1955; Buhler, 1959; Erikson, 1950; Maslow, 1954; Rogers, 1951). Such innate drives, in both blacks and women, are certainly in conflict with becoming adjusted to a social environment with associated restrictive stereotypes. Acceptance of an adjustment notion of health, then, places women in the conflictual position of having to decide whether to exhibit those positive characteristics considered desirable for men and adults, and thus have their "femininity" questioned, that is, be deviant in terms of being a woman; or to behave in the prescribed feminine manner, accept second-class adult status, and possibly live a lie to boot.

Another problem with the adjustment notion of health lies in the conflict between the overt laws and ethics existing in our society versus the covert but real customs and mores which significantly shape an individual's behavior. Thus, while American society continually emphasizes equality of opportunity and freedom of choice, social pressures toward conformity to the sex-role stereotypes tend to restrict the

> These authors present an early version of cultural criticism. They criticize therapists for endorsing the prevailing point of view, which seems to justify lower status for an identifiable group (women) due to innate psychological weaknesses.

actual career choices open to women, and, to a lesser extent, men. A girl who wants to become an engineer or business executive, or a boy who aspires to a career as a ballet dancer or a nurse, will at least encounter raised eyebrows. More likely, considerable obstacles will be put in the path of each by parents, teachers, and counselors. We are not suggesting that it is the clinicians who pose this dilemma for women. Rather, we see the judgments of our sample of clinicians as merely reflecting the sex-role stereotypes, and the differing valuations of these stereotypes, prevalent in our society. It is the attitudes of our society that create the difficulty. However, the present study does provide evidence that clinicians *do* accept these sex-role stereotypes, at least implicitly, and, by so doing, help to perpetuate the stereotypes. Therapists should be concerned about whether the influence of the sex-role stereotypes on their professional activities acts to reinforce social and intrapsychic conflict. Clinicians undoubtedly exert an influence on social standards and attitudes beyond that of other groups. This influence arises not only from their effect on many individuals through conventional clinical functioning, but also out of their role as "expert" which leads to consultation to governmental and private agencies of all kinds, as well as guidance of the general public.

It may be worthwhile for clinicians to critically examine their attitudes concerning sex-stereotypes, as well as their position with respect to an adjustment notion of health. A cause of mental health may be better served if both men and women are encouraged toward maximum realization of individual potential, rather than to an adjustment to existing restrictive sex roles.

> Many of these references will be valuable to you if you do research on historical views of psychological sex differences.

References

Allport, G. W. *Becoming.* New Haven: Yale University Press, 1955.

Anastasi, A., & Foley, J. P., JR. *Differential psychology.* New York: Macmillan, 1949.

Broverman, D. M., Klaiber, E. L., Kobayashi, Y., Vogel, W. Roles of activation and inhibition in sex differences in cognitive abilities. *Psychological Review, 1968, 75,* 23–50.

Buhler, C. Theoretical observations about life's basic tendencies. *American Journal of Psychotherapy, 1959, 13,* 561–581.

Cowen, E. L. The social desirability of trait descriptive terms: Preliminary norms and sex differences. *Journal of Social Psychology, 1961, 53,* 225–233.

Erikson, E. H. *Childhood and society.* New York: Norton, 1950.

Fernberger, S. W. Persistence of stereotypes concerning sex differences. *Journal of Abnormal and Social Psychology, 1948, 43,* 97–101.

Kitay, P. M. A comparison of the sexes in their attitudes and beliefs about women. *Sociometry, 1940, 34, 399–407.*

Kogan, W. S., Quinn, R., Ax, A. F., & Rifley, H. S. Some methodological problems in the quantification of clinical assessment by Q array. *Journal of Consulting Psychology, 1957, 21, 57–62.*

Komarovsxy, M. Functional analysis of sex roles. *American Sociological Interview, 1950, 15, 508–516.*

Lynn, D. B. A note on sex differences in the development of masculine and feminine identification. *Psychological Review, 1959, 66, 126–135.*

Maslow, A. H. *Motivation and personality.* New York: Harper, 1954.

Mckee, J. P., & Sherriffs, A. C. The differential evaluation of males and females. *Journal of Personality, 1957, 25, 356–371.*

Mckee, J. P., & Sherriffs, A. C. Men's and women's beliefs, ideals, and self-concepts. *American Journal of Sociology, 1959, 64, 356–363.*

Rogers, C. R. *Client-centered therapy; Its current practice, implications, and theory.* Boston: Houghton, 1951.

Rosenkrantz, p., Vogel, s., Bee, h., Broverman, i., & Broverman, D. Sex-role stereotypes and self-concepts in college students. *Journal of Consulting and Clinical Psychology, 1968, 32, 287–295.*

Seward, G. H. *Sex and the social order.* New York: McGraw-Hill, 1946.

Seward, G. H. , & Larson, W. R. Adolescent concepts of social sex roles in the United States and the two Germanics. *Human Development, 1968, 11, 217–248.*

White, L., Jr. *Educating our daughters.* New York: Harper, 1950.

Wiener, M., Blumbeko, A., Segman, S., & Cooker, A. A judgment of adjustment by psychologists, psychiatric social workers, and college students, and its relationship to social desirability. *Journal of Abnormal Social Psychology, 1959, 59, 315–321.*

Wylie, R. *The self concept.* Lincoln: University of Nebraska Press, 1961.

Discussion Ideas

1. Apply the concept of **mirror image stereotyping** to the design of this experiment. Do you think mirror image stereotyping frequently occurs in descriptions of men and women?

2. The researchers used a sample of college students to develop their questionnaire. What are some potential problems with using the students this way?

3. Why was it important to have helping professionals as participants in this study? For what other career professionals would you like to see the results of the same study?

4. The authors say that acceptance of the adjustment notion puts women in a conflictual position. To what conflict are they referring?

5. This research was done more than thirty years ago. Would the results be the same today, do you think? How could you discover whether any modern research has investigated the same question?

6. The Broverman et al. study demonstrated how cultural attitudes may be studied without the participants knowing exactly what was being pinpointed. What other cultural attitudes would need to be studied without participants' full knowledge of what was being tested? Have you seen other techniques for doing so?

Answer Key for Practice Test Questions

True/False

1. F
2. F
3. F
4. F
5. F
6. F
7. T
8. T
9. F
10. F

Multiple Choice

1.	b	11.	c
2.	e	12.	f
3.	e	13.	a
4.	b	14.	c
5.	c	15.	f
6.	d		
7.	a		
8.	f		
9.	b		
10.	c		

CHAPTER 12

Transpersonal Development

Chapter Review

Transpersonal counseling seeks to expand the client's awareness of self to a developmental stage beyond establishing ego strength. Borrowing from Eastern traditions, a personal sense of self is considered merely the result of mental constructions that block an awareness of the divine within all living things and of the interdependent unity of all life. Life is seen as transient, happening from moment to moment in a flow that denies a rigidity of uniform patterns that never change, including a personality structure known as "me" or "I." A greater Self, the individual in relation to a universal consciousness, builds awareness beyond the personal through practices that encourage letting go of self-absorbing thoughts and feelings. An expanded awareness comes to a sense of well-being, compassion for others, and an acceptance of reality for what it is, without the resistance that things need to be as the individual defines them to be.

The goal of spirituality in transpersonal psychology is to transcend or rise above a focus on daily activities and the mental chatter typically cluttering the mind. Meditation concentrates the mind's attention to the breath as it flows into the body and moves out of the lungs. The rhythm of breathing mimics an exchange from the external to the internal and from the internal back to the external, as in the concept of universal life and flow. The concentration of attention is interrupted by distracting thoughts and feelings, but as the meditator notes the interference, he gently returns attention to focus on the breath. Many forms of concentrated attention vary across meditation practices, sometimes focusing on a mantra, or an emotion, or a particular insight. The purpose of concentration practice is to learn to manage the distractions and to free the mind from negative habits. The self-absorbed mind clings to personal preferences and concepts in a process called *attachment*; or the undisciplined mind rejects what it defines as negative in a habit called *aversion*; or the mind craves positive experiences in an addictive process. Delusions define the self and reality according to personal fantasies or to polarities that project mirror image opposites onto what actually is. With concentrated attention, the meditator recognizes the mind's distortions and is able to let go of the self's negative thinking patterns and to loosen emotional demands. *Disidentification* refers to the releasing impact that occurs when observing the workings of the mind. The meditative observer is no longer identified with the mind's attachments. An internal life without the capacity to redirect its attention is considered the cause of human suffering and the source of many psychological problems. With mindfulness, the practitioner can set aside the negative habits of the mind and be open to a full experience of what actually is present in the moment. External reality can be viewed in all its beauty, others can be seen with compassion, the limited self can gain perspective, and blocks to experience can be removed.

238

Several forms of yoga stem from the same meditative traditions. Hatha-yoga practices gentle exercises that position the body in stances called *asanas*. Asanas open the flow of vital energies, or pranas, and reformulate internal blocks. Raja-yoga practice includes motionless body positions and meditation. Karma is what is left after a person has acted—for good or for ill. Karma-yoga emphasizes positive behavior that will return good will for the practitioner.

Specific therapies developed in Japan construct a series of activities designed to help clients move away from self-absorbed living toward constructive living. Morita therapy establishes a routine of journal writing to record neurotic thoughts and perceptions and a regime of performing tasks no matter what one's personal reactions are. Simple tasks are assigned at first and gradually the demands are increased. Feedback from teachers encourages focusing on the doing and on gaining joy from small accomplishments and events. Support is also gained from small group discussions. Over time, clients learn to react within the context of task completion and to redirect their focus from self-constructed views. Naikan therapy requires clients to review their relationships and to recognize what others have done for them, how they returned the kindnesses, and how they inconvenienced others. In facing their own inconsiderate behavior, without focusing on the flaws of others, clients develop loving kindness.

Critiques of transpersonal approaches confuse the discipline of focusing attention with mysticism, and the direction away from the self as promoting ego dissolution. The spiritual experience of concentrated attention can be integrated with most religions. The approach is generally confined to clients who have established ego strength and who seek a constructive life.

Practice Test Questions

True or False: Consider each statement and try to explain in your own mind why it might not be fully true. Be sure to take into account any qualifying factors that might make the statement untrue. If you decide that the statement is fully true, circle **T**. Otherwise, circle **F**.

T F 1. According to Freud, we get depressed or rebellious against the facts because we are trapped by our own mind's self-absorption.

T F 2. Transpersonal psychology is called the *third-force of psychology.*

T F 3. Self-transcendence is dangerous because people could enter psychosis if they let go of their sense of self.

T F 4. The Eastern philosophical point of view emphasizes the value of stable personality traits and habits.

T F 5. Disidentification is a process where a person identifies emotions and thoughts as only thinking and feeling, not as defining the self.

T F 6. Transpersonal counselors agree that their own practice is too personal to serve any function in assisting clients.

T F 7. Mahayna and Theraveda are two forms of yoga practice.

T F 8. A practitioner chastises himself severely for loosing focus when meditating.

T F 9. Breathing techniques cannot be used with children.

T F 10. Hatha-yoga and Raja-yoga involve no physical activity; just sitting meditation is used.

Multiple Choice: Circle the one letter next to the best answer to the following questions or to complete the sentence stems.

1. *Mindfulness* is a term representing which of the following?
   a. full attention to essential facts so you can demonstrate what you know, as on a test
   b. full involvement in the experience of the here-and-now
   c. paying attention and strongly attaching to emotions to keep from getting upset
   d. ignoring the freshness and novelty of each moment
   e. b and d

2. Which of the following is a reason that a therapist might encourage a client to do physical exercise daily?
   a. Exercise improves cardiovascular and respiratory fitness and also relieves depression.
   b. Regular exercise improves psychological mood and cognitive functioning.
   c. Exercise provides a sense of self-mastery and the ability to manage negative thoughts and emotions.
   d. People who maintain an exercise routine are able to immerse themselves in pleasant activities.
   e. all of the above

3. Morita therapy is designed for clients with a diagnosis of neurasthenia, which is NOT characterized by
   a. worry and nervousness.
   b. fears and psychosomatic pain.
   c. attention deficits and hyperactivity.
   d. perfectionism and self-criticism.

4. Naikan practice includes daily examination of the conscience that does NOT focus on which of the following?
   a. What did another person do for me?
   b. What faults did the other person demonstrate?
   c. What did I do for that person in return?
   d. What trouble and inconvenience did I cause that person?
   e. a, b, and c
   f. a, c, and d

5. Meditation practice has been shown to be helpful to nursing home residents in which of the following ways?
   a. improvement of blood pressure, word fluency, and feelings of effectiveness
   b. better coping abilities, feeling less old and less impatient
   c. meditators as a group live longer than nonmeditators
   d. a and b
   e. a, b, and c

6. Physicians in training who practiced meditation were shown to experience less anxiety and which of the following?
   a. less depression
   b. increases in empathy
   c. increases in concentration
   d. a and b
   e. a and c

7. According to the Buddha, which of the following habits of the mind cause human suffering?
   a. craving and attachment
   b. compassion and selflessness
   c. aversion/avoidance
   d. a and c
   e. a and b

8. Which of the following remedies to human suffering does the Buddha NOT suggest?
   a. moral discipline
   b. pure mind without distractions
   c. careful control of giving
   d. seeing through false pretenses

9. The Eastern point of view characterizes the self as a
   a. shifting sense of impressions.
   b. clear identity with appropriate boundaries.
   c. coherent sense of boundaries and ego strength.
   d. stable, complex sense of experiences across time.

10. The processes of transpersonal therapy and meditative practices are NOT characterized as
    a. escaping from the heavy sense of reality by practicing a foggy reverie.
    b. gaining a sense of wholeness rather than feeling fragmented.
    c. freeing the self from illusions and distortions.
    d. recognizing the potential of life in an unfolding manner.

11. Development from a transpersonal perspective could be described as
    a. human beings are naturally able to find a balance in life but are blocked by bad habits of the mind.
    b. when a person recognizes his own mental disarray and he starts to return to natural joys.
    c. when, with the discipline of regular practice, the mind self-corrects perceptions.
    d. peak experiences that stabilize to a point where mindfulness occurs in everyday life.
    e. all of the above

12. Meditative practices combined with other psychotherapy interventions offer which of the following advantages?
    a. Meditative practice, such as yoga, and centered attention, can be taught in groups—serving a number of clients in a cost-effective manner.
    b. Meditative practices can serve a proactive, preventative purpose.
    c. Therapists could benefit by increasing empathy and preventing burnout.
    d. a and b
    e. a, b, and c

13. *Karma* is a word that does NOT convey which of the following?
    a. What we do has an impact on the universe that interconnects all life into one unity.
    b. How we live returns to us in kind.
    c. If we focus our lives on positive endeavors, we gain a positive sense of being.
    d. A meditative life is not concerned with doing; it only emphasizes sitting.

14. Which of the following is a correct definition?
    a. delusions are false pretenses.
    b. craving is attachment to positive stimuli.
    c. aversion is avoidance of negative stimuli.
    d. a and c
    e. a, b, and c

15. *Content-less awareness* is the goal of meditations. Which of the following does NOT describe what is meant by this phrase?
    a. suchness or thusness
    b. the experience of pure being—what is
    c. the experience of knowing nothing about a subject
    d. the absence of self-directed mental chatter

Key Terms and Essential Concepts

Self: In Western psychology the self (small s) denotes a permanent coalition of stable traits, maintained over time, that characterize an individual. An Eastern concept suggests Self with a capitalized S is where the individual lets go of ego-defined separateness to become interconnected to the Oneness of all life. The Self transcends personally constructed attitudes that maintain a rigid point of view to accept the transience of experience, realistically acknowledging whatever the external world presents and whatever internal changes occur, living within the flow of life. The transcendent Self represents a developmental stage occurring after the self has achieved a nondefensive ego strength—open to compassion and wisdom without pretense.

Transcendental reality: To rise above the cares of everyday existence requires a shift in consciousness. Instead of preoccupied thoughts of "me" and what "I" think or feel, the mind lets go of personal striving and idiosyncratic illusions. Spiritual experience leads to an awareness of moral thoughts and compassionate behavior.

Peak experiences: Moments of deep inspiration, wonder, ecstasy, and spiritual awareness that are clearly different than ordinary daily routine experiences.

Transpersonal psychology: Psychological approaches encouraging growth beyond an emphasis on the self are said to be transpersonal. Transpersonal is called the fourth source of psychological theory; psychoanalytic, behavioral, and humanistic are considered the first three types. Most often the spiritual practices of transpersonal approaches stem from Eastern traditions and lead to an awareness of the interconnection among all forms of life.

Egoism: Characterized as self-absorption, egoism refers to being stuck in the ego in a point of view that is limited by personal awareness. Defining life solely by personal experience blocks the recognition of a reality separate from the self and beyond the self. Egocentric attitudes prevent compassion for others and acceptance of life as it actually is outside personal delusions. The rigidity of mind that insists on a self-centered position creates emotional difficulties and relational problems, and from a Buddhist perspective: life suffering.

Being-needs: Allport defined psychological needs that go beyond basic security, belonging, and self-esteem. Being-needs enhance an appreciation of life through creativity, beauty, connecting to others, enjoying the natural flow of experience, learning for learning's sake, adding knowledge and contributing to society. Being becomes a sense of self beyond one's own needs.

Self-actualization: In Western psychology becoming all one can be represents the epitome of development. Actualizing one's true nature leads to a feeling of wholeness and fulfillment.

Interdependence: A systemic network of mutually dependent living beings implies an inherent unity in which all life is interconnected.

Altered states of consciousness: Transient states of heightened awareness offer glimpses into reality beyond self and everyday experience. Altered states can occur naturally and spontaneously and through regular practice of focused attention as in meditation.

Relaxation response: A technique that teaches people to evoke a calm and focused mind-body reaction. The program includes the repetition of a personally meaningful word, awareness of the breath, and focused attention while the person is performing a preferred activity such as running, praying, physical exercise, or meditation.

Concentration: Focusing on what is present in the here-and-now, resisting the common chatter that typically takes place in the mind. The mind calmly pays attention to a specific object, such as a mantra, the breath, or a defined emotion or thought. As distracting thoughts occur, or as emotional diversions such as boredom and irritations take place, the focus is gently renewed. A peaceful rhythm is maintained, building a feeling of well-being when this moment in life is experienced in full appreciation.

Attention: Maintaining attention means to resist distractions and the wandering mind's senseless chatter. Returning the mind to concentrated focus can occur gently, simply noting the distraction and coming back into focus. Meditative awareness grows with fewer and fewer interruptions and with regular practice and can eventually allow a person to call forth a sense of inner peace in many situations. Attending to the moment opens awareness to a self-adjusting mechanism, where balance and harmony are experienced, with the external world accepted simply as it is, and with an internal sense of calm.

Mindfulness: Focusing on just what is, right now, each moment, experiencing the freshness of color, sound, physical sensation, external objects, and movement, without attachment or judgment, will allow the mind to be fully aware. Mindfulness reveals a sense of self in time and space with full involvement and with full awareness of the flow of the experience. Mindfulness can take place in meditative movement, such as with yoga or walking, or in everyday experiences where intense attention is paid.

Attachment: A negative habit of the mind, attachment indicates clinging to a person, idea, experience, or aspect of the self without allowing the natural flow of change, contradiction or movement. Rigidly holding on leads to closing the mind and cutting off natural feelings, ultimately creating a sense of isolation and despondency. Attachment is a refusal to be in touch with life as it actually is and to resist the flow of life.

Aversion: Another negative habit of the mind in which reality is rejected and a rebellion against the facts is felt. The mind avoids what it deems negative and the reality is denied. Refusal to accept negatives also cuts off actual feelings and leads to delusions. Aversion is the negative twin of attachment.

Craving: Attaching to desired positive stimuli is another negative habit of the mind. Passion and longing warp realistic awareness and prevent the flow of experience as it is. Even taking behavioral steps to obtain what is desired can be impeded by the reverie of craving.

Delusions: The mind creates personal constructs that distort perceptions, block development, and maintain false pretenses. Obviously maintaining a private view of reality prevents awareness of the moment and honest interactions with others.

Dichotomies: Conceiving reality in opposing dualities labels objects in extremes as mirror images. Dichotomies deny both the complexity of life as systemic and the unity of life. Meanings are better placed on a continuum with subtle shadings. Although experience is easier to describe in contrasting terms, the richness of reality is lost.

Disidentification: A method of removing mind attachments to conceptual labels entails focusing attention on how the mind is working and recognizing how feelings and perceptions are distorting reality to meet personal constructs or desires. Detaching occurs by stepping back and watching thoughts and feelings from a distance, and observing what is happening in the internal process. Emotional clinging is loosened and the mind can regain a fluidity of experiencing.

Hatha-yoga: A method of cultivating maximum well-being, hatha-yoga includes gentle exercises that induce a meditative balance of physical action and a peaceful mind.

Vital energy: In hatha-yoga, health is maintained with the proper flow of various energies throughout the body which consequently order the mind.

Pranas: Vital energies are called *pranas*.

Asana: Hatha-yoga positions are called *asanas*. The body positions limber the body and encourage all physical parts to work in harmony and balance. Body positioning is practiced daily along with a system that includes healthy diet, breathing exercises, and meditative concentration.

Raja-yoga: Raja-yoga emphasizes body positions that hold the body still. Raja-yoga also includes meditation, maintaining mental control by focusing on the breath, and letting go of external intrusions to the mind.

Karma-yoga: In addition to physical yoga practice, yoga philosophy prescribes behavior that results in an inner sense of well-being. Thinking of others, practicing ethical actions, and meeting responsibilities are considered appropriate outlets for spiritual balance.

Karma: Karma is the residue of what is left from previous behavior. How a person acts affects the whole world, and what a person sends out to the universe will return to her.

Constructive living: The Japanese have designed several therapeutic systems to teach how to live in a positive way. Morita and Naikan therapy methods help individuals turn away from unhealthy self-preoccupation, determine a higher purpose for living, and practice behaviors that are in concert with higher goals.

Morita therapy: In the Morita residential program clients rest, work, write journal entries, receive feedback, and participate in group discussions. Neurotic symptoms are acknowledged, but the focus remains on doing the tasks at hand anyway. Simple limited tasks are emphasized at first, and then gradually more tasks are added. Clients learn to appreciate small accomplishments and to maintain awareness of the details and quality of work. The discipline of doing becomes the focus rather than individual reactions until reactions are interwoven with tasks. Clients learn to share amusement for minor events and to appreciate patience and the joy of consistent effort. An attitude of gratitude is developed, accepting the self and linking the action of doing to mental and emotional reactions. Similar activities are utilized for clients in nonresidential programs.

Naikan therapy: Clients in Naikan therapy review their relationships, asking themselves, what have others done for me? What have I done in return? and What difficulties have I caused for the other person? In answering the questions, no reference to the other person's flaws is allowed; answers describe only what the client has done. Clients learn to appreciate others and to live with an attitude of repaying kindness, rather than viewing others as in the service of their egos. Naikan methods increase awareness of love received and of the value of admitting mistakes. The desire to give to others develops.

Representative Case: Carey Roberts

As in previous cases, **D** designates **Data, A** designates **Assessment,** and **P** designates **Plan.**

D: Carey Roberts has been a client suffering from recurrent severe depression for much of her adult life. She has received inpatient treatment and several years of counseling. Several members of her family over three generations were also diagnosed with depression. She has struggled with several combinations of medication, some of which resulted in difficult side effects and others that had no effect in reducing symptoms. She has worked hard with cognitive restructuring methods and knows the signs that indicate when a new episode is approaching. She participates in an ongoing support group and returns to individual counseling as she sinks into new depressive episodes. Individual counseling helps her review the thought patterns that recur with chemical changes. Carey requires reminding that some thought patterns increase her sadness, and she needs encouragement to maintain some hope such as remembering that depression does not last over time without a break, and she can look forward to some times without symptoms. She also requires adjustments to her medication as an episode develops. Lifestyle changes have been made to reduce stress, including a job change, regular exercise, and a healthy diet. She has not been able to fully avoid recurring episodes, but she does her best to manage the depression.

A: Clearly this is a case of genetically-based recurring depression where clinical interventions have been only partially effective. The prognosis suggests a lifelong battle that has endured the suffering of periodic episodes. A proactive measure is needed.

P: Empirical research has supported the use of mindfulness meditation as a proactive intervention for the prevention of relapse. After this episode subsides, Carey will learn to concentrate on the breath and to return attention to the breath when interfering thoughts intrude. Once concentrated attention is established, Carey will observe her thoughts, cognitive patterns and emotional attachments. The loosening of patterns will allow her to maintain an attitude that such reactions are just thoughts, or simply feelings, not who she is. It is important for Carey to continue counseling with a counselor who also practices meditation and who can offer encouragement, suggestions, and a growing insight into the process.

Thinking About Carey

1. How would it be for you as a counselor to work with a client with such a severe case of depression? What methods would you use to deal with the impact on your mood and to maintain your effectiveness?

2. The case is written as individual therapy. As a counselor drawing from multiple theories and practices, would you think it appropriate to suggest family counseling or to determine the impact Carey's illness may have on her husband or others?

3. Carey has considered having a child. As her counselor would you feel it appropriate to make a recommendation regarding this decision?

4. What do you think about meditation practice for Carey? How could focused attention, mind/feeling observations, and disidentification serve as proactive measures for depression?

Check Your Thinking About Carey

1. Working with Carey could be draining, given the repetitive nature of recurring episodes. However, if the counselor could keep a perspective on thoughts requiring a curative change, being with Carey could be a practice in meaningful empathy for a suffering client. Meditation practice would be helpful in retaining loving kindness for someone who truly needs it.

2. Carey's husband certainly needs support also and recommending a group would definitely be in order. Other relatives might be consulted too. Psychoeducational interventions could help family members understand the nature of Carey's depression and coping mechanisms for interacting with her. The counselor might also learn of interactional patterns that may be associated with Carey's depression.

3. Bringing a child into Carey's world would add stressful demands for her life and could expose the child to periods of time when her mother would withdraw. Although having a child might represent a meaningful experience for Carey, her maternal desire may cause more suffering for her and her child, as well as her husband. It would be appropriate for the counselor to raise such issues with Carey and her husband, though the decision would rest with the perspective parents.

4. When Carey is well, a meditative practice could serve as a means to enhance the cognitive work she has already experienced. Concentrated attention and observing her thoughts and feelings from a distance could loosen her attachment to negative patterns in a way that refuting and reframing could not. She might also discover other patterns not identified in therapy. It is possible she would recognize depressive slipping sooner with meditation.

Finding a Balance

Do transpersonal approaches suit your personality and theoretical preferences? Here are some of the qualities we've noticed in transpersonal counselors.

Key Counselor Preferences

1. The counselor who integrates transpersonal approaches is likely to practice them herself. Meditators, for example, often see how meditation could assist their clients. Many practitioners would say that personally experiencing yoga, meditation, prayer, and so forth is requisite if a counselor is going to suggest it to clients.

2. Transpersonal counselors are calm and patient. Many of the techniques are nonverbal, so highly verbal types of people sometimes find themselves bored or distracted. These people may be just the ones to benefit from the silence, but as counselors they will prefer approaches that are more actively verbal.

3. Transpersonal counselors do not usually elevate scientific, rational ways of knowing over other more spiritual ways.

4. Transpersonal counselors are glad to add other experts such as yoga instructors, meditation instructors, gurus, and religious figures to the client's treatment plan. Counselors who like to maintain control over the whole therapeutic situation will be uncomfortable with the addition of outside healers.

Core Case: George Gordon

George Gordon was first seen as a case for the Finding a Balance section in Chapter 5, Adlerian Psychology. Now we view the case from a transpersonal development perspective.

The Adlerian lifestyle analysis revealed a values system based on materialism and achieving a leadership role above others and led to no insight on George's part, suggesting his self-absorption. Dreams of watching trains go by intensified. The therapist then prescribed doing exactly as the dream suggested: sit and do nothing. Doing nothing in session was excruciating for George as he described his thoughts and feelings of helplessness since he had no projects, plans, or strategic conversations to consider. The counselor taught him a method of centering where he could count his breathing. On one, breathe in; two, breathe out; three, breathe in; four, breathe out. He was instructed to count to ten and then return to one, while breathing in on odd numbers and out on even numbers. If other thoughts or feelings interrupted the counting, distracting his attention from the rhythm of breathing, he was to return to the number one. The practice in session calmed George, and he reported feeling refreshed. He seemed to relish the prospect of continuing the practice as homework. When he returned, however, he reported his concentration was constantly interrupted by his "to do" list and his fears that the "lazy" activity was just wasting the time he needed to find a new business venture. The counselor encouraged George to continue his practice, suggesting that his inability to envision a new project was blocked by the insistent chatter cluttering his mind. Thoughts were calling for productivity in the absence of meaningful tasks. George began to realize his life was filled with a driven quality that offered little joy. He found a health resort where he practiced meditation in a group that sat for several hours a day. He began to realize the art of letting go of his demanding thoughts and his ambitious activities.

Eventually, George had a dream in which he found the courage to get on a slow moving train that stopped in a small mountain town where a group of students greeted him. In describing the dream to the counselor, George said he had come to a vision of his "retirement" venture. He would establish an institute teaching young business leaders how to gain their own visions of success. He would share stories of his business experience but more importantly, he would listen to his students and encourage them to create their own dreams. He would also continue his meditation practice since his life now contained joy and a calm inner peace. He hoped his students would learn to combine productive achievement along with life enjoyment.

Applying Counselor Preferences

1. With George Gordon, the counselor assigned first just sitting and then a meditation technique of counting the breath. The counselor's own meditation practice allowed her to know the value of "just being" rather than "doing." It appeared George could benefit from a new practice since his driven style of living had limited his sense of purpose or meaning.

2. Only a fellow meditator would have been able to patiently listen to George's complaints regarding meditation and still support him in continuing to try the technique. George's reactions are not uncommon for those beginning meditation, and another's support is vital to maintain the practice until rewards become apparent.

3. The counselor does not offer evidence from scientific studies or lengthy philosophical rationales in supporting George. The experience in and of itself is the point, not the intellectual justification.

4. The counselor encouraged George to attend the health spa where extended meditations were held. Rather than assume that continued exploration of psychological insight was the only therapeutic endeavor to help George change, the counselor facilitated the referral to a practice that reinforced a new lifestyle.

Comparison with Other Approaches

Adlerian and other Psychodynamic approaches: Psychodynamic approaches would offer interpretations regarding George's driven lifestyle. For example, George may be the oldest sibling in his family of origin.

Person-Centered approach: A Rogerian counselor would patiently wait for George to determine the effect of his excessive achievement activities. George's dream would be self-interpreted for meaning.

Existential approach: An existential therapist would directly interpret George's dream as evidence for the need to examine the meaning of his life path and would challenge George to determine his spiritual needs.

Behavioralists and Cognitive-Behaviorists: Such practitioners would determine if George wanted to set a goal of changing his behavior and if so, would set up behavioral learning contingencies. A cognitive approach would also identify self-talk behind George's driven behavior.

Example of a Published Research Article on Meditation Research

Here is an example of a published article on meditation research. Commentary in boxes to the left of the article will help you understand the research and the format of the piece.

Transcendental Meditation
in the Treatment
of Post-Vietnam Adjustment

James S. Brooks and Thomas Scarano

In a randomized, prospective study at the Denver Vietnam Veterans Outreach Program, the Transcendental Meditation (TM) program was compared with psychotherapy in the treatment of post-Vietnam adjustment. Nine dependent variables were measured both before and after a 3-month treatment period. The TM treatment group improved significantly from pretest to posttest on eight variables; the therapy group showed no significant improvement on any measure. This study indicates that the TM program is a useful therapeutic modality for the treatment of post-Vietnam adjustment problems.

James S. Brooks and Thomas Scarano, "Transcendental Meditation in the Treatment of Post-Vietnam Adjustment," from *Journal of Counseling and Development*, 64 (1985), pp. 212–215. Copyright © ACA. Reprinted with permission. No further reproduction authorized without written permission of the American Psychological Association.

PTSD (in the DSM-IV-TR, coded 309.81) comprises a group of symptoms that follow an extreme traumatic stressor. War experiences can be such stressors, as well as violent personal assaults, being kidnapped, terrorist attacks, and natural disasters. Intense fear, helplessness, and horror in response to these stressors may predict the development of PTSD.

The physiological correlates of TM listed here are also signs of relaxation.

The authors imply that case reports are not as trustworthy as scientific studies. A *prospective* study like this one applies a treatment and measures what happens at a future time; a *retrospective* study comes to conclusions based on what already happened. For example, looking for common features in the childhoods of convicted violent criminals is a *retrospective* study.

In July 1981 we began a research project at the Denver Vietnam Veterans Outreach Program ("Vet Center") to determine if the Transcendental Meditation (TM) program would be useful in the treatment of Vietnam veterans who were having difficulty readjusting to civilian life. The hypothesis was that because many of the symptoms of post-traumatic stress disorder (PTSD), including insomnia, depression, outbursts of anger, somatization, emotional numbness, anxiety, substance abuse, difficulty holding onto a job, and problems in interpersonal relationships, have been relieved by the regular practice of TM (Banquet, 1974; Bielefeld, 1981; Bloomfield, 1977; Ferguson & Gowan, 1976; Frew, 1974; Glueck & Stroebel, 1975; Hjelle, 1974; Miskiman, 1977a, 1977b, 1977c; Nidich, Seeman, & Dreskin, 1973; Shafii, 1974, 1975), this technique should prove to be a useful adjunct in the treatment of PTSD.

Transcendental Meditation is a simple mental technique that comes from the Vedic tradition of India. During TM, the mind periodically transcends or experiences a state of pure consciousness in which it is completely devoid of thought and yet remains fully awake within itself. This subjective state is physiologically correlated with electroencephalogram (EEC) coherence (Banquet, 1974), reduced metabolic rate and blood lactate (Wallace, Benson, & Wilson, 1972), increased skin resistance (Glueck & Stroebel, 1975), and reduced cortisol (Jevning, 1975). Additionally, the TM technique has been shown to be superior to relaxation techniques and other meditation techniques in its physiological and psychological benefits (Alexander, Langer, Newman, Chandler, & Davies, 1984; Eppley, Abrams, & Shear, 1984).

To date, the TM program has not been studied as a form of treatment of PTSD. Hypnotherapy, systematic desensitization/behavior modification, individual psychotherapy, marriage and family counseling, group therapy, small group living, phenelzine, and hospital treatment have all been reported as being beneficial in the treatment of PTSD (Brende & Benedict, 1980; Egendorf, 1975; Figley & Sprenkle, 1978; Geer & Silverman, 1967; Goldsmith & Cretekos, 1969; Hogben & Cornfield, 1981; Howard, 1981; Keane & Kaloupek, in press; Kentsmith, 1980; Klipper, 1977; O'Neill & Fontaine, 1973; Rado, 1942; Silverman & Geer, 1968; Williams & Jackson, 1972). Most of these studies are case reports, however, and there have been few well-designed, controlled prospective studies attempting to measure the comparative effectiveness of these various treatments.

Method

Participants

A group of 18 male Vietnam veterans seeking treatment at the Denver Vet Center were randomly selected to be in one of two treatment groups. From November 1981 through March 1982 each incoming client at the Vet Center was assigned a number. Odd-numbered participants were assigned to the TM group and even-numbered clients were assigned to the psychotherapy group. During the intake evaluation, each client was evaluated to determine whether or not he met the criteria of the study. The criteria for selection were that the participant (a) was not on major tranquilizers (e.g., Haldol, Thorazine), antidepressants (e.g., Nardil, Elavil, Tofranil), or lithium carbonate (Eskalith); (b) had no history of previous psychiatric hospitalizations; (c) was not actively suicidal or homicidal; (d) had no record of inpatient treatment for alcoholism or drug abuse during the past year; and (e) was not practicing Transcendental Meditation.

Procedure

Those individuals with odd numbers who qualified for the study were invited to participate in a stress management workshop where they would learn the TM program. It consisted of initial 4-day instruction period of 1-1/2 hours per day and weekly follow-up meetings over a 3-month period. (Participants were also informed that after the 3-month period they could get further treatment if they desired.) They were told that should they decide to participate in the workshop, they would be asked to fill out a questionnaire and to undergo a physiological measurement of their stress levels.

Those clients with even numbers who met the criteria for the study were told: "We are conducting a study to measure how effective our program is in reducing stress. In this study, we would like our clients to fill out a questionnaire and have their stress level measured prior to and after 3 months of treatment. Would you be interested in participating in this study?" Neither group knew of the existence of the other group throughout the study.

Over a 3-month period before the start of the study, the seven therapists at the Vet Center were trained to answer concise questions clients might have with regard to the workshop, the physiological measurement (Stimulus GSR), and the questionnaire. After pretesting, clients were taught the TM technique by an instructor trained and qualified to teach TM by Maharishi Jahesh Yogi. Each client was instructed to meditate twice daily for a period of 20 minutes. Also, weekly follow-up meetings of about an hour each were held. These meetings were similar to the advanced lectures held each week at the local TM center that consisted of a "meditation check" and a discussion period in which questions that may have come up between sessions were answered.

Clients assigned to the therapy group participated in weekly, individual psychotherapy sessions conducted by the Vet Center staff and, when appropriate, were given the option of participation in group or family counseling. The approach of the

---

Each group must remain in the dark about the other group. If they are in contact, the treatment might be contaminated. For example, in this experiment a TM member might befriend a member of the other group and teach him TM techniques.

The therapy group served as the control group, while the TM group was the experimental group. Both groups did receive treatment at the Vet Center.

therapists was eclectic; various theoretical approaches were used, including behavioral, existential, cognitive, somatic, and psychodynamic, depending on the training of the therapist. The full-time staff members at the Vet Center were Vietnam veterans, and each had at least a master's degree in either psychology or social work.

Dependent Variables

The questionnaire was scored by an independent evaluator not otherwise involved in the study. Dependent variables were measured in all 18 participants, both at pretest and posttest. The variables consisted of:

This experiment used a *pretest-posttest* design. By comparing before-and-after scores, researchers derive evidence of the effects of the treatment. In this case, symptoms, behavioral data (like employment status), and physiological data were all collected before and after treatment.

1. A measurement of degree of PTSD, designed by Charles Figley, that was modeled after DSM III criteria and that included a subscale measuring emotional numbness. This subscale was analyzed separately because it is considered to be one of the salient features of PTSD.
2. A measurement of anxiety using the Taylor Manifest Anxiety Scale (Taylor, 1953).
3. A measurement of degree of depression using the Beck Depression Inventory (Beck, 1967).
4. Individual questions taken from a questionnaire designed by Figley to measure post-Vietnam adjustment by addressing (a) amount of alcohol consumption, (b) degree of insomnia, (c) employment status, and (d) extent of family problems.
5. A physiological measurement using Stimulus GSR to measure rapidity of habituation to a stressful stimulus.

The procedure for the habituation measurement followed standard protocol (Orme-Johnson, 1973):

1. An initial hearing test was administered so that appropriate adjustments could be made in the decibel level of the tone if needed.
2. The participant sat in a comfortable chair and was given the following instructions: "Just sit comfortably with your eyes open. After about 10 minutes you'll be hearing some loud tones. I'll be measuring small changes in the amount of sweat on your palm in response to the tone. You will not feel a shock or any pain throughout the procedure. Do you have any questions?"

The tones were delivered monaurally through earphones via a Beltone Audiometer at a frequency of 3,000 Hz and at a decibel level of 85. The tones lasted .5 seconds and were administered at an average of every 45 seconds, with a range of 5 to 120 seconds between stimulus presentations. The GSR was allowed to stabilize before the next tone was presented. Skin resistance was measured by silver-plated, contoured electrodes systematically placed on the palm of the left hand. A 12-channel Grass polygraph machine was used to record fluctuations in skin resistance. Tones were presented until three consecutive responses of an amplitude of less than .4 kilohms occurred; this was the criterion for habituation.

This measurement was used to physiologically quantify an individual's ability to handle stress. There is evidence to suggest that individuals who are manifestly anxious are more autonomically labile as measured by how quickly they habituate to a recurrent stressful stimulus (Katkin, 1965; Orme-Johnson, 1973). We postulated that those suffering from PTSD could have a high anxiety level and could therefore be autonomically labile. We also postulated that after successful treatment of this condition, one might see a faster habituation response. Therefore, pre-habituation and post-habituation were measured for each participant.

> The expectation is that anxious people find it physically more difficult to get used to a stressful stimulus, and thus their habituation times are longer. Becoming less anxious would shorten their habituation time.

Participants who responded "not a problem" (score of 4) at pretest to the individual post-Vietnam adjustment questionnaire items (alcohol use, insomnia, employment status, and family problems) were not included in the statistical analysis unless they scored below a 4 at posttest. This eliminates potential ambiguity of results attributable to ceiling effects, because 4 was the maximum positive score available and a pretest score of 4 left no opportunity for improvement to be measured. Additionally, one participant from the therapy group was not included in the depression scale data because of his failure to complete that section of the questionnaire. Two therapy participants were not included in the GSR analysis because they refused to participate in the habituation posttesting.

Results

Pretest and posttest group means and the results of the statistical analysis are reported in Table 1. A comparison of the two groups before treatment showed no significant differences for the demographic variables of age (M = 33.3 years), sex (all male), marital status, annual income, time spent in the military, degree of combat, race, and location of service. There were also no significant differences between the two groups on any of the dependent variables ($p < .10$, two-tailed t test) at the pretest, with the exception of insomnia, $t(13) = 3.27$, $p < .01$. The therapy group reported greater difficulty sleeping.

> Before treatment, the two groups were comparable on almost every pretest. Therefore, they started the treatments at about the same level of distress.

Analysis of covariance with the pretest used as the covariate revealed a significant positive treatment effect for TM as compared to psychotherapy on degree of PTSD, $F(1, 14) = 5.26$, $p < .05$; the PTSD subscale for emotional numbness, $F(1, 15) = 6.64$, $p < .025$; anxiety, $F(1, 15) = 14.74$, $p < .005$; depression, $F(1, 15) = 7.05$, $p < .025$; alcohol consumption, $F(1, 19) = 16.05$, $p < .005$; insomnia, $F(1, 11) = 30.29$, $p < .001$; and family problems, $F(1, 12) = 5.48$, $p < .05$. Despite the large variance in the measure of GSR habituation, it was found that the TM group had a faster habituation response to a stressful stimulus, $F_{(1, 13)} = 3.44$, $p < .10$.

No significant difference was found between treatments on the measure of employment status, $F_{(1, 6)} = 1.61$, n.s.; however, a *t* test for related measures showed that the TM group improved significantly from pretest to posttest, $t_{(3)} = 5.000$, $p < .01$, whereas there was no such improvement for the therapy group, $t_{(4)} = .785$, n.s. Comparable pretest to posttest, within group results were found on all of the dependent variables (see Table 1). The TM group showed significant improvements on all self-report items and a trend toward significant improvement on the physiological measure of habituation to a stressful stimulus (GSR); the therapy group did not change significantly on any measure.

> The analysis of variance compared the two groups' scores with each other. The *t* tests compared pre and post scores within each group to see whether individuals improved more than might be expected by chance.

Discussion

We would have preferred to include a control group but did not because we felt it would be unethical to make Vietnam veterans who were in a crisis and seeking treatment wait for 3 months before being offered any formal treatment at the Vet Center. We found that the Vietnam veterans were willing to participate in both the TM group and the therapy group. Out of 14 veterans who were given the chance to participate in the TM group, 13 volunteered to do so (92%); out of 14 veterans given the chance to participate in the therapy group, 12 volunteered to do so (85%). The high initial participation in

> Dropout rates from both groups were about the same. Many researchers would check to see whether people dropped out of each group for different reasons, or whether there were any systematic patterns to who dropped out.

Table 1

Comparison Between the Two Groups on Pre/Post Measurements

Measure	TM Group				Psychotherapy Group			
	Pre		Post		Pre		Post	
	Mean	SD	Mean	SD	Mean	SD	Mean	SD
Post-Vietnam Stress Disorder	9.70	2.98	5.80[b,z]	4.26	11.71	2.63	10.86	2.85
Emotional Numbness Scale	3.70	1.64	1.70[b,y]	1.95	3.75	1.03	3.50	1.41
Taylor Anxiety Scale	16.50	4.72	9.10[d,z]	5.34	18.25	4.43	18.62	5.01
Beck Depression Scale	16.60	6.80	7.60[b,z]	7.49	20.62	7.94	19.75	3.84
Alcohol Consumption (4 = no problem)	2.00	.63	3.67[d,x]	.82	2.17	.41	2.17	.41
Insomnia (4 = no problem)	2.71	.76	3.71[e,w]	.49	1.57	.53	1.43	.53
Employment (4 = no problem)	2.25	.50	3.50[x]	.58	2.40	1.14	2.80	1.30
Family Problems (4 = no problem)	2.12	.83	3.25[b,x]	.89	2.14	.90	2.29	.76
Sensitivity to Stress (GSR)	18.80	19.46	10.50[a,v]	10.92	19.16	16.95	23.00	21.11

[a]$p < .10$; [b]$p < .05$; [c]$p < .01$; [d]$p < .005$; [e]$p < .001$. (ANCOVA; pretest as the covariate)
[v]$p < .10$; [w]$p < .05$; [x]$p < .01$; [y]$p < .005$; [z]$p < .001$. (paired *t* test, one tailed; pre/post)

The superscripts *a* through *e* show probabilities for the comparison between the two groups. The superscripts *v* through *z* show probabilities for the comparison of pre and post scores within a group. For example, the TM group improved more than the therapy group on Emotional Numbness at the .05 level of probability. People in the TM group improved (on average) pre to post treatment on Emotional Numbness at the .005 level. This means that the probability that these people would improve this much by chance is 5 out of 1000.

both groups increased the randomness of the selection method and hence decreased the possibility of selection bias. Three people in the TM group and four people in the therapy group dropped out of the study before its completion.

Because the number of participants in each group was small (8 in the therapy group and 10 in the TM group), caution must be exercised about generalizing the findings of this study to others with PTSD. In this study, however, the TM program was found to be beneficial in the treatment of PTSD. The participants in the TM group reported significant reductions in depression, anxiety, emotional numbness, alcohol consumption, family problems, difficulty in getting a job, insomnia, and overall symptoms of PTSD.

The phenomenon of *transcending* may be responsible for the TM group improving so significantly. Past research has shown that when the mind transcends during TM, the body achieves a deeply restful state and the mind remains fully alert. It seems that the deep level of rest produced during TM allows the body to spontaneously heal itself or rid itself of the deep impressions incurred from past stressful experiences. Veterans in the TM group commonly reported that, "I feel after I meditate that I no longer have the same intensity of tension, rage, and guilt inside—it's as if a huge burden has been lifted."

The therapy group showed little improvement over the 3-month period. It could be that measurable benefits of psychotherapy for PTSD are seen only after an extended period of time. After 3 months of treatment, 7 out of 10 participants in the TM group felt improved enough that they saw no further need for the services of the Vet Center. Three members of the TM group, however, still wanted to work on some issues pertaining to their Vietnam experience. Therefore, these individuals decided to remain in therapy in addition to practicing TM regularly. The TM program may sufficiently relieve the symptoms of many individuals with PTSD. In some cases, however, a combined approach of both TM and psychotherapy (or other approaches) may be the preferred treatment.

References

Alexander, C. N., Langer, E. J., Newman, R. I., Chandler, H. M., & Davies, J.L. (1984). *T.M., mindfulness and the elderly.* Manuscript in preparation.

Banquet, J. P. (1974). EEC analysis of spontaneous and induced states of consciousness. *Revue d'electroencephalotraphie el de neurophysiolozie clinique, 4,* 445–453.

Beck, A. T. (1967). *Depression: Clinical, experimental and theoretical aspects.* New York: Harper & Row.

Bielefeld, M. (1981, August 24). *TM: A stress reducing self-help support system.* Paper presented at the annual meeting of the American Psychological Association, Los Angeles.

Bloomfield, H. H. (1977). Some observations on the uses of the transcendental meditation program in psychiatry. In *Scientific research m the transcendental meditation program: Collected papers* (Vol. 1, pp. 605–622).

Brende, J. O., & Benedict, B. D. (1980). The Vietnam combat delayed stress syndrome: Hypnotherapy of "dissociative symptoms." *American Journal of Clinical Hypnosis, 23,* 34–40.

Egendorf, A. (1975). Vietnam veteran rap groups and themes of postwar life. *Journal of Social Issues, 31,* 111–124.

Eppley, K., Abrams, A., & Shear, J. (1984). The effects of meditation and relaxation techniques on trait anxiety: A meta-analysis. Manuscript in preparation.

Ferguson, P. C., & Gowan, J .C. (1976). Psychological findings on transcendental meditation. *Journal of Humanistic Psychology, 16,* 3.

Figley, C. R., & Sprenkle, D. H. (1978). Delayed stress response syndrome: Family therapy indications. *Journal of Marriage and Family Counseling, 4,* 53–60.

Frew, D. R. (1974). Transcendental meditation and productivity. *Academy of Management Journal, 17,* 362–368.

Geer, J. H., & Silverman, I. (1967). Treatment of a recurrent nightmare by behavior-modification procedures: A case study. *Journal of Abnormal Psychology, 72,* 188–190.

Glueck, B. C., & Stroebel, C. F. (1975). Biofeedback and meditation in the treatment of psychiatric illnesses. *Comprehensive Psychiatry, 16,* 303–321.

Goldsmith, W., & Cretekos, C. (1969). Unhappy odysseys: Psychiatric hospitalization among Vietnam returnees. *Archives of General Psychiatry, 38,* 440–445.

Hjelle, L. A. (1974). Transcendental meditation and psychological health. *Perceptual and Motor Skills, 39,* 623–628.

Hogben, G. L., & Cornfield, R. B. (1981). Treatment of traumatic war neurosis with phenelzine. *Archives of General Psychiatry, 38,* 440–445.

Howard, S. (1981). The Vietnam warrior; His experience and implications for psychotherapy. *American Journal of Psychotherapy, 30,* 121–135.

Jevning, R. (1975, June). *Plasma prolactin anacortisol during transcendental meditation.* Paper presented at the 57th annual meeting of the Endocrine Society, New York.

Katkin, E. S. (1965). Relationship between manifest anxiety and two indices of autonomic response to stress. *Journal of Personality and Social Psychology, 2,* 324–333.

When you see a *meta-analysis*, you have a source that puts together the results of several different research studies on the same topic. You couldn't find the article from this reference list, but you could look up each author's name and find it, since by now it is published somewhere.

The Glueck and Stroebel article sounds like another study of meditation versus another treatment.

Keane, T. M., & Kaloupek, D. G. (in press). Imagined flooding in the treatment of post-traumatic stress disorder. *Journal of Consulting and Clinical Psychology*.

Kentsmith, U. K. (1980). Minimizing the psychological effects of a war-time disaster on an individual. *Aviation, Space, and Environmental Medicine, 51,* 409–413.

Klipper, D. A. (1977). Behavior therapy for fear brought on by war experiences. *Journal of Consulting and Clinical Psychology, 45,* 216–222.

Miskiman, D. E. (1977a). The effect of the transcendental meditation program on compensatory paradoxical sleep. In D. O. Johnson & J. T. Farrow (Eds.), *Scientific research on the transcendental meditation program: Collected papers* (Vol. 1, pp. 292–295). Scelisberg, Switzerland: Meru Press.

Miskiman, D. E. (1977b). The treatment of insomnia by the transcendental meditation program. In D.O. Johnson & J.T. Farrow (Eds.), *Scientific research on the transcendental meditation program: Collected papers* (Vol. 1, pp. 296–298). Scelisberg, Switzerland: Meru Press.

Miskiman, D. E. (1977c). Long-term effects of the transcendental meditation program in the treatment of insomnia. In D. O. Johnson & J. T. Farrow (Eds.), *Scientific research on the transcendental meditation program: Collected papers* (Vol. 1, p. 299). Scelisberg, Switzerland: Meru Press.

Nidich, S. I., Seeman, W., & Dreskin, T. (1973). Influence of transcendental meditation on self-actualization: A replication. *Journal of Counseling Psychology, 20,* 565–566.

O'Neill, D. J., & Fontaine, G. D. (1973). Counseling for the Vietnam veterans. *Journal of College Student Personnel, 14,* 153–155.

Orme-Johnson, D. W. (1973). Autonomic stability and transcendental meditation. *Psychosomatic Medicine, 35,* 341–349.

Rado, S. (1942). Pathodynamics and treatment of traumatic war neurosis. *Psychosomatic Medicine, 42,* 362–368.

Shafii, M. (1974). Meditation and marijuana. *American Journal of Psychiatry, 131,* 60–63.

Shafii, M. (1975). Meditation and the prevention of alcohol abuse. *American Journal of Psychiatry, 132,* 942–945.

Silverman, I., & Geer, J. H. (1968). The elimination of a recurrent nightmare by desensitization of a related phobia. *Behavior Research and Therapy, 6,* 109–111.

Taylor, J. A. (1953). A personality scale of manifest anxiety. *Journal of Abnormal and Social Psychology, 48,* 285–290.

The Orme-Johnson article would provide more detail on the physiology of TM. In a library search, you could type Orme-Johnson's name in as an author to find more recent research, and also follow up on Orme-Johnson's co-authors and reference list.

Wallace, R. K., Benson, H., & Wilson, A. F. (1972). A wakeful hypo-metabolic physiologic state. *American Journal of Physiology, 221,* 795–799.

Williams, M., & Jackson, R. D. (1972). A small group living program for Vietnam-era veterans. *Hospital and Community Psychiatry, 23,* 141–144.

Discussion Ideas

1. What were the selection criteria for participants in this experiment? Explain the probable reasoning behind each criterion. What potential drawbacks do these criteria bring with them?

2. As you can see from the description, collecting the physiological data was complicated. What is the advantage of collecting this data in the experiment?

3. If you wanted to see whether an individual participant improved from pre to post test, what would you look at in Table 1? If you wanted to see whether one group fared better than another on a dependent variable, what would you look at?

4. The authors say that the small number of participants (18) indicate caution in generalizing the results of the study. Why is that?

5. What is the researchers' theory about why TM worked? Can you think of other reasons for the results of their experiment?

Answer Key for Practice Test Questions

True/False	Multiple Choice	
1. T	1. b	11. e
2. T	2. e	12. e
3. F	3. c	13. d
4. F	4. b	14. e
5. T	5. e	15. c
6. F	6. b	
7. T	7. d	
8. F	8. c	
9. F	9. a	
10. F	10. a	

CHAPTER 13

Integrative Innovation: The Example of Cognitive-Interpersonal Therapy

Chapter Review

Integrative therapy approaches synthesize concepts and techniques from two or more therapeutic models. Since the 1970s counselors have individualized the counseling process to meet client needs by borrowing methods across schools of thought. Empirical studies have supported the effort to determine the most effective techniques considering client characteristics and presenting concerns. Cross-cultural adjustments to therapy approaches have also influenced eclectic practice. The counseling literature reveals several major integrative approaches that thoughtfully fashion the merger of multiple conceptual frameworks.

Research findings show similar counseling outcomes for interventions stemming from different approaches, leading some authors to suggest it is the common factors across theoretical orientations that create positive client change. One point of consensus across all theories is the necessity of an effective therapeutic alliance between the counselor and the client. Such transtheoretical thinking suggests that most counselors support the value of instilling hope, providing corrective emotional experiences or new experiences, and giving accurate feedback. Prochaska and colleagues also propose stages for client change: precontemplation, contemplation, preparation, action, maintenance, and termination. Counselors vary interventions according to the client's stage of readiness for change.

Some counselors, technical eclectics, may retain a singular theoretical orientation but borrow techniques from others. Other approaches, such as the multimodel approach and STS (Systematic Treatment approach), eliminate higher levels of abstract theory altogether but depend on research to define specific interventions at particular choice points in therapy. In these methods, counselors depend on clinical strategies, or principles, that guide the course of counseling and determine the techniques of choice.

Theoretical integration takes several approaches and blends multiple concepts to build a unified view that improves the explanations given by each theory separately. The cognitive-interpersonal approach combines concepts regarding relationship patterns with ideas regarding dysfunctional thoughts. Terms are taken from each theory. *Self-system*, a term taken from interpersonal theory, denotes how we see ourselves and our relation to others. *Self-schemas*, taken from cognitive theory, is a term for the internal structures formed in childhood that create a sense of satisfaction, security, and anxiety, and that dictate personal preferences. Another phrase, *security operations*, is used to describe defense mechanisms designed to protect an individual's self-system. We screen out evidence that would invalidate our self-systems and cause anxiety, and pay attention only to factors that confirm our self-schemas and help us feel secure. Individuals also maintain an interpersonal schema to define expectations regarding relationships. In a cognitive-interpersonal cycle, we choose those people for relationships that allow us to maintain behavior and thoughts that are carried over from past experiences. Dysfunctional thoughts about ourselves and others in relationships are confirmed when we behave in such a way that others respond as we expect. For example, I might believe I have nothing worthwhile to say and say very little. When others rarely talk to me, it confirms my belief that no one talks to me because I have nothing important to say.

In counseling, cognitive-interpersonal therapists observe client interaction styles looking for clues, or interpersonal markers, that reveal behavioral and cognitive patterns. Counselors may also ask clients to describe their current relationships using a method called an *interpersonal inventory*. Collaboratively, the client and counselor determine how relationships meet expectations, if they are satisfying, and what changes might be beneficial. Through a transference process, the client will likely enact typical interaction patterns used with others outside counseling. The client's manner of communicating invokes a reaction from the counselor who shares these feelings with the client, thereby helping the client gain an understanding of her impact on others. Such metacommunication, talking about talking, also provides a chance to examine the client's internal cognitions that are related to her interactive style. The counselor is careful to respond in helpful ways and not according to typical interpersonal patterns, where the client's remarks would bring into play complementary responses, such as anger invoking anger. When the counselor discontinues the expected interactional patterns, the client experiences a new type of exchange, and the typical pattern the client has used in most relationships is disconfirmed. Homework assignments can provide further experiential disconfirmation to build and maintain client change. The client's interpersonal world is the focus of counseling. Examining dysfunctional beliefs, negative behavior patterns, and links between current and childhood experiences integrates concepts and techniques from cognitive and psychodynamic approaches.

Integrative therapy is criticized as inordinately complex. To avoid shallow eclecticism that does not synchronize multiple approaches, or is syncretic, counselors must think through how and why different principles might work together. Research validating combined approaches is also difficult. Therapists are ethically bound to be able to define the scope of their practice, to document their work, and to describe to clients what it is they do. The more varied and complex the therapist's orientation is, the more difficult it may be to explain clearly.

Practice Test Questions

True or False: Consider each statement and try to explain in your own mind why it might not be fully true. Be sure to take into account any qualifying factors that might make the statement untrue. If you decide that the statement is fully true, circle **T**. Otherwise, circle **F**.

T F 1. Using any technique that intuitively seems right to a counselor in the moment during therapy represents how integrative approaches work.

T F 2. Problems with public speaking are most successfully treated with insight therapy.

T F 3. Integrative approaches tailor treatment to client characteristics, including cultural background, situational factors, and stages of change.

T F 4. The more years of experience counselors have, the more likely they adhere to a single theoretical approach.

T F 5. Empirical studies have shown that different counseling approaches share common factors that are effective in creating client change.

T F   6. Technical eclecticism suggests some techniques may work well for reasons other than the explanations given by a theoretical model.

T F   7. According to the STS approach, the likelihood of client change is greatest when the client's stress level is high.

T F   8. Transtheoretical therapy uses specific techniques dictated by the preferred counseling approach.

T F   9. Bandura's triadic reciprocity suggests an interactive effect among behavior, cognitive, and other intrapersonal factors with environmental factors.

T F 10. Metacommunication is defined as reflecting on interactions.

Multiple Choice: Circle the one letter next to the best answer to the following questions or to complete the sentence stems.

1. Harry Stack Sullivan wrote that preadolescence is an important stage of development because
   a. preteens share mutual daydreams, validate each other and learn to communicate as peers.
   b. by interacting with chums, egocentric childhood interactions can change to meet a maturational need for intimacy.
   c. preteens prepare for adolescence when teens begin to separate from their parents.
   d. a, b, and c
   e. b and c

2. Atkinson, Thompson, and Grant's theory of cultural interaction does NOT propose which of the following as considerations for the role of the counselor?
   a. the client's level of acculturation
   b. internal or external etiology
   c. the client's intelligence
   d. goals of helping

3. Individual preferences of clients can be factors affecting therapeutic collaboration. Which of the following is a factor determining counseling approaches?
   a. tolerance for ambiguity
   b. rational vs. emotional processing
   c. expectations for counseling
   d. all of the above
   e. none of the above

4. Which of the following is an effective common factor for creating client change?
   a. fifty-minute counseling sessions
   b. the therapeutic alliance
   c. corrective emotional experience
   d. instilling hope
   e. b, c, and d

5. The Dayton Family Institute performed research determining effective factors for difficult cases. Which of the following represents their findings?
   a. The counseling relationship was less important than the techniques used.
   b. Accommodating the client's schedule improved outcome.
   c. Adapting to the client's view regarding the nature of the problem, its causes, and its solution created a successful outcome.
   d. all of the above

6. *Security operations* can be defined and characterized by which of the following?
   a. strategies that maintain self-systems and a sense of poor self-esteem
   b. constructs that screen out anxiety-provoking elements of interactions
   c. selective inattention that ignores experiences that don't conform to biases
   d. tuning into possible opportunities to relatedness
   e. all of the above

7. Persistence of poor interactional habits are maintained regardless of the negative consequence of losing friends and loneliness. Which of the following explains this phenomena?
   a. cognitive-interpersonal cycle
   b. dysfunctional etiology
   c. confirmation of positive self-esteem
   d. poor feedback from counselors

8. *Interpersonal markers* are the objects of counselor's observations and interventions. Which of the following is true of interpersonal markers?
   a. The counselor can be seen as rudely telling the client something undesirable to hear.
   b. The counselor points out interaction patterns that may cause the client difficulties.
   c. The counselor corrects the client's language errors to improve accuracy.
   d. a and b
   e. a and c

9. A cognitive-interpersonal therapist uses his own reactions to the client's communication to
   a. understand the client's intrapersonal dynamics.
   b. communicate to the client how her pathology originated in childhood.
   c. tease out aspects of the client's interpersonal schemas.
   d. all of the above

10. From a cognitive-interpersonal point of view, *decentering* allows a person to
    a. be aware of the immediacy of the moment.
    b. recognize the errors of parents' cognitions.
    c. identify interpersonal patterns that require change.
    d. look at one's self from the outside.
    e. c and d

11. *Discontinuation of complementary responding* is a counseling technique characterized by
    a. completing the circle of one person responding to another person.
    b. the wrong prediction of what a response will draw out from another person.
    c. complimentary responses between the counselor and the client.
    d. the counselor choosing a response that is not complimentary to the client's lead.

12. *Experiential disconfirmation* means that the
    a. person has experiences that lead to a lack of self esteem.
    b. client learns to take disappointments in stride.
    c. client has a new experience that does not confirm her beliefs.
    d. counselor confirms the client's interpretation of negative experiences.

13. Cognitive-interpersonal therapy for depression is characterized by which of the following?
    a. It includes a manual with clear instructions for counseling interventions across the course of therapy.
    b. It is often used in combination with antidepressant medication.
    c. It focuses on long-term problems in interpersonal relatedness.
    d. It focuses on one or two areas including: grief, interpersonal disputes, role transitions, loneliness, and social isolation.
    e. all of the above

14. *Syncretic eclecticism* is NOT characterized by which of the following?
    a. a synchronized blending of concepts and techniques clearly defining how concepts and techniques work together
    b. a bag of tricks or techniques that allow the counselor to vary counseling interventions according to intuitive responses to the client
    c. an awareness of the empirical evidence showing what techniques work based on client characteristics, situational determinants, and client stage of change
    d. all of the above

15. Defining the scope of practice involves a risk when using an integrated approach in what ways?
    a. A firm professional identity is easier when subscribing to multiple theories.
    b. Describing an integration of concepts can sound substantive or very knowledgeable.
    c. Telling the client what to expect in therapy could be confusing if specific contingencies are given.
    d. Describing therapy to a client could be so vague that the client doesn't know what to expect.
    e. c and d

Key Terms and Essential Concepts

Theoretical integration: Blending two or more theoretical approaches, therapists conceptualize clients' issues and personalities with greater complexity than only one approach would offer. The goal of integrating theories is to gain a synergistic effect in which the more multifaceted explanations provide more understanding of individual dynamics and more flexibility in determining appropriate interventions.

Technical eclecticism: A collection of techniques used in counseling offers the counselor a variety of tools for facilitating client change. A therapist can maintain a singular focus for case conceptualization and borrow techniques from multiple theories, if care is taken to smoothly blend the use of interventions within the counseling process without a jarring effect. Interventions can be chosen on the basis of empirical research validating the use of specific methods for changing specific concerns for clients with particular characteristics. In fact, technical eclecticism can go as far as relegating abstract theory to less importance than considering the proven clinical strategies that guide the counselor's choice of interventions.

Common factors orientation: A recognition that regardless of theoretical approach, therapists employ similar healing practices. The quality of the counselor-client interaction and the pattern established by therapeutic process has been shown by empirical research and by counselor agreement to be instrumental in positive client change. In addition to warmth, empathy and unconditional positive regard, counselors facilitate corrective emotional experiences by enhancing hope and trust. Client change is encouraged through persuasion, challenging misperceptions, maintaining morale, providing new experiences, and offering accurate feedback.

Transtheoretical therapy: Using a common factors approach to counseling can be described as conceptualizing case management across theories without specifying which theory or theories are the major focus. Prochaska and other collaborators define specific stages to client change and choose counseling interventions appropriate to the client's particular level of readiness. The Dayton Institute's research found that abiding by the client's analysis of problems gave counselors clues for determining intervention strategies across theoretical explanations.

Systematic Treatment Selection: Empirical validation for counseling interventions based on client characteristics and treatment variables offer nontheoretical technical choices at particular points in the course of therapy. STS creators reviewed research studies to determine eighteen principles and guidelines for determining what interventions work or don't work under specific conditions.

Syncretism: Nonsystematic use of multiple techniques and theoretical concepts is labeled syncretic and characterized as random and lacking thoughtfulness. The theoretical approaches are not synchronized to form a meaningful theoretical orientation, but instead, ill-fitting ideas and practice are used without careful consideration.

Eclecticism: Use of theories or techniques (or both) from more than one traditional school of thought.

Collaboration: The counselor and the client work together to achieve client goals. Collaborating implies that the client is made aware of treatment choices and of the purpose of different methods for achieving change.

Therapeutic alliance: The counselor and the client join together in a relationship with both parties working toward positive client change. The alliance includes agreement on goals, agreement on tasks, and the affective bond between client and therapist. It is also called the *helping alliance.*

Three-dimensional model: To encourage the therapeutic practice of adapting to the client's cultural background Atkinson, Thompson, and Grant developed a model for deciding on the counselor's interactive stance that included three dimensions: the client's level of acculturation, the locus of problem etiology, and the goals of helping.

Helper roles: The function counselors serve in order to provide the needed intervention that will assist client change can be defined as particular roles. In addition to counselor or therapist roles, a helper could act as an advocate, advisor, change agent, consultant, or could facilitate indigenous support or healing systems. These roles were defined by Atkinson and colleagues in their research regarding cross-cultural issues, but the same roles might apply regardless of clients' and counselors' cultural backgrounds.

Complementary responding: When a person interacts in ways that reinforce another person's interaction style, the person is responding in a complementary way. Such interactions are called an *interpersonal cycle* where the first communication elicits a predictable response. So, an angry statement brings forth an angry response. A submissive act brings forth a dominant act.

Discontinuation of complementary responding: In therapy, the counselor is aware of the typical response that would follow a client's statement and deliberately chooses to respond in an unexpected way, thus forcing the client to consider a different response in turn.

Experiential disconfirmation: The counselor who chooses to interact with the client in nontypical ways does not confirm the client's interpersonal schema and this new experience helps break the client's pattern.

Triadic reciprocity: Bandura wrote that behavioral, cognitive, and interpersonal factors influence human experience and that the three factors interact. Consequently, counseling outcome can be viewed as the interaction of the therapeutic relationship with cognitive and behavioral interventions.

Self-schema: Cognitive theorists describe the mind's construction of habitual patterns of thinking and behavior. The structural framework defines a person's sense of security, satisfaction, and anxiety and provides a basis for preferences, beliefs, avoidances, and behavioral patterns.

Self-system: The self-system as defined by Harry Stack Sullivan is similar to the individual's self-concept, extended to emphasize the person's typical and expected interactions with other people.

Security operations: Individuals determine methods to maintain psychological consistency and dependable interactions with others in an attempt to gain a sense of stability.

Anxiety: Interpersonal relations theorists define personal security as an expectation of consistent relating with others and anxiety as habitually predicting relationships as destabilizing.

Interpersonal schema: Individuals develop cognitive constructs over time that describe their expectations and responses in interpersonal relationships.

Selective inattention: Interpersonal schemas serve as screening structures that permit the person to pay attention to relevant occurrences and to ignore other events. Selecting relevant observations creates a bias that screens out information that does not fit with the schematic view.

Cognitive-interpersonal cycle: Once people develop interpersonal schemas for viewing relationships, they maintain the constructs by behaving in ways that conform to their expectations and elicit predictable responses from others. The views carried forward from past relations are also maintained by choosing others who interact in particular ways. For example, I blurt out my opinions, trying to show I care about the group, and others are annoyed. I believe no one wants me in the group, and this idea is confirmed when others ask me to wait to talk until others are finished talking.

Interpersonal markers: In session, counselors working within an interpersonal relations approach observes the client's typical habits of interacting and describes out loud what these stylistic behaviors are and then offers feedback to clients. With the client's interactive style as a topic for counseling, the client can explore the internal experience associated with interactive behaviors.

Interpersonal inventory: Interpersonal therapy counselors may use a technique of reviewing with the client a description of the current relationships in the client's life. Such a review allows the client to determine his interpersonal schema and what cognitive-interpersonal cycles may be operating. When the interactive patterns are repeated in the counseling relationship, the counselor can bring out into the open the presence of the pattern and its impact on interactions.

Transference: When the client interacts with the counselor, she will undoubtedly behave in similar ways as she would with other people in his life. The client is said to transfer emotions and behaviors that define her sense of self and her relations to others onto the counseling relationship. The counselor, attuned to the implications of the client's interactions, responds with empathy and appropriate feedback, so the client's cognitive assumptions regarding relationships can be opened to change. This is a broader definition of the term *transference* than a psychodynamic usage of the term, which assumes that clients transfer parental relationships onto the counselor.

Metacommunication: Discussing aspects of how people are communicating to each other is talking about their talking—*metacommunication*. The term denotes an approach that makes the communication itself the topic of discussion, rather than other content. The impact of how each person reacts to the words of the other person can reveal interpersonal patterns arising from internal responses.

Decentering: When a client hears feedback regarding how the counselor feels when the client says or does something in their interactions, the client is able to view how he is coming across to others. The client can see his self from the outside view, rather than experiencing himself as the primary center of the interaction. Such an external view can be a powerful means to understand both self and others from a perspective that is not common in most relationships.

Scope of practice: Counselors are ethically bound to define what counseling issues and treatments they are competent to deliver and to inform clients of what to expect in therapy.

Core Case: Barbara Scheman

The Barbara Scheman case was seen in Chapter 9, Cognitive-Behavioral Therapies, in the Finding a Balance section. The following is a script showing both cognitive and interpersonal interventions.

BARBARA:	I dreamed about high school last night. My father was drunk. He ripped my prom dress right down the middle. . . . And then, he laughed. He said I didn't deserve to go to prom. He yelled, "Who do you think you are, you're no princess!"
COUNSELOR:	You were hurt . . . and scared?
BARBARA:	I didn't know what he was going to do. I was terrified. I just went to my room and cried. What kind of father does that?
COUNSELOR:	I notice you cry each and every time you talk about your father.
BARBARA:	I can't get away from it. My memories, over and over again.
COUNSELOR:	You suffered so much in your relationship with your father. You still suffer as memories replay hurtful scenes.
BARBARA:	No one understands. My sisters say, forget it. My mother says, what's done is done; it's in the past.
COUNSELOR:	It's important to you that I understand how much your father hurt you; how you still hurt.
BARBARA:	Yes. Maybe if at least you can understand . . .
BARBARA:	And John, he's up to his tricks again! I tiptoe around to keep him from getting angry. For the children.
COUNSELOR:	The way you describe your husband, he sounds like your father.
BARBARA:	Yah, they're alike in so many ways. He must be drinking again.
COUNSELOR:	When you talk about your father, you cry, but when you talk about your husband, you are energized, almost angry.
BARBARA:	I won't be the enabler!! I won't, I won't.
COUNSELOR:	Is it important that you make sure your husband does not treat you like your father did? That you protect yourself?

BARBARA:	I've suffered enough.
COUNSELOR:	Is it important that you prove to me that your husband is an alcoholic?
BARBARA:	Yes. If you can understand, I can relax. . . . At least, it explains everything. All the signs are there.
COUNSELOR:	You understand how families suffer when there is alcoholism.
BARBARA:	Yes.
COUNSELOR:	When you describe you husband's alcoholic behavior, I feel like you're listing the symptoms. Like you're teaching me what alcoholics do. Yet "his tricks" don't necessarily indicate alcoholism. Does it matter? If your husband is an alcoholic?
BARBARA:	Of course it matters. How will everyone understand? How can I understand?
COUNSELOR:	It's important to you that I understand your husband is an alcoholic?
BARBARA:	I want you to understand. It's alcohol. John has to be sneaking around drinking. He's angry half the time. I've been enabling him. I've been denying the problems for years. It's O.K. when John's away. The children and I together are just fine.
COUNSELOR:	The children and you together, like you and your brother and sisters, and your mother.
BARBARA:	Exactly.
COUNSELOR:	Could it be that you carry a pattern in your mind of bad marriages, and that pattern has alcoholism. Like what you experienced as a child. Like what you hear about in AlAnon?
BARBARA:	It all fits. My past. My memories. And now, John.
COUNSELOR:	If there was no alcohol involved, how do you see your marriage?
BARBARA:	Bad. We don't talk. Just go through the motions. Sleep separately. John's gone all the time. He comes home; everything changes. I hate it!!!!
COUNSELOR:	When you say that you hate your marriage and your husband's behavior, I keep feeling that these are just words, I keep feeling that these are just words—you don't really intend to do anything about it.
BARBARA:	I don't know. What would you think of me?
COUNSELOR:	I think you're a strong woman who can make her own decisions. Stay married? Or not. Evaluate your marriage as good. Or bad.
BARBARA:	I just don't love him, respect him.
COUNSELOR:	Alcohol or not? So does it matter if he's an alcoholic? Would it be O.K. if you just don't want to be married to John?
BARBARA:	Alcohol or not. I don't want to be married to him.
COUNSELOR:	That comes through loud and clear. What I think when you say that, though, is that you're getting it off your chest, not making a plan. Is that right?
BARBARA:	Yes, I'm just complaining. I do that all the time. You're right. I don't have anything to back up my threats and complaints because I never do anything. Nobody believes me.

Example of a Published Research Article on Counseling Theories

The following article is important background when you think about how you will integrate theories and techniques.

The Face of 2010: A Delphi Poll
on the Future of Psychotherapy

John C. Norcross, Melissa Hedges, and James O. Prochaska

Abstract

A panel of 62 psychotherapy experts using Delphi methodology predicted psychotherapy trends in the next decade. The observers forecasted changes in theoretical orientations, therapeutic interventions, psychotherapy providers, treatment formats, and future scenarios. Cognitive-behavior, culture-sensitive, cognitive, and eclectic/integrative theories were predicted to increase the most, whereas classical psychoanalysis, solution-focused theories, and transactional analysis were expected to decline. Directive, self-change, and technological interventions were judged to be in the ascendancy. Master's-level psychotherapists along with "virtual" therapy services were expected to flourish. Forecast scenarios with the highest likelihood centered on expansion of evidence-based therapy, practice guidelines, behavioral medicine, and pharmacotherapy.

What might the future of psychotherapy look like? What is hot and what is not in the new millennium? Where are the growth opportunities for psychologists? As we transition from the industrial era to an information era, it is imperative that we remain knowledgeable of how changes will impact psychotherapy, psychologists, and our patients (Lesse, 1987). As we move through the dawn of the new millennium, it is advantageous to reflect on where psychotherapy is heading.

Every 10 years, starting in 1980 (Norcross, Alford, & DeMichele, 1992; Prochaska & Norcross, 1982), we have conducted a Delphi poll on the future of psychotherapy. The 36 experts in the initial poll anticipated a variety of changes in psychotherapy, such as the shift in theoretical orientation from psychoanalytic to cognitive-behavioral and the replacement of long-term therapy with briefer therapy. Their optimistic forecasts included an increase in female and minority therapists, accelerated services to underserved populations, coverage under national health insurance, and standard implementation of peer review. The 75 experts in our second Delphi poll, 10 years later, opined that self-help groups and social workers would proliferate and that the proportion of psychotherapy provided by psychiatrists would diminish. The results also predicted the centrality of program accreditation, psychotherapists becoming specialists rather than general practitioners, and mandatory certification/licensure of master's-level mental health professionals. Although not without erroneous predictions (such as coverage under national health insurance), these studies have highlighted core forces that gradually but persistently shape the face of psychotherapy.

This updated and expanded study was designed to garner expert consensual predictions on psychotherapy during the next decade. What will the face of psychotherapy look like in the year 2010?

The Delphi Method

The Delphi methodology, developed in the early 1950s as a part of military research on expert opinion, structures communication so that a group of individuals, as a whole, can deal with a complex problem (Linstone & Turoff, 1975). A panel of experts answers the same questions at least twice. In the first round, the experts answer the questions anonymously and without knowledge of the responses of their peers. During subsequent rounds, the experts are provided with the responses of the entire panel and are given the opportunity to revise their predictions in light of the group judgment. The use of Delphi methodology has increased in such diverse fields as family therapy (Fish & Busby, 1996, Levine & Fish, 1999), education research (Boberg & Morris-Khoo, 1992) and water resource development (Malcolm Pirnie, Inc., 1980).

Delphi polls are an economical, time-efficient, and accurate means of gathering the opinions of a group of experts on future events or directions. Cumulative research indicates that the results of Delphi polls usually provide the most accurate answers to difficult questions compared with other prognostication techniques (Boronson, 1980). The group Delphi consensus also consistently outperforms the opinions of individual experts (Ascher, 1978; Linstone & Turoff, 1975). Another advantage of the technique, particularly relevant to our study, is that "the Delphi method attempts to negotiate a reality that can then be useful in moving a particular field forward, planning for the future or even changing the future by forecasting its events" (Fish & Busby, 1996).

We adapted a five-page questionnaire from our previous Delphi polls (Norcross, Alford, & DeMichele, 1992; Prochaska & Norcross, 1982). Dated items were eliminated (e. g., neurolinguistic programming), and the questionnaire was augmented with new items (e.g., computerized therapies, neurobiofeedback) concerning recent developments. The questionnaire comprised five sections: theoretical orientations (29 items), therapeutic interventions (38 items), psychotherapists (14 items), therapy formats (9 items), and forecast scenarios (24 items). The panel was repeatedly asked to predict the probability of each item occurring during the next decade according to what *will* happen, as opposed to what they would personally *like* to happen. Responses on the first four sections were recorded on a 7-point, Likert-type scale where 1 = *great decrease*, 4 = *remain the same*, and 7 = *great increase*. Responses to the final section were recorded in a similar fashion, where 1 = *very unlikely*, 4 = *uncertain*, and 7 = *very likely*.

Questionnaires were mailed with a cover letter and a stamped, return envelope in January 2001. The responses were then pooled and analyzed. The same instrument was then redistributed to the panelists in April 2001, along with feedback on the responses of the panel as a whole. Feedback was provided for each item in terms of means and standard deviations, which were depicted both numerically and graphically.

The Expert Panel

Members of the expert panel were selected from two samples, the 54 living participants from our previous Delphi study and 30 editors of leading mental health journals. These samples were combined for a pool of 84 possible participants. Sixty-five (77%) returned the first round of the questionnaire, but three were not usable, leaving 62 participants. Sixty-two of the 65 participants (95%) completed the second round of the study and served as the panel of experts. Individual responses were not (and cannot be) associated with them personally.

The panel consisted of distinguished mental health professionals. All 62 participants held a doctorate (58 Ph.D.s, 3 M.D.s, and 1 Ed.D.) and reported an average of 30 years (*SD* = 9.77) of postdoctoral clinical experience. The panel was composed of 15 women and 44 men (3 did not indicate gender). On average, they devoted their professional time to clinical work (30% of their time), research (28%), teaching (18%), administration (11%), and supervision (9%). The most prevalent employment settings were university departments (58%), independent practices (26%), and medical schools (11%). The experts represented a diversity of self-reported theoretical orientations: cognitive-behavioral (32%), eclectic/integrative (26%), psychodynamic (18%), humanistic/experiential (9%), behavioral (5%), feminist (5%), and systems/family systems (4%).

A *Likert scale* asks the respondent to choose from values on a 1 to 5 scale with 1 meaning "completely disagree" and 5 meaning "completely agree." A *Likert-type scale* is similar in format but may use a different value range (1 to 7, for example) and different meanings assigned ("very unlikely" to "very unlikely," for example). Researchers hope that respondents view the scale points as representing regular intervals of meaning intensity. Many researchers no longer use the term *Likert-type*, just calling a scale a scale.

The return rate is important to report. If only half of the respondents mailed back the first questionnaire and then only half of those mailed back the second round, only 25% of the experts are represented in the results. You would have to wonder whether there were systematic differences between who stayed in and who dropped out.

The uneven sex composition of the expert panel is of interest. There might be several reasons for it. Later, the researchers test whether men's answers differed systematically from women's.

Notice that both of the top categories of orientation are integrative in nature.

Methodology and Its Discontents

The primary goal of Delphi methodology is to reach a consensus among the experts. The achievement of this goal was illustrated by consistent decreases in standard deviations from the first to second round for 103 of the 114 items (90%). Providing feedback to the panel of experts thus reduced disparity and encouraged consensus concerning future directions in psychotherapy.

At the same time, there are several limitations to this type of research and to this study in particular. First, our panel was composed solely of psychotherapists living inside the United States; generalizations to other countries are unwarranted. Second, these distinguished psychotherapy researchers and practitioners may be committed to the status quo and thus inclined to favor those therapies and theories currently in favor. Third, our experts' predictions do not of Congress unnecessaryges but rather relative increases and decreases in the orientations, techniques, and providers. That is, we asked about change as opposed to final status. A theoretical orientation or a clinical method could increase substantially in the next decade but still not be a frequent or common event. Fourth, our sample included only 15 women and 3 psychiatrists, and thus we undersampled women and psychiatrists relative to their numbers in the mental health professions. However, statistical analyses revealed few differences between the responses of men and women in this sample (fewer than expected by chance), so gender did not exert an appreciable impact. And fifth, although the item standard deviations did decrease from the first to second round of data collection, congruent with Delphi methodology, they were still rather large and reflected considerable variation in experts' forecasts.

The following tables present the item means and standard deviations from both data waves, but the items are rank-ordered in terms of the results of the second wave. Rules in the tables divide the items into three rationally created categories: those items the experts expect to increase (item mean of 4.5 and greater), those items predicted to remain about the same (mean ranging from 3.5 to 4.49), and those predicted to decrease (mean of 3.49 and less) in the next decade.

Theoretical Orientations

Our experts rated the extent to which a variety of theoretical orientations will be employed over the next decade. As presented in Table 1, cognitive-behavior therapy, culture-sensitive/multicultural, cognitive (Beck), interpersonal therapy, technical eclecticism, and theoretical integration were expected to increase the most. By contrast, classical psychoanalysis, implosive therapy, transactional analysis, and Adlerian therapy were expected to decrease.

The standard deviations reflect the average distance from the mean among the individual respondents. So when the standard deviations went down, the respondents agreed more closely with each other.

Explanations within the text of the article help you understand the accompanying tables. In this case, the horizontal lines across the tables are meaningful.

Table 1

Predicted Changes in Theoretical Orientations in Rank Order

Theoretical Orientation	Round 1		Round 2		
	M	SD	M	SD	Rank
Cognitive-behavioral therapy	5.54	1.42	5.67	0.99	1
Culture-sensitive/multicultural	5.41	1.23	5.40	0.98	2
Cognitive therapy (Beckian)	5.20	1.38	5.07	1.18	3
Interpersonal therapy (IPT)	4.88	1.18	5.05	1.11	4
Technical eclecticism	4.72	1.33	4.89	1.20	5
Theoretical integration	4.84	1.07	4.89	1.07	6
Behavior therapy	4.53	1.67	4.81	1.09	7
Systems/family systems therapy	4.57	1.14	4.80	0.96	8
Exposure therapies	4.88	1.51	4.70	1.34	9
Solution-focused therapy	4.47	1.26	4.70	0.99	10
Motivational interviewing	4.58	1.45	4.47	1.35	11
Feminist therapy	4.22	1.22	3.92	1.27	12
Rational-emotive behavior therapy	3.82	1.37	3.83	1.24	13
Narrative therapy	4.07	1.47	3.83	1.15	14
Psychodynamic therapy	3.88	1.39	3.80	1.19	15
Male-sensitive therapy	4.08	1.34	3.58	1.36	16
Experiential therapy	3.51	1.49	3.58	1.12	17
Transtheoretical therapy	3.83	1.45	3.56	1.46	18
Client/person-centered therapy	3.38	1.39	3.20	1.24	19
Eye movement desensitization and reprocessing (EMDR)	3.66	1.66	3.18	1.43	20
Humanistic therapy	3.05	1.21	2.02	1.03	21
Realistic therapy	3.37	1.16	2.95	1.06	22
Existential therapy	3.02	1.24	2.85	1.09	23
Gestalt therapy	2.93	1.10	2.78	0.88	24
Jungian	2.72	1.39	2.33	0.95	25
Adlerian	2.43	1.25	2.25	0.89	26
Transactional analysis	2.55	1.02	2.13	0.77	27
Implosive therapy	2.47	1.47	1.91	0.94	28
Psychoanalysis (classical)	2.14	1.11	1.16	1.07	29

Note: 1 = great decrease, 4 = remain the same, 7 = great increase

We repeatedly emphasized that participants should predict what would happen rather than what they would like to happen. However, in addition to being experts, our observers might have been prone to present their own preferred theories in a more favorable light. To investigate the possibility of a rating bias, we compared the mean predictions on three superordinate orientations (i.e., psychodynamic/ psychoanalytic, cognitive-behavior, and eclectic/ integrative) as a function of the panelist's theoretical orientation. Participants who identified themselves as psychoanalytic/psychodynamic rated the future of classical psychoanalysis significantly more favorably (p <.05) than did the cognitive-behaviorists and eclectic/integrationists (a difference of 1.02 and 1.67 points on the 1–7 rating scale). Cognitive-behavior therapists, in addition, rated the future of psychodynamic therapy significantly lower (p <.05) than did the other groups (a difference of 1.23 and 1.40). However, no differential ratings were made on the future of cognitive-behavior or eclectic/integrative therapies. Thus, there was robust convergence in predictions for the future but modest allegiance bias with regard to psychodynamic and psychoanalytic therapies.

Therapeutic Interventions

As Table 2 shows, 18 of the 38 interventions were predicted to increase in the next decade. Those methods characterized by computer technology (virtual reality, computerized therapies), client self-change (self-change, self-help resources, self-control procedures), and therapist didactic-direction (homework assignments, relapse prevention, problem-solving techniques, and cognitive restructuring) were forecast to increase. Panel members forecasted that free association, encounter exercises, emotional flooding/implosion, and dream interpretation would diminish.

Psychotherapists

As displayed in Table 3, over half of the 14 different types of psychotherapists were expected to expand in the future and only one to decrease. Master's-level practitioners, clinical social workers, and technological therapy services (e.g., Internet and telephone services) should expand in the first decade of the millennium. The use of self-help groups was also judged to be on the rise as compared with other psychotherapy providers, such as primary-care providers, peer counselors, and psychologists, who were judged to remain about the same. Psychiatrists as psychotherapists, by contrast, were expected to experience a marked decline.

Therapy Formats

Our experts foresaw four therapy formats increasing, three remaining about the same, and only one decreasing in the next decade. Short-term therapy (second-round $M = 5.70$), psychoeducational groups for specific disorders ($M = 5.56$), crisis intervention ($M = 4.95$), group therapy ($M = 4.82$), and couples/marital therapy ($M = 4.56$) were predicted to increase, in that order. Three therapy formats—conjoint family therapy ($M— 4.16$), individual therapy ($M = 4.07$), and single-session therapy ($M = 4.03$) were expected to experience essentially no change in the future. Our panel members forecasted that only one format on our list would decline: long-term therapy ($M = 2.70$).

Forecast Scenarios

The panel's collective projections on 23 scenarios are summarized in Table 4. Future scenarios with the highest likelihood centered on the expansion of evidence-based therapies, master's-level psychotherapists (including mandatory licensure/certification), practice guidelines, technology in psychotherapy, behavioral medicine, and pharmacotherapy. The experts thought it slightly likely that a number of states would legislatively allow psychologists to prescribe psychotropic medications in the next decade. Several future scenarios were judged to experience no change in the future. Among these were the integration of spirituality into therapy and funding for psychotherapy research. Scenarios least likely to be seen in the future were increased funding for psychotherapy training, psychotherapy regulation by a federal agency, and the number of doctoral-level specialists in the field increasing at the expense of master's-level therapists.

Panel members were generally doubtful of the group's ability to accurately predict the future of psychotherapy. When asked the likelihood that a panel of expert psychotherapists could accurately predict the future of psychotherapy, the average response was slightly unlikely ($M = 3.26$, $SD = 1.50$). This prediction provides an important caveat that our experts were not confident in the forecasts of the entire panel.

Whither the Future?

What will the face of psychotherapy resemble in the new millennium? Four themes account for the majority of changes predicted by our Delphi panel of experts. *Efficiency* is an economic theme that emphasizes the briefest therapies, the cheapest therapists, and the least expensive techniques. *Evidence* is a scientific theme that rewards research on the efficacy of treatments, therapists, and clinical interventions.

Table 2

Predicted Changes in Therapeutic Interventions in Rank Order

Therapeutic Intervention	Round 1		Round 2		Rank
	M	SD	M	SD	
Homework assignments	5.25	1.18	5.52	0.94	1
Relapse prevention	5.25	1.11	5.44	0.92	2
Use of virtual reality	5.42	1.07	5.32	1.20	3
Problem-solving techniques	5.05	1.07	5.30	0.85	4
Computerized therapies	5.50	1.21	5.28	1.16	5
Cognitive restructuring	5.07	1.25	5.25	1.00	6
Self-change techniques	5.10	1.08	5.07	0.93	7
Solution-focused methods	4.97	0.94	5.10	0.93	8
Recommending self-help resources (beyond books)	4.92	1.27	4.98	0.85	9
Teaching/advising	4.80	1.19	4.87	0.90	10
Interpersonal support	4.70	1.01	4.85	0.78	11
Relaxation techniques	4.60	1.08	4.80	0.98	12
Communication skills	4.76	1.01	4.79	0.82	13
Assertion/social skills training	4.62	0.99	4.77	0.78	14
Expressing caring and warmth	4.55	1.08	4.75	1.07	15
Self-control procedures	4.65	1.09	4.70	0.99	16
In vivo exposure	4.77	1.14	4.68	1.14	17
Bibliography	4.55	1.16	4.63	1.06	18
Population-based interventions	4.75	1.21	4.49	1.06	19
Behavioral contracting	4.30	1.17	4.42	0.88	20
Imagery and fantasy	4.31	1.05	4.33	0.94	21
Acceptance methods	4.44	1.19	4.27	1.09	22
Therapist self-disclosure	4.25	1.10	4.27	1.01	23
Forgiveness methods	4.12	1.12	4.17	1.11	24
Neurobiofeedback	4.53	1.28	4.16	1.24	25
Accurate empathy	4.05	1.02	4.07	1.04	26
Biofeedback	4.02	1.05	3.92	0.95	27
Confrontation	3.83	1.04	3.57	0.83	28
Systemic desensitization	3.73	1.01	3.52	1.13	29

Table 2 (continued)

Predicted Changes in Therapeutic Interventions in Rank Order

Therapeutic Intervention	Round 1		Round 2		Rank
	M	SD	M	SD	
Analysis of resistance	3.44	1.33	3.35	1.18	30
Hypothesis	3.48	1.31	3.34	0.83	31
Transference interpretation	3.27	1.29	3.24	1.10	32
Paradoxical interventions	3.33	1.04	3.20	1.03	33
Cathartic methods	3.27	1.21	3.02	1.10	34
Dream interpretation	2.78	1.18	2.69	0.99	35
Emotional flooding/implosion	3.02	1.27	2.68	1.21	36
Encounter exercises	2.95	1.13	2.68	0.95	37
Free association	2.68	1.37	2.54	1.06	38

Note: 1 = great decrease, 4 = remain the same, 7 = great increase

Table 3

Predicted Changes in Psychotherapists in Rank Order

Type of Therapist	Round 1		Round 2		Rank
	M	SD	M	SD	
Master's-level counselors	5.30	1.15	5.44	0.81	1
Internet therapy services	5.55	1.21	5.39	0.92	2
Clinical social workers	5.10	1.26	5.38	0.78	3
Telephone therapy services	5.17	1.24	5.20	0.96	4
Master's-level family therapists	5.02	1.09	5.10	0.83	5
Self-help groups	5.05	0.98	5.11	0.90	6
Psychiatric nurses	4.97	1.16	5.07	1.04	7
Paraprofessionals	4.85	1.12	4.50	1.18	8
Peer counselors	4.60	1.06	4.43	0.92	9
Pastoral counselors	4.49	0.94	4.39	0.84	10
Primary care providers	4.17	1.22	4.11	0.97	11
Mass media "therapy" shows	4.33	1.30	4.12	1.03	12
Psychologists	4.07	1.45	3.92	1.13	13
Psychiatrists	2.48	1.10	2.15	0.85	14

Note: 1 = great decrease, 4 = remain the same, 7 = great increase

Evolution is a theoretical theme that supports gradual change that builds on, rather than breaks with, historical trends in therapeutic theories and techniques. And *integration* is a knowledge theme that seeks increasing cohesion to counter historical fragmentation. These four themes are the key drivers of change in the profession of psychotherapy.

Economic efficiency is the primary driver in all of health care, so it is not surprising that it should be the primary driver of predicted changes in mental health care. Of the 114 ratings, short-term therapy received the highest absolute rating in terms of expected increases. Long-term therapy was the only format predicted to decrease. Almost all of the theoretical orientations predicted to increase supported the use of short-term therapy. Psychoanalysis was the theory predicted to decrease the most. The psychotherapists predicted to increase the most were master's-level (counselors, social workers, psychiatric nurses), those using lower cost Internet services or telephones, paraprofessionals, and self-help groups. The most costly therapists, namely psychiatrists, were the only professional group expected to decrease, and psychologists were next in line for the least growth. The therapeutic interventions predicted to increase included those that can be used at home (e.g., homework, computers, self-help resources, and self-control) and those that contribute to short-term treatments (e.g., problem solving, cognitive restructuring, solution-focused, and skill training). Techniques predicted to decrease precipitously were those that are part of long-term therapies (e.g., free association, analysis of resistance, transference and dream interpretations).

In the first round of the Delphi poll the most likely scenario in all of psychotherapy was that evidence-based psychotherapies would be required by health care systems. In the second round this scenario slipped to number two, but four of the top six scenarios all supported evidence-based practice (e.g., research generates prescriptive treatments, practice guidelines become standard, and therapists increasingly treat health-related behaviors). For the most part, the ascending theoretical orientations were those with the most intense involvement in controlled research. This does not necessarily mean that these therapies have greater efficacy, but they do have greater evidence. So the Dodo bird prediction (Luborsky, Singer, & Luborsky, 1975) from the past is probably untrue in the health care market, and it is unlikely to be the case that "All have won and all must receive prizes." Theories that will win the most prizes are those that have won the support of the most researchers.

The history of psychotherapy indicates that old theories and therapies do not fade away; instead, they typically evolve into what the next generation believes to be new theories and therapies (Prochaska & Norcross, 2002). The Delphi poll predicted a similar form of evolution rather than a revolution.

Table 4

Predicted Scenarios in Rank Order

Scenario	Round 1		Round 2		
	M	SD	M	SD	Rank
Licensure or certification becomes mandatory for the mental health specialist at the master's level	3.63	1.23	5.67	0.85	1
Evidence-based psychotherapies are required by health care systems	5.75	0.99	5.48	1.23	2
Psychotherapy research provides prescriptive "treatments of choice" for certain disorders and people	5.32	1.48	5.31	1.13	3
Practice guidelines become a standard part of daily psychotherapy	5.12	1.23	5.30	0.92	4
Psychotherapists routinely treat the behavioral components of health problems and chronic illnesses	5.28	1.21	5.25	1.01	5
A growing percentage of psychotherapy will be offered by telephone, videophone, or e-mail	5.39	1.27	5.20	1.18	6
Psychopharmacology expands at the expense of psychotherapy	4.92	1.57	4.98	1.12	7
Master's-level mental health specialists flood the job market, making it difficult for Ph.D.s to find work	4.95	1.44	4.90	1.27	8
Master's-level graduate training for the mental health specialist becomes highly specialized	5.03	1.17	4.79	1.02	9
Psychotherapists become specialists rather than general practitioners	4.80	1.29	4.77	1.06	10
Psychiatry as a mental health specialty within the medical profession declines in popularity	4.62	1.69	4.74	1.49	11
A number of states legislatively allow psychologists to prescribe psychotropic medications	4.66	1.64	4.66	1.33	12

Table 4 (continued)

Predicted Scenarios in Rank Order

Scenario	Round 1		Round 2		Rank
	M	SD	M	SD	
The overall effectiveness of psychotherapy improves appreciably	4.47	1.70	4.52	1.31	13
A renewed emphasis emerges on the creation and centrality of the therapeutic relationship	4.50	1.63	4.39	1.26	14
Psychotherapists increasingly integrate spiritual and religious content into treatment	4.22	1.56	4.20	1.12	15
Psychotherapists become more involved in community action, e.g., politics, social change	4.17	1.49	4.15	1.24	16
Funding for psychotherapy research increases (relative to inflation)	3.95	1.48	3.95	1.91	17
Master's-level therapists conduct virtually all of the psychotherapy in the public sphere	4.03	2.04	3.85	1.74	18
The number of positions will keep pace with the number of new psychotherapists entering the field	3.03	1.55	3.18	1.16	20
Psychotherapy is regulated by a federal agency, e.g., the FDA	3010	1.65	2.85	1.31	21
Psychotherapy is regulated by a federal agency, e.g., the FDA	3.10	1.65	2.85	1.31	22
Revolutionary new techniques of psychotherapy are discovered and replace traditional treatments	3.07	1.81	2.62	1.24	23
Doctoral-level mental health specialists flood the job market, making it difficult for M.A.s to find work	2.86	1.72	2.46	1.16	24

Note: 1 = great decrease, 4 = remain the same, 7 = great increase

The second least likely scenario in the study was that revolutionary psychotherapy techniques will be discovered and will replace traditional treatments. Historically, Adlerian therapy preceded rational-emotive behavior therapy, which contributed to cognitive-behavioral and cognitive therapies. Similarly, psychoanalysis led to psychodynamic therapy, which led to certain forms of interpersonal therapy. Person-centered therapy had a profound influence on contemporary experiential therapies and motivational interviewing. Feminist therapy has been an important contributor to multicultural therapy. Some therapies, like solution-focused and reality therapies, may be devolving into therapeutic methods.

Integration could be seen as a more intentional and inclusive approach to evolution. The integration movement seeks to combine the best ideas and the efficacious methods of leading systems of psychotherapy. On a smaller scale, cognitive-behavioral therapies have synthesized some of the best of behavior and cognitive therapies. More ambitious integrations are found in theoretical integration and technical eclecticism, which are predicted to be two of the top six growth areas in the next decade. Theoretical integration seeks systematic ways to conceptually combine processes and principles across systems of psychotherapy, whereas technical eclecticism seeks systematic ways to empirically identify which treatment methods and relationship stances work best with which patients. Ideally, such integration would serve as a framework for evidence-based approaches to practice.

If the economic value of efficiency, the scientific value of evidence, and change values of gradual evolution and growing integration do in fact increase as predicted, then psychotherapy approaches that cannot adapt to these change drivers are likely to decline. Therapies such as classical psychoanalysis that are least efficient in terms of time and training, have limited empirical evidence, are most resistant to integration, and are likely to lose the most. Therapies that are fundamentally more conceptual and value-based, such as humanistic, existential, Gestalt and Jungian, are also expected to have diminishing influence, especially as the field relies increasingly on techniques like the Internet and telephone. Such technologies tend to be anathema to therapies that value human relationships as the essence of healthy functioning. A major exception to this trend is the predicted growth of culturally sensitive and multicultural therapies, which rely more on constructivist principles and cultural values that seek to protect the experiences of minority groups from being dominated by the worldviews of powerful groups that dominate the discourse of mental health.

A major challenge for the field of psychotherapy will be to discover creative ways to integrate the values and worldviews of multiple cultures within the discourse of efficiency and evidence that currently dominate health care. Such integration would produce a healthier future for the field and for populations that turn to psychotherapy to help them develop healthier and more balanced approaches to life.

References

Ascher, W. (1978). *Forecasting*. (Baltimore: Johns Hopkins University Press).

Boberg, A. L. & Morris-Khoo, S. A. (1992). The Delphi method: A review of methodology and an application in the evaluation of a higher education program. *The Canadian Journal of Program Evaluation, 7, 37–39.*

Boronson, W. (1980). The secret of the Delphi oracle. *Next, 1,* 50.

Fish, L. S. & Busby, D. M. (1996). The Delphi method. (In D. H. Sprenkle (Ed.), *Research methods in family therapy.* (New York: Guilford Press).

Lesse, S. (1987). Psychotherapy in a changing postindustrial society. *American Journal of Psychotherapy, 41,* 336–348.

Levine, L. B. & Fish, L. S. (1999). The integration of constructivism and social constructionist theory in family therapy: A Delphi study. *Journal of Systemic Therapies, J8,* 58–84.

Linstone, H. A. & Turoff, M. (Eds.) (1975). *The Delphi method: Techniques and applications.* (Reading, MA: Addison Wesley).

Luborsky, L., Singer, B. & Luborsky, L. (1975). Comparative studies of psychotherapies. *Archives of General Psychiatry, 32,* 995–1008.

Malcolm Pirnie, Inc. (1980). *A view of the future's most critical water issues: As developed in a modified Delphi poll,* (White Plains, NY: Author).

Norcross, J. C., Alford, B. A. & DeMichele, J. T. (1992). The future of psychotherapy: Delphi data and concluding observations. *Psychotherapy, 29,* 150–158.

Prochaska. J. O. & Norcross, J. C. (1982). The future of psychotherapy: A Delphi poll. *Professional Psychology, 13,* 620–627.

Prochaska, J. O. & Norcross, J. C. (2002). *Systems of psychotherapy: A transtheoretical analysis (5th ed).* (Pacific Grove, CA: Brooks/Cole).

It is standard practice in a Delphi poll to acknowledge the panel of experts. We are indebted to the following; Neil Altaian, PhD; Hal Arkowitz, PhD; Diane B. Amkoff, PhD; Allan E. Bergin, PhD; Ervin Berts, PhD; Larry E. Beutler, PhD; Annette M. Brodsky, PhD; Laura S. Brown, PhD; James F. T. Bugental, PhD; Gerald C. Davison, PhD; Patrick Henry DeLeon, PhD; E. Thomas Dowd, PhD; Paul Emmelkamp, PhD; Gary M. Farkas, PhD; Cyril M. Franks, PhD; Dolores E. Gallagher-Thompson, PhD; Sol L. Garfield, PhD; Earl Ginter, PhD; Carol R Glass, PhD; Jerold Gold, PhD; Marvin R. Goldfried, PhD; Leslie S. Greenberg, PhD;

Thomas Greening, PhD; Alan S. Gurman, PhD; David A. Haaga, PhD; William A. Hargreaves, PhD; Michel Hersen, PhD; Marcia Hill, EdD; Kenneth A. Holroyd, PhD; Mardi J. Horowitz, MD; T. Byram Karasu, MD; Paul Karoly, PhD; Jerald Kay, MD; Sharon M. Keigher, PhD; Philip C. Kendall, PhD; Mary Beth Kenkel, PhD; David P. Kniskern, PhD; Gerald P. Koocher, PhD; Arnold A. Lazarus, PhD; Peter Lewinsohn, PhD; Zanvel A. Liff, PhD; Lester Luborsky, PhD; Michael J. Mahoney, PhD; Barbara S. McCrady, PhD; Stanley B. Messer, PhD; Dana L. Moore, PhD; Thomas H. Ollendick, PhD; Donald R. Peterson, PhD; Nancy Porter-Steele, PhD; Malcolm H. Robertson, PhD; Richard Sauber, PhD; Monique Savlin, PhD; Robert T. Segraves, PhD; Wade H. Silverman, PhD; John J. Steffen, PhD; William B. Stiles, PhD; George Stricker, PhD; Phoebus N Tongas, PhD; Robert Ursano, PhD; Gary R. VandenBos, PhD; Paul L. Wachtel, PhD; and G. Terence Wilson, PhD. Correspondence may be addressed to John C. Norcross, Department of Psychology, University of Scranton, Scranton, Pennsylvania, 18510–4596. Electronic mail may be sent to norcross@scrantonb.edu

Discussion Ideas

1. What predictions were made in 1980? In 1990? From your point of view, how were they accurate? How were they erroneous?

2. Describe briefly the Delphi method. What are its advantages? Why are the first expert responses anonymous? Why do they revise their opinions in a second round? Why is the method better than consulting individual experts?

3. Of the limitations listed in Methods and Discussion, which strikes you as most significant? Which limitations seem minor to you? Why?

4. After studying *Theory and Design in Counseling and Psychotherapy*, what do you think of the ranks in Table 1? Any surprises?

5. Was there evidence of allegiance bias on the part of the experts? What was it, if any?

6. Can you think of a situation or problem in your work or school setting that could benefit from a study using Delphi methodology?

Answer Key for Practice Test Questions

True/False		*Multiple Choice*			
1.	F	1.	d	11.	d
2.	F	2.	c	12.	c
3.	T	3.	d	13.	e
4.	F	4.	e	14.	b
5.	T	5.	c	15.	e
6.	T	6.	b		
7.	F	7.	a		
8.	F	8.	d		
9.	T	9.	c		
10.	T	10.	d		